PRAISE FOR *CLIMATE CHANGE ENTERPRISE RISK MANAGEMENT*

"A must-read for anyone managing climate risk. The book is insightful, informative and a great one-stop shop among a plethora of thought leadership out there on the topic. Most importantly, the book contains excellent practical guidance on how to incorporate climate risk management into existing risk management frameworks and, equally, how to start from scratch. I will certainly be consulting it."
Susan Young, CRO, R&Q

"Building on the existing tools and techniques of risk management, Martin Massey methodically shows the reader how to encompass and embrace the challenges that climate change will bring to us all. The book is readily accessible for those new to risk management but will also bring fresh insight to those familiar with the concepts"
Roy Boukins, Group Risk Officer, Accelerant Holdings

"Finally, here is a book which provides risk and financial professionals with a roadmap for implementing climate risk into their thinking. The book contains a host of comprehensive detail to equip readers with everything they need to achieve the business transformation that is required."
Rachel Johnson, ACCA Global

"This book provides great insight for risk managers needing to navigate the challenges of climate change, particularly during this early exploratory stage as firms start to ramp up their expertise to improve understanding of risks and opportunities."
Judith Ellison, Business Development Manager, JBA Risk Management

"This book explains in a very clear and methodically way how to integrate climate risks into an existing ERM and Governance Framework."
Alfa Falconi, Director Enterprise Risk | Governance, Risk & Compliance (GRC), NEOM

'Martin Massey has written a book which will be welcomed by the risk management community, but more importantly by their children and grandchildren as we wrestle with the changes required for a net zero future. I am confident that the book will greatly help the reader to bring climate risk into their thinking including the opportunities that climate change presents to us all.'
Paul Mahon, Head of Technical Development, Cornish Mutual

"Addressing the overarching issue of how we inhabit the planet, Martin Massey's book informs and equips us superbly to develop a culture that unites everyone's positive efforts around a core consensus on climate risk. He draws together a superb array of expert insights, shows us all how to take reassuringly practical steps, and finds new opportunities for enterprise even as we engage with an existential threat."
Roger Miles, Head of Faculty, UK Finance: Conduct Leaders Academy

"Building on existing tools and techniques of risk management, Martin Massey methodically shows the reader how to encompass and embrace the challenges that climate change will bring to us all. The book is readily accessible for those new to risk management but I am sure it will also bring fresh insight to those familiar with the concepts."
Derek Thrumble, Head of Analytics, Gallagher Specialty

Climate Change Enterprise Risk Management

A practical guide to reaching net zero goals

Martin Massey

KoganPage

Publisher's note
Every possible effort has been made to ensure that the information contained in this book is accurate at the time of going to press, and the publishers and authors cannot accept responsibility for any errors or omissions, however caused. No responsibility for loss or damage occasioned to any person acting, or refraining from action, as a result of the material in this publication can be accepted by the editor, the publisher or the author.

First published in Great Britain and the United States in 2023 by Kogan Page Limited

2nd Floor, 45 Gee Street
London
EC1V 3RS
United Kingdom
www.koganpage.com

8 W 38th Street, Suite 902
New York, NY 10018
USA

4737/23 Ansari Road
Daryaganj
New Delhi 110002
India

Kogan Page books are printed on paper from sustainable forests.

ISBNs

Hardback 978 1 3986 0872 6
Paperback 978 1 3986 0870 2
Ebook 978 1 3986 0871 9

British Library Cataloguing-in-Publication Data

A CIP record for this book is available from the British Library.

Library of Congress Control Number

2022948343

Typeset by Integra Software Services, Pondicherry
Print production managed by Jellyfish
Printed and bound by CPI Group (UK) Ltd, Croydon, CR0 4YY

To my wonderful children, Sebastian and Francesca.

I hope that this book helps in some small way to protect their futures from the impacts of a worsening climate.

CONTENTS

ACKNOWLEDGEMENTS

I'd like to thank the Institute of Risk Management (IRM) for their trust and support, and in particular Clive Thompson (Technical Adviser, IRM) who provided significant guidance in structuring and reviewing the book.

I have received considerable support from a number of my fellow risk professionals and organizations, including several major risk companies such as Aon, Swiss Re and S&P.

Specific thanks to those who have provided me with either contributions or specific case studies to the book, including Roger Miles, Judith Ellison, Luke Watts, Simon Ashworth, Bogdan Pletea, Andrew Smith, Oliver Schelske, Patrick Saner, Thanasis Chasapis, Peter Moar, Rebecca Marra, Laurent Sabatie, Mark Heath, Graham Findlater, Paul Mahon, Gregory Hutton-Squire, Derek Thrumble, Samuel Lucas, Chris Ewing, Susan Young, Shiva Keihaninejad, Rachael Johnson and Tom Osborne.

One of the main challenges in producing the book was developing the risk management frameworks for this new and rapidly evolving field. Therefore, I want to give special thanks to Iain Felstead for his significant technical assistance and support, also Vishakha Joshi my research assistant and Cherish Hewes my graphics designer, for helping to develop a range of visual risk management frameworks used in the book.

I'd like to recognize the importance of a number of mentors that have guided me in my career who have truly inspired me, particularly in the early part of my career. These include Derek Thrumble, Crawford Paul, Pauline Margrett and David Scott, who I consider to have been visionaries in the risk management profession.

I'd like to dedicate this book to my wonderful children, Sebastian and Francesca. I hope that this book helps in some small way to protect their futures from the impacts of a worsening climate.

FOREWORD

Climate change and the route to net zero

The key to success for people and organizations in the 21st century will be their ability to adapt to and navigate through complexity, uncertainty, and disruption. Climate change is now recognized as an existential crisis of humanity and addressing this huge adaptive challenge will require a transformation in how we live and work.

The first step is to understand and assess current and future risks and accurately price external costs. Decarbonizing our economy and learning to live sustainably will open up extraordinary new opportunities for entrepreneurs and organizations. A massive overhaul of everything we do and the systems that support our lives is required over the next decade to pivot towards net zero and the upside this offers. The route to net zero is also a route to net benefit.

Together we have the knowledge and ability to address the climate crisis, but we desperately lack understanding, will, and active leadership at every level. It therefore falls to us all to do extraordinary things. In some ways this book is a call to duty for risk professionals, an opportunity for them to step up and lead. After all, there is no Planet B.

The fundamental nature of climate risk affecting every organization is the reason the Institute of Risk Management (IRM) commissioned this book and worked with our members and the wider community to explore how climate change risks can be identified and managed.

For risk managers this call to leadership means a call to create a successful climate change Enterprise Risk Management (ERM) perspective to energize and focus their organization, large or small, on its journey to reduce carbon and achieve sustainability based on transparent, ethical, and socially responsible behaviours.

The IRM has long supported the development of ERM to enable and deliver successful business strategy. This book follows on from the climate change risk management training programme developed with the Grantham Institute at Imperial College, and, combined with the qualifications offered by the IRM, enables risk professionals and others to support their employer or clients in taking the first step, no matter how small, on their journeys to net zero.

This book outlines approaches to achieving successful climate change ERM that will support any type of organization in its efforts to address the climate crisis and create sustainable growth. I hope it will be a valuable resource for everyone committed to addressing climate change through risk management leadership in action.

Stephen Sidebottom

Stephen Sidebottom is Chair of the Institute of Risk Management, risk management's leading worldwide professional education, training and knowledge body. Further information about the Institute and its training and qualifications is available from the IRM website, www.theirm.org.

Introduction

Climate change enterprise risk management in context

This book is intended for all who want a comprehensive introduction to current and new enterprise risk management practices aimed at integrating climate change into the risk strategy of organizations. The main objective is to provide guidance to risk management professionals in supporting their organizations in the transition to a sustainable future through explaining a range of practical risk frameworks as well as tools and techniques.

The book provides examples and 'best practice' methodology for all organizations and geographies. It has been informed through consultation across different sectors as to their current practices and the reader will find that case studies and illustrative examples have been drawn from both public and private sector, primary, tertiary and consumer-facing industries.

The book builds on the work undertaken by the Institute of Risk Management (IRM). It expands the work of the original guidance documents issued by the Climate Change Special Interest Group (SIG), which has, for example, identified key enablers that would require the most attention to facilitate the development and execution of a climate change risk management strategy.

The reader will find that many of the examples have been drawn from the financial services industry. This is only because the sector has been leading some of the main developments of risk management practices in this field, driven mainly by regulatory requirements. We have used the learnings from those examples to apply to wider fields. For example, the categorization of climate risks into physical, transition and liability risk was initially developed by the Financial Stability Board but has been taken up widely and is accepted as the taxonomy to address these issues. These and other examples will equip the reader with models they can apply to their own specific context.

The book focuses on two foundational components of climate change risk management, namely 'resilience', and 'sustainability'. It provides insights into how to integrate climate change into an existing risk appetite and emerging risk management framework. It also explains some of the complexities in the design of stress and scenario tests through risk modelling tools and techniques. These are particularly important in the context of management and mitigation of climate change risks.

Vision and philosophy

The management of climate risks includes both threats and opportunities. It is now perceived to be crucial to most organizations. The main purpose and vision of the book is to provide practical insights to enable the development and execution of a climate change risk management strategy in any organization.

Climate change and wider environmental, social and governance (ESG) issues are becoming the single most important business driver of the decade. Although it has been an emerging issue for many organizations, there is currently little formal risk management guidance on this topic. This book therefore aims to address this and we hope it will provide insight and intelligence for all key stakeholders concerned with the challenge of climate change facing organizations:

- Boards require assurance that significant risks have been identified and appropriate controls put in place. In order to ensure that correct business decisions are taken, risk management activity is undertaken to provide structured information to assist business decision-making. Risk managers need to enhance existing practices to integrate climate risks so that boards can make those decisions in the context of the most challenging issue facing society, climate change. Members of boards may find this book useful to identify and inform their climate change journey.
- Regulators will increasingly impose net zero ambitions on their sectors and require the organizations operating within that sector to demonstrate a transition to a more sustainable low-carbon economy through transparent disclosures.
- Wider society is calling for organizations to embrace the green agenda, creating the enhanced need for environmental, social and governance goals or sustainability targets. This book should help engaged citizens to increase their understanding of the issues and provide constructive ways to increase pressure on any 'errant' organization that needs to contribute more to a carbon-free future.

The specific goals of climate risk management include:

- Ensuring that there is a robust framework in place to identify and manage climate risks and opportunities
- Ensuring that there is adequate visibility of risk management activities at the board level
- Enabling strategic discussions to support the right risk/reward decisions
- Integrating climate change into existing risk frameworks in order to become business as usual (BAU)

One of the objectives of this book is to develop the use of consistent approaches and methodologies for climate risk management. Its aim is to promote, within context, an established way of identifying, assessing and managing climate risks. The reader should be equipped after reading this to formalize the integration of these techniques within their existing ERM framework.

Book structure and key features

The book focuses on existing risk management tools and techniques and explains how they can be tailored for managing climate change. For example, the reader will find discussions of how established techniques such as risk radars, 'bow tie' analysis, stress and scenario testing, risk maturity models, risk reporting dashboards, etc can be easily modified to encompass climate-related issues. It also includes new risk management theory and concepts such as 'stakeholder mapping', which are often perceived to be strategic management tools.

The book is presented in 12 chapters, focusing on developing the integration of climate change into an existing ERM framework to support decision making:

- Chapter 1 sets the scene by outlining the main components and enablers that organizations need to develop and embed within their existing ERM framework and introduces the development of a climate risk taxonomy and a climate risk maturity model.
- Chapter 2 builds on this to discuss the development of a climate risk strategy, which will typically be a subset of corporate strategy. It also includes how organizations can achieve their strategic goals in a sustainable and climate-friendly way.
- Chapter 3 discusses how to build a strong and documented governance approach within organizations to help manage climate change risks.
- Chapter 4 explores stakeholder expectations, particularly in the context of the Paris Agreement, and highlights the importance of stakeholder analysis and mapping as a key risk identification tool for organizations to utilize. This also includes discussion of a climate change risk radar as a key tool to enhance the resilience of organizations.
- Chapter 5 covers transition risks, providing a global perspective on carbon emissions and mitigation strategies and what government and regulators are doing to meet their net zero targets.
- Chapter 6 then delves into how organizations can build improved resilience from an operational, financial and strategic perspective due to the increased uncertainty of future weather patterns.

- Chapter 7 provides an overview of climate risk data sources and how they are used to help organizations and businesses in climate-related risk management. This chapter focuses on the opportunities and challenges linked to data and how the data and tools/models can be best used in a changing climate.
- Chapter 8 examines global economic climate trends and consequences in detail in light of the fact that 'climate action failure' has been identified by the World Economic Forum as the risk with potential to inflict the most damage at a global scale over the next decade.
- Chapter 9 provides examples of some of the main emerging climate trends across physical, transition and liability risks, including legal cases that are important for organizations to consider in the context of climate change.
- Chapter 10 explains how organizations can assess the materiality of the climate risks and opportunities that they have identified, through the use of stress and scenario analysis.
- Chapter 11 aims to bring the previous topics together and discusses taking the methods discussed into a BAU context. This includes consideration of customer requirements, third-party procurement processes, and financial and investment planning.
- Chapter 12 scrutinizes how governments and regulators worldwide are introducing requirements for transparent disclosures. These will become mandatory soon in the UK and this is expected to be the route many countries will follow.

In order to bring the subject to life and provide context to the ideas and concepts that are described, short illustrative examples are used throughout the text. In addition to these general examples, real-life situations and examples are also used. It should be noted that while some references to individual organizations' annual reports have been cited in this book, the requirement for companies to disclose detail is changing so fast that the reader is encouraged to investigate topical reports on high-profile companies to increase their understanding further.

Climate change risk management in the future

The world is facing an increasingly volatile and uncertain future; the Covid-19 pandemic, war in Ukraine and rapid changes in the way work is conducted have introduced change at an ever-faster pace. These pressures combine with the need for all of us, in whatever field, to contribute to a more sustainable future. The consequences of failure to adequately manage climate change risk will be disastrous and are potentially existential.

Whenever change occurs at a rapid pace there are increased risks. These may be seen as threats but for those with the foresight to implement risk management techniques in full they present a world of opportunity. The transition to a carbon-neutral and sustainable future is full of opportunity.

Achieving those opportunities is a key feature of this book. By setting out an integrated approach to climate change risk management, this book provides a description of the fundamental components of successful management of the transition to a net zero future. It describes a wealth of risk management tools and techniques and provides information on successful delivery of an integrated and enterprise-wide approach to climate change risk management.

1

Climate change risk landscape and ERM maturity

This chapter sets the scene for the book in that it outlines the main enterprise risk management (ERM) framework components and enablers for climate change that organizations need to develop and embed within their existing ERM framework. We start with the development of a climate risk taxonomy and a climate risk maturity model.

The main learning outcomes from this chapter are to:

- Understand the key areas that require attention to enable the development and execution of a climate change risk management strategy in any organization.
- Be aware of the relationship between climate change and the wider set of environmental, social and governance (ESG) criteria that are increasingly prominent features of regulation and supervision globally.
- Recognize the main causes and consequences of climate change including the natural catastrophe losses and trends across different perils
- Provide an overview of the main global drivers and expectations for organizations, including the Paris Agreement and Task Force on Climate-related Financial Disclosures (TCFD)
- Appreciate the importance of developing a climate risk taxonomy that includes physical and transition risks.
- Acknowledge the conditions and benefits of embedding climate change into an existing ERM framework.
- Understand how to develop a climate change risk maturity model to support the assessment of the current maturity status and to set targets across a range of key criteria that will be covered within the book.

The chapter provides an overview of why organizations need to address climate change and integrate the risk within their ERM framework. In order to do so an organization should develop a climate change taxonomy that can be discussed externally and used internally to ensure that all risks and opportunities are addressed and that there is a consistent approach and understanding.

Introduction

Climate change is unlike any other environmental or public policy problem and is characterized by a combination of four unique issues:

- Its global nature
- Its long-term nature
- The fact that it is potentially irreversible
- The almost overwhelming uncertainty surrounding its progression and effects

Climate change is a global trend as temperature and sea levels rise and contribute to amplifying certain global risks such as extreme weather events and altering the relationship between them. The leading cause of climate change has been the increase in the concentration of atmospheric greenhouse gas (GHG) emissions, including carbon dioxide, which has led to a range of major impacts including an increase in storms and floods, heatwaves and droughts, as well as impacts on human health, biodiversity, ocean acidification and global food supplies.

In recent years, climate change risk has shifted from being an emerging risk to a public risk that all firms are expected to manage and mitigate.

The recent Covid-19 pandemic crisis provides us with an indication of what a fully-fledged climate crisis could entail. Both can be considered 'grey swans'. Experts have been warning about these threats for years and both indicate that the world at large is generally ill-prepared to deal with either. What has been encouraging is how scientists and health professionals have been collaborating and reinventing how they work. Integration of scientific knowledge into risk management is also crucial to building resilience to climate risk.

Climate risk management is complex and there is a difference between thinking you know your risks and fully understanding the potential magnitude and their implications. Given the ongoing changing climate and associated risks, organizations need to continually seek to identify, assess, mitigate, monitor and report climate risks in a formal way using the latest tools and techniques where appropriate.

A famous quotation on risk came from Theodore Roosevelt, the former US President, who stated that 'Risk is like fire: if controlled it will help you; if uncontrolled it will rise up and destroy you.'[1] The point here is that he recognized the opportunity angle to risk and being able to exploit risk situations. This is particularly valid for climate change risks given the transition risks and opportunities to gain competitive advantage through, for example, being an industry leader or first mover in areas such as product innovation.

The impact of climate change also poses a financial stability risk to the global financial system. Various international, national and industry bodies, driven by the Financial Stability Board representing the G20 countries, are working together to achieve long-term regulatory alignment. Although it is easy to feel overwhelmed by the complexity of the problem there are a range of solutions available including the need to replace fossil fuels with cleaner, renewable energy like wind and solar power.

Companies therefore need to integrate climate change within their existing ERM framework. The tools and techniques covered in this book can also be adopted or adapted in order to cover some of the wider risks and issues across an organization's risk profile. To do this it is important to establish a climate change risk taxonomy, which is discussed in section 1.5 of this chapter. This taxonomy, which covers climate physical, transition and liability risks, will be the focus and content of this book.

During the Covid-19 pandemic, there has been discussion of a 'tilt to the green' in future investments. It is argued that organizations that are 'front-runners' – that adjust to future structural changes and put sustainability at the heart of their strategies more rapidly – will be able to reap the potential benefits that it will bring. These will include enhanced brand image, heightened employee engagement, enhanced innovation, new sources of revenue, improved relationships with stakeholders and greater operational resilience.

1.1 Climate change risk management enablers

Climate change presents several distinctive elements (which are non-linear, irreversible and occur over extended time horizons), which, when considered together, present firms with unique challenges.

The dynamic and interconnected nature of climate risk, in addition to limitations in data sets and methodologies, will require firms to adopt an iterative approach. Perhaps one of the most important considerations will be the adoption of a proactive approach to assessing the resilience of a firm's business strategy and to be able to adapt quickly to climate change.

The design of a climate change strategy should therefore align to an existing enterprise risk management (ERM) framework and the wider group business and strategic objectives. In terms of being able to evidence successful implementation, risk managers need to integrate and embed climate change into existing business processes and protocols.

Figure 1.1 outlines the themes of the 12 chapters of the book, each of which is a key and distinct area, and can be considered a key enabler that requires attention to enable the development and execution of a climate change risk management strategy in any organization.

This chapter focuses on the use and articulation of a consistent climate risk taxonomy that can be discussed externally and used internally within organizations to ensure that all risks and opportunities are addressed and that there is a consistent approach and understanding.

Chapter 4 provides further insights into how the risk taxonomy can be developed into a climate change risk radar across the organization's risk profile that describes the risk landscape for climate-related risks covering both threats and opportunities.

FIGURE 1.1 Climate change enterprise risk management – key enablers

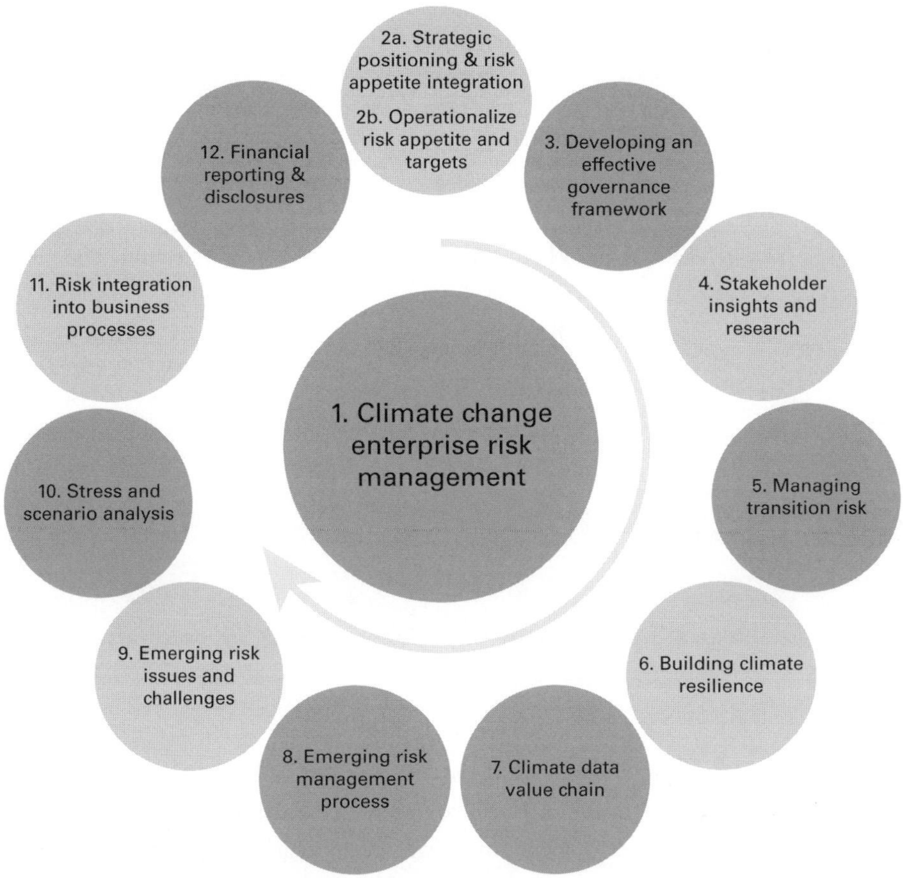

SOURCE © OneRisk Consulting. All rights reserved, 2022

1.2 Climate change and ESG integration

Although this book will be focusing on climate change it is important to understand the relationship and relevance to the wider environmental, social and governance (ESG) agenda that is becoming an increasingly prominent feature of regulation and conducting business.

Sustainability issues are becoming core considerations in business. ESG criteria are increasingly valued by shareholders, employees and customers. In recent years there has been an increasing number of corporate pledges on mitigating climate change: on average one new company joined the Science Based Targets initiative each day and committed to emission reduction goals.[2]

This momentum raises the bar for corporate governance. The growing focus on climate change also extends to corporate disclosure, and there has been significant progress on this front. Europe is taking the lead on climate-related financial disclosures, and other jurisdictions are following suit. Figure 1.2 outlines the main ESG factors used by S&P's Global Ratings agency.

FIGURE 1.2 Environmental, social and governance criteria

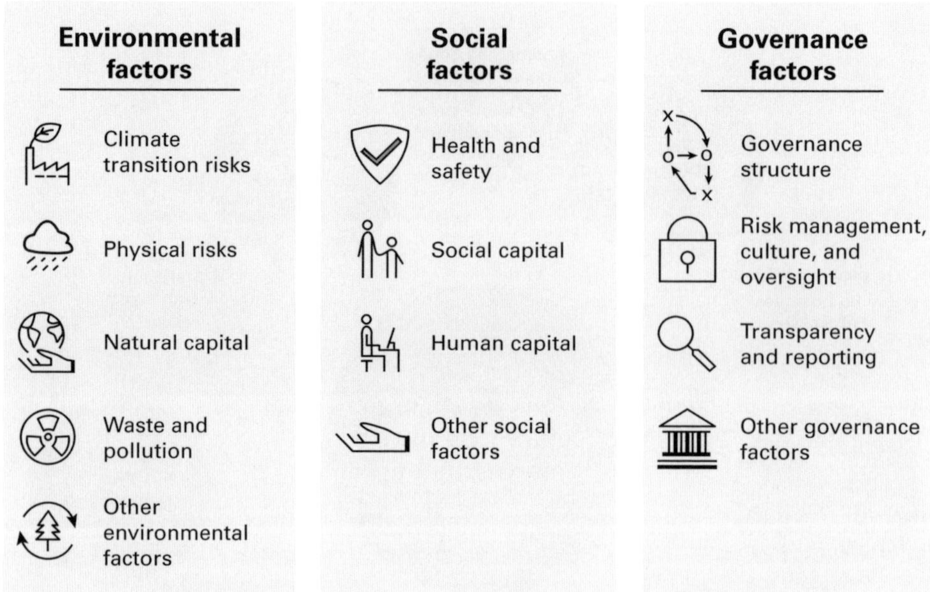

SOURCE S&P Global Ratings © 2021 by Standard & Poor's Financial Services LLC. All rights reserved

1.2.1 Use of ESG factors

ESG factors that are applied across all three components of ESG are generally used to support the assessment of compliance and performance against a set of risk indicators, typically used in the context of benchmarking, in areas such as investment strategy and supplier procurement processes, which are discussed in more detail in Chapter 11.

From a credit ratings perspective, S&P use ESG rating factors to provide an opinion on the exposure and management in respect of any material and relevant impact on the company's creditworthiness. More details of the influence and importance of credit rating agencies in respect to climate change are provided in Chapter 4 under stakeholder analysis and mapping.

1.3 Global macro risk and climate change

It is important to remember that climate change is a set of global trends. One of the best publications on emerging risks is the Global Risks Report published by the World Economic Forum.

In recent years, the World Economic Forum's top risks have been dominated by environmental risks. In their most recent report (2022), climate change accounted for the top three global risks:

- Climate action failure

- Extreme weather
- Biodiversity loss

'Climate action failure' is the risk with potential to inflict the most damage at a global scale over the next decade and climate change therefore continues to be perceived as the gravest threat to humanity.

Global economic climate trends and consequences are discussed in more detail in Chapter 9.

1.3.1 The main causes of climate change

The effects of the dramatic intensification of human activity are clearly visible in an array of indicators that monitor the Earth's living systems. This intensification has been the main cause of climate change over the last half century, leading to increases in concentration of atmospheric greenhouse gas (GHG) emissions, including carbon dioxide.

Scientists state that to avoid dangerous climate change we need to keep concentration of CO_2 below 350 parts per million. 'It is over 400 ppm and still rising, pushing us towards a hotter, drier and more hostile climate along with a rise in sea levels that threaten the future of islands and coastal cities worldwide.'[3]

According to the UN Environment Programme (UNEP) report, global greenhouse gas emissions need to fall by 7.6 per cent each year between 2020 and 2030, to stay on track towards the 1.5°C temperature goal of the Paris Agreement, and the world is not meeting these targets.[4]

1.3.2 The main impacts of climate change

The main effects of climate change include an increase in storms, floods, wildfires, heatwaves and droughts, as well as impacts on human health, biodiversity, ocean acidification and food supply. The increase in storms, floods and wildfiresin the last decade, according to Swiss Re, have been responsible for 75 per cent of all global catastrophe losses insured by the insurance industry, with wildfires becoming a particular concern. The historical information is a valuable indicator of future climate trends in respect to events and types of hazards from a global perspective set out in Figure 1.3.

In July 2020, in the Swiss Re sigma 1/2021 report 'Natural Catastrophes in 2020', the Group Chief Economist of Swiss Re, Jerome Haegeli, stated that 'climate change is a systemic risk for the whole world. Unlike the COVID-19 crisis, it does not have an expiry date'.

Figure 1.3 highlights the increasing cost of weather-related losses that are twice as high now than ten years ago. In a 2021 Swiss Re Report, it states that 'severe floods in Australia, ice storms in Texas and wildfires in California – the latest series of natural catastrophes point to a world increasingly at risk from extreme weather and climate change.'[5]

FIGURE 1.3 Global insured natural catastrophe losses by peril

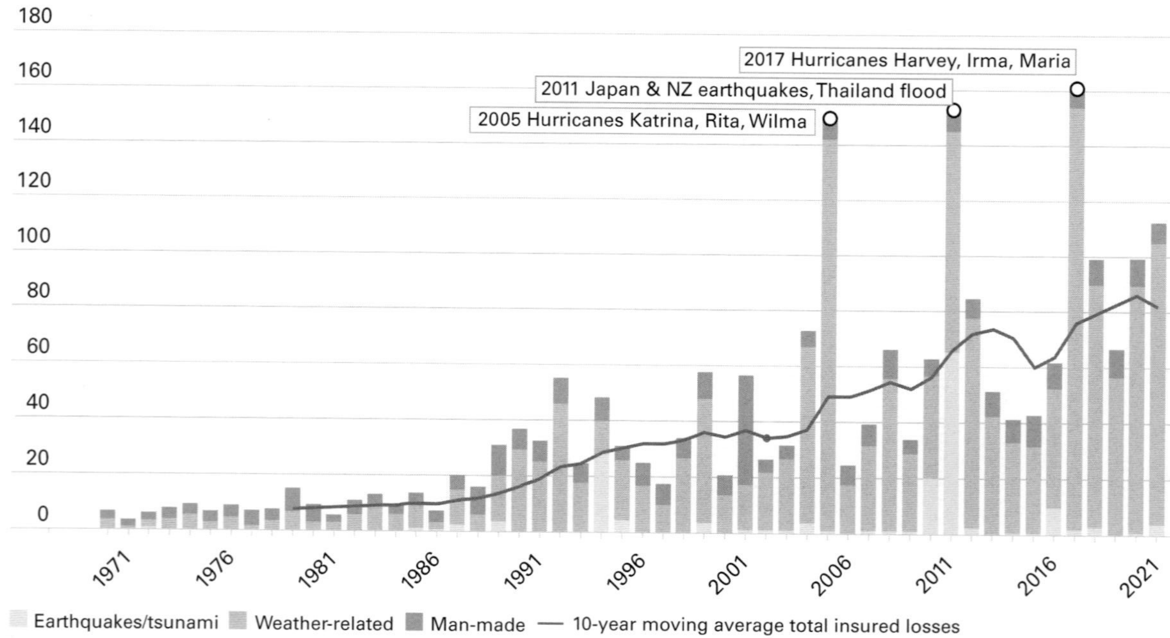

SOURCE Swiss Re Institute

It also points out that secondary perils have been rising steadily, driven by urban sprawl and climate change that include localized weather events such as thunderstorms, flooding and wildfires which are pushing up insurance losses.

In 2005, Hurricane Katrina cost the US economy $105 billion. There is an ongoing progression of climate change effects that will occur without adequate adaptation and mitigation by organizations. An extreme example of this was in 2020 when Pacific Gas & Electric, a US energy company, was heralded as the first 'climate change bankruptcy' when it filed for bankruptcy in the face of liabilities from wildfires, which reportedly amounted to $30 billion.

1.3.3 Climate change and weather distribution

Climate change from a statistical perspective can be simplified and defined as a change in the weather distribution curve, with extreme weather events reflecting the tails of the distribution curve.

Figure 1.4 provides a simplistic explanation of how small shifts in average temperature can create greater extremes in the tail of the distribution of temperature that are leading to, for example, hotter and longer heatwaves.

FIGURE 1.4 Climate change and weather distribution

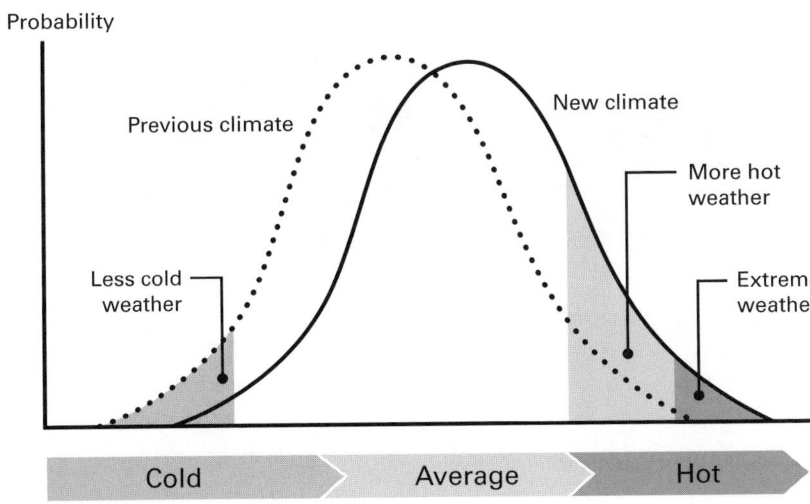

SOURCE US Environmental Protection Agency (EPA

REVIEW OF 2021 DIRECT ECONOMIC LOSSES FROM NATURAL CATASTROPHE – AON

Direct economic losses and physical damage resulting from natural disasters are increasing and estimated at $343 billion in 2021. It is important to recognize that events from weather and climate-related events, which are defined as events caused by atmospheric-driven phenomena, totalled $329 billion. This represents over 95 per cent of total economic losses, and is 45 per cent higher than the average and 52 per cent higher than the median in the last century. This clearly highlights an alarming upward trend.

The most notable takeaway from the economic costs of natural disasters in 2021 was the frequency of large-scale and highly impactful events. Four individual events topped the $20 billion economic loss threshold: Hurricane Ida, July flooding in Europe (Bernd), summer seasonal flooding in China and the February polar vortex in North America (US/Mexico). This was just the second time on record in which four $20+ billion events had been registered in a calendar year, but the first time that four events were weather/climate related.

Figure 1.5 provides an overview of the events in 2021 split by hazard and highlights the four events that generated economic losses above $20 billion.

FIGURE 1.5 Significant economic loss events in 2021 – > $1 billion

SOURCE Data: Aon (Catastrophe Insight)

When viewing economic losses on an aggregate basis since the start of the 21st century, tropical cyclone is the costliest global hazard. It is worth noting that 41 per cent of tropical cyclone losses in this century occurred within the last five years (2017–2021).

FIGURE 1.6 Cumulative economic losses split by peril

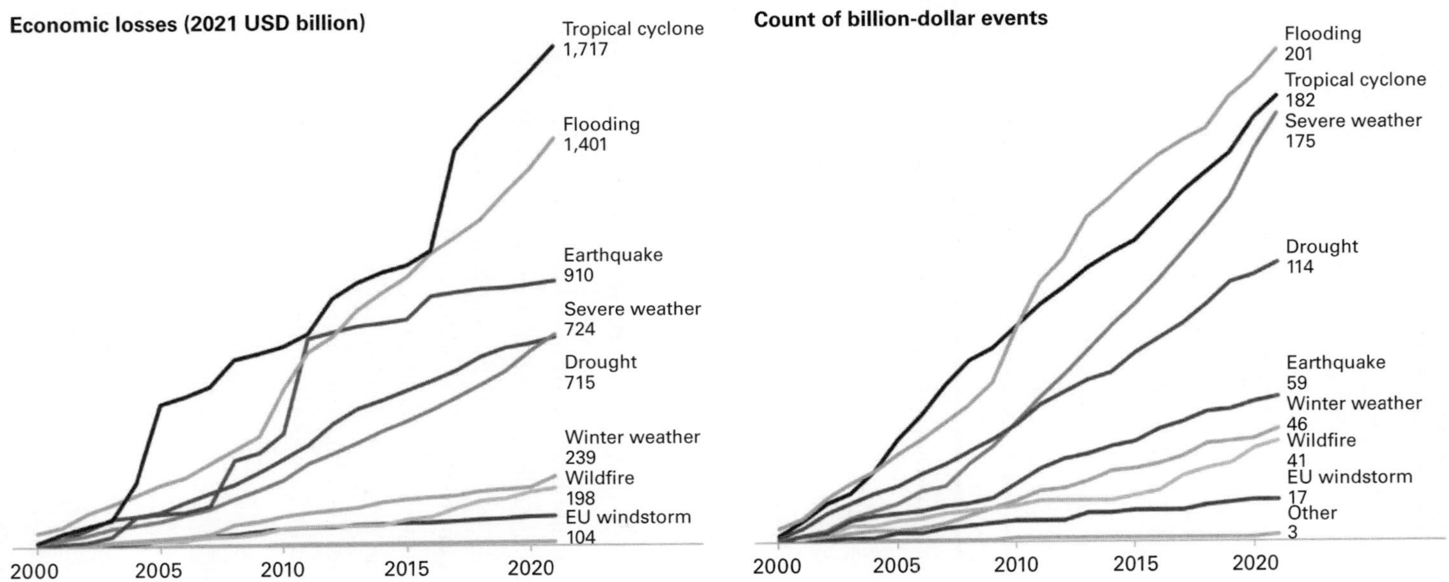

SOURCE Data: Aon (Catastrophe Insight)

FIGURE 1.7 The top six areas of physical climate change risks in the UK

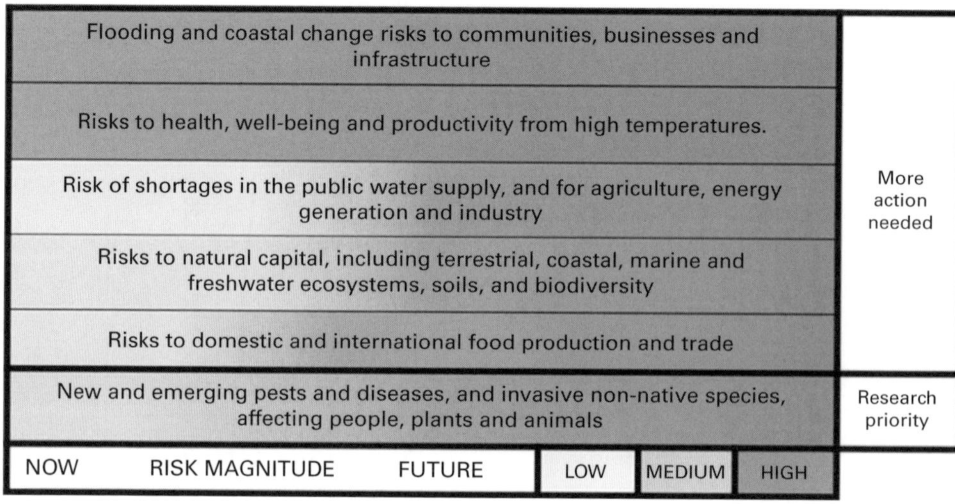

SOURCE Committee on Climate Change (2016) UK Climate Change Risk Assessment 2017 synthesis report

If we get more localized a different set of specific risks are applicable. A good example is from the UK's Climate Risk Assessment report, which highlights the top six physical climate risks outlined in Figure 1.7 from a government perspective.[6]

1.4 Key drivers and expectations for organizations

There has been a significant shift in recent years from governments and organizations to tackle climate change and manage risks as both threats and opportunities. This is due to many external drivers, expectations and pressures.

Organizations must therefore address a growing number of critical drivers of change and expectations, including new international and national legislation and regulation and the voluntary disclosure approach led by the Task Force on Climate-related Disclosures (TCFD). Other major drivers include increasing public concerns and pressure from lobby groups, activists, regulators and investors.

1.4.1 The Paris Agreement 2015

The main change driver is the Paris Agreement , which was adopted by 196 parties at COP21 in Paris in 2015 and came into force in 2016. The agreement sets out with long-term goals to keep the increase in global average temperature to well below 2°C above pre-industrial levels and to pursue efforts to limit the rise to 1.5°C. The climate ambition alliance was set up by United Nations Framework Convention on Climate Change to achieve net-zero CO_2 emissions by 2050 at the latest.

FIGURE 1.8 Ambition mechanism and targets in the Paris Agreement

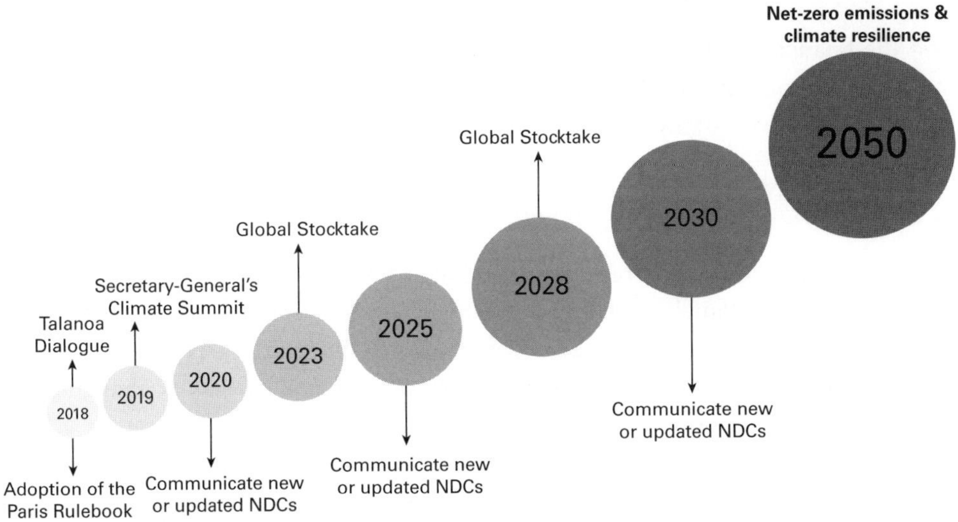

SOURCE World Resources Institute

We heard at COP26 in 2021 that we are now on course for global temperatures to reach 2.4°C above pre-industrial levels by the end of the century. This is concerning for governments and policy makers. The key question is how societies worldwide put in place the steps outlined under the agreed global action plan.

The Paris Agreement sets out energy pathways consistent with nationally determined contributions (NDCs) from signatory countries that need to report on their efforts and progress to the international community. Every five years the international community will take stock of collective progress towards the Paris Agreement's long-term goals ('ambition mechanism'). Chapter 4 explores stakeholder expectations in more detail and highlights the importance of stakeholder analysis and mapping as a key risk identification tool for organizations to utilize.

The two main outcomes from COP26 were the signing of the Glasgow Climate Pact and agreeing the Paris Rulebook. The Glasgow Climate Pact is a 'series of decisions and resolutions that build on the Paris accord', setting out what needs to be done to tackle climate change. However, it does not stipulate what each country must do and is not legally binding.

The Paris Rulebook[7] provides guidelines on how the Paris Agreement is delivered. A focus of COP26 was to secure agreement between all the Paris signatories on how they would set out their NDCs to reduce emissions. The finalized Rulebook includes agreements on:

- An enhanced transparency framework for reporting emissions
- Common timeframes for emissions reductions targets
- Mechanisms and standards for international carbon markets

It is important to note that the economic overhang of the Covid-19 crisis and weakened social cohesion – in advanced and developing economies alike – may further limit the financial and political capital available for stronger climate action. China and India, for example, lobbied at COP26 to change the Pact's wording from 'phase out' to 'phase down' of 'unabated coal power and inefficient fossil fuel subsidies'.

1.4.2 Intergovernmental Panel on Climate Change (IPCC)

There are many excellent reports on climate change and the United Nations Intergovernmental Panel on Climate Change (IPCC) released the 'The Physical Science Basis Report' in 2021 in advance of COP26, which the UN chief has stated 'is a code red for humanity'. The report states that human activity is changing the climate in unprecedented and sometimes irreversible ways.

The landmark study warns of increasingly extreme heatwaves, droughts and flooding, and a key temperature limit being broken in just over a decade.

1.4.3 Global regulators (including the Bank of England)

Supervisory and regulatory authorities have many aims but they typically include protecting customers, ensuring market stability and supporting market development. Climate-related changes threaten each of these aims.

The speed of this change has meant best practice and regulation have evolved very rapidly and are continuing to develop, particularly in the financial sector. We have witnessed a significant change and improvement in best practices in recent years that can be largely attributed to the development of regulatory expectations and guidance.

In July 2020 the Prudential Regulation Authority (PRA) sent a letter to all CEOs in the UK across all financial institutions, which stated that 'Climate change represents a material financial risk to regulated firms in the financial system'.

The letter stated that organizations need to consider the far-reaching breadth and magnitude that climate change represents, distinguishing between financial and non-financial risk management, corporate responsibility (particularly in respect to reputational risk), customers' behaviours and legal risk.

Regulation is evolving quite rapidly and there has been a shift in emphases in recent years to adaption and the need to reduce carbon emissions to reach net-zero targets for organizations to align their strategies to meet government targets.

Evidence of this shift can be seen through the Bank of England's climate change adaptation report issued in October 2021 entitled 'Climate-related financial risk management and the role of capital requirements' in which it stated 'a proactive response is needed to ensure financial institutions are resilient to the financial risks from climate change and able to support an economy-wide transition to net-zero emissions'.

Government guidance has been helpful to organizations. For example, the PRA set out four key pillars for financial organizations. Each of these pillars has sub-themes, and these components are covered in various chapters in this book so that regulatory best practice expectations are addressed. Some of the most important requirements set out by the regulator that organizations can seek to develop under each pillar are as follows:

Under Governance

✓ Appoint a 'Senior Management Function' to take lead responsibility for climate change risks.

Under Risk management

✓ Formally consider climate change within an organization's risk management framework.

For Scenario analysis

✓ Conduct regular scenario analysis covering a range of timescales to different transition paths.

For Disclosures

✓ Ensure that they reflect the firm's evolving understanding of the financial risks.

The PRA expectations are that organizations should have developed a robust framework to manage climate-related financial risks by the of end of 2021. But for risk practitioners that implement best practice ERM it's a journey and it is important to design a robust road map for implementation.

1.4.4 Task Force on Climate-related Financial Disclosures (TCFD)

Organizations increasingly need to meet new international and national legislation and regulations including the voluntary approach led by the Task Force on Climate-related Financial Disclosures (TCFD). These disclosures are becoming mandatory in many countries such as the UK from 2023 for certain organizations. Reporting and disclosures will be covered in detail in Chapter 12.

These key drivers and increased public pressure have led to a step change in momentum and action by governments and organizations around the world.

The Task Force encourages organizations to undertake both historical and forward-looking analyses when considering the potential financial impacts of climate change, with a greater focus on forward-looking analyses as the efforts to mitigate and adapt to climate change are without historical precedent.[8] Its assessment framework is set out in Figure 1.9 and we will cover scenario analysis in more detail in Chapter 10.

FIGURE 1.9 TCFD guidance

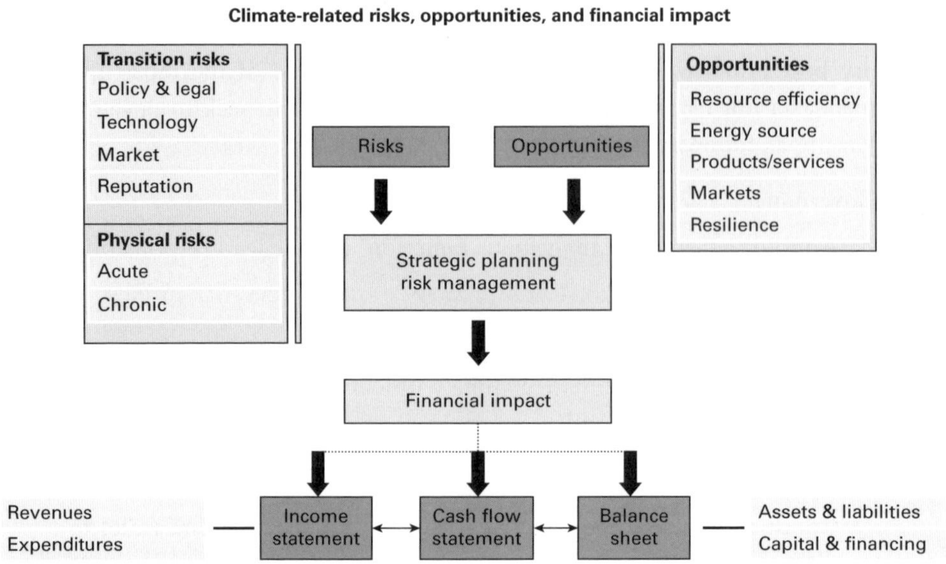

SOURCE TCFD Final Report, 2017

1.4.5 Climate change and society's responses

These drivers and expectations have led to a step change in momentum and action by governments and organizations worldwide. There is a growing recognition that climate change is not just a matter for the future and in order to fully understand risks faced now and in the future, we need to understand the history and development of those risks.

This has led government and corporations to set emissions targets, which are becoming central to organizations' strategic objectives and included within their risk appetite metrics to manage and monitor.

For example, Microsoft hit the headlines recently with its pledge to become 'carbon negative' by 2030, and to remove all carbon emitted since the company was founded in 1974 by 2050. They have set up a new $1 billion Climate Innovation Fund to stimulate and accelerate development of carbon removal technology.

With respect to the energy sector, BP's CEO Bernard Looney has pledged net zero emissions by 2050. In the words of this CEO, 'the world's carbon budget is finite and running out fast'.[9] To meet the targets, energy companies need to reduce existing production over time, develop technologies to capture carbon and invest more heavily in renewables such as wind farms and solar power.

Chapter 5 covers management of transition risks, providing a global perspective on carbon emissions and mitigation strategies and what government and regulators are doing to meet their net zero targets. A sample of organizational responses and targets are set out in Figure 1.10.

Companies need a robust framework in place to identify and manage both climate risks and opportunities across different risk types.

Climate plans and associated management information should be communicated regularly to the board, which will allow for strategic discussions that support decision making in terms of evaluating risk and rewards tradeoffs.

ERM integration considerations should include risk policies, risk mitigation strategies, and improvements in monitoring capabilities and design of risk appetite metrics and targets.

1.5 Developing a climate change risk taxonomy

While it is important to treat climate-related risks as drivers of existing risks and map them to their existing risk categories, it is also important to develop a consistent taxonomy that can be discussed externally and used internally within organizations

FIGURE 1.10 Organizational responses – examples to meet net zero emissions goals

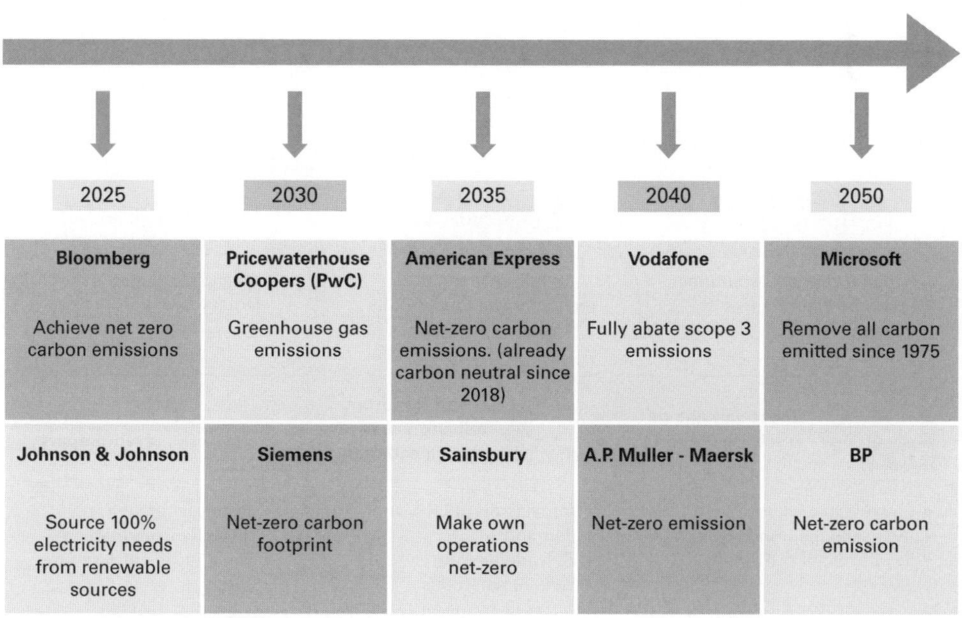

SOURCE

to ensure that all risks and opportunities are addressed and that there is a consistent approach and understanding.

A new climate risk taxonomy developed initially by the Financial Stability Board and adopted by many regulators such as the Australian Prudential Regulatory Authority (APRA), is shown in Figure 1.11.[10] It provides a clear delineation of the financial risks associated with climate change, namely physical, transition and liability risks.

Physical risks include direct damage to assets and indirect impacts of supply chain disruption. Physical risks can be event-driven (acute) or longer-term shifts (chronic). Specific examples include:

- **Acute physical risks**, which arise from particular events, especially weather-related events such as storms, floods, fires or heatwaves that may damage production facilities and disrupt value chains.
- **Chronic physical risks**, which arise from longer-term changes in the climate, such as temperature changes, rising sea levels, reduced water availability, biodiversity loss and changes in land and soil productivity.

For example, the intensity and frequency of wildfires, often driven by drought, are becoming an increasing concern particularly for Australia, southern Europe and parts of the US, including California. Other noted examples relate to property portfolios for banks and insurers that will become increasingly susceptible to climate risk from acute or chronic perils: flooding; storms; mudslides; water-level rise.

Transition risks relate to financial risks that arise as a consequence of transitioning to a lower-carbon or 'green' economy. These risks arise from related transformations

FIGURE 1.11 Climate change risk taxonomy

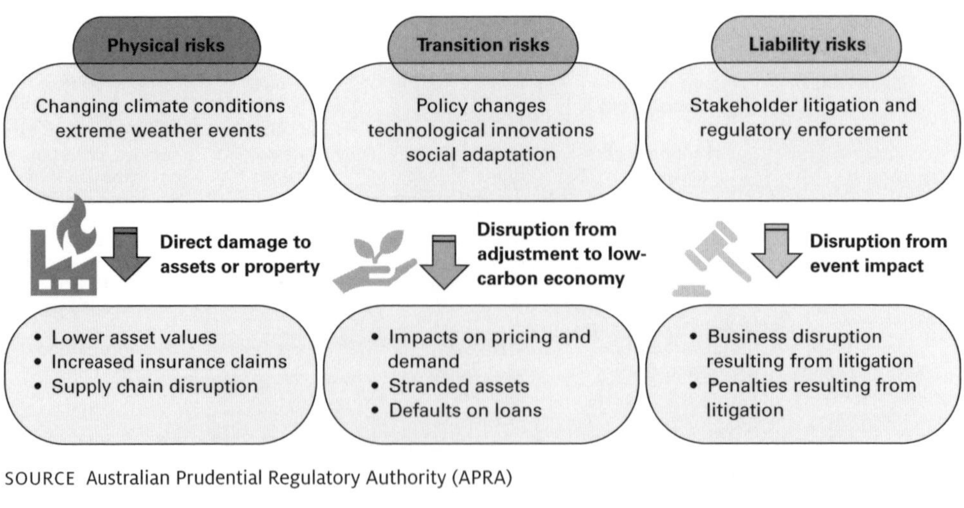

SOURCE Australian Prudential Regulatory Authority (APRA)

including regulatory policy such as carbon taxes, technology and market disruption that will include innovation in renewable energy.

Transition risks are developing as governments support and subsidize low-carbon industries and regulate and tax high-carbon ones. They are also developing as public attitudes and preferences change. They can include legal risk as well, but for some organizations it may make sense to treat liability risks separately, since they may be exposed to liability risks from past activities that are not directly related to the transition itself.

Liability risks stem from the potential for litigation if entities and boards do not adequately consider or respond to the impacts of climate change, as well as stakeholders that are seeking compensation from past climate inactivity or misrepresentation.

This may include the potential breaching of directors' duties. In February 2020, the UK Government's decision to allow plans for a third runway at Heathrow airport was ruled unlawful by the UK Court of Appeal because it did not take climate commitments into account. This was the first judgment in the world to be based on the Paris Agreement and will have an impact both in the UK and globally by inspiring challenges against other high-carbon projects.

Some of the main legal challenges can arise from:

- Failure to mitigate GHG emissions
- Failure to adapt to the physical impacts of climate change
- Failure to adapt investment strategies

Chapter 9 outlines some of the latest emerging liability risks and legal cases that are important for organizations to consider.

1.5.1 Other climate risk taxonomies

It is important to recognize that there are other climate taxonomies being used that cover the wider scope of environment risks such as waste and pollution. Other risk descriptors that are being used by credit rating agencies, for example, include 'natural capital' risks, which relate to the stock or availability of renewable and non-renewable resources available in the world. These are made up of elements such as animals, water and air, and biodiversity, which are all features of natural capital.

Throughout the book the main focus is to cover the broad risk taxonomy of physical and transition risks, including some reference to emerging liability risks in Chapter 9. However, the main objective is to explain how the climate-related risks can be integrated into an organization's existing ERM framework as well as business-as-usual practices.

1.6 Climate change integration into an existing ERM framework

To successfully embed climate risk management within an organization and to align the climate risk strategy to the wider group business and strategic objectives, it makes sense to leverage the various facets of the enterprise risk management framework that already exist and to incorporate and align climate risk considerations whenever appropriate.

A robust ERM framework should ensure that an organization meets the following three key goals:

- ✓ Provide a framework to ensure that corporate risks are managed and mitigated.
- ✓ Grow shareholder value through making smart risk–return-based decisions.
- ✓ Enhance the company's reputation across a wide range of stakeholders.

According to the most recent COSO (Committee of Sponsoring Organizations – a body founded in 1985 focused on the design and implementation of internal controls) framework, 'Enterprise risk management is no longer focused principally on preventing the erosion of value and minimizing risk to an acceptable level. Rather, it is viewed as integral to strategy setting and the identification of opportunities to create and maintain value.'

So how can risk managers integrate climate change into their ERM frameworks? The design of a climate change strategy should align to the existing ERM framework and wider group business and strategic objectives

1.6.1 Specific integration challenges and benefits

Risk managers, through collaboration with a range of stakeholders, will need to play an increasing role in supporting organizations in identifying, assessing and managing their climate-related risks and opportunities and integrating them within existing ERM frameworks.

This integration of emerging risk information and analysis will provide a number of benefits, including an improved risk appetite framework and risk mitigation strategies across most areas considered within an organization's risk profile.

One of the biggest challenges and focus areas for organizations is how to develop a climate change risk appetite strategy with supporting qualitative statements and quantitative metrics, to manage and monitor risk in line with risk tolerances. This is set out in more detail in Chapter 2.

It is essential, therefore, that a centralized ERM approach with a robust governance structure be utilized at all levels throughout the organization in managing risks and opportunities. This will enable the organization to be in a stronger position to make more informed decisions, deliver on its objectives and meet strategic climate ambitions such as net zero targets.

FIGURE 1.12 Conditions and outcomes of embedding climate change into an ERM framework

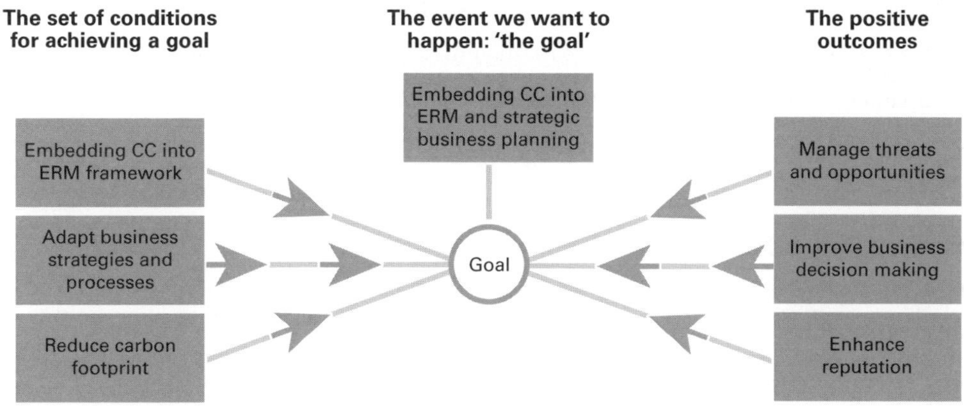

SOURCE © OneRisk Consulting. All rights reserved, 2022

The overall goal should be to embed the various actions into business as usual (BAU) and to support business decision-making. The conditions and positive outcomes of doing so are illustrated at a high level in Figure 1.12.

With these steps in place, the development of a climate risk strategy can begin. This is typically a subset of the corporate strategy (but not always – for some firms it will be the corporate strategy). This should be complemented by outlining how the company achieves the corporate strategy in a sustainable and climate-friendly way. Climate strategic positioning and risk appetite integration is covered in Chapter 2.

The benefits of such an approach are that it fits within the existing risk management infrastructure, which is already understood and used by the business. It also prevents duplication of effort, minimizes unnecessary reporting and saves time. This will:

- ensure that there is a robust framework in place to identify and manage climate risks and opportunities across different risk types
- ensure that the climate plan, actions and associated management information, which allow for strategic discussions that support decision making in terms of evaluating risk and rewards trade-offs, are communicated regularly to the board
- integrate ERM considerations, which should include policies, thresholds, mitigation strategies, monitoring capabilities, and risk appetite metrics and targets

The discipline of climate risk management should be considered an extension of standard enterprise risk management and align with the risk frameworks, policies and taxonomies. It should also integrate with the key risk management tools such as risk appetite statements, risk policies, scenario analysis, etc. Developing risk mitigation plans and improving the control environment is also critical and organizations need to align them with stakeholder expectations and to their strategic objectives, core operations and processes.

This approach to risk management will support the company's integration of risk management within the business processes, including:

- Sustainability strategy including management of carbon footprint (Chapter 5)
- Business continuity and disaster recovery planning (Chapter 6)
- Financial and investment planning (Chapter 11)
- Third-party procurement processes including suppliers and customers (Chapter 11)
- Performance management (Chapter 3)
- Insurance procurement (Chapter 6)
- Product innovation (Chapter 9; Chapter 11)
- Risk modelling and concentration management (Chapter 7)
- Capital management (Chapter 6)
- Credit risk management (Chapter 2; Chapter 11)
- Human resources and employee benefits (Chapter 3)
- Litigation risk (Chapter 9)

1.7 Developing a climate change risk maturity model

In setting ambition and targets in respect to climate change and integration into an existing ERM framework, an organization should consider developing or adapting a risk maturity model for climate change.

As well as deciding on its level of climate ambition and strategic positioning, it is also important to consider the level of long-term climate risk maturity and goals that the organization wants to achieve against specific criteria that are set out in Figure 1.13.

There are various risk maturity models that have been designed to assist organizations in assessing their maturity against a set of best practice criteria in the form of ERM components.

Risk maturity models typically have an assessment level of between 1 and 5, which helps to determine where the organization is and set a target level for each of the main components within the model.

The descriptions of the five levels to determine the performance and capabilities of an organization's enterprise risk management maturity vary. An example is outlined here with key descriptors:

1. Ad hoc or underdeveloped
2. Initial or formalized

3 Repeatable or established
4 Managed or embedded
5 Leadership or optimized

Example definitions for Levels 4 and 5, which are the most aspirational, would constitute the following:

- **Embedded** – The 'embedded' level is defined as measuring and managing risks quantitively and on an aggregated basis throughout the organization. Essentially this entails a proactive approach to the management of risk at all levels of the organization with management having a clear understanding of the risks and the process.
- **Optimized** – The optimized level states that risk management is a source of competitive advantage for the organization and that the organization undertakes continuous risk improvement. This level implies that the risk is integral to strategic and business decision-making and capital optimization and that ERM is backed by a single IT platform and knowledge management system.

In order to successfully achieve an organization's desired ERM target state, a full review of the current status against maturity models should be undertaken.

The main steps in developing a formalized process would be to:

- Agree maturity model categories
- Review of current framework/infrastructure
- Discussion with key stakeholders
- Review regulatory requirements
- Rate the current maturity on a scale of 1–5
- Develop a future state vision for each category/sub-category

ILLUSTRATIVE EXAMPLE

Climate risk maturity model

An approach that can be adapted to specifically evaluate the maturity of an organization's climate change enterprise risk management programme is outlined in Figure 1.13.

This approach can seek to ascertain the organization's existing and target levels of climate risk ambition and target climate maturity. The process can be benchmarked against, for example, TCFD and other regulatory requirements and standards including best practice risk management standards.

The process provides a basis for risk professionals to engage with management and agree on a set of management action and mitigation plans to support areas that need most attention and build a road map for improvements in order to reach the target risk maturity level for each criteria.

FIGURE 1.13 Climate risk maturity model illustration

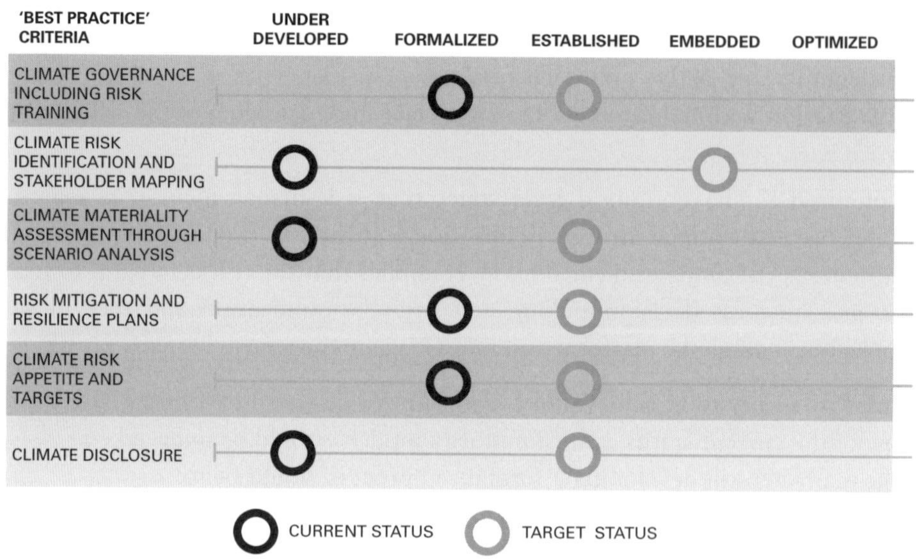

SOURCE © OneRisk Consulting. All rights reserved, 2022

This book addresses and discusses each of the main criteria shown in Figure 1.13, which represent the most important climate ERM framework components. For example, developing an effective climate governance framework is outlined in Chapter 3, and climate risk identification and stakeholder mapping is included in Chapter 4.

Conclusion

Climate change continues to be perceived as the gravest threat to humanity and in the latest Global Risks Report (2022) respondents rated 'climate action failure' as the risk with potential to inflict the most damage at a global scale over the next decade.

Risk managers, through collaboration with a range of stakeholders, will need to play an increasing role in supporting organizations in identifying, assessing and managing their climate-related risks and opportunities and integrating them within existing ERM frameworks in order to support strategic business decisions.

This chapter has set the scene for the rest of the book in outlining the main components of a climate risk management framework, which can be developed into a risk maturity model to support the implementation of climate change plans within an organization. Specific case studies and examples of best practice processes and tools and techniques will be used throughout the book to provide additional detail on each of these aspects.

Notes

1 R J Chapman (2012) Monitoring and review: Stage 6, in *Simple Tools and Techniques for Enterprise Risk Management*, 2nd edn, 233–40. doi:10.1002/9781118467206 (archived at https://perma.cc/8EC9-36T3), Ch 13

2 Swiss Re Institute. Sigma 4/2021 – More risk: the changing nature of P&C insurance opportunities to 2040, 2021. www.swissre.com/institute/research/sigma-research/sigma-2021-04.html (archived at https://perma.cc/8ALG-APKS)

3 K Raworth (2018) *Doughnut Economics: Seven ways to think like a 21st-century economist*, Random House Business Books, London

4 UN Environment Programme. Cut global emissions by 7.6 percent every year for next decade to meet 1.5°C Paris target, 2019. www.unep.org/news-and-stories/press-release/cut-global-emissions-76-percent-every-year-next-decade-meet-15degc (archived at https://perma.cc/42DE-K5WC)

5 Swiss Re. In 5 charts: natural catastrophes in a changing climate, 2021. www.swissre.com/risk-knowledge/mitigating-climate-risk/sigma-in-5-charts.html (archived at https://perma.cc/CAP6-RAHZ)

6 HM Government. UK Climate Change Risk Assessment 2017. https://assets.publishing.service.gov.uk/government/uploads/system/uploads/attachment_data/file/584281/uk-climate-change-risk-assess-2017.pdf (archived at https://perma.cc/J4JT-3WZA)

7 UN Climate Change Conference UK 2021. COP26 keeps 1.5C alive and finalises Paris Agreement, 2021. https://ukcop26.org/cop26-keeps-1-5c-alive-and-finalises-paris-agreement/ (archived at https://perma.cc/2TRM-5BY9)

8 TCFD. Recommendations of the Task Force on Climate-related Financial Disclosures. Final Report, 2017. https://assets.bbhub.io/company/sites/60/2020/10/FINAL-2017-TCFD-Report-11052018.pdf (archived at https://perma.cc/AA65-E8GQ)

9 BP. BP sets ambition for net zero by 2050, fundamentally changing organisation to deliver, 2020. www.bp.com/en/global/corporate/news-and-insights/press-releases/bernard-looney-announces-new-ambition-for-bp.html (archived at https://perma.cc/HU4U-PCZH)

10 APRA. Information Paper: Climate change: Awareness to action, 2019. www.apra.gov.au/sites/default/files/climate_change_awareness_to_action_march_2019.pdf (archived at https://perma.cc/A72G-9KW7)

2

Climate strategic positioning and risk appetite integration

This chapter explains the importance of developing a stand-alone climate change strategy, including the setting of the ambition for change for the organization, which should be aligned to the overall corporate strategy. As well as covering the need to develop a strategy focused on both sustainability and resilience, the chapter provides a detailed insight into how an organization should develop its climate risk appetite strategy, supporting both qualitative and quantitative metrics and targets.

The main learning outcomes from this chapter are to:

- Explain how organizations can set their strategic positioning and ambition in respect to climate change.
- Recognize the importance of the influence that risk leaders can exert in their boards and board risk committees in developing and supporting a climate change strategy for the organization with an impact on wider society.
- Understand the four levels of ambition that an organization can adopt in terms of its strategic positioning that is dictated by the board.
- Appreciate the key dimensions of establishing a climate strategy that will be underpinned by the two foundation components, namely resilience and sustainability.
- Understand the importance of developing a climate change plan and road map that allocates and prioritizes actions to specific workstreams with timelines to completion.
- Be able to design and implement an organization's risk appetite strategy that can help to articulate and shape its overall strategy, including the development of climate risk principles and objectives.
- Be able to design and embed key climate change risk indicators across the organization's risk profile, to help to measure and monitor its climate change-related exposures.

Introduction

Upon the establishment of the consistent climate risk taxonomy that was discussed in Chapter 1, the next step is to align this with the climate risk strategy, determine priorities and develop a detailed plan in order to meet the climate risk objectives. In the context of aligning risk management with strategic planning, Norman Marks states:

> Businesses should set objectives and strategies only after thinking carefully about where you are, what is happening around you, and what may happen in the future. These objectives and strategies should then be executed on, with an eye kept on what is happening as you progress on that may affect the success of your journey.[1]

In almost all recent risk surveys, climate risk features in the top 10 risks facing organizations (this includes surveys from the CRO Forum, WEF, Swiss Re, Zurich and McKinsey). Many organizations now have climate change as a strategic or principal risk with an assigned owner and are developing associated risk appetite strategies, including key risk indicators, to manage the risks.

It is reasonable to say that climate risk has now emerged and needs addressing now (as opposed to requiring mitigation in the future). It is indisputable that climate risk is a strategic risk facing almost all businesses. Consequently, it requires executive ownership, governance arrangements that support the management of climate risk and for there to be appropriate resourcing.

In terms of alignment to strategy and the positioning of climate change within that strategy it is important to remember that missed organizational goals often result from ineffectively managed risk(s) or from taking the wrong amount of risk.

Risk professionals can support the climate ambitions of an organization by applying their expertise in providing a structured approach (that helps the business manage the risk) and aligning the overall corporate ambition with the enterprise risk management framework.

The CRO of BHP (an Australian multinational mining, metals and petroleum company) stated in an interview for this book that 'Competent people don't take undue risks'. In this chapter we explore how organizations need to develop their climate risk appetite strategy across different dimensions to enable them to better manage and mitigate the risks from climate change. It can be argued that the level of ambition and risk maturity of an organization is linked to the competence and long-term reputation of the organization. This is being played out with climate-related disclosures, which are discussed in Chapter 12.

2.1 Corporate strategy and purpose

Most organizations have a defined corporate strategy, which outlines the goals and ambitions of the organization (i.e., what they do and why they do it), the markets and industry in which they operate, their competitive positioning and goals for the future. This provides a direction of travel for the firm and its employees and should significantly influence decision making. The corporate strategy needs to align with an organization climate strategy.

It is important at the outset that risk leaders discuss the genuine role and purpose of the firm in society with their boards and board risk committees.[2] Risk leaders must facilitate a dialogue that focuses on the WHY and avoid the temptation to immediately focus on the HOW. Purpose can be described simply as why you exist.

2.1.1 Alignment of climate strategy with corporate strategy

Designing a climate strategy involves the actual and potential impacts on the organization's strategy, business and financial planning, while climate risk management deals with the processes used by the organization to identify, assess and manage climate-related risks. It can be argued that the 'glue' between the corporate strategy and the ERM strategy is the risk appetite of the organization.

Figure 2.1 sets out the main components of designing climate strategy that will be covered in this chapter.

2.2 Developing a climate risk strategy

The risk management function can play a critical role in designing the overall climate change risk appetite of the organization and ensure that it aligns with the overall corporate strategy of the organization.

The breadth of climate change presents firms with challenges when assessing the actual and potential impacts on the strategic position of the firm. This may require firms to repurpose and re-evaluate business strategy and financial planning

FIGURE 2.1 Climate change strategy – the three core components

SOURCE OneRisk Consulting

over the short, medium and long term. This will likely have negative impacts in terms of, for example, increases in operational costs but it also provides positive implications for the firm's existing business and operating models.

It is important for risk leaders to consider the uncertainties associated with each strategic option. As the awareness of climate change risk increases, business strategy cannot be fully developed without factoring in climate change opportunities.

Some of the most important questions that need to be considered in developing the strategy include the following:

- Does the board consider the actual and potential impacts of climate-related risks and opportunities on the firm's business, strategy and financial planning?[3]
- Has the board positioned evaluating and addressing climate change implications as a priority?[4]

In developing a climate strategy and broader ESG strategy, recent experience indicates that while the climate strategy needs to align with the corporate strategy, the climate strategy itself supports and develops the corporate strategy. Effectively the alignment of these components enables the development of a sustainability strategy.

In order to align a combination of corporate, ESG, climate and sustainability strategy (the balance and importance of these will differ from firm to firm), a set of additional strategic questions for senior management to consider are set out here:

- How could climate change risk affect the strategic plan or the company's mission?
- Have you developed a climate change plan that meets regular expectations about the impacts across your operations?
- What is the board's role in this?
- Has your organization defined and communicated its beliefs relating to climate change risk?
- How does the company integrate climate-related risks into its risk policies and overall approach to risk management?
- Has the company conducted an assessment of its stated climate positions and benchmarked itself against its trade and industry associations and other industry sectors?
- What are your climate risk objectives?
- Within what time frame will this be achieved?

2.2.1 *Strategic positioning and levels of ambition*

In terms of strategy, firms will need to decide on their level of ambition with regard to climate risk. The level of ambition should align with the target level of climate risk maturity that was discussed in Chapter 1. Firms will need to decide whether to take a passive role in managing the risks and effecting change, or if the ambition is to make active changes to the way the business is run in response to climate change and be a 'force for good' that leads the industry and supports the wider society in which it operates.

By creating a climate risk ambition, executives become accountable for its delivery and senior management have an informed view of what they are trying to achieve. This then infuses the decision making in the business with regard to the options for how it can be achieved, and the actual and potential impacts of climate-related risks on the business processes, strategic objectives and financial plans of the firm. This then influences the work required to achieve those goals, the understanding the relative priorities of these actions, and to formulate plans to address gaps or areas of weakness.

In terms of climate ambition, there are generally four levels of ambition that organizations are adopting for the strategic positioning that should be set by the board. These ambitions need to be proportionate and will be influenced by the profitability of the firm, the industry sector in which it operates (which will require peer comparison and benchmarking), the size of the organization and the expectations of other stakeholder groups.

These ambitions are generally termed as follows:

- Follower – reactive to requirements
- Adapter – proactively adopts new standards
- Champion – advocate for industry
- Leader – climate is core to strategy

These categories generally reflect the amount of investment and resource the organization can allocate to climate change. For example, having an aggressive net zero ambition that requires the organization to quickly adapt its business models will put that organization into the 'leader' category. This may require it to invest in product innovation in order to gain competitive advantage and be seen to be an early adopter of change.

Many organizations have the ambition to be a 'leader' but do not have the ability in terms of resources and capabilities. Often their ambition will be limited to being an 'adapter' to make sure that they adhere to minimum stakeholder expectations. This will often include meeting regulatory requirements, which can be quite onerous.

Organizations are often described in the context of climate change ambition and position, as noted above, for example from industry 'leaders' to industry 'followers'. This clearly has implications in respect to the reputational risk perspective if an organization is, for example, being a follower and effectively playing a 'wait and see game' and this means that it could lose competitiveness in its respective marketplace.

In order to develop an organization positioning strategy, there are a number of steps and implementation options to be considered. These include:

- Define the level of ambition your firm wants to achieve.
- Understand what 'net zero' means for your firm and set appropriate targets and metrics.
- Develop a clear strategic response to the financial risks of climate change and tools that help to inform business decisions.
- Less complex firms may adopt a qualitative 'walk-through' that considers a possible sequence of events (shocks and responses) as a basis for developing the climate change strategy.
- More complex firms may need to adopt quantitative metrics to substantiate the risk appetite statement.

2.2.2 Types of strategic integration

Before beginning the integration of climate change ambitions, organizations should ask themselves 'Is your chosen approach to climate risks and opportunities management responsible, responsive or strategic?'

- **Responsible** – the approach driven primarily by corporate social responsibility (that focuses on reputational risks).
- **Responsive** – an approach that views climate change as a financial risk, albeit from a relatively narrow, short-term perspective.
- **Strategic** – a more comprehensive approach adopted that takes a long-term view of the financial risks, with board engagement.

It is important that the risk function works with senior leaders to consider the uncertainties associated with each option. As the awareness of the climate change risk increases, business strategy cannot be fully developed without factoring in climate change risks and opportunities. It is important to note that climate-related opportunities are expected to have more significant impact on business strategies going forward than climate-related threats.

A good example is the automotive industry in moving to electric and hybrid vehicles, driven to some extent by transition risks, due to regulatory changes and all the organizations that are involved in the supply chain. If the organization decides to take a 'strategic' approach, for example, they may be able to harness suppliers that can repair electric vehicles, while their competitors may not, given the potential lack of specialist suppliers of spare parts for electric vehicles.

2.3 Core dimensions of climate strategy

The development of a climate risk strategy is contingent on understanding the corporate strategy, the wide array of climate risk terminology, the drivers of climate change and how it can affect your organization (i.e., the outcomes, both positive and negative).

As a climate risk strategy is developed there are three dimensions that most organizations will need to consider, covering different aspects of the 'challenge' that is shown in Figure 2.2.

In isolation, the principle of 'climate change ambition' will be underpinned by the two foundational components 'resilience', and 'sustainability'. Sustainability is the focus on how the organization operates (i.e. the 'business as usual') in reducing emissions and is more aligned to transition risks. Resilience is the ability of the organization to survive and continue to operate (with regard to physical risks) and this has both financial and operational considerations. In isolation, these will not ensure success in achieving the strategic aims. However, when aligned they complement each other and provide a robust foundation for achieving both strategic and climate risk objectives.

2.3.1 Sustainability strategy

Developing a sustainable strategy for most organizations relates to the need to decarbonize and manage and mitigate transition risks, a broad risk type that affects

FIGURE 2.2 The main dimensions underpinning climate change strategy

SOURCE © OneRisk Consulting. All rights reserved, 2022

organizations across all industries, and relates to a range of risks as a consequence of transitioning to a lower-carbon or 'green' economy.

The sustainability strategy in respect to climate action plans should include an inventory of existing emissions, reduction goals or targets, and analysed and prioritized reduction actions. Ideally, a climate action plan should also include an implementation strategy that identifies required resources and funding mechanisms.

Factors that influence this include adjusting to climate-related developments in policy and regulation, emergence of disruptive technology or business models, shifting sentiment and societal preferences and evolving evidence, frameworks and legal interpretations. Managing transition risks is covered in detail in Chapter 5.

There are many questions that organizations need to address, including how much to invest, what to invest in and over what time horizon, in terms of meeting climate net zero targets, such as the development of new technologies.

Organizations that are 'front-runners', that adjust to future structural changes and put sustainability at the heart of their strategies more rapidly, should be well positioned to reap the potential benefits, such as enhanced brand image, that it will bring.

2.3.1.1 PRACTICALITIES – ESTABLISHING A BASELINE FOR CHANGE

One of the first practical steps is the need to establish a baseline. This means that firms will need to think about the different types of emissions being generated:

- Scope 1 emissions – these are direct emissions from owned or controlled sources.
- Scope 2 emissions – these are indirect emissions from the generation of purchased electricity, steam, heating and cooling consumed by the firm.
- Scope 3 emissions – these are all other indirect emissions that occur in a company's value chain.

At the outset, organizations will need to understand the factors that contribute to their carbon footprint before they can define their level of ambition and then set targets and plans. Currently many organizations are seeking to understand their carbon footprint and the options available to them, prior to formulating a climate risk strategy. Agreement on a climate risk strategy will influence the establishment of targets and metrics (against which the business can be managed going forward).

There are various levels of ambition ranging from becoming fully carbon negative to achieving carbon neutrality. This will depend on a number of factors such as:

- The corporate culture and the extent to which carbon considerations are incorporated into how the organization operates
- Expectations of the various stakeholder groups
- The industry in which they operate

- Timeframes established
- Work required to achieve these goals (while accepting this can change over time)

Sustainability plans should encompass a broader scope and address environmental, economic and social considerations beyond those directly related to climate change.

The climate crisis is changing the competitive landscape and existing business models will need to adapt if an organization is to survive and to thrive. This represents an opportunity for organizations to create competitive advantage and differentiate themselves from competitors through, for example, product innovation.

It is important for risk leaders to consider the uncertainties associated with each strategic option. As awareness of the climate change risk increases, business strategy cannot be fully developed without factoring in climate change risks and opportunities. Climate-related opportunities are expected to have more significant impact on business strategy than climate-related risks.

2.3.1.2 SUSTAINABILITY STRATEGY – DEVELOPING A ROAD MAP

In order to develop the risk appetite statement (and incorporate its stated climate risk ambitions into the organization's strategy) it is important to develop a comprehensive long-term road map.

The plan should have a variety of interim targets and workstreams.

Chapter Zero (the community of business leaders focused on climate change) proposes the approach shown in Figure 2.3,where the initiatives identified are sequenced and grouped into planning horizons on a road map.[5] The figure breaks down actions by emission types (i.e. Scopes 1, 2 and 3) and by the differing time frames (near term, medium term and longer term).

Some of the concepts and terminology raised in this chapter link to further detail in subsequent chapters, for example Chapter 5 provides a global perspective on carbon emissions and mitigation strategies. Chapter 11 will cover examples of integration reduction strategies within existing 'business as usual' processes.

FIGURE 2.3 Carbon footprint – illustrative road map

Time to impact	Under 2 years	2–5 years	5+ years
Scope 1 emissions	Drive low emissions, etc		
Scope 2 emissions			
Scope 3 emissions			
	Good business practice	Competitive differentiation	Game-changing innovation

SOURCE Principles and frameworks for climate change strategy and action, Chapter Zero

2.3.2 Business resilience strategy

At the highest level, in order to grow and operate profitably organizations need to be built on solid foundations. These foundations include an underlying ability to respond to adversity by building operational and financial resilience to climate change impacts.

Operational resilience is defined as the ability of an organization to deliver critical operations through disruption. Reactive resilience is most commonly managed through business continuity, incident response management and crisis/recovery planning, which are backward-looking and focus on recovery from specific individual high-impact risk events. For example, a flood event driven by climate change can impact on the supply chain of an organization.

From a financial resilience viewpoint, organizations need to consider how climate scenarios could impact on the financial position and design appropriate control such as pre-and post-loss financing mechanisms through, for example, insurance and hedging strategies. These risk transfer techniques typically seek to reduce volatility of earnings within the risk appetite of the organization. This will be covered in more detail in Chapter 6.

2.4 Developing a climate risk strategy plan and road map

For most organizations, in order to implement their climate change strategy they need to develop a formalized strategic climate change plan and associated road map that may be over a 3–5-year period. This is partly covered in section 2.3, with respect to developing a sustainability strategy. However, organizations need to build out a more comprehensive strategy and plan, covering both ERM integration and BAU integration.

This should allocate prioritized actions to specific workstreams with timelines to completion, actions owners who should be involved, and regular status updates to risk committee and boards.

2.4.1 Establishing a working group

Establishing a working group is often the best governance approach to support the implementation and monitoring of the progress of the plan. They can help generate healthy discussions with a wide range of stakeholders, both internal and external, to provide external opinion and subject-matter expertise.

As firms develop their approach to climate change risk management, the complexity and scale of the exercise will become apparent. This will need to be proportionate to the size of the organization, the jurisdictions in which it operates, the regulatory environment and the organization's operating model, and its approach to project management (which may necessitate multiple project workstreams progressing simultaneously).

Feedback from industry participants indicates that an approach that works well is to set out specific workstreams that cover, for example, ERM core components such as governance, risk management integration and scenario analysis. It is also important to recognize the need to develop additional plans to manage an organization's carbon footprint as well as ensuring compliance with reporting and disclosure requirements such as TCFD.

From a practical perspective these workstreams can then develop stand-alone plans that can be broken down into specific actions along with timelines to completion and allocation of action owners.

An example output is shown in Table 2.1 – it can be a good way to summarize the actions in order to report back internally to risk committees, and ultimately to boards, on progress. It is important to rate the actions as high/medium/low to assist in prioritization.

To be effective this will benefit from executive ownership and sponsorship, the setting of appropriate time frames, the allocation of project resources including senior management from the relevant business areas, and appropriate budget being available to support the plans.

2.4.2 Alignment with regulatory expectations

Many organizations are developing their plans in line with regulatory expectation in order to review gaps and develop mitigation plans against specific criteria.

In designing strategic plans it is important to incorporate some of the general sound guidance and advice from regulators. For example, as stated in the PRA's Supervisory Statement SS3/19, 'The PRA expects a firm's response to the financial risks from climate change to be proportionate to the nature, scale, and complexity of its business. As a firm's expertise develops, the PRA expects the firm's approach to managing the financial risks from climate change to mature over time.'[6]

The implementation and embedding of the recommendations will take time. Organizations need to make sure that recommended mitigation actions, controls and measures are integrated into their high-level climate change plans.

The plans should also align with the TCFD requirements. The idea of disclosures is that they will help companies prepare for climate change impacts, and help investors understand risks so that they can make more informed investment decisions. Chapter 12 covers financial disclosure requirements in detail.

TABLE 2.1 Indicative action plan output

Workstream component	Summary of completed actions	Treatment initiative	Treatment actions	Timeline to completion	Action owner	Priority
Governance	✓ The board has allocated SMF responsibility for managing climate change financial risks to its chief risk officer. ✓ The company has established a cross functional climate change working group who have identified a comprehensive set of key climate related financial risks, the details of which was shared with the board risk committee. ✓ The company established **initial plan** to meet regulatory requirements.	o Board training	o Create suitable training material to be presented to the board to ensure that they understand the risks and how it might impact the company and strategic decision making	TBA	CRO	High
		o Climate risk appetite strategy	o Create a risk appetite statement o Update risk appetite policy seek management risk committee o Approval for statement & policy amendments o Seek board approval for risk appetite	TBA	CRO	High
		o other				

SOURCE

2.5 Risk appetite strategy

Organizations acknowledge that the delivery of their vision and mission and the achievement of their strategic objectives cannot be achieved without taking risk. Therefore, the importance of defining the company's risk appetite is recognized as the foundation of a robust ERM framework.

The board should set the risk appetite of the organization, determine those risks that could threaten the company's business objectives, and define risk tolerance levels. The governance framework, including risk committees, should then examine and monitor all aspects of risk in sufficient detail to advise the board appropriately.

The risk appetite strategy should be a clear articulation of the amount and type of risk the company will accept in the pursuit of its strategic goals. The risk appetite strategy lays out aggregate enterprise risk tolerances and appetites for specific risk-taking activities and different risk types. Additionally, the strategy provides principles and guidelines for linking risk appetite to risk tolerances and for a risk limit management system.

A risk appetite strategy should specifically aim to:

- Avoid financial distress and provide comfort to policyholders, counterparties, regulators and rating agencies
- For a private company, optimize profitability by allocating capital and risk-taking capacity to areas where the organization has competitive advantages
- Improve transparency of goals and authorities that can be understood and executed at all levels of the organization through actionable limits, processes and procedures

The risk appetite strategy helps to inform all the company's stakeholders that the company has clearly established boundaries for overall risk taking and decision making.

The role of the ERM function is to ensure that an organization's risk appetite is clearly communicated, understood by all stakeholders and consistently applied by all involved within the risk management process. Enterprise risk tolerance and risk appetite for specific risk types needs to be flexible and reactive to the changing market conditions, the company's financial strength and the competitive landscape.

2.5.1 Risk appetite definitions

Risk appetite is the total value of the corporate resources that the board of directors of the organization is willing to put at risk at any given point in time. It is important to understand and distinguish between related definitions that are applicable to the design of a climate risk appetite strategy.

- **Risk appetite** is the overall framework that establishes the risks that the organization wishes to acquire, avoid, retain and/or reduce.

- **Risk preferences** are qualitative risk appetite statements that guide the insurer in the selection of risks.
- **Risk tolerances** are quantitative risk appetite statements that guide the organization in the selection of risks. These statements typically specify maximum acceptable losses. They help the organization to translate the qualitative risk preferences into actions by constraining the insurer's exposures to risks.

2.5.2 Climate risk appetite guidance from regulators

Governments set the overall parameters with regard to climate change aims and regulators are responsible for determining the accompanying framework(s), rules and principles. This provides the basis on which firms can operate in a coherent and efficient manner and highlights how the public and private sectors have complementary roles to play in the management of climate risks.

Supervisory and regulatory authorities have many aims but they typically include protecting customers, ensuring market stability and supporting market development, and climate-related changes threaten each of these aims.

The Prudential Regulation Authority (PRA), through its supervisory statement SS3/19 issued in April 2019, has provided specific guidance in respect to risk appetite strategy. It states that where appropriate it would expect to see evidence of how a firm monitors and manages the financial risks from climate change in line with its risk appetite statement.

Furthermore, it states that a risk appetite statement should include the risk exposure limits and thresholds for the financial risks that the firm is willing to bear, and should take into account factors such as:

- Long-term financial interests of the firm, and how decisions today affect future financial risks
- Results of stress and scenario testing, for shorter and longer time horizons
- Uncertainty around the timing and the channels through which the financial risks from climate change may materialize
- Sensitivity of the balance sheet to changes in key risk drivers and external conditions

Under the section on risk management the PRA specifies the needs in respect to risk monitoring and the development of key risk indicators and states that 'Firms should also use these metrics to monitor progress against their overall business strategy and risk appetite.'

It must be pointed out that many have not built out key risk indicators to monitor for climate risks, given the lack of both design of metrics and data availability. The PRA acknowledges in its own statement that these metrics and tools will evolve and mature over time as firms gain experience.

2.6 Integration of climate change into risk appetite

The implementation of an organization's risk appetite strategy is perhaps the most complex and challenging component of an ERM framework. In respect of climate change it is proving quite difficult for some organizations to design specific metrics and targets. This is partly driven by the lack of data to track and monitor exposures. This is a common concern raised by risk managers.

Some organizations are developing stand-alone risk appetite statements (RAS) for climate change, which can cover, for example, the ambition of reducing their own GHG emissions to net zero.

Figure 2.4 contains one of the results from a survey conducted by the Institute of Risk Management (IRM) in February 2022. The survey included the question 'Are climate risks explicitly reflected in your organization's risk appetite framework?'

The survey shows that only 6 per cent of the IRM Special Interest Group (SIG) respondents have fully embedded their climate risk within their existing risk appetite framework and nearly half of respondents are either in the early stages of discussions or have not addressed the issue to date, highlighting the complexity and time it takes to fully embed the process, including risk metrics. It can be assumed that this is a representative sample.

FIGURE 2.4 Climate risk appetite integration maturity

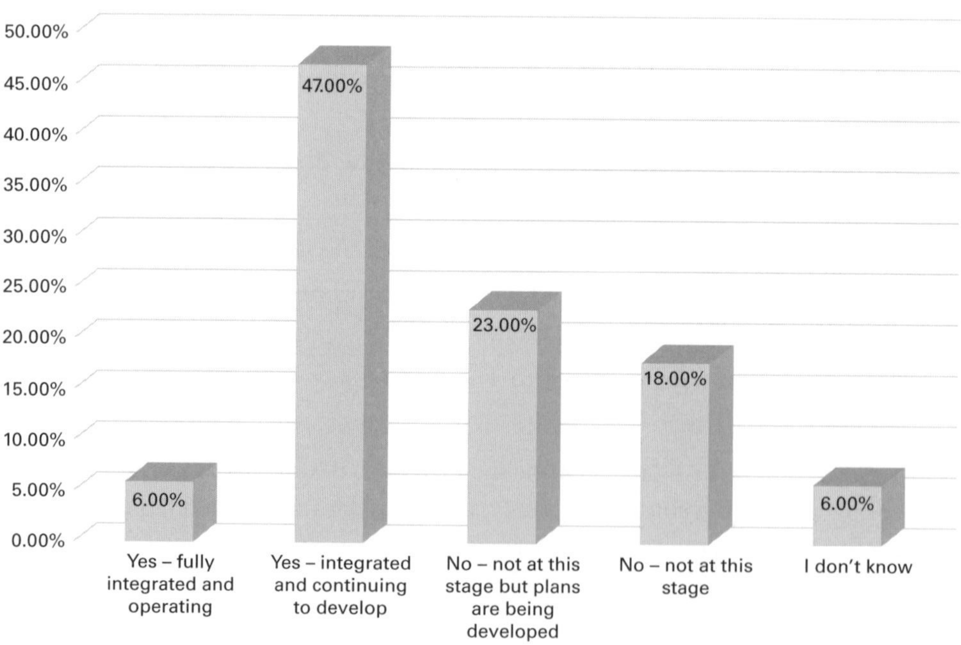

SOURCE IRM Climate Change Special Interest Group (SIG) survey results

2.6.1 Risk appetite components

The risk appetite strategy should document the risks organizations wish to seek, minimize or avoid and should define the boundaries within which risk taking can occur. These metrics and guidelines provide a central view on risk taking with which the whole organization can agree.

The four main components of an organization's risk appetite strategy that can help an organization to articulate and shape its overall strategy are as follows:

1. Risk principles: overarching climate risk philosophy (see section 2.6.2).
2. Strategic risk metrics: the primary set of risk metrics aligned to stakeholder expectations (section 2.6.3).
3. Risk preferences: qualitative statements that guide the company in the selection of risks it seeks versus those it wishes to minimize or avoid (section 2.6.4).
4. Risk tolerances/limits: quantitative risk appetite statements that guide the company in the selection of risks. These statements may typically specify maximum acceptable losses or exposure. They will help the company to translate the qualitative risk preferences into action by constraining its exposure to risks (section 2.6.5).

Climate risk appetite can be integrated into the main components of the prevailing risk appetite framework of the organization, which will be covered in this section.

In respect to climate change, organizations should design relevant metrics and set risk indicators across the different risk profiles, and it is important to consider metrics that manage physical risks from those that manage transition risks.

2.6.2 Component 1: Risk principles – overarching climate risk objectives

The high-level specific climate risk principles (or a 'climate risk philosophy') that determine how an organization responds to climate risk are set out here. Some of these are general principles that can be applicable to climate change integration while others are climate change specific to help differentiate between them:

- **Example of general principles**
  - Play an important role in society and take responsibility for acting in a fair and honest manner towards all our stakeholders, enhancing our reputation by acting as a role model in our industry.
  - Business activities and risk taking are consistent with our strategy and expectations from stakeholders including shareholders, regulators and rating agencies.

- Recognize the importance of a robust risk culture and strive to continually improve risk awareness across the business.

- **Example of climate-specific principles**
  - Our organization supports scientific consensus that climate change is a reality of increasing global concern and that it is a key strategic risk to our organization and we are therefore seeking to play our part in tackling the climate crisis that we all face.
  - In transitioning to a net zero economy, we recognize the vital importance of industry collaboration and coordination and seek ways to transition away from fossil fuels to more sustainable sources of energy across our value chain.
  - Our organization is taking a proportionate approach to climate risk relative to the nature, scale and complexity of our business and is committed to managing climate change risk through integration into its existing risk management and governance framework.

2.6.3 Component 2: Primary strategic risk metrics – risk appetite dimensions

It is important that an organization sets out a primary set of strategic risk metrics that align to stakeholder expectations. For financial services companies these would typically include capital adequacy, earnings volatility, liquidity and franchise (or brand) value metrics.

Organizations will need to consider the amount of climate volatility they are willing to accept on earnings in respect to, say, an acute physical risk such as a major hurricane or flood event. Chapter 7 provides a case study of setting earnings risk appetite against a mild winter for a utility company. This analysis will also then need to consider future time horizons and possible adjustments to the risk appetite for any potential future increases in volatility in respect of physical risk on a like-for-like basis.

This would include the need to limit the impact on specific financial metrics of the organization such as capital adequacy and earnings volatility to an acceptable level. Examples of natural catastrophe key risk indicators are given in section 2.6.5.2. Financial resilience will be covered in more detail in Chapter 6.

The franchise value encapsulates the desire to build and sustain a business in the medium to long term. It can be seen in terms of brand and reputation of its key stakeholders in order to ensure people remain satisfied to do business with the organization. Managing and mitigating climate change is very much aligned to protecting the reputation in, for example, managing transition and liability risks in respect to key stakeholders such as:

- Public and media
- Regulators

- Policymakers
- Third-party suppliers
- Customers

Organizations in their statements would seek to monitor and manage the elements that impact these risk appetite dimensions, through the direct linkage of these dimensions to the company's performance targets and objectives, so that the company is in effect monitoring and managing the drivers of key performance objectives. Stakeholder analysis and mapping of climate risk is covered in detail in Chapter 4.

2.6.3.1 SETTING SPECIFIC METRICS AND TARGETS FOR CLIMATE EMISSIONS

Setting the ambition and targets for emissions is one of the key strategic risk appetite metrics that many organizations are including as a new metric to manage their risk appetite in respect to climate change.

An example of how this could practicably be applied would be:

1. Operational net zero carbon (for Scopes 1 and 2) by 2030 with carbon offsets being applied for any residual emissions (this is in part due to the availability and quality of Scope 3 emission data being limited currently)
2. Getting to the point of net zero carbon (for Scope 1, 2 and 3) by 2050

An example of how this has been applied in industry is provided by Cornish Mutual (a UK insurer of the agricultural sector) (see case study).

CASE STUDY

Cornish Mutual: Level 1 risk appetite strategy – statement

- Our ambition is to be a net zero company by 2050 (interim targets to 2050 will be developed in due course).
    - We will determine the carbon footprint of our investments and will reduce them with the aim to transition all assets to be net zero by 2050.
    - We will determine the carbon footprint of our insurance portfolio and will support members with the aim to transition the portfolio to be net zero by 2050.
- We are working to minimize our directly controlled emissions (Scopes 1 and 2) (annual targets to 2025 have been developed).
- We will offset any remaining emissions (Scopes 1 and 2) by supporting credible local projects.
- As a measure of staff climate risk awareness and 'buy in' we are seeking an average score of at least '7' (scale of 1 to 10) to the following two questions as per our annual staff survey:

To what extent do you feel Cornish Mutual is:

- Aware of our responsibilities as a business in relation to climate change?
- Taking appropriate action in relation to climate change?

2.6.4 Component 3: Risk preferences

Risk preferences are a set of qualitative risk appetite statements that guide an organization in the selection of risks. One of the best ways to do this is to define a set of risk preferences that specifies the types of risk an organization seeks versus those it would like to minimize or avoid as described below:

- **Seek** – Our organization actively seeks this risk type as a consequence of the products we choose to sell and our investment decisions. We retain this risk type on our book and do not actively transfer or hedge it.
- **Minimize** – Our organization must take on this risk as part of its day-to-day operations. We actively minimize this risk subject to cost–benefit trade-off of implementing appropriate policies, processes and controls to do so. These preferences generally relate to the management of operational risks.
- **Avoid** – Our organization actively avoids having exposure to this risk. However, should we become exposed to this risk as a consequence of our strategy and business model, we will actively transfer or hedge it.

In line with best practice organizations should seek to develop risk preferences across all the main risk types such as investment, credit and operational risks. More details of how an organization manages these risks should then be included within separate risk policies for managing major risk types.

Some examples of risk preferences in respect to 'Seek', to help guide an organization in the selection of climate-related risks are set out in Table 2.2.

2.6.5 Component 4: Risk tolerances and limits

The quantitative risk appetite metrics help to translate the qualitative risk preferences into actions by constraining the company's exposures to risks in terms of agreeing specific metrics to manage and monitor. Risk metrics levels called key risk indicators (KRIs) are typically set using a red/amber/green (RAG) assignment for each.

Essentially KRIs provide metrics around risks and their potential impact on business performance and objectives. They act as early warnings to ultimately support management in making business decisions.

The RAG status typically drives the process of escalation. An amber rating should act as an early warning while a red would imply the activity is outside of risk tolerance. If this is agreed, then there needs to be immediate action to bring the rating

TABLE 2.2 Climate risk preferences – examples of 'Seek'

Risk grouping	Risk	Description
Legal and regulatory	Failure to observe legal and regulatory requirements	We seek to observe all legal and regulatory climate requirements, monitoring developments through the Climate Change Strategy Committee and via our trade bodies. We seek full and transparent disclosures in our annual report aligned with the recommendations of the Financial Stability Board's Task Force on Climate-related Financial Disclosures (TCFD) and will monitor development of industry best practice disclosures.
Operational	Vendor risk management	We seek to use suppliers who are climate change active, aligned with our own plans and meeting regulatory standards through a robust supplier procurement process and proactive relationship management.
Operational	Business disruption through systems failure, natural disaster or unexpected events	We will maintain contingency plans including the ability for employees to work from home. We will seek to review the appropriateness of our head office being on the side of a river in view of the operational impact should the office flood (the operational risk is mitigated by flood defences, a second office, duplicate servers, and physical damage and business interruption insurance placed with another insurer).
People	Failure to attract and retain employees with appropriate skills	We seek to attract and upskill our people to ensure they are climate risk aware and have the capabilities to innovate and develop products and services that integrate consideration of long-term sustainability issues and cater for members' requirements. We seek to fully engage our people in how we are playing our part in tackling the climate crisis that we all face including reduction of the company's carbon footprint. We seek to support our employees in their transition to a low-carbon economy (e.g. availability of 'green' pension investment options).
Prudential	Market (investment) risk	We seek to be in a position where we have a sustainable investment approach and where we can determine whether we have an excessive accumulation of financial risks from climate change in our investment portfolio.

back to amber and then green. Mechanisms need to be in place to communicate and report both amber and red issues so management, including the risk function, can agree appropriate mitigation actions to rectify the underlying issue.

Amber threshold breaches should be reported to the board, typically at the next scheduled meeting, together with a summary of the agreed action plan. Red threshold breaches that are perceived to be of high importance should ideally be communicated directly to the board, within a certain number of days (typically a week) to raise awareness at an early stage.

KRIs should be forward looking in nature to assist with providing guidance to operating or business units to monitor potential breaches and support escalation processes to be able to present updates at risk committees. It is important to consider contingency plans that have been agreed up front with stakeholders in advance of breaches to help ensure mitigation actions can be taken more quickly.

2.6.5.1 DESIGNING AND INTEGRATING CLIMATE CHANGE KRIS

Organizations need to review their risk profile carefully and consider ways to measure and monitor their climate change-related exposures.

The principles of designing KRIs are similar for most risk types. For investment strategy for example, it is important to consider setting limits in high carbon risk industries or setting targets to invest in sustainable funds within the asset portfolio. Organizations are often using external organizations to help manage and monitor their exposures. Accountability for the implementation, monitoring and oversight of risk appetite should be aligned with individual owners and facilitated by the risk function.

For monitoring and reporting of KRIs to be effective they need to be specific and measurable, available on a regular frequency, reportable and ideally based on forward-looking assumptions. KRIs should be quantifiable and one of the key challenges particular to climate change is to collect the relevant data, so internal IT systems and processes may need to be changed.

When monitoring and reporting, organizations should seek to align the metrics to the overall high 'level 1' strategic principles that have been discussed in section 2.6.2. They should take into account the stakeholder interests of customers and shareholders as well as investors and regulatory requirements.

In developing KRIs risk professionals can play a vital role in designing bespoke KRIs that can be developed and cascaded across the organization. It is important in developing the KRIs to consider the following factors that could form part of an internal project:

- To set at a level to constrain risk taking within risk appetite, taking into account the interests of stakeholders such as customers to meet capital and regulatory requirements.

- A mix of hard and soft boundaries constraining the risk-taking activities. Soft boundaries are used as early warning signs to avoid breaking hard boundaries.
- Limits should be defined on indicators that can be controlled.
- Be established for business lines and legal entities as relevant, and generally expressed relative to specific metrics such as earnings, capital, liquidity or other relevant measures (e.g. growth, volatility).
- Include material risk concentrations at the institution or group-wide, business line and legal entity levels as relevant (e.g. counterparty, industry, country/region, collateral type, product).
- Although referenced to market best practices and benchmarks, should not be strictly based on comparison to peers or default to regulatory limits.
- Not be overly complicated, ambiguous or subjective.
- Be monitored regularly.

2.6.5.2 DESIGN OF KRIS FOR BAU PROCESSES – EXAMPLE FOR SUPPLIER DUE DILIGENCE

Risk tolerances and associated KRIs are typically aligned to the business processes and risk preference that will have been identified and outlined in Component 3.

A good example of this is the integration of KRIs into supplier due diligence processes. With this approach most organizations are seeking to integrate automated processes to develop KRIs against climate-related questions that link to a score that equates to a target level of acceptance.

The target itself can also then be linked to, say, the percentage of suppliers that align with the organization's climate risk appetite.

There also needs to be a mechanism to review suppliers that do not align with the organization's criteria, through a RAG scoring system, with the first step often being to develop a bespoke mitigation plan. This is a helpful process that supports the engagement with suppliers to discuss climate-related issues.

As outlined in the risk preferences section, this process should help to ensure that suppliers used by the company are 'climate change active' and demonstrate that the supplier has a good rating against set criteria.

Chapter 11 provides a detailed plan of how organizations should approach integrating a climate due diligence process.

Two specific examples are provided here to explain the process for designing KRIs across natural catastrophe and/or credit risk in loan portfolios to help illustrate the principles that can then be applied across other risk types.

EXAMPLE 1

Risk aggregation exposures to natural catastrophe

Many organizations have exposures to natural catastrophes caused by climate change such as floods or windstorm.

Risk aggregation in this context refers to the aggregation of exposures to a single loss event. So a flood event for example, might impact an organization across multiple assets such as properties or motor vehicles across a geographical area or zone.

In designing a KRI, it should generally be set to track the probable maximum loss (PML) at a set return period, for example 1 in 100 years, against a specific metric. For financial institutions this would typically be capital at risk on the legal entity's balance sheet that in turn should relate to the risk appetite for natural catastrophe perils.

The approach can be tailored for all natural or man-made catastrophe events so that an organization can make sure there is consistency of approach in managing and mitigating risks from catastrophe events.

In developing KRIs for climate change in this context organizations should consider the following:

1. The inclusion of new or emerging material perils such as wildfire that have not yet been considered or modelled.
2. Multiple events in the same year due to the increased frequency of events linked to climate change. The point here is that two or three medium-size events may have much more material impact on the organization than a single loss event and could be more likely to breach the risk appetite of an organization.
3. The impact of future climate change should support future financial planning, which may in turn lead to the need to change the risk appetite metrics themselves.

In respect to the third point, organizations can seek to adjust their net natural peril tolerance thresholds in light of future climate change. Adjustment factors can be linked to the future predicted aggregate loss forecasts of the specific geographic area or country or region.

A key risk indicators metric would typically be stated as 'Net exposure to a single natural catastrophe hazard not to exceed X at the 1 in 100 return period' and a RAG status would be developed to signify if the organization was below, close to or above the target. For financial institutions the target metric would typically be a percentage of capital. With climate change integration the prevailing metric may be adjusted to reflect future increase in the 1 in 100 loss event, so that the organization readjusts to the future exposure levels, for example a flood event whose 1 in 100 return period impact may be calculated to be X per cent greater in 2030.

EXAMPLE 2

Designing credit risk management metrics and KRIs

When considering the loan books of an organization that lends to purchase a property, it is possible that flood risks will affect the loan portfolios as house prices devalue and that can lead to negative equity for homeowners. Chapter 10 provides a specific example of a flood risk scenario for a bank.

Credit risk management policies need to be revised to explicitly reference and consider climate risk (or as part of a wider 'responsible lending policy'). Climate risk is becoming a standing agenda item at credit risk committees (and included in meeting papers) and the monitoring of credit portfolios is being expanded to cover a variety of additional variables. Examples of metrics for monitoring include:

TABLE 2.3 Credit portfolio risk metrics examples for mortgage lenders

Physical risk considerations	Metrics
Assessment of an organization's exposure to mortgages in high-risk flood areas.	Percentage of mortgage credit exposure linked to properties in high-risk flood areas.
Assessment of an organization's corporate credit exposure to companies in sectors affected by extreme weather events.	Percentage of corporate credit exposure in sectors affected by extreme weather events.
Assessment of any collateral provided that is in a high-risk flood area or of heightened likelihood of being affected by extreme weather events.	Percentage of collateral provided (assets or property) that is linked to high-risk flood areas or is of heightened likelihood of being affected by extreme weather events.
Transition risk considerations	**Metrics**
Assessment of an organization's exposure to mortgages with low energy performance.	Percentage of mortgage book linked to low energy performance properties.
Assessment of an organization's corporate credit risk exposure to companies/sectors sensitive to transition risk.	Percentage of corporate credit exposure in sectors affected by transition risk.

A relatively recent development among some mortgage providers has been the offering of discounted-rate mortgages for those properties with a higher energy performance certificate (EPC) rating (thus promoting the purchase of more energy-efficient properties). An example of this in the UK mortgage market is Tandem Bank, which offers discounts of up to 0.5% on mortgages for the most energy-efficient properties.[7]

Alternatively, if real estate is provided as collateral for a loan, the approach to valuing such collateral can also influence behaviours over time (i.e if properties with higher EPC rating are valued more competitively).

Another consideration is the realization among mortgage lenders that as climate change risk worsens, the likelihood of extreme weather events occurring increases. This could lead to asset prices falling (in this instance the value of the property), which may mean that the value of an asset at the end of the mortgage term is less than the value of the outstanding loan and hence the mortgage cannot be repaid.

All of these factors will influence the level of credit risk the lending organizations are exposed to and consequently these variables will need to be factored into the overall credit risk management policy and the pricing methodology.

2.7 Climate change risk appetite reporting

While all of the work discussed here focuses on developing and aligning the corporate and climate risk strategies with a set of cohesive relevant risk appetite statements, it is important that an appropriate mechanism is in place to be able to report this effectively to senior management and the board.

The reporting of risk exposure against risk appetite typically comprises:

- **High-level summary** – A one page overview of the risk appetite strategic risk metrics designed to give a clear snapshot of the current red/amber/green (RAG) rating of the constituent KRIs' status to the audit and risk committee.
- **Individual KRI dashboards** – A more detailed overview of the KRIs by risk types that can be presented at corporate risk committee meetings. Individual risk owners should seek to provide comments, particularly in relation to any red or amber ratings, together with the response. A remediation plan can then be developed and escalated for all amber and red KRIs.

Conclusion

This chapter has outlined how risk professionals can support the climate ambitions of an organization by applying their expertise in aligning the overall corporate ambition with the enterprise risk management framework. The strategy needs to be underpinned by the two foundational components, *resilience* and *sustainability*.

One of the most important roles of the risk function is to design the overall climate change risk appetite strategy of the organization and ensure that it aligns with the overall corporate strategy, which is generally best designed and articulated through a risk appetite policy or statement that drives the company's overall risk taking and mitigating behaviours.

In designing a risk appetite strategy, it is important to set out a set of risk principles, review and agree additional strategy risk metrics such as stating the company's ambition in alignment to the government's net zero emissions targets.

The risk appetite strategy should also include a set of qualitative risk preferences across risk types as well as a set of quantitative key risk indictors that it can measure and monitor that align to the interests of key stakeholders and that typically would constrain the company's exposure to risks.

Accountability for the implementation, monitoring and oversight or risk appetite should be aligned with individual owners and facilitated by the risk function.

Notes

1 N Marks. Uniting risk management with strategic planning, CMSWire, 18 October 2018. www.cmswire.com/information-management/uniting-risk-management-with-strategic-planning/ (archived at https://perma.cc/LZD6-PRSL)

2 The Risk Coalition. Guidance: Raising the bar, 2019. www.riskcoalition.org.uk/the-guidance (archived at https://perma.cc/HY5U-PAWM)

3 Chapter Zero. Chapter Zero: A climate change boardroom toolkit, 2019, p 35. www.chapterzero.org.uk/wp-content/uploads/2021/09/Chapter-Zero-Board-Toolkit-2020.pdf (archived at https://perma.cc/RAC3-EQS4)

4 Chapter Zero. Principles and frameworks for climate change strategy and action: Executive summary, 2020, p 3. www.chapterzero.org.uk/wp-content/uploads/2021/09/Chapter-Zero-Change-Management-Toolkit-Summary.pdf (archived at https://perma.cc/PAG3-L52X)

5 Chapter Zero. Principles and frameworks for climate change strategy and action: Executive summary, 2020, p 22. www.chapterzero.org.uk/wp-content/uploads/2021/09/Chapter-Zero-Change-Management-Toolkit-Summary.pdf (archived at https://perma.cc/NL4H-T886)

6 Bank of England Prudential Regulation Authority. Enhancing banks' and insurers' approaches to managing the financial risks from climate change, 2019. www.bankofengland.co.uk/-/media/boe/files/prudential-regulation/supervisory-statement/2019/ss319 (archived at https://perma.cc/D4J2-TMH8)

7 Tandem. New 2nd charge mortgage feature offers rate reductions based on EPC rating, 3 May 2022, https://www.tandem.co.uk/newsroom/new-2nd-charge-mortgage-feature-offers-rate-reductions-based-on-epc-rating (archived at https://perma.cc/L77H-85AZ)

3

Developing an effective climate governance framework

Governance is one of the main pillars that organizations need to develop to assist in the development of a robust climate action plan and road map. This chapter will cover how organizations should develop an effective climate governance framework by explaining how they can incorporate climate risk considerations into their existing corporate governance framework.

The main learning outcomes from this chapter are to:

- Understand and appreciate the importance and role of the board in developing and overseeing a robust governance framework.
- Explain the importance of developing a strong climate governance framework for managing and mitigating climate change risks.
- Outline the main foundational components and underlying enablers of developing an effective climate change governance framework through explaining each of core best practice components, which include risk ownership and accountability and risk reporting and communication.
- Explain how climate governance activities and responsibilities fall under the three lines of the defence model.
- Explain how organizations manage and report climate risks through their governance structures by providing some practical examples.
- Evaluate the importance of developing a good organizational and risk culture framework, to support effective risk management.

The chapter will discuss the key climate components that organizations need to consider across five core governance pillars in order to make sure that climate risk is effectively embedded.

Introduction

Risk governance is sometimes referred to as the 'risk architecture'. Within an organization it specifies the roles, responsibilities, communication and risk reporting structures (including the individuals and committees) that support the risk management process throughout the organization.

An effective and efficient corporate governance framework should focus on accountability and responsibility, create the conditions for value creation and encourage ethical behaviour. Contributing to the organizational culture, the leadership should create a positive working environment for all employees, from executive level to front-line staff, helping them to undertake their day-to-day duties and achieve their objectives. From an external perspective, corporate governance should provide assurance to all stakeholders in the ability of the organization to deliver its objectives and meet their expectations.

Corporate governance should focus primarily on the responsibilities and authorities of senior management in the context of the organizational reporting structures that should seek to encourage open communication, and stimulate integrity and accountability in decision making. In achieving an organization's strategic objectives, risk management plays a critical role in the overall corporate governance structure.

To have a common understanding of climate-related risks, their particularities and potential impact on an organization, an effective governance approach should ensure that it has a full oversight and top-down accountability for the materiality of climate-related risks. The board has the ultimate accountability to deliver the long-term objectives, financial stability and resilience of the organization. From this perspective, it is critical for the board to have a deep understanding and clear overview of the organization's exposure to climate-related risks.

Having a full oversight of the management of all interconnected risks will create the foundation to embed effective governance in the entire organization. A top-down approach to how climate-related risks are integrated into the risk management process and a comprehensive perspective of them will allow a common understanding of these risks, a clear allocation of responsibilities, and effective tools and processes to identify, assess and manage them at the right levels.

3.1 Role of the board in risk management

Mainly due to the rising moral, societal and fiduciary as well as regulatory responsibilities to integrate climate change into the strategic plans and business management of an organization, it is becoming increasingly important that management of climate change risk (and the associated opportunities) becomes central to the roles and responsibilities of directors who lead the organization.

A board of directors must ensure that the organization is making decisions with regard to the interests of all its relevant stakeholders and is not driven by the interests of senior management or a dominant individual.

A company looks to develop and grow a business in a way that balances the expectations, risks and rewards of all stakeholders through taking opportunities for which the outcome will have a level of uncertainty in a marketplace that continuously evolves and changes. The board's role is to ensure it is in a position in which it can provide confidence and assurance to investors and other stakeholders that these uncertainties are understood and are being managed – that is, that the business has an effective risk management capability.

3.1.1 Corporate governance and climate change

One of the main challenges for organizations and risk managers is how to integrate climate change and wider ESG risks within the existing governance framework. Most of the guidance that is available is directed at corporate boards, with one of most helpful guides being the World Economic Forum's publication 'How to Set Up Effective Climate Governance on Corporate Boards: Guiding principles and questions'.

This publication states that it 'seeks to provide useful guidance to boards, acknowledging that climate governance is both integral to basic good governance and fraught with complexity. The result is a set of principles and questions to guide the development of good climate governance – designed to help the reader practically assess and debate their organization's approach to climate governance and frame their thinking about how the latter could be made more robust.'[1]

The publication sets out eight climate governance principles:

Principle 1 – Climate accountability on boards

Principle 2 – Command of the subject

Principle 3 – Board structure

Principle 4 – Material risk and opportunity assessment

Principle 5 – Strategic integration

Principle 6 – Incentivization

Principle 7 – Reporting and disclosure

Principle 8 – Exchange

These governance principles are designed to increase directors' climate awareness, embed climate considerations into board structures and processes and improve navigation of the risks and opportunities that climate change poses to businesses.

Because the role of the board is to hold management accountable for the resilience of the company and the long-term value creation for its shareholders, directors need to be able to articulate the climate change strategy, how climate change risks are being managed, how compliant the company is today, and what the path to full compliance looks like.

In Chapter 4 we will cover external drivers and expectations, including stakeholder analysis and mapping. It is becoming increasingly important to consider and factor in the wider interests of stakeholders (including customers, employees and the wider community).

From a wider society perspective, as we transition into a low-carbon economy, boards will also need to reassess their role and purpose, and we covered this in Chapter 2.

3.1.2 Duty of care

Directors need to exercise 'reasonable care, skill and diligence' when conducting their duties and they therefore must find the most effective way of integrating climate change into governance. Failure to do so may subject some directors to liability for breaching their duty of care and we will cover some of the latest legal cases in Chapter 9.

Directors also need to exercise independent judgement when assessing the impact of climate change within their organizations. They should take a proactive approach and have an open mind to considering how climate change threats and opportunities can be managed.

They will also need to embrace any potential material risks that may be emerging on the horizon and will need to investigate these issues to support their decision making. Odgers Berndtson have said that 'given the widespread availability of knowledge about climate change's current and anticipated impact on people, countries and businesses, directors can no longer plead ignorance about the topic and the risks it poses for their company.'[2]

3.2 Alignment to stakeholder expectations

Organizations need to align their governance to meet external stakeholder expectations. Companies will need to understand the regulatory expectations as well as the recommendations of the G20 Financial Stability Board's Task Force on Climate-related Financial Disclosures (TCFD). These are a recognized benchmark against which companies can assess their strategic approach to managing climate change risk.

3.2.1 *Task Force on Climate-related Financial Disclosures (TCFD)*

Although we provide a comprehensive overview of climate disclosures and regulatory requirements in Chapter 12 it is important to note that the TCFD highlights governance as a building block for effective climate-related risk and opportunity management. Without effective climate-related governance structures in place, a company will not be able to make informed strategic decisions or appropriately manage the risks.

Investors, regulators and other stakeholders increasingly expect the TCFD recommendations to be used to navigate the physical, economic transition and liability risk exposures relevant to their organizations. In addition, disclosure in accordance with the TCFD recommendations could in fact be used as a strategy to publicly demonstrate compliance with directors' duties and disclosure obligations and to highlight your corporate climate credentials.

TCFD state that, in respect to governance, disclosures should:

- Describe the board's oversight of climate-related risks and opportunities.
- Describe management's role in assessing and managing climate-related risks and opportunities.

3.2.2 *Regulatory requirements and expectations*

The Prudential Regulation Authority (PRA) in the UK, in its ground-breaking supervisory statement issued in April 2019 for financial services organizations, states that in respect of governance they expect:

> a firm's board to understand and assess the financial risks from climate change that affect the firm, and to be able to address and oversee these risks within the firm's overall business strategy and risk appetite. The approach should demonstrate an understanding of the distinctive elements of the financial risks from climate change and a sufficiently long-term view of the financial risks that can arise beyond standard business planning horizons.[3]

One of the most important aspects of the statement above was to require all regulated financial services firms to request that the board assign a senior management function holder (SMF) to take responsibility for identifying and managing financial risks from climate change and to ensure that these responsibilities are included in the SMF's statement of responsibilities.

This change has helped to ensure that climate change is seen as a key strategic risk for organizations to manage.

3.3 Climate change governance risk framework

The governance structure should include a robust risk management process in order to be able to anticipate, respond and adapt to any event or situation that might impact its objectives in delivering and meeting shareholder expectations. This is how it delivers value to its shareholders.

The main foundational components of a robust corporate governance framework are equally applicable for managing climate change and include the following:

- Board oversight
- Risk ownership and accountability
- Risk reporting and communication
- Performance and incentive compensation management
- Training and education accountability

In order to manage climate risks effectively, it is vital that organizations establish a clear governance framework in terms of establishing clear accountability, appropriate structures and the allocation of sufficient resources. We discuss the components of a climate governance framework that align with the five core pillars in detail in this section.

In respect to developing an effective climate governance framework it is important to address some best practice questions. Some examples from leading authorities are provided below.

The Australian Institute of Company Directors suggests organizations need to address the following questions:[4]

- How are issues associated with climate change integrated within our board governance (strategic and oversight) responsibilities? Is this issue receiving adequate time and focus within the board/committee agenda?
- Who is responsible and accountable for this issue within management? Are we satisfied that relevant staff (or experts that they consult) have the appropriate competence and resources?
- How do we as a board, and senior management (including legal, governance, finance and risk teams), ensure that we are staying up to date in this dynamic area?
- Are our remuneration structures aligned with our strategic approach to climate change?

FIGURE 3.1 Climate change governance risk framework

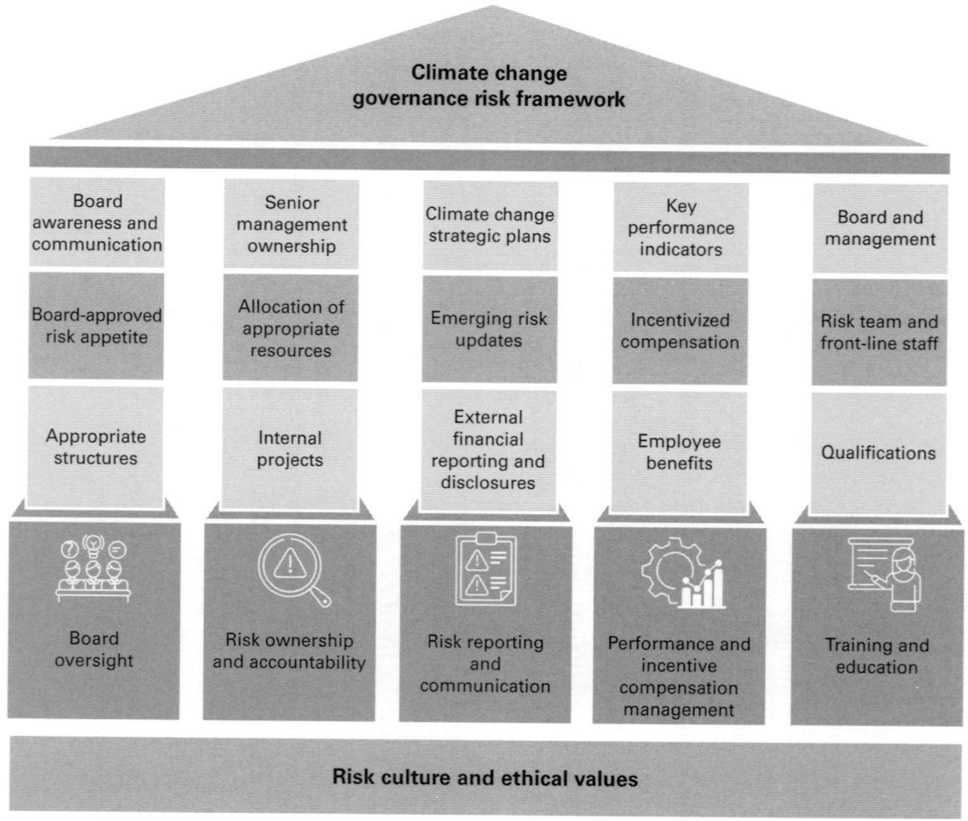

SOURCE © OneRisk Consulting. All rights reserved, 2022

The National Audit Office in the UK in its report on good practice guidance for audit and risk assurance committees states that boards will need to be able to provide assurance in respect to the following:[5]

- Assessing the organization's approach to managing climate-related risks
- Reviewing board briefings on relevant climate change matters including results of climate risk 'deep dives'
- Assessing management's use of data and consideration of data integrity to gain assurance over any potential impact

In respect to climate governance and integration within an ERM framework, the following is a climate change governance framework that covers the main components that risk leaders should seek to review and embed, which will support the organization in integrating climate change within its governance framework. The components are split into five areas of focus that align with regulatory expectations and best practices, which are reflected in Figure 3.1.

This section provides insights into each of these focus areas.

3.3.1 Board oversight

Boards are expected to understand and assess climate change risks that affect the organization and be able to address and oversee these risks. Therefore, one of the critical areas of focus is to make sure that the board and its relevant sub-committees exercise effective oversight of risk management and controls.

Boards should ensure that the right depth of oversight is given to climate change. Often a separate committee may be needed, a committee that can fully discuss the material aspects and elevate discussions about climate and other ESG issues to the general board agenda.

On an important and practical point, climate change strategic plans and updates and associated management information should be communicated regularly to the board in order to allow for strategic discussions and to support decision making in terms of evaluating risk and rewards.

Advisory boards An advisory board can provide a dynamic perspective, counsel and guidance in climate and wider ESG matters. Before making long-term strategy decisions, boards and executives need to have a detailed understanding of the impacts that climate change will have on the business model of the company, its product and its assets. Advisory boards can serve this function. Additionally, it's important to monitor foreseeable policy changes related to climate change to anticipate both risks and opportunities.

Board oversight themes and expectations Three key governance themes relating to boards oversight are:

a. Board awareness and communication
b. Board approved risk appetite
c. Appropriate structures

One of the World Economic Forum's principles of climate governance is that directors have 'command of the subject'. Regulators also expect that boards will receive ongoing awareness training. The risk function can therefore play an important role in developing and facilitating ongoing training and communication to the board to increase their awareness of climate change risks, impacts and possible responses.

3.3.1.1 BOARD AWARENESS AND COMMUNICATION

A firm's board needs to understand and assess the risks from climate change that affect the firm, and be able to address and oversee these risks within the firm's overall business strategy and risk appetite.

It is important that there is adequate time and focus to discuss climate change risks within board and sub-committees and that the board themselves have appropriate training that addresses objectives such as:

- Increase board awareness of climate change risks, impacts and possible responses.
- Ensure understanding of regulatory expectations and limitations thereof.
- Prompt discussion of appropriate strategy re risk, investments, disclosure, et al.
- Define objectives to be achieved by the organization's climate implementation strategic plan.

The outcome of such training should provide:

- Increased board awareness of breadth and magnitude of climate change risks, the potential impacts and the opportunities it may present.
- Appreciation of the importance of climate change risk management and understanding of relevant regulatory requirements.
- Defined parameters and constraints within which the organization's climate change strategy can be developed.

INDUSTRY FEEDBACK AND OBSERVATIONS

It is important that organizations don't simply provide a one-off awareness training to their boards, as the risk landscape is fast changing, with new regulations coming into focus on a regular basis. It is vital that boards receive ongoing training as well as regular communications to increase board awareness of climate change risks, impacts and possible responses.

Learning and development teams/departments can support in developing a more structured range of training to the board, using, for example, external subject-matter experts across different climate-related themes and topics such as product innovation.

3.3.1.2 BOARD-APPROVED RISK APPETITE

Organizations need an approved climate risk appetite strategy and a board-approved climate risk appetite statement that considers a combination of quantitative and qualitative risk appetite guidelines that cover both risk preferences and risk tolerances across the risk profile. Chapter 2 provides details of how to operationalize an organization's climate risk appetite strategy.

INDUSTRY FEEDBACK AND OBSERVATIONS

Many organizations are in the process of developing their risk appetite strategies. One of the main components for many companies has been to set their carbon emissions ambition to align with the Paris Agreement's objective of limiting global warming to below 2°C (relative to pre-industrial times).

3.3.1.3 APPROPRIATE STRUCTURES

Organizations should set up relevant structures including sub-committees and working groups that can exercise effective oversight. Given the importance and complexity of managing climate-related risks many organizations have decided to establish a stand-alone climate risk committee or steering group, with many also establishing separate committees to cover the wider corporate social responsibility risks.

The alternative approach is using the existing committee structures and setting up a central working group and sub-working groups that report back to the pre-existing committees to coordinate activities and implement climate plans.

It is critical that in respect to setting up a new climate governance structure, organizations seek to:

- Define the role and terms of reference for the committee
- Define the decision-making process
- Agree the terms on which the climate risk committee contributes to other committees

Two alternative approaches and examples are highlighted in the following sections. In the first example the organization set up a stand-alone climate strategy committee and in the second example climate change has been developed and coordinated through the organization's pre-existing emerging risk committee.

EXAMPLE 1

Structure: establishment of a new climate change strategy group (CCSG)

This institution recognized that the changing climate would impact their operations in both physical and transition risks. Its aim was to create an effective climate risk management strategy supported by climate awareness across the organization. It was cognizant of needing to take a proportionate approach to climate risk relative to the nature, scale and complexity of its business.

Governance structure

Responsibility for managing climate risk was allocated to a 'senior management function' being the chief risk officer (CRO). They have been set climate change-related performance objectives.

The organization formed a climate change strategy group (CCSG), which drew from a wide representation from across the business, outlined in Figure 3.2. This group reports through the CRO to the audit and risk committee and then to the board specifically on climate change as a formal matter, which must be considered at every meeting.

The organization provided climate risk training to all employees and ensured it had provided board awareness training to its leadership.

Climate change strategy group – purpose

The climate change strategy group (CCSG) whose members are appointed by, and are accountable to, the CRO has as its purpose to enable the CRO to:

- Assist the board and risk and audit committee to understand the possible impacts of climate change on the company.
- Communicate progress made across the company and report matters arising from committee deliberations to the risk and audit committee (RAC) and board as appropriate.
- Ensure all business decisions take climate change into account including:
  - Engagement with board and executive committees
  - Training – help to identify requirements and provide content where needed
- Maintain an awareness of and feed into climate change-related investment discussions.

FIGURE 3.2 Climate change strategy group (CCSG) – structure

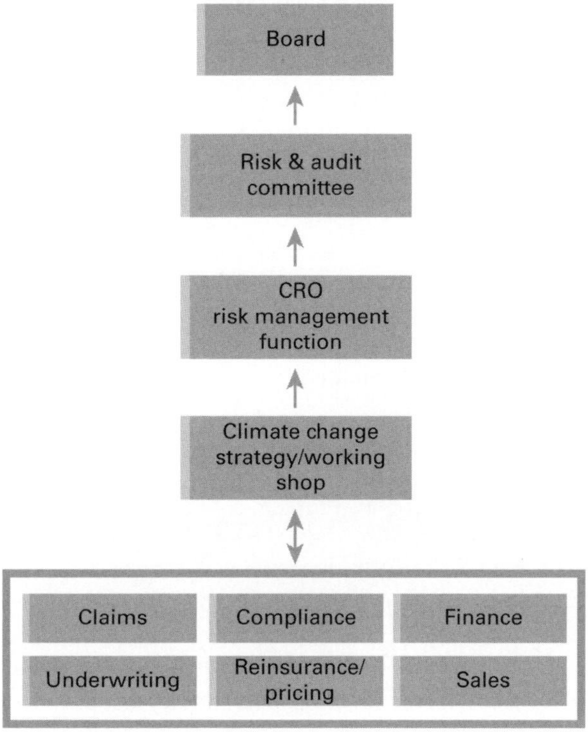

SOURCE © OneRisk Consulting. All rights reserved, 2022

- Develop a carbon footprint reduction plan and monitor and communicate progress against the plan.

Specifically relating to risk management this group will:

- Ensure that the approach to financial risks from climate change is embedded within the risk management framework.
- Confirm compliance with climate-related legal and regulatory obligations.
- Highlight, identify and where appropriate develop climate-related product and service opportunities.
- Implement effective scenario analysis over short- and long-term time horizons to help determine all material exposures.

Working methods

- The CCSG will meet at least six times per year.
- Minutes of the CCSG meetings will be circulated promptly.
- The CCSG chair will report on the meeting to the RAC and board.

Standing agenda – schedule of matters

The committee developed a list of standing agenda items for each meeting:

- Review of the previous CCSG minutes and action points
- Carbon footprint plan progression
- Scenario analysis
- Risk management
- Disclosures
- Training
- Communication
  - Internal to board/board committees
  - External

EXAMPLE 2

Structure: pre-existing emerging risk focus group (ERFG)

This organization decided to use its pre-existing emerging risk committee as a structure that best suited its needs in order to develop its strategy and plans in respect to climate change.

Table 3.1 outlines the development and milestones as to how the focus group has operated since its formation in 2019. Its main purpose has been to identify, manage and monitor its emerging risks, in its words, where it sees 'a risk that is evolving in areas and ways where the body of available knowledge is weak, and one of the most significant of these in recent years, and arguably still emerging, is climate change'.

The focus group undertook a number of 'deep dives' on climate change in 2021 that have been instrumental in harnessing the wider emerging risks framework to develop a holistic, enterprise-wide approach to managing its climate risks.

Owners, actions and timescales for each of these have been identified and progress is monitored by the risk management function and the ERFG, with oversight by the organization's group- and subsidiary-level risk and compliance committees. This activity has also underpinned the organization's sustainability efforts and facilitated ongoing compliance with the variety of climate-related regulatory requirements.

TABLE 3.1 Development and milestones of the emerging risk focus group

Pre 2019	Q2 2019	2020	2021	2022 and beyond
• Process was largely informal	• Established a groupwide, multidisciplinary emerging risks focus group (ERFG)	• ERFG met twice, in January and July	• ERFG met twice, in January and July	• First ERFG meeting held in January
• Risk management function conducted horizon scanning from external sources	• Initial meeting comprised a workshop to consider the whole emerging risks universe and identify prioritize those top emerging risks relevant to the organization	• Identified new risks and reprioritized others	• Membership of the group reviewed and amended commensurate with changes to organization's risk profile	• Action plan for addressing risks of climate change including owners and timescales
• Emerging risks identified from quarterly meetings with senior management, functional heads and risks and control owners, as well as incident reporting process	• Established a methodology for assessing emerging risks based on anticipated velocity/timeline to crystallization	• Reported to group risk committee majoring on those emerging risks identified as key (climate change, emerging cyber and pandemic fallout)	• Conducted climate change 'deep dive' area of focus in 2021	• Development of climate change and other emerging risks stress and scenario testing
• Emerging risks were reported by exception to the group risk committee where deemed material	• Biannual report to the group risk committee	• Incorporated/formalized approach into group risk policy, processes and procedures	• More formal horizon scanning as part of the ERFG process	• Formal deep dive workshops on other emerging risks such as emerging cyber planned for H2 2022

(continued)

TABLE 3.1 (Continued)

Pre 2019	Q2 2019	2020	2021	2022 and beyond
		• Education of Board members (general approach)	• Formally cascaded emerging risks assessment to key operating subsidiaries	• Ongoing education programme under the auspices of the ESG framework
			• Workshopped TCFD requirements and dovetailed into outputs of earlier deep dive	
			• Developed a plan for specific consideration of the requirements of TCFD and the need for strategic approach	
			• Continued education of Board members on specific emerging risks	
			• Facilitated alignment with the organization's Environmental, Social and Governance (ESG) framework	

Emerging risk management is covered in Chapter 8, and specifically emerging climate risks and opportunities are covered in Chapter 9.

3.3.2 Risk ownership and accountability

The main role of the risk function is to help embed risk management within its business's activities and it seeks to promote a culture of risk awareness across the organization. All employees have a responsibility for the management of risk; as such, each employee should take due care to ensure compliance with the risk management policy and procedures and work to help the organization manage risk effectively. It's not enough that risk and control functions exist, it's equally important to assign specific roles, define clear responsibilities and coordinate efficiently and effectively among the groups to avoid duplication or gaps.

Three key governance themes relating to risk ownership, accountability and assurance include:

- Senior management ownership
- Allocation of appropriate resources
- Internal projects

Before discussing the specific themes here in more detail, it is important to discuss the three lines of defence operating model and outline how climate change can be allocated between the three lines. While there are other approaches this is a best practice approach that we recommend.

Three lines of defence operating model The three lines of defence model (3LOD) provides a simple and effective way to enhance communication on embedding risk management and controls by defining roles and responsibilities. Each of the three lines plays a distinct role within the organization's overall governance framework. The three lines of defence are illustrated in Figure 3.3 together with the main areas of responsibility.

First line of defence The first line of defence (1LOD) is where the risks are taken and the controls performed within the business. Risk management is the day-to-day management of risk exposures in accordance with frameworks, policies, standards and risk appetite (as agreed upon by the board and on advice from the risk function).

Second line of defence The second line (2LOD) comprises the risk function that is responsible for developing an enterprise risk management framework within which authority can be delegated from the board to the front-line staff to enable them to deliver on the strategy efficiently and effectively. This comprises setting the policy, issuing minimum requirements and providing guidance and challenge. These are then left to the 1LOD on a day-to-day basis to operate, albeit within boundaries and limits that have been established.

FIGURE 3.3 Risk management – three lines of defence and main climate responsibilities

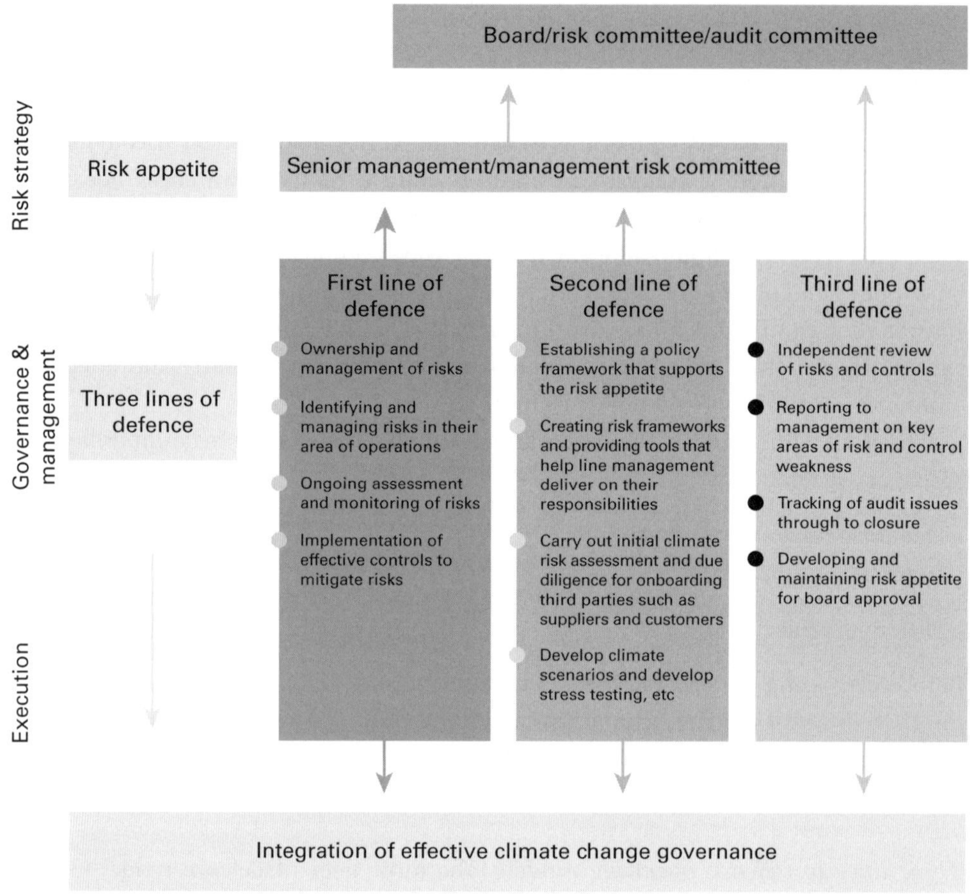

While the 2LOD supports the business in risk-based activities, to ensure independent oversight and challenge is possible, the team does not own risks. The main role is to help ensure the 1LOD business functions appropriately manage their risks and that their own self assessments of the organization's exposures to risk are accurate.

The compliance and risk functions may have their own management and governance committees that are part of the ERM framework, or they may have direct reporting lines into appropriate ERM framework structures.

Third line of defence The third line is the internal audit function who provide assurance that the people, processes and controls within the organization are appropriately designed and operating effectively (and as represented to the board). Boards set risk appetite and oversight whereas audit provides independent and objective assurance on the overall effectiveness of risk governance.

Three lines of defence and main climate change responsibilities Figure 3.3 was developed from the Orange Book, which sets out the main principles underlying effective risk management in all government departments and arm's length public bodies with responsibility derived from central government for public funds.[6]

Applying the 3LOD principles to climate change, Table 3.2 provides a breakdown of responsibilities across the 1LOD and 2LOD. The 3LOD would be largely unchanged by the incorporation of climate change into the risk framework.

3.3.2.1 SENIOR MANAGEMENT OWNERSHIP AND ACCOUNTABILITY

The board should seek to appoint someone from senior management to take ownership for managing and mitigating climate change financial risks. For financial services organizations this should be an SMF.

TABLE 3.2 First line and second line climate change responsibilities

	First line of defence identification, measuring and mitigation		Second line of defence policy, oversight and reporting
A	Manage the business in accordance with the policies (Links to 3)	**1**	Develop climate risk policies, frameworks and risk appetite statements
B	Identification and assessment of risks (Links to 4)	**2**	Integrate climate risk policies and frameworks into existing erm framework (follows from 1)
C	Design and operation of controls (Links to 4)	**3**	Oversee adherence of Climate Risk policies/ Frameworks (Links to A)
D	Manage climate risk exposures within agreed limits/thresholds (Links to 5)	**4**	Oversight of risks managed in 1LOD (Follows B & C)
E	Sourcing and management of relevant climate risk data	**5**	Develop climate risk limits/thresholds (Precedes D)
F	Collation and submission of regulatory reporting/disclosures	**6**	Monitor breaches of limits/thresholds
G	Management and escalation of risk events	**7**	Develop reporting requirements for Risk Committee
H	Development of new products with consideration for climate risk (Links to 8)	**8**	Review and approval of new products (Links to H)

SOURCE

FIGURE 3.4 Senior management accountability for climate risks

The responsibility for the identification, management and oversight of the financial risks from CC is overseen by the Chief Risk Officer (CRO), with day-to-day management of the risks carried out by the relevant individuals in the business

Financial risk from CC	Responsibility	Responsible SMF
Operational	Oversee operational impact of CC risks	SMF: 24 Chief operating officer
Credit	Oversee potential for CC related financial losses stemming from counterpart default	SMF: 2 Chief financial officer
Liquidity, reserving and solvency	Oversee impacts of CC risks that might jeopardize our reserving approach solvency of liquidity	SMF: 2 Chief finance
Legal and compliance	Oversee CC risks stemming from legal and compliance issues	SMF: 16 Compliance oversight
Reputational	Oversee actual/potential for reputational damage stemming from CC risks	SMF: 1 Chief executive
Market (investment)	Oversee impacts that CC risks may have on the investment portfolio	SMF: 2 Chief finance

SOURCE © OneRisk Consulting. All rights reserved, 2022

The day-to-day management of the risks are carried out by the relevant senior individuals in the business. An example is shown in Figure 3.4.

INDUSTRY FEEDBACK AND OBSERVATIONS

Many companies have allocated overall responsibility to a member of the executive team given the strategic importance of managing climate change, but it is also important that responsibilities are allocated throughout the organization across the risk profile for day-to-day management of the risks.

As per the survey conducted by the IRM Climate Change Special Interest Group (February 2022), the main executive responsible for climate change was the CRO or the CEO of an organization. However, the responses were surprisingly wide ranging and included the finance director, facilities director, chief impact officer and chief human resources officer under the auspices of ESG.

3.3.2.2 ALLOCATION OF APPROPRIATE RESOURCES

Organizations will need to allocate adequate resources and sufficient skills and expertise devoted to managing climate change as it becomes established as a component of the overall risk universe. It is important that organizations review whether they have adequate resources from both a capacity and capability perspective among existing staff and plan accordingly with regard to future positions and headcount.

> **INDUSTRY FEEDBACK AND OBSERVATIONS**
>
> In designing and implementing climate change plans the organization needs to carefully consider whether there are adequate ongoing internal resources available and if not, consider using external subject-matter expertise. There is a general view that insufficient resources are being allocated to deal with the wide range of threats and opportunities that need to be managed. This is partly related to the lack of adequate skills and experience.

3.3.2.3 INTERNAL PROJECTS

As the business integrates emerging climate risks into the corporate strategy, initiates projects to incorporate climate risk considerations into existing processes, and introduces new processes and procedures, the risk function is well positioned to support the successful implementation of these changes due to their visibility across the entire organization.

This can ensure the leveraging of the existing infrastructure (both operational and with regard to governance), the establishment of a robust internal control environment and the transfer of knowledge across the end-to-end process. This will deliver far-reaching benefits (ranging from product design to regulatory reporting, and business planning to the management of their own emissions).

> **INDUSTRY FEEDBACK AND OBSERVATIONS**
>
> In order to gain traction and buy-in from key stakeholders it is clear that formal working groups supplemented by questionnaires, interviews and workshops can really assist organizations in knowledge transfer, and help to embed climate change into their ERM framework and support meeting business objectives.

3.3.3 Risk reporting and communication

Three key governance themes relating to risk reporting and communication are:

a Climate change strategic plans
b Emerging risk updates (which will include climate change risks)
c Reporting and disclosures (both internal and external)

3.3.3.1 CLIMATE CHANGE STRATEGIC PLANS

Climate change plans and status progress updates need to be regularly reported and communicated within the organization's governance framework and ultimately be presented to the board.

Risk practitioners should also seek to design risk dashboards that can present updates on short-, medium- and long-term climate risks and opportunities that can then be presented to their risk committee.

3.3.3.2 EMERGING RISK UPDATES

In Chapter 8 we will discuss the importance of developing a formal emerging risk management framework to support an organization in understanding its future risk profile and for organizations to have an early warning system in place to improve their resilience. In Chapter 9 we discuss the main emerging climate trends, issues and challenges in climate change, as well as interconnected risks related to climate change and then, in Chapter 10 we discuss the importance of scenario analysis that can be used to assess emerging climate risks.

It is clearly important for risk practitioners to provide updates on emerging climate risk themes to risk committees and ultimately to the board on those that have a direct or indirect impact on future strategic and business planning. This should include deep-dive research on emerging risks and opportunities across physical, transition and liability risks.

3.3.3.3 REPORTING AND DISCLOSURES (BOTH INTERNAL AND EXTERNAL)

Internal reporting The risk function should seek to design an internal climate reporting process such as using the climate risk radar that will be discussed in Chapter 4. It is also helpful to develop a bespoke risk-reporting dashboard that can be updated and presented to the board on a regular basis. This could be developed to cover different time horizons covering short-, medium- and long-term climate risk and opportunities that are then presented to the risk committee and board.

Here is an excerpt from a case study provided by North of England P&I club (NEPIA) (from within the insurance industry) that includes how they developed and designed their internal reporting dashboard for climate change.

CASE STUDY

North of England P&I Club (NEPIA) – design of climate reporting dashboard

At NEPIA cross-cutting approach demanded that risk owners would need to regularly report on CC risk. Our approach (on a quarterly basis) asked risk owners a set of questions alongside their other risk components to assess their exposure to CC risks, covering product, market and operational risks.

FIGURE 3.5 Dashboard example – long-term risk examples (10+ years)

Physical risks - the impact of more regular and more severe extreme weather events		
A	Underwriting/claims/operational	*Rising sea levels and changes in storm patterns and their severity result in changes to current voyageroutes, increased claims (including increased incidents at ports) *Fishing stock migrate to areas inaccessible to fishing *Potential decrease in property values if considered to be within an area of increased flood risk
Y	Underwriting/claims	The use of different technologies and fuel types may result in different claims which may increase in value if not subject to appropriate underwriting discipline (policy terms and limitations)

Transition risks - the impact of adjustment to a low carbon economy		
R	Underwriting/claims	Coal and oil sector will change significantly and the current levels of transportation will be significantly reduced and may not be replaced with another energy commodity

Opportunities		Threats or new liabilities	
B	Offshore carbon storage transportation market	A	What was previously not considered a pollutant becomes a pollutant, causing claims

BRAYG impact assessment (expert judgement with limited data) possible increase in claims and costs/reduction in premium/reduction in investment asset values			
B	Positive gains or potential opportunities	Y	Moderate between w% and x%
R	High above y%	G	Low up to w%
A	Medium between x% and y%		

SOURCE North of England P&I Club

Risk owner reporting question examples:

- **Underwriting**
  - Have any climate-related developments occurred in the last reporting period relevant to pricing risks underwritten by us?
  - Have any new potential opportunities arisen from CC over the last reporting period?
- **Claims**
  - Have business lines in the last reporting period been exposed to changes in claim liability, in relation to the type, frequency and severity stemming from climate risks?
- **Market investments**
  - During the last reporting period, have investment advisors flagged any climate-related issues which, for example, could have an adverse effect on the value of our investment assets?

Risk-owner responses to questions rated moderate to high impact would then go on to be reported in the risk reporting dashboard. Given the long-term nature of climate change risk we recognized that we needed to incorporate a new reporting tool in the Risk Management Framework to capture medium and long-term climate change risks. We decided that the initial assessment CC dashboard covering short-, medium- and long-term risks should be updated annually and presented to the risk committee. This would provide guidance and reference to the sustainability strategy, stress testing scenarios and risk appetite statements.

An example of the dashboard follows in Figure 3.5.

External reporting including disclosures The board should ensure that material climate-related risks, opportunities and strategic decisions are consistently and transparently disclosed to all stakeholders. A number of the disclosures also need to be included in documents such as the annual reports and accounts.

Disclosure reporting consists primarily of four core elements: governance, strategy, risk management, and metrics and targets, which we also cover in different chapters within this book.

In Chapter 12 we provide details of how organizations increasingly need to provide detailed and insightful disclosures to meet both the evolving current and future disclosure requirements.

As organizations build and implement their climate change strategies and as their climate risk maturity develops, they can concurrently provide improved disclosures (in line with requirements from regulators and other stakeholder groups).

3.3.4 Performance and incentive compensation management

Organizations should seek to ensure that performance against climate-related objectives is incorporated into variable remuneration for specific executives accountable for implementing and integrating the climate change strategy.

Three key governance themes relating to performance and incentive compensation management are:

- Key performance indicators
- Incentivized compensation for executives
- Employee benefits

3.3.4.1 KEY PERFORMANCE INDICATORS

Organizations should seek to develop climate change strategic objectives and then align them with individual performance management objectives.

These should incorporate specific environmental key performance indicators (KPIs) that can cover the move towards sustainable consumption, the monitoring of emissions and any production efficiencies (all of which can facilitate the shift towards lower impacts on the environment).

3.3.4.2 INCENTIVIZED COMPENSATION FOR EXECUTIVES

Once a set of specific KPIs has been developed, these should be integrated into short- and long-term pay and incentives, in particular for senior executives.

Regulators such as the Prudential Regulation Authority (PRA – one of the primary financial services regulators in the UK) state that the performance of the senior management functions should be monitored against these objectives and reflected in variable remuneration.

The board should therefore seek to set climate-related targets as part of its executive incentive schemes where appropriate.

3.3.4.3 EMPLOYEE BENEFITS

Employee benefits can also provide a win–win for both employers and their workforce in helping promote a base from which to provide a positive impact on the environment.

Clear reporting of an organization's efforts to manage its environmental performance helps to attract high-calibre employees, as good environmental reputation and performance can be an important factor influencing an employee's choice of employer.

In respect to employee benefits, organizations should seek to add a greater range of flexible benefits aligned to reducing carbon emissions.

Some specific examples are shown in Table 3.3:

TABLE 3.3 Examples of employee benefits for staff supporting net zero targets

Staff benefits	Details
Company cars	Organizations can promote the use of electric vehicles (as a company car option)
Tax schemes	Employers can participate in a variety of tax-efficient schemes that offer tax breaks to staff to purchase bicycles ('Bike to Work' scheme) or promote electric vehicles via various lease-back schemes
Interest-free season ticket loans	Companies can offer interest-free season ticket loans to cover the costs of commuting to work on public transport. This reduces the overall cost of travel and encourages the use of more environmentally friendly modes of transportation (rather than driving to work)
Car-pooling initiatives	Some companies arrange car-pooling schemes to reduce transportation cost for staff and to reduce overall emissions

3.3.5 Training and education

There are three key governance approaches relating to training and education (all of which are intended to raise awareness):

- Board and senior management-focused development
- Training for risk and compliance functions (in order to enhance oversight) and staff on the front line (in order to support embedding it into business as usual)
- Complementing the in-house training with support for professional/academic qualifications

3.3.5.1 BOARD AND MANAGEMENT

One of the World Economic Forum's climate governance principles is that directors have command of the subject. Regulators also expect that boards receive ongoing awareness training.

The risk function can therefore play an important role in developing and facilitating ongoing training and communication to the board to increase awareness of climate change risks, impacts and possible responses.

3.3.5.2 RISK TEAMS AND FRONT-LINE STAFF

The focus for many organizations has been to train the board initially, and regulators such as the PRA advocate providing awareness training on an ongoing basis, but it is also very important to facilitate training and brainstorming sessions across the risk and compliance functions, senior management and ultimately across all employees.

For front-line staff some base-level training is important, and it is important to provide some form of introductory training for all staff.

Increased demand for training There is an increasing demand for training as evidenced from the IRM's Climate Change SIG Survey undertaken in 2020, in which 64 per cent of attendees at their first event stated an interest in training. This is driven primarily by the increasing pressure from stakeholders (which include regulators) for organizations to act and meet global emissions targets and use risk management techniques to help their organizations to achieve this.

IRM'S CLIMATE CHANGE TRAINING COURSE

IRM's training started in 2021 in conjunction with Imperial College and Grantham Institute.

The course was designed primarily for risk managers and risk professionals who need to adapt to changing standards and guidelines of climate change risk management and ensure they remain up to date and are able to apply best practice principles within their organizations.

The course is also applicable to all senior managers who have accountability for managing climate change risk as well as risk champions and coordinators that have risk management responsibility.

Overall course objectives

The main course objective is to help equip risk managers with knowledge and the latest tools and techniques to help translate the complexity and uncertainty of climate change to inform key internal and external stakeholders.

The course also aims to balance theory with practical real-life examples covering case studies across different industry sectors, and increase awareness of climate change threats and opportunities.

3.3.5.3 QUALIFICATIONS

Recognizing the strategic importance of this subject there are a number of organizations, including training companies, that are developing qualifications in climate change, including the IRM who plan to launch a qualification in 2023. The Chartered Body Alliance and the Global Association of Risk Professionals (GARP) have both developed a Certificate in Climate Risk. These are aimed primarily at the financial service industry with a focus on sustainable finance.

Overall, there is a recognition that qualifications will become more important, especially for those that are considering careers in related fields or already have roles in their organizations for managing and mitigating climate change.

3.4 Building a good risk culture

In this section of the chapter, we provide some additional thoughts in respect to the development of a good risk culture, focusing on aspects that are specifically relevant for climate change.

The development of a risk culture throughout the firm is perhaps the most fundamental tool for effective risk management.[7] Therefore, developing a good risk culture is a key enabler and prerequisite to enable a firm to embed enterprise risk management, including climate risks, into its business practices.

Risk culture is now referred to in most risk management standards and regulations and is a key focus of rating agencies. Examples are the ISO 31000 risk management standard that refers several times to the need for managing risk to be integrated into the organization's culture. A much greater emphasis has been placed on the development of a good risk culture since the global financial crisis and driven by increased regulation that has been aligned with the development of conduct risk management practices.

In supporting the development of a good risk culture many organizations have set out a code of ethics outlining the behaviours that they expect employees to uphold, and this should include the need to treat others with fairness, dignity and respect, free from harassment (verbal and physical) and discrimination.

Before outlining some standard approaches and components that help support the development of a good risk culture, many organizations as we have stated, need to refocus their business strategies and objectives in implementing their climate change plans and that will often need senior management support and buy-in.

A very helpful approach has been developed by Australian mining company BHP that can support the implementation of strategic changes such as climate change through the acronym 'RSVP'. The components and explanation of how it is applied are described by Robb Eadie, the CRO who was interviewed.

3.4.1 Change management – use of 'RSVP' approach

Implementing change in an organization is often challenging unless behaviour and incentives are aligned. Robb Eadie, the CRO of BHP, uses this acronym and says that 'unless you deal with RSVP nothing will ever change'.

He has applied this across the risk spectrum within BHP and especially for its climate change strategic plans. The acronym stands for rewards, structure, values and process:

- R = Rewards (mechanisms need to be in place to reward the desired behaviours)
- S = Structure (the structure or architecture of how risks are managed within an organization, i.e., architecture, accountabilities, authorities and limitations)
- V = Values (staff need to live your values)
- P = Process (the policies, processes, procedures and practices that the organization adopts)

With regard to climate at BHP this is achieved as follows:

In terms of the reward component, this is defined by the global scorecard for the group, which focuses on desired outcomes in the areas of greatest risk to the group. Included here are specific metrics relating to delivery against climate change targets.

In terms of structure, the material risks related to climate change are defined as a group risk in their own right, categorized under the group risk category 'Environment, climate change & community', monitored and measured through the risk appetite (three KRIs) and the accountability of a senior member of the executive leadership team (chief external affairs officer).

In terms of values, climate change is implicit in BHP's purpose and charter values:

- **Purpose:** To bring people and resources together to build a better world.
- **Our Values:** Putting health and safety first, being environmentally responsible and supporting our communities.

It is also explicitly detailed in BHP's Charter, where BHP details the requirement to demonstrate its environmental responsibility by minimizing impacts through every stage of its operations and contributing to resilience of the natural environment.

And finally, processes – BHP manages its highest risks through mandates processes called 'Our requirements', and 'Our requirements for the environment & climate change' is one of 30 or so specific mandated processes that apply enterprise-wide.

3.4.2 Why is risk culture important in the board room?

All organizations need to take risks to achieve their objectives. The prevailing risk culture within an organization can make it significantly better or worse at managing these risks. Risk culture significantly affects the capability to take strategic risk decisions and deliver on performance promises.

Organizations with inappropriate risk cultures will inadvertently find themselves allowing activities that are at odds with stated policies and procedures or operating completely outside these policies. An inappropriate risk culture means not only that certain individuals or teams will undertake these inappropriate activities but that the rest of the organization ignores, condones or does not see what is going on. At best this will hamper the achievement of strategic, tactical and operational goals. At worst it will lead to serious reputational and financial damage.

Some of the main examples that are often cited are the abilities of an organization to seek out risk information in supporting business decisions and thus it is critical that leaders support those actively seeking to understand and manage risks. One of the main tools is performance management, which needs to be aligned to risk-taking activities.

The Financial Stability Board (FSB) in their report framework for assessing risk culture (2014) said that risk culture is important because it ensures that:[8]

- an appropriate risk-reward balance consistent with the organization's risk appetite is achieved when taking on risks
- an effective system of controls commensurate with the scale and complexity of the financial institution is properly put in place
- the quality of risk models, data accuracy, capability of available tools to accurately measure risks, and justifications for risk taking can be challenged; and
- all limit breaches, deviations from established policies, and operational incidents are thoroughly followed up with proportionate disciplinary actions when necessary

All these components are important in the context of climate change. The establishment of a robust risk appetite strategy was explained in Chapter 2 and the quality of risk models and model risk are covered in Chapter 7.

3.4.3 Organizational culture – definitions and behaviours

It is important to first understand organizational culture and then explain the interrelationship to risk culture. Culture is the combination of repeated behaviours of people in the organization that drives the way decisions are taken at all levels in the organization. The goal is to become like driving a car – ultimately doing the right thing without having to think about it.

Two important definitions are shown below:

> A system of shared values (that define what is important) and norms that define appropriate attitudes and behaviours for organizational members (how to feel and behave).[9]

> An organization's culture is reflected by what is valued, the dominant leadership styles, the language and symbols, the procedures and routines, and the definitions of success that make an organization unique.[10]

Cameron and Quinn state 'it is difficult to name even a single highly successful company, one that is a recognized leader in its industry, that does not have a distinctive, readily identifiable organizational culture'.[11] Personal beliefs and values of staff that underpin culture cannot be changed by senior management directly; management must rely on influence, which we discuss in the next section.

In the context of climate change, we are seeing a shift in the purpose of an organization, which we discussed in Chapter 2, through, for example, setting the organization's ambition to be a net zero company by 2040.

3.4.4 Organizational culture and risk culture

Much of the literature written on this subject does not fully explain or explore the link between organizational culture and risk culture. 'Risk culture refines the concept of organizational culture to focus particularly on the collective ability to take managed risk and to minimize threats but the organizational culture itself is an active backstop determining, and itself influenced by, risk culture.'[12]

This is one of the main intentions of this chapter, to explain the importance of developing a strong climate governance framework for managing and mitigating climate change risks.

The linkage between organizational and risk culture is the behaviours and attitudes of the staff, as set out in Figure 3.6. It is critical for an organization to direct the right attitudes and behaviours of most employees to focus on risk taking and risk control activities, which we now explore in more detail.

3.4.5 Developing a good risk culture

A risk culture manifests itself through the way things are done, that is, how employees behave in identifying, understanding and acting on the risks the organization

FIGURE 3.6 Organizational and risk culture

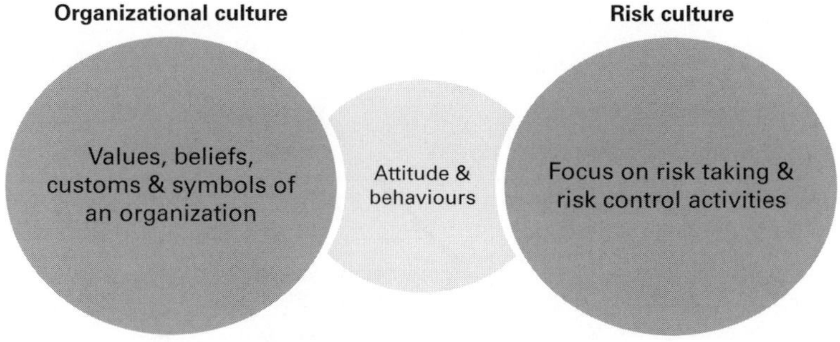

SOURCE

confronts on a day-to-day basis. The sign of a good risk culture is that the sense of responding by 'doing the right thing' is valued and encouraged more than 'doing whatever it takes to get on'.

Having understood the difference between organization and risk culture above, organizations can seek to develop and use a risk culture model.

3.5 Integrated risk culture model

In respect to the development of a good risk culture there appear to be three separate but specific drivers that make up a risk culture and that can ultimately change it:

1. Employees
2. Management
3. The ERM function

A risk culture model is illustrated in Figure 3.7 and uses the analogy of a bicycle. This analogy has been designed first to reflect the importance of all employees working

FIGURE 3.7 Integrated risk culture model

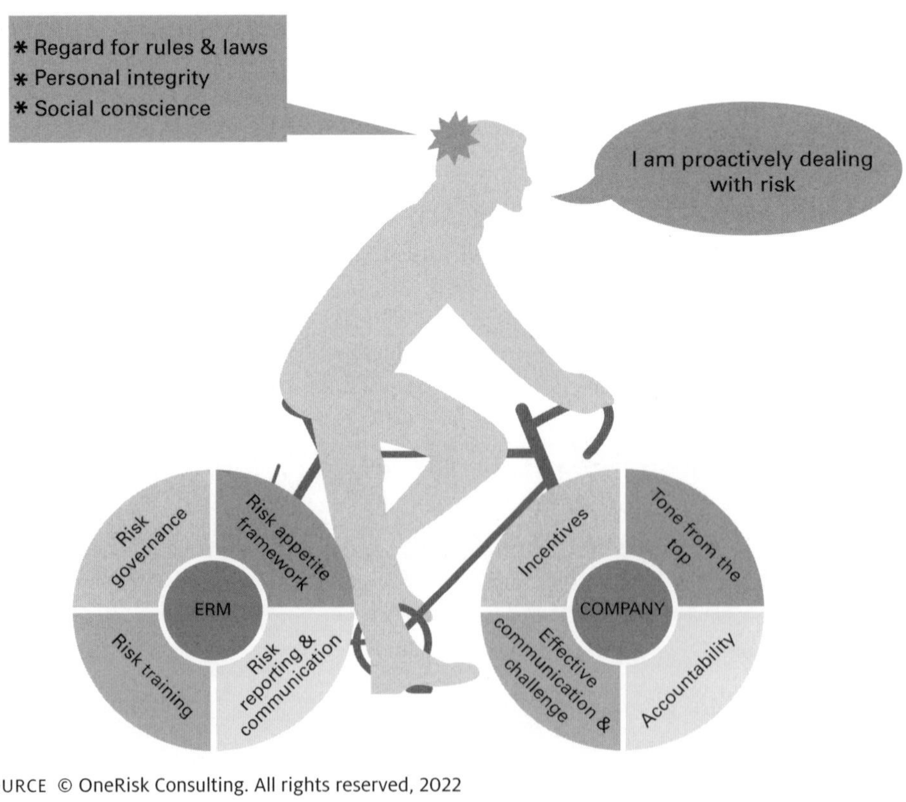

SOURCE © OneRisk Consulting. All rights reserved, 2022

collectively with a common purpose and set of values, and second to reflect the need for the organization to become sustainable and to reduce its carbon footprint.

Let's explore each of these three components in turn, starting with people.

3.5.1 Components: 1 Individuals' core attributes

Each employee has a set of core values, beliefs and ambitions, whether these are dominated by integrity and security or money and position. These in turn affect an employee's attitudes, behaviours and perceptions towards the working environment. Equally, aspects of the working environment impact employees' attitudes, behaviours and perceptions.

Management needs to recruit those individuals who possess the preferred values, beliefs and ambitions, and seek to evidence that the working environment mutually reinforces their attitudes, behaviours and perceptions. Motivating changes in employees' attitudes, behaviours and perceptions requires investment in demonstrating what the company values.

Therefore, organizations should seek ways to recruit and retain employees that align with values, and support sustainability with the employees' daily work and the company's operation.

In an article entitled 'Engaging employees to create a sustainable future' Polman and Bhattacharya (2016) explain that successfully integrating sustainability into a business requires management to reconcile the gap between personal and corporate values in three dimensions:[13]

> In the formal dimension, employees observe whether sustainability is integrated into job descriptions and training programs and whether sustainability targets are tied to employees' variable compensation.
>
> In the psychological dimension, employees observe whether sustainability performance is rewarded and recognized and whether superiors set performance expectations that align with sustainability.
>
> And in the social dimension, which is key, employees observe whether there is consistency between what the company says about its values in its mission statement and what it practices.

3.5.2 Components: 2 Management – the front wheel

What drives the risk culture is the attitudes and behaviours of management. Most of the current models, such as the IRM's model, focus on the organizational components. The Financial Stability Board as part of their risk culture framework set out four key components as outlined in Figure 3.8.

3.5.2.1 TONE FROM THE TOP

The key influence on the culture of an organization comes from the top because staff will reflect the signals they receive from their leaders in order to secure and advance

FIGURE 3.8 Financial Stability Board – risk culture framework

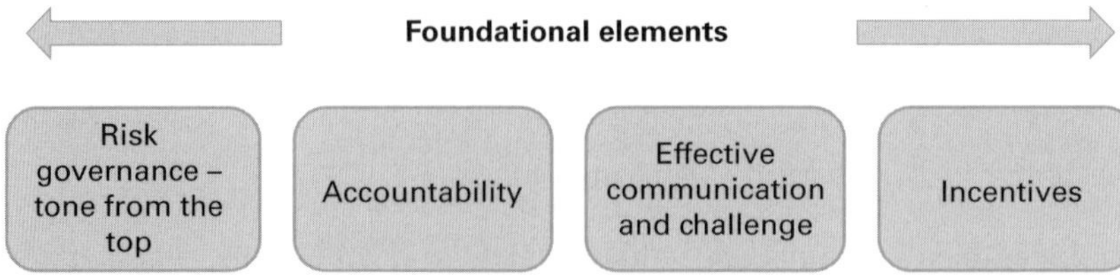

SOURCE Financial Stability Board. A Framework for Assessing Risk Culture, Climate Disclosure Standards Board

their ambitions, which is often referred to as the 'tone from the top'. Management must therefore rely on influence to change the way culture manifests itself.

It is critical that the board and senior management demonstrate adherence to sound risk management. Examples in practice include the board and senior management being committed to establishing, monitoring, and adhering to an effective risk appetite framework, which is supported by appropriate risk appetite statement(s) that underpin the financial institution's risk management strategy, and is integrated with the overall business strategy.

Indicators of 'tone from the top' include the promotion, through behaviours, actions and words, of a risk culture that displays integrity and a sound approach to risk management, as well as embracing an open exchange of views, challenge and debate. It is critical to provide alternative views and opinions, which will often result in better decision-making.

3.5.2.2 ACCOUNTABILITY AND ESCALATION OF RISK

Accountability is one of the most difficult issues for risk managers to embed and this often relates to the lack of a good risk culture.

In developing a good culture, the board and senior management need to establish a policy of ownership of risk where employees are held accountable for their actions and are aware of the consequences for not adhering to the desired behaviours towards risk. In particular, business lines, the risk management function, compliance, internal audit and other control functions have clearly delineated responsibilities with regard to monitoring, identification, management and mitigation of risk.

One of the most important risk management processes is designing appropriate escalation processes. In the context of climate change many organizations are looking at, for example, their incident reporting processes or onboarding and ongoing monitoring of customers, suppliers and counterparties, to make sure that they adhere to their risk appetite and tolerance levels for managing climate and wider ESG issues.

It is important to develop and design effective escalation processes using risk triggers that allow management to review and agree effective management actions and develop risk mitigation plans.

Integrating climate change into BAU practices and processes is discussed in detail in Chapter 11.

3.5.2.3 EFFECTIVE COMMUNICATION AND CHALLENGE

A culture of open communication and collaboration is constantly promoted to ensure each employee's view is valued to strengthen risk-related decision-making.

One way to accomplish this is through strong control functions. Control functions should share the same stature as the business lines, actively participating in committees and relevant risk decisions and activities. They need to also operate independently and have appropriate direct access to the board.

Organizations need to review and improve their control environment to manage and mitigate climate risks.

3.5.2.4 REMUNERATION AND PERFORMANCE

It is important that reward systems are evaluated to make sure that they promote the greater good and long-term interests of the company and its clients, including sustained profitability as opposed to short-term revenue generation.

An objective-setting process should be linked to core values and risk culture including treatment of customers, cooperation with internal control functions, respect of risk limits, etc. It would be beneficial to promote the development of individuals through a talent management programme that embraces risk management as a core skill (and a critical skill set for senior management).

> Only when good corporate culture and the incentive system align with each other will there be sustainable impact that helps reduce misconduct risks, a crucial element in gaining the trust of customers in the long run. (Norman Chan, Chief Executive of the Hong Kong Monetary Authority (Sept 2007))

There is a lot of literature on the topic and it is important to recognize that while rewards can be used to influence risk culture, they have their limitations.

Rewards do drive behaviour, particularly variable compensation. However, they won't always drive the right behaviours, as we have seen in areas such as customer sales where bad practices can and often do lead to mis-selling in industries such as financial services and consumer goods.

One of the controls that can be undertaken by ERM is to review the incentive programmes by making an inventory and reviewing the design, and assessing any weaknesses and potential impacts using a traditional risk-assessment approach.

3.5.3 Components: 3 ERM function – the back wheel

The ERM function can support the implementation of a good risk culture but needs support from the organization and this is particularly important for managing strategic risks such as climate change. The main components that an organization needs to develop are set out in Figure 3.9, from Standard & Poor's ERM evaluation criteria.

FIGURE 3.9 ERM evaluation criteria

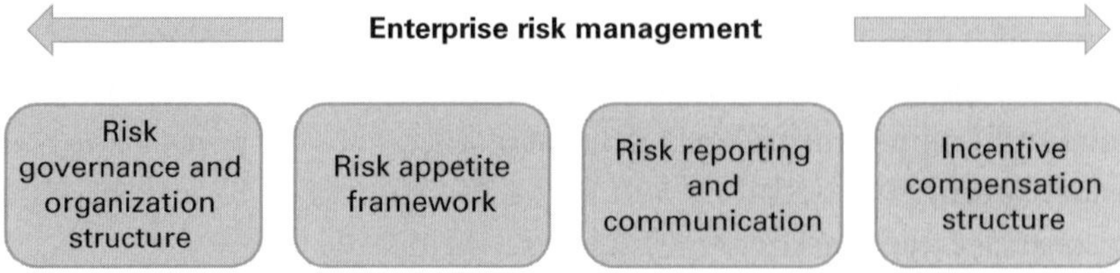

SOURCE OneRisk Consulting

3.5.3.1 RISK GOVERNANCE AND ORGANIZATION STRUCTURE

The fundamental component that drives a risk culture is risk governance. The COSO (Committee of Sponsoring Organizations) Framework is a system used to establish internal controls to be integrated into business processes.

In 2017, the committee introduced their COSO Enterprise Risk Management Framework. The COSO ERM framework aims to help organizations understand and prioritize risks and create a strong link between risk, strategy and how a business performs.

As per the new COSO standard, the first main component or pillar is entitled 'Governance and culture'. It states that governance sets the tone for the organization and establishes oversight responsibilities for ERM. It also states that culture relates to ethical values, desired behaviours and understanding of risk.

The COSO ERM framework states that the board also needs to make sure that all decisions made, in the interests of all stakeholders, include consideration of risk and reward including the appointment of the CEO.

The focus of the CRO is moving away from the compliance role to a business advisory role. In terms of governance this means more closely aligning the role to the business needs and business decisions. To do this ERM must act analogously to a football team, and play more as an attacking midfield supporting the front line in passing on information in order for the front line to make better decisions. The point here is that the ERM function needs to be part of the decision-making team that drives a better risk culture.

3.5.3.2 RISK APPETITE FRAMEWORK

The COSO ERM framework states that the organization needs to define risk appetite in the context of creating, preserving and realizing value. The framework explains the importance of designing a risk appetite statement that considers the strategic setting that is then communicated by management, embraced by the board and integrated across the organization.

3.5.3.3 RISK REPORTING AND COMMUNICATION

Risk reporting and communication is covered in more detail in Chapter 12. The new COSO framework covers this within the fifth main pillar of the new standard, entitled 'Information, communication and reporting'.

To develop a good risk culture, it is critical to share information. The COSO framework states that the information should flow up, down and across the organization and provide insight to key stakeholders. The COSO framework states that ERM should report not only on risk but also on culture directly, as well as performance, which is a real directional development. As the saying goes, 'what gets measured gets done'.

3.5.3.4 RISK TRAINING

The COSO standard states that management must define the knowledge, skills and experience needed to execute strategy; set appropriate performance targets; attract, develop and retain appropriate personal and strategic partners; and arrange for succession.

The standard does not implicitly refer to training of staff in risk management. In our experience, risk training is one of the fundamental objectives of an ERM department.

3.5.3.5 RISK ATTITUDES AND JOB ROLES

What is perhaps overlooked by organizations is that risk attitudes can be a good indication as to whether an employee is a good fit for a particular role in the organization. For example, it is known that a person with a risk-averse attitude typically makes a good middle manager or administrator or an engineer. Risk-seeking attitudes typically make good entrepreneurs and negotiators. Risk-neutral attitudes tend to make good executives and group leaders. Thus, risk tolerances should in theory align to an individual's role in an organization in respect to risk taking.

There is an obvious and wide perception divide between the risk manager and the strategist. It is important to note the perception of risk as a tactical function with a low tolerance for risk. Does the CFO's (and by extension, the organization's) perception of enterprise risk roles create any obstacles to communicating about and acting on risks?

As stated already, climate change is now a key strategic risk for many organizations to manage and the understanding of the concept of risk perception outlined above is important in the context of accountability and having the right level of leadership that is required to develop and implement the climate change strategic plans and associated mitigation strategies.

Conclusion

In this chapter we have explained the importance of having a robust and effective climate governance framework that is critical to the role of risk practitioners in integrating climate change risk and opportunities into an existing ERM framework.

We have explored the main ingredients and components that can support the design of a robust climate governance framework and also explained the relevance and importance of having a good corporate and risk culture that requires specific behaviours and processes from the board, management team, risk function and individuals to make a mature risk culture.

The main requirement is that the board and the CRO clearly articulate a balanced, business-oriented view of climate risk as a basis for educating and advising the rest of the business as well as having effective ongoing communication and reporting processes and an education programme involving operational first-line management.

The ERM function can play a major role in developing a good governance framework and associated risk culture but is reliant on the underlying cultural characteristics, which are difficult to change and are often intangible items but need to be carefully considered, particularly in managing the complexity of climate change risk.

Notes

1 World Economic Forum. How to Set Up Effective Climate Governance on Corporate Boards: Guiding principles and questions, January 2019. www3.weforum.org/docs/WEF_Creating_effective_climate_governance_on_corporate_boards.pdf (archived at https://perma.cc/UV9Z-L8K7)

2 Odgers Berndtson. Corporate governance and climate change, 19 August 2020. www.odgersberndtson.com/en-us/insights/corporate-governance-climate-change (archived at https://perma.cc/ZR3Q-NWGL)

3 Bank of England Prudential Regulation Authority. Enhancing banks' and insurers' approaches to managing the financial risks from climate change, 2019. www.bankofengland.co.uk/-/media/boe/files/prudential-regulation/supervisory-statement/2019/ss319 (archived at https://perma.cc/9TTY-HN3Q)

4 Australian Institute of Company Directors. Climate Risk Governance Guide, 2021. www.aicd.com.au/risk-management/framework/climate/climate-risk-governance-guide.html (archived at https://perma.cc/3DTS-SEL8)

5 The National Audit Office. Climate change risk: a good practice guide for Audit and Risk Assurance Committees, 2021. www.nao.org.uk/insights/climate-change-risk-a-good-practice-guide-for-audit-and-risk-assurance-committees/ (archived at https://perma.cc/6DKJ-L7FV)

6 https://assets.publishing.service.gov.uk/government/uploads/system/uploads/attachment_data/file/866117/6.6266_HMT_Orange_Book_Update_v6_WEB.PDF (archived at https://perma.cc/7KBD-29XW)

7 Institute of International Finance. Final Report of the IIF Committee on Market Best Practices: Principles of conduct and best practice recommendations. Financial Services Industry Response to the Market Turmoil of 2007-2008, p 38. https://www.iif.com/portals/0/Files/private/iif_final_report_of_the_committee_on_market_best_practices.pdf (archived at https://perma.cc/4XYU-Z949)

8 Financial Stability Board. Guidance on Supervisory Interaction with Financial Institutions on Risk Culture, 7 April 2014. www.fsb.org/wp-content/uploads/140407.pdf (archived at https://perma.cc/FE9T-MVEP)

9 C A O'Reilly and J Chatman. Organizational commitment and psychological attachment: the effects of compliance, identification, and internalization on prosocial behavior, *Journal of Applied Psychology*, 1986, 71 (3), pp 492–499. https://doi.org/10.1037/0021-9010.71.3.492 (archived at https://perma.cc/TV2S-BU3B)

10 K S Cameron and R E Quinn (2005). *Diagnosing and Changing Organizational Culture: Based on the Competing Values Framework*, revised edition, Chapter 1, Jossey Bass, San Francisco

11 K S Cameron and R E Quinn (2005). *Diagnosing and Changing Organizational Culture: Based on the Competing Values Framework*, revised edition, Chapter 1, Jossey Bass, San Francisco

12 The Institute of Risk Management. Risk Culture: Under the Microscope Guidance for Boards, 2012. https://www.theirm.org/media/4703/risk_culture_a5_web15_oct_2012.pdf (archived at https://perma.cc/4LDH-FKZU)

13 P Polman and C B Bhattacharya. Engaging Employees to Create a Sustainable Business. Stanford Social Innovation Review, 2016, Fall. https://ssir.org/articles/entry/engaging_employees_to_create_a_sustainable_business (archived at https://perma.cc/BTS8-R52M)

4

Climate change risk identification techniques, including stakeholder mapping

This chapter covers the way an organization can develop a climate risk radar to map its climate risks into its existing risk profile through a range of best practice risk identification processes, techniques and risk management tools.

This chapter focuses on the use of stakeholder analysis and mapping for all the main climate-related stakeholders across the organization's value chain that should be considered when identifying climate risks (both threats and opportunities).

The main learning outcomes from this chapter are to:

- Evaluate the practical processes and techniques involved in the identification of climate risks.
- Establish an understanding of different approaches and the benefits and challenges of risk identification.
- Understand how to develop a climate 'risk radar' that maps out a climate risk taxonomy to an organization's risk categories.
- Compare specific risk identification techniques that include a risk review process that can be tailored to focus on climate risk through the use of risk questionnaires and workshops.
- Understand the use of stakeholder analysis and mapping, which is a key management tool for identifying and addressing climate change risks and opportunities.

In Chapters 8 and 10 we provide further detailed insights into using specific risk identification techniques, including the use of horizon scanning and stress and scenario analysis which assist in addressing emerging climate risks and in the design of climate scenarios (which are covered in chapter 10).

Introduction

By identifying and proactively addressing risks and opportunities, all enterprises endeavour to protect and create value for their stakeholders, including owners, employees, customers, regulators and society overall.

The rationale is that one of the greatest dangers to any organization is not recognizing a threat until it is too late. It is no longer acceptable for an organization to find itself in a position whereby unexpected events or trends that could have been anticipated cause financial loss, disruption to normal operations, damage to reputation, regulatory censure, loss of market presence or adverse human impacts.

The purpose of risk identification is to generate a comprehensive inventory of risks based on those events that might create, prevent, accelerate or delay the achievement of an organization's objectives. When identifying risks, an organization needs to consider not only its processes and systems, but also its relationships with its clients, the nature of its products and the wider business environment.

Based on the context and understanding of the business environment, risk managers need to translate external trends and drivers into identified risks and assess the impact and severity to the organization. Effective risk identification is critically important because it underpins the risk management process and determines those risks to which management will seek to allocate resources.

In the context of climate change and the risk taxonomy that was described in Chapter 1 organizations need to identify physical, transition and liability risks, both threats and opportunities, across the risk profile. The process needs to make sure that both strategic climate-related risks as well as the risks facing each department or business area are captured to ensure a complete risk profile of the organization is built.

It is also important to separately identify and manage emerging climate risks and trends, such as government legislation and technology shifts, which can be better controlled through an enterprise risk management framework based on future time horizons.

The risk identification process can be a difficult exercise due to the diverse nature of risks and the difficulty in distinguishing cause and effect.

4.1 Risk identification process

An adequate risk identification and assessment process for climate risks should address key portfolios and geographic areas related to products and services of the organization, but will need to be tailored depending on the size, nature and complexity of the organization involved. It is important to understand the importance of the risk identification process and the various techniques and tools that are available for risk managers.

Risk identification is the process of finding, recognizing and describing risks. A risk identification process should include the following:

- Identify risk sources, events, their causes and their potential consequences.
- Utilize historical data, theoretical analysis, informed and expert opinions, and stakeholder's needs.

A comprehensive risk identification process should consider the following:

- Involve all relevant stakeholders in the process. This ensures:
  - Risks are comprehensively assessed
  - A group-wide perspective and ownership of the risks
- Risks should be properly articulated in order to ensure:
  - Everyone understands the risk, its causes and consequences
  - Effective controls can be put in place
- Risks are appropriately recorded in a risk register (or equivalent)
- Attitudes, behaviours and risk perceptions
- Consider the risks of major decisions, projects, investments, functions, etc
- Think about 'grey swan' and 'black swan' events

4.1.1 Main benefits of risk identification

The main benefits of developing a formal risk identification process include the following:

- Provides information to management on which decisions to make, which can be actioned on to ensure a controlled environment
- Provides a basis for risk measurement and assessment, which may, for example, be used for capital allocation purposes
- Sets boundaries to differentiate between risk types and assign ownership for their mitigation
- Helps develop a common language for discussing, assessing and managing risks that allows clear and transparent communication, which will support decision making

4.1.2 Risk identification – common observations and issues

Some of the main practical issues for risk managers to consider include the following:

- The amount of time required of the risk function, senior management and staff to develop a comprehensive profile of the risks (it is an iterative process at the outset)

- Getting buy-in throughout the firm (which comes from quality communication)
- The environment in which you operate, the operating model and the activities undertaken
- Ongoing changes that occur that hinder the identification of risks (i.e. regulatory environment, technological and system developments, client-led requirements and new products and markets)
- Availability of historical risk data (i.e. availability, consistency of the formats and completeness of the data)
- The existence of appropriate frameworks, policies, taxonomies, categorizations and procedures
- The prevailing awareness of and appetites for risk (i.e. are they consistent?)
- Engagement of staff and how their opinions are captured

4.2 Risk articulation

A common issue that many organizations have is not articulating the risks correctly. Quite simply, if an organization is unable to describe the risks they face, this is an immediate impediment to managing and mitigating the risk.

Some common examples are highlighted here:

- Poor risk descriptions that fail to identify the cause and therefore prevent effective mitigation (which can be achieved by addressing the cause)
- An inability to make the distinction between issues of the day and the risks facing the business on an ongoing basis
- Risk descriptions being too generic (e.g. failure of strategy) and lacking sufficient detail
- Risks focused towards one particular business discipline (e.g. financial, legal, operational) depending on the influence of senior executives, project sponsors or coordinator
- Risk descriptions that focus on a control failure rather than a specific risk (e.g. lack of business continuity plan, poor staff induction)

In respect to effective risk articulation, it is important that a consistent risk language is developed within the organization to help describe risks. Some examples of risks or threats descriptors are shown in Table 4.1.

Risk events do not occur in isolation; there is an order that results in the adverse outcome. This starts with the root cause, then the risk event and the subsequent impact (i.e. root cause – risk event – effect). The root causes (and their triggers) are a useful way to identify risk events and Table 4.2 provides some useful descriptors of these triggers.

TABLE 4.1 Examples of risk trigger descriptors

Examples of risk trigger descriptors	
Failure to...	Reduction of...
Loss of...	Disruption to...
Inability to...	Increase in...
Inappropriate...	Lack of...

TABLE 4.2 Risk events and risk descriptors – climate change examples

Root cause	Risk event (scenario of concern)	Risk impact(s)
Define the underlying root cause of the risk event	Describe concisely what the risk is	What impacts would the risk occurring have?
Examples • Failure to identify impact of trends in long-term weather patterns • Inability to respond to climate-related risks causes damage to the brand (insurance of polluting vehicles, use of plastic, company and insured fleet carbon footprint, failure to use energy efficient technology). • Reduction in the creditworthiness of our investments portfolio due to over-exposure to sectors adversely revalued as a consequence of climate change • Inappropriate use of services from suppliers who are climate change inactive, e.g. have poor climate/ ESG ratings	Examples • Our offices are affected by climate change, e.g., major flood, meaning they cannot be used or can only be used in a limited way • Inadequate insurance cover in the light of more frequent flooding events in a calendar year • Stranded assets in the investment portfolio • Products and services are mispriced	Examples • Reduced profitability • Increased earnings volatility • Regulatory fines/ penalties • Major business interruption • Reputational/brand damage • Reduced investment performance • Loss of market share • Failure to meet net zero targets

Risk practitioners should be cognizant of the danger of mistaking a cause or trigger as a risk event. If this occurs, attention may be focused on introducing additional controls whereas it may be more effective to focus on addressing the underlying root cause (and why any associated controls failed).

Consequently, when the triggers have been identified, if these can be prevented, the risk event may not actually occur.

Preventative controls operate to prevent the risk event occurring (thus reducing the likelihood).

Detective controls operate after the risk event has occurred and are there primarily to minimize/reduce the impact. Earlier detection of the risk event is key in order to minimize the severity. Figure 4.1 provides a visualization of the process.

This approach is akin to the commonly used risk management tool of bow tie analysis, which aims to depict a series of threats or causes, the undesirable or hazardous event and the negative effects or consequence. However, as mentioned elsewhere in this book, it is important not to overlook the flip side of risks and to consider the opportunities that may arise as a consequence of events occurring.

The management consultant Peter Moar has developed an approach in this regard, which aims to accentuate the positive and leverages a more positive mindset that looks at the bow tie method through a different lens.[1] If the root causes are instead thought of as conditions and the more positive risk event is considered as an organizational goal, this can switch the focus on positive effects for an organization. This can be depicted as shown in Figure 4.2.

FIGURE 4.1 Risk events and risk descriptors

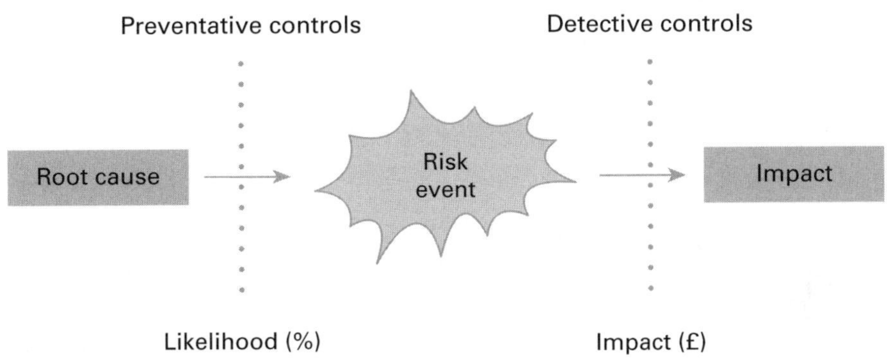

SOURCE © OneRisk Consulting. All rights reserved 2022

FIGURE 4.2 Negative and positive conceptual risk identification processes

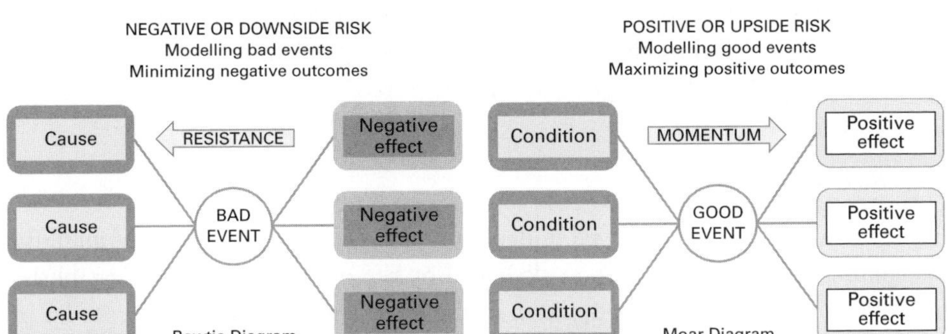

SOURCE Peter Moar Accentuate the positive. RMIA Year Book 2016

This can be particularly useful when applied within a context of climate change, where both physical risks and transition risks will generate significant upheaval in corporate value chains, consumer demands and the competitive landscape. Consequently, this is where the opportunities present themselves for organizations. A few examples that are relevant to climate change include:

- Organizations planning and restructuring their supply chains to ensure continuity of supply (of both the raw materials they need and the supply of their own products).
- Companies being early adopters of changes in consumer patterns borne out of environmental concerns (e.g. the production of electric vehicles but also the subsequent maintenance and insurance of these vehicles).
- Firms reviewing their disaster recovery arrangements in response to concerns about floods and moving to the cloud or remote working arrangements.

This change in perspective and the subsequent forward planning provides an opportunity for organizations to gain a competitive advantage, can reduce costs in the long run, ensures resilience and can potentially change the dynamics of the marketplace by seizing the momentum from the uncertainty created by climate change.

4.3 Risk universe and risk taxonomy – definitions and importance

Let's begin this section with an understanding of what a risk universe and a risk taxonomy are.

4.3.1 Risk universe

The risk universe includes all risks that could affect an organization. These can be categorized into different risk types to aid in the understanding and appropriate actioning of risks. Once these high-level classifications are established, a lower level of granularity is required and this is where they can be allocated to appropriate areas of the business in order to assign ownership and the design of controls (as required). This will be influenced by the risk appetite of the organization and how the risk(s) are to be treated (i.e., avoided, managed, transferred, etc).

4.3.2 Risk taxonomy

Establishing a consistent and well understood risk taxonomy provides a foundation for defining and categorizing the risks faced by the organization. Once established this helps ensure a consistent approach to the treatment of certain risk types (as per the risk framework and risk appetite of the firm) and all employees can follow the risk management process in place. Chapter 1 provided an overview of how to describe climate risk in terms of physical, transition and liability risks.

The importance of developing a consistent risk taxonomy is to make sure that whatever is decided upon is well communicated throughout the organization to ensure that the focus is on the risks and how they are managed and time is not wasted discussing how they are categorized.

4.3.3 Developing an organizational climate change risk radar

Developing a 'risk radar' is one of the key objectives of risk management and a fundamental principle of resilience. The ability to anticipate problems and see things differently will help an organization develop an early warning system and seize new opportunities.

The risk radar is a key diagnostic tool used to help identify an organization's key risks.[2] It can be easily updated on an ongoing basis to facilitate discussion and help management prioritize risk remediation activity and the allocation of resources.

In developing an organization's climate risk radar, it is important to seek out information from outside the organization, for example by using PESTLE analysis covering political, economic, sociological, technological, legal and environmental issues. A PESTLE analysis describes a framework of macro-environmental factors used in the environmental scanning component of strategic management, to gain insights in respect of global trends such as climate change. One of the main benefits of doing this is to build consensus among a range of stakeholders about future threats and opportunities and how to tackle or profit from them.

Threats: What is emerging on the horizon that could adversely affect future commercial or other defined success factors?

Opportunities: What trends and directions do data and information gathering reveal and indicate as areas of potential competitive advantage in the future marketplace?

The schematic in Figure 4.3 provides a climate change risk radar that seeks to align some of the main physical, transition and liability risks and opportunities associated with climate change and adapt it with a traditional risk management risk radar. The development of such a schematic can help enable risk managers to better articulate and inform senior management about the risks of climate change that pervade many organizations' entire risk profiles and risk categories.

FIGURE 4.3 Climate change risk radar framework

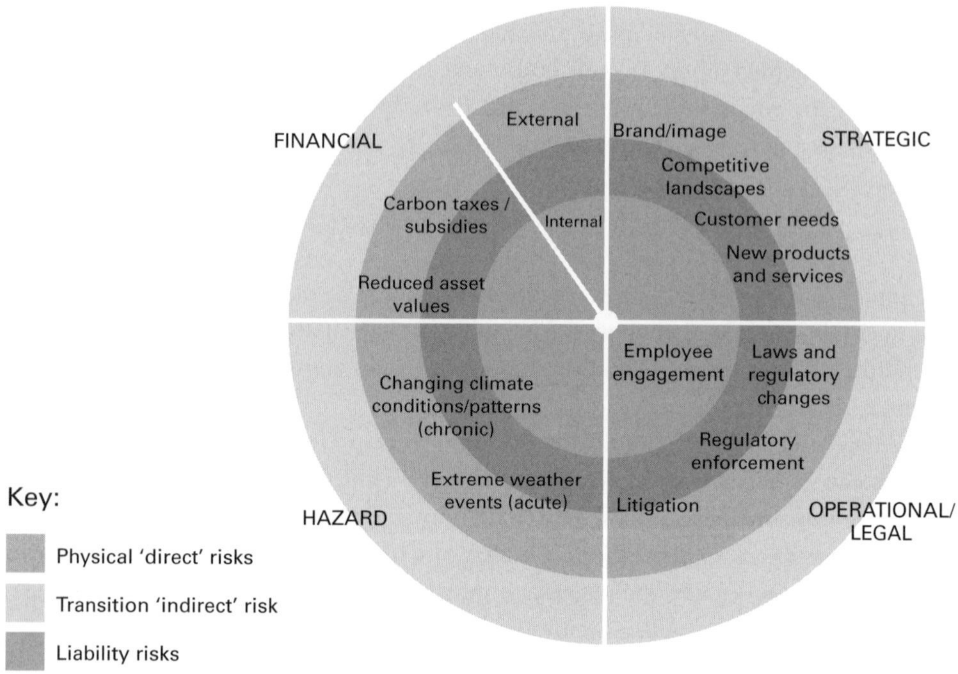

SOURCE © OneRisk Consulting. All rights reserved 2022

An organization will need to align climate risks and opportunities to its own risk categories that cover the risk profile of the organization. The above highlights the risks and opportunities aligned to the three main climate risk types and split between strategic, financial, operational/legal and hazard.

4.4 Risk identification processes, techniques and enablers

Organizations need to consider a variety of processes and techniques to identify and capture relevant climate risks. Risk identification should be an ongoing process that can be supported through employees identifying and communicating risks to the risk function and through regular quarterly risk management committee and working group meetings.

However, it is important to recognize and develop formal risk identification processes and use of specific techniques that are underpinned by specific enablers or tools that can assist in the process.

FIGURE 4.4 Risk identification processes and techniques

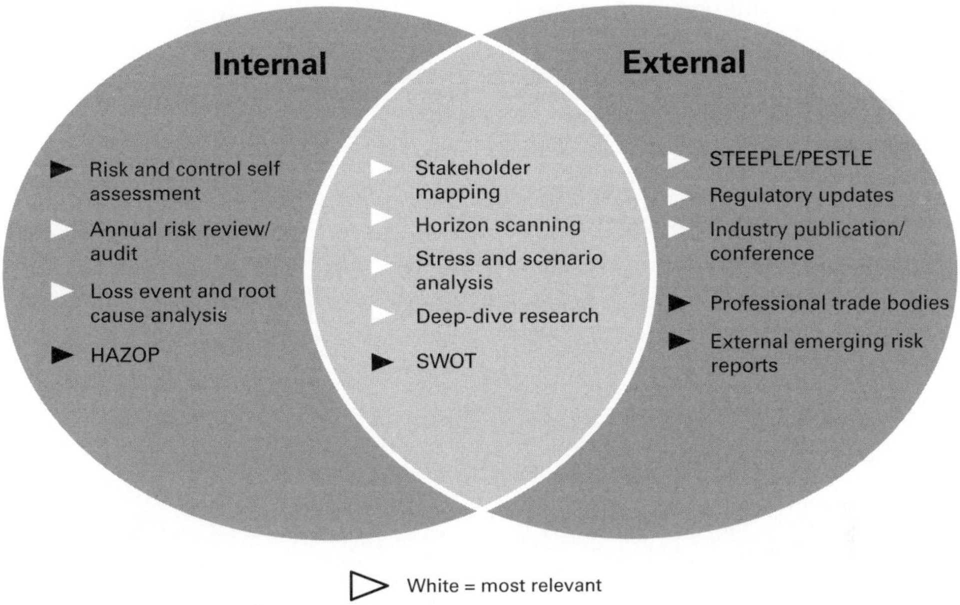

SOURCE © OneRisk Consulting. All rights reserved 2022

Figure 4.4 provides a summary of some of the risk identification processes and techniques for organizations to consider, some of which are focused primarily on an internal scan or risk; others focus on the external environment and then there are some that can be used for both purposes.

In the diagram we highlight those techniques in white that are considered to be most relevant for identifying climate change risks. While some are covered in this chapter, specifically stakeholder mapping, other techniques such as horizon scanning and stress and scenario analysis are included in other chapters.

While Figure 4.4 provides a range of processes and techniques it does not provide details of specific risk management tools or enablers that risk professionals can use to implement the techniques, as well as recording and reporting them. The traditional risk identification tools or enablers include the following.[3]

Internal interviewing and discussion:

- Interviews
- Questionnaires
- Brainstorming
- Self-assessment and other facilitated workshops
- SWOT analysis (strengths, weaknesses, opportunities and threats)

External sources:

- Comparison with other organizations
- Discussion with peers
- Benchmarking
- Risk consultants

Tools, diagnostics and processes:

- Checklists
- Flowcharts
- Scenario analysis
- Value chain analysis
- Business process analysis
- Systems engineering
- Process mapping

The most widely used reporting tool is a risk register that is often part of a risk management system and as this is a standard risk management process this will not be covered in this book (we suggest readers refer to the IRM *Fundamentals of Risk Management*.[4])

The following is a summary of each of the main internal risk identification processes and techniques.

4.4.1 Internal identification techniques

Referring back to Figure 4.4, the main internal risk identification techniques are as follows.

4.4.1.1 RISK AND CONTROL SELF-ASSESSMENT (RCSA)

This process captures and assesses the risks and controls of a given activity or process with the personnel involved in the day-to-day operation of the activity or process. It can also be applied at a strategic level. This is most useful when aligned to the objectives of the strategy, process or activity. An additional benefit is that the RCSA process can be expanded to encompass an entire end-to-end process spanning multiple teams.

4.4.1.2 ANNUAL RISK REVIEW – TYPICALLY CORPORATE OR STRATEGIC RISKS

An annual review is facilitated by the risk function where the risk expert will work together with management and staff in order to produce a risk profile that can be used in the risk measurement or assessment phase. This review is often supported through the development of a risk questionnaire and structured interviews with key stakeholders. These are discussed in more detail in section 4.4.3.2.

A review will typically consider the following:

- Clarity of risk ownership
- Adequacy of the existing controls
- Any material changes to the internal control environment
- Potential impact to the organization of losses or control failures
- Changes in the business model
- Any significant audit or compliance reviews
- Key projects delivered in the previous year
- Existence of a suitable mechanism for monitoring the risk

4.4.1.3 LOSS EVENT AND ROOT CAUSE ANALYSIS

After a particular loss event has occurred within an organization it can be analysed by key staff to help to identify the reasons and root causes for the occurrence and how future loss events can be avoided. The organization may learn more about the way it operates and question its own practices to help develop its risk policy further. Additionally, if there are any recurring themes arising over a prolonged period with regard to smaller risk events, this provides an opportunity for an organization to learn from these and introduce improvements to the internal control environment and to make any necessary adjustments to the overall risk profile.

4.4.1.4 HAZOP (HAZARD AND OPERABILITY ANALYSIS)

HAZOP is often used as a technique for identifying potential hazards in a system and identifying operability problems likely to lead to nonconforming products.

4.4.2 External identification/scanning processes

External risk identification processes and techniques are particularly appropriate for the identification of emerging risks, which we discuss in more detail in Chapter 8 when we cover designing an effective emerging climate risk management process. Chapter 8 will also cover the use of horizon scanning.

4.4.3 Internal and external risk identification processes

Some of the most important risk identification techniques for climate change risk involve the use of processes that need to consider both internal and external environments.

4.4.3.1 SCENARIO ANALYSIS

Scenario analysis is a process of identifying and assessing several plausible future events or 'what if' scenarios by considering alternative possible outcomes (sometimes called alternative worlds).

Risk managers need to play an increasing role in driving the identification of scenario selection and design decisions to assess future climate scenarios in a rapidly changing world. In Chapter 10 we will discuss the use and design of climate stress and scenarios.

In this chapter we will now focus and provide more details of two of the other best techniques for identifying climate risks:

1. Risk review using risk questionnaires and workshops
2. Stakeholder analysis and mapping

4.4.3.2 ANNUAL RISK REVIEW/AUDIT USING RISK QUESTIONNAIRES AND WORKSHOPS

Risk professionals often undertake an annual review of their risk registers in order to reflect the revised risk profile, which is often focused on updating existing and including new risks that can then be used in the risk measurement or assessment phases.

As part of this process and in order to identify a list of climate risks that can lead to scenarios to be used within, for example, workshops, the design of bespoke risk questionnaires is an important risk management tool that can support various techniques.

The questionnaire from a risk management perspective should seek to understand the business strategy, objectives and process, and activities of the business areas and then ask the question: What climate risks (threats and opportunities) could prevent or support your department in achieving its objectives, and individual business processes in functioning effectively, i.e. what are the key climate risks? (Referring to the organization's climate risk taxonomy and climate risk radar.)

Through the questionnaire and workshop process, the aim should be to develop and agree a number of potential risks, threats and scenarios for each department. The questionnaire needs to be completed in advance of planned workshops where responses will be validated, and loss scenarios developed.

This process affords an opportunity to provide input and direction for senior management that will help shape how the company deals with climate risks and risk management in the future.

Senior executives It is important to differentiate the approach and design of risk questionnaires for internal purposes. The approach for senior management is to set out a high-level set of questions that align with the business strategy and objectives.

The involvement of senior management in both the risk questionnaire and workshop process is critical as they can provide valuable insights in identifying climate risks that can impact on the organization's objectives.

Senior management (responsible for climate risks) A second, more detailed questionnaire that generates more in-depth responses can be designed and sent out for those employees that have greater knowledge or accountability for managing climate risks.

This type of questionnaire would be used as part of an annual risk identification exercise but can be used as a one-off exercise for identifying climate risks.

The questionnaire and workshop processes should be designed to explore:

- The main climate risks, threats and opportunities in relation to an individual's own function/directorate or specialist area
- The factors that could cause these risks to materialize
- The probability of these risks materializing
- The impact if the risks did materialize in terms of financial impact, and/or reputation with stakeholders, etc
- The current control environment to manage these risks, their effectiveness and if not fully effective, the reasons why this may be the case

An example of a simple questionnaire approach that can be used and adapted is provided here.

RISK IDENTIFICATION

Risk questionnaire for selected department – development of scenario synopsis

Using the template in Table 4.3 (physical risks only):

1. Provide risk description of the top three climate scenarios of most concern both for the organization as a whole and for your area of responsibility
2. Provide initial risk impact/business process impacted

Additional questions can be designed, adapted and tailored to cover other climate risks such as transition and liability, and to cover details of risk treatment improvements/ action plans. In addition, the questions can be developed to explore relevant time horizons.

TABLE 4.3 Sample risk identification template (to be completed) – climate physical risks

Name & job title:			
Examples Please refer to climate risk taxonomy.	Risk cause/key driver	Scenario description	Risk impact/business process impacted
	1. Extreme weather event (acute), or 2. Changing climate conditions/ patterns (chronic) Examples: Major flood event, prolonged heatwave, extended wildfire, etc.		

What are the top three climate risks (physical threats) facing the organization as a whole?			
1			
2			
3			

What are the top three climate risks (physical threats) affecting your area of organization, i.e. risk pillar?			
1			
2			
3			

This process of identification is very helpful in the design of climate scenarios that we discuss in detail in Chapter 10. The outputs of this process can be used to prioritize the design of climate scenarios. Now let's look at stakeholder analysis and mapping.

4.5 Stakeholder analysis and mapping

In this section we discuss one of the main risk identification techniques for climate change risks that can help support the development of a climate 'risk radar' for identifying both risks and opportunities through the use of stakeholder mapping.

Organizations will need to identify risks and opportunities that emanate from stakeholder expectations and then align them with their strategic objectives, core operations and processes.

4.5.1 Developing a stakeholder map (internal and external stakeholders)

Stakeholder analysis is often considered the first step in strategic planning activities on an organizational level. The concept of stakeholder awareness and the need for analysis is prevalent among project management principles.[5] This is equally applicable to climate change risk management but with a differing set of requirements/expectations.

An approach to climate change-related risk based on stakeholder expectations has many advantages. It facilitates a full and thorough validation of the core processes of the organization (strategic, operations and compliance) while considering the environment/climate change expectations that each stakeholder places on each core process.

Stakeholder expectations are shifting and there is a strong customer and investor focus today on corporate purpose, fulfilling regulatory requirements and pledging to meet emissions targets. It is becoming increasingly apparent that, as well as profit, non-financial key performance indicators such as ESG ratings, customer satisfaction, etc, are also going to be important drivers for stakeholders (including lenders, pension funds, insurers, shareholders, regulators and consumers).

4.5.2 Range of stakeholders

Organizations will have a wide range of stakeholders, some of whom may indeed be unwanted as far as the organization is concerned. ISO Guide 83[6] suggests that the term 'interested party' is preferred, but stakeholder is an acceptable, all-encompassing and a commonly understood alternative. ISO Guide 73[7] defines a stakeholder as a 'person or group concerned with, affected by, or perceiving themselves to be affected by an organization'. ISO Guides are documents that provide advice to:

- **Standards writers** on how to deal with specific issues when drafting standards; or
- **National Standards Bodies** on how to deal with issues specific to standardization principles

For organizations in different sectors, the range of stakeholders will be different.

For government agencies, the general public will be a major stakeholder. Specific groups within the general public will be stakeholders in different agencies, depending on the purpose of each particular agency. For organizations that have significant environmental interests or exposures, a different range of stakeholders would need

FIGURE 4.5 Climate change stakeholder map

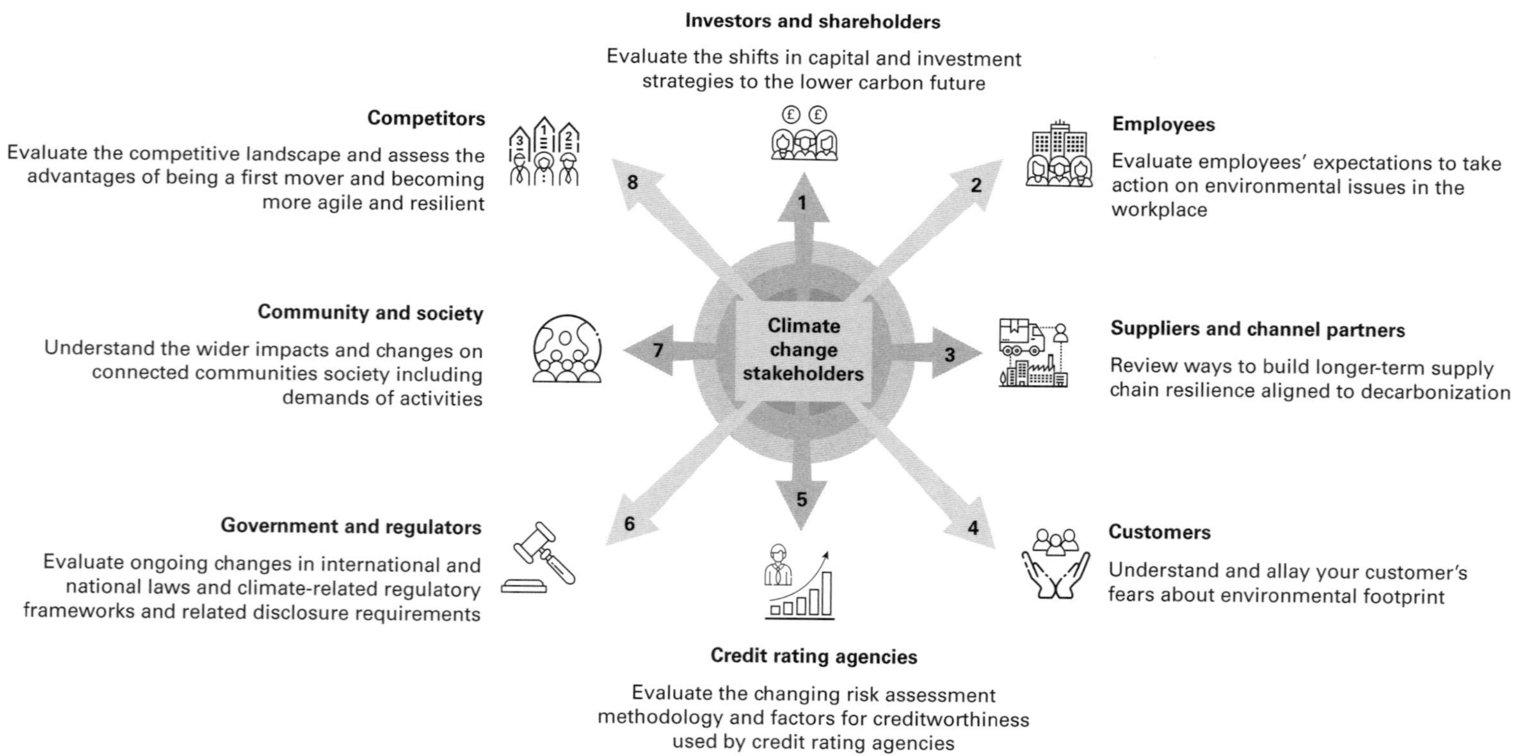

SOURCE

to be considered. For energy or mining companies, environmental pressure groups are higher-profile key stakeholders.

Figure 4.5 provides a depiction of the main stakeholder groups who may have requirements/expectations with regard to climate change. It is not a definitive list and will differ depending on the industry in which your organization operates, the size and ownership structure of the firm, the value chain of your service/product offering and the strategic objectives.

Let's take a look at each of these groups in more detail.

4.5.3 *Investors and shareholders*

Organizations need to evaluate the impact of shifts in capital and investment strategies on the lower-carbon future. In early 2021, Larry Fink, the CEO of BlackRock, one of the world's largest asset managers, expressed a clear conviction that climate change will drive a fundamental reshaping of finance and, therefore, BlackRock's strategy.[8]

Despite the pandemic, 2020 proved to be a landmark year for investor action on climate change and investments pouring into sustainable funds. With regulators and clients increasingly calling for change, asset managers are broadening their remit beyond energy/carbon-intensive industries such as oil.

The pandemic has served to raise awareness of corporate fragilities. As Mirza Baig noted, 'Rather than drive investor attention away from climate change, the pandemic has cemented interest, with many investors fearing the economic fallout seen during the pandemic could be replicated if the world fails to halt global warming.'[9]

Regulators such as Mark Carney, former head of the Bank of England, have also warned of significant investment risk from 'stranded assets', where investors have holdings that become unsellable because of climate change.

There have been many groups established, such as the Net-Zero Asset Owner Alliance, which have set out asset portfolio decarbonization targets and exert influence by becoming vocal shareholders in these listed organizations.

'The Alliance sees engagement as potentially the most important mechanism asset owners must contribute to a net-zero transformation.'[10] One of the most recent developments is that all members are required to set engagement targets.

The members' approach to engagement varies but includes: corporate, sector and value chain, alliance position paper contribution, and asset manager engagement. Their desired outcome of any engagement type is alignment with 1.5°C no/low overshoot trajectories.

4.5.4 *Employees*

Addressing social issues like climate change is increasingly becoming an employee expectation. Gen Z have grown up amid an unending litany of social and political unrest, and place a high value on the ethics, authenticity and social impact of employers today.[11]

Employers need to evaluate the expectations of employees, particularly younger generations, concerning climate change. It is important to acknowledge that employees may be at a point where there is a blurring of the lines between the E and S of ESG. Organizations must consider the increased risk of not being able to attract and retain employees if, for example, they are not seen to be aligning with their values and any expectations of greening their operations, as well as being more proactive in complying with climate change regulations. Other significant and related risks could also extend to strikes and reputational damage leading to lost business.

There have been some specific recent examples. In 2021, thousands of cleaning workers in Minneapolis marched in what's believed to have been the first union-authorized climate strike in the United States.[12] Their demands ranged from a guarantee of more environmentally friendly cleaning products to funding for a 'green technician janitorial training program', which could help them push for more substantial changes during their day-to-day operations rather than wait for top-down measures.

4.5.4.1 HR POLICIES AND RESKILLING

The Covid-19 pandemic has led to significant changes in respect of shifting HR policies to better meet the needs of employees and can be viewed as a 'practice run' for climate change. Employers will need to focus on looking at the impact of their remote and flexible working policies as one example.

Some of the additional HR policies for HR departments to consider include 'adjustments to indoor workplaces (cooling, additional breaks, supply of refreshments, adjusted dress code etc) and to outdoor workplaces (adapted working times to avoid high heat for those in the construction and agriculture industries etc).'[13]

Other areas of focus are changes to employee benefits, and training and reskilling of staff, which we cover in more detail in Chapter 3 under governance and in Chapter 11 under climate integration.

4.5.4.2 MIGRATION AND TALENT ATTRACTION AND RETENTION

Climate-induced migration is also now a rising concern for organizations, with employees increasingly expected to move away from high-risk zones. Recruitment, working practices and retention policies may need to be adjusted to reflect these challenges, otherwise talent could become increasingly concentrated in certain jurisdictions or business sectors.

Additionally, employees are starting to focus more on working for organizations that align with their own values as well as traditional employee concerns around pay, benefits and working conditions. Employers that are high profile and have positive climate change credentials will be more appealing to candidates and it can be a differentiator in the market for talent.

The role of employees in mitigating climate risk (i.e. reducing carbon emissions) should also not be underestimated. Promoting environmental awareness and aligning this with a clear corporate climate risk strategy can be a powerful tool in the management of this risk, and can contribute to marked reduction in emissions while also increasing employee engagement. Examples of how organizations have attempted to address this include:[14]

- Aviva – Initiated weekly internal climate change updates to inform employees about climate change developments for the insurance sector and globally. This was complemented by 'snapbriefs' for staff, where specific details were provided about what Aviva is doing about climate change and within the domain of influencing public policy.
- Allianz – Runs an annual group-wide sustainability forum for all staff to attend and launched an app that allows staff to track their emissions and carbon savings. These then feed into an offset process.

Such initiatives are vital to increase engagement, to raise the profile of climate change risk and to empower and enable staff to think about how climate risk emissions can be reduced, the risks can be better mitigated or operational processes can be made more efficient.

4.5.5 Suppliers and channel partners

Organizations need to review ways to build sustainable supply chain resilience aligned to decarbonization.

In terms of risk and opportunity, businesses should be accelerating efforts to reduce the carbon intensity of their operations and that of their supply chains, to manage their climate-related investment risks, and innovate to refocus their business models for growth in a decarbonized world. This is equally applicable to outsourced providers. Practical steps can include an evaluation of the vulnerability of suppliers that may be affected, for example, by emission regulations and also an assessment of the geographical distribution of the supplier network.

Additionally, climate change considerations are becoming increasingly important criteria when undertaking due diligence of suppliers, channel partners, service providers or outsourcers. This can be at the initial selection stage, during ongoing service reviews or as part of periodic views (which are typically linked to contract renewals). Climate change also raises the potential for significant supply and demand shocks.

One of the main impacts will be a shrinking, or shorter, supply chain footprint as companies seek a different cost/resilience trade-off and look to localize production and sourcing. We will also see changes in outsourcing arrangements. The supply chain disruptions in the food supply are opening up other potential risks such as food security concerns and safety breaches.

4.5.5.1 SUPPLIER DUE DILIGENCE PROCESSES

Many organizations are now focusing on the development of robust supplier procurement processes, which include assessing the climate change and wider ESG credentials of the key suppliers in order to meet certain regulatory standards, to align with their own corporate values and in order to track their Scope 3 emissions (which may form part of their own strategic net zero goals/emission targets).

A detailed outline of how to develop an end-to-end process is provided in Chapter 11 when we discuss how to integrate climate change into business processes.

It is important to recognize that this is a circular process and that your own organization becomes part of the process. This could mean that your own organization could be dropped from a preferred supplier or tender list if you don't meet your customer expectations, which we discuss in more detail in the next section.

4.5.6 Clients and customers

One of the key strategic challenges that climate change poses is to understand changing customer behaviours and the potential for reduced or increased demand for goods and services due to shifts in consumer preferences. This creates opportunities, and many organizations are seeking to meet these demand shifts through developing greener products, for example shifting to electric cars in the automotive sector.

There are related risks to disclosure and information sharing with customers on specific products where legal challenges may arise in the future. As an example, from the property loan sector, climate change will impact properties in future flood-related zones and there will be increasing potential for customers who are given long-term loans to sue lenders if they suffer financial loss and information known to the lender about the property's potential flood risk exposure was withheld. On the flipside, there is the risk that the underlying asset loses all of its value and does not cover the value of the loan at the end of its term.

A national survey commissioned by sustainability charity WRAP in the UK in 2021 states 'a majority of consumers believe companies across industry need to do more when it comes to tackling emissions to help the UK meet tough, binding environmental targets for 2050'.[15]

Dr David Moon, Director of Collaboration & Change at WRAP, commented:

> People are making it clear that they expect businesses to lead the way on tackling climate change and are prepared to walk away from brands if they don't change. It's also apparent that there is a willingness and desire for business to collaborate and work together on the best ways of combating climate change and guiding the UK along the path to 'Net Zero'. Bringing down emissions and adapting to the concerns of customers should now be at the forefront of business thinking. Time is running out for companies to act.

There are also wider strategic issues that organizations need to address in terms of clients and customers that they want to deal with (and vice versa). This also extends to engagement and a good example is in the insurance industry where insurers are developing 'responsible underwriting strategies' across their client base.

4.5.7 Rating agencies

The world's efforts to hit emissions targets will pose a threat to many more industries' creditworthiness, including some that do not directly emit much carbon, according to the top rating agencies. Moody's Investor Services in its environmental heat map states that thirteen sectors with a combined $3.4 trillion in debt have 'very high' or 'high' environmental credit risk as the transition to a low-carbon economy gathers pace.[16]

This stakeholder group will not be applicable to all because it is primarily (although not exclusively) relevant to larger publicly traded firms that are looking to raise capital in global markets. It is nevertheless relevant to a significant percentage of organizations and thus exerts a large amount of influence and is key in promoting a consistency of approach.

Typically, they ask questions around the performance of the ERM framework and embedding of the framework within the respective organization that include:

- Give an update on developments in your risk management framework in the past 12 months.
- Explain your risk appetite and tolerances, the key risk controls you have in place and how these are monitored.
- What do you consider to be the strengths and weaknesses of your organization's risk management programme?

Managing climate change is increasingly being seen as an important risk to manage and mitigate along with other key risks. What is different with climate change is the fact that rating agencies have already signalled that the rating of certain industries will decline because climate change will drive a move to a low-carbon economy.

Organizations that take a long time to adjust could experience a decline in creditworthiness. This 'transition risk' is particularly high for financial institutions with high exposure to carbon-intensive sectors such as automotive, oil and energy as they are vulnerable to climate policies and restrictions. Yet the Moody's rating agency's heat map report states that transition towards a low-carbon economy may also present business opportunities for the financial sector.

4.5.7.1 CLIMATE ESG RATINGS

Many rating agencies are developing their own approach to the assessment of climate change as part of a wider assessment of ESG factors that they consider to have an impact on the company's overall rating and consequently it may affect their assessed creditworthiness.

4.5.7.2 INTERSECTION OF ESG FACTORS AND CREDIT RISK

According to S&P:

> ESG factors typically incorporate an entity's effect on and impact from the natural and social environment and the quality of its governance. ESG credit factors are those ESG factors that can materially influence the creditworthiness of a rated entity or issue and for which we have sufficient visibility and certainty to include in our credit rating analysis. Importantly, not all ESG factors materially influence creditworthiness, and thus credit ratings.[17]

Figure 4.6 is an output from S&P that outlines the current ESG factors that have the most influence on global ratings of insurers.

The most important ESG factor for insurance companies is environmental factors associated with physical risks. According to S&P they represent over 50 per cent of the total rating due mainly to non-life re/insurers that are exposed to natural disasters, which can impact upon both their capital and earnings.

S&P also set out and explain the importance for organizations to consider their entire value chain, as we discussed earlier. They state that organizations need to

FIGURE 4.6 Rating factors that have the most influence

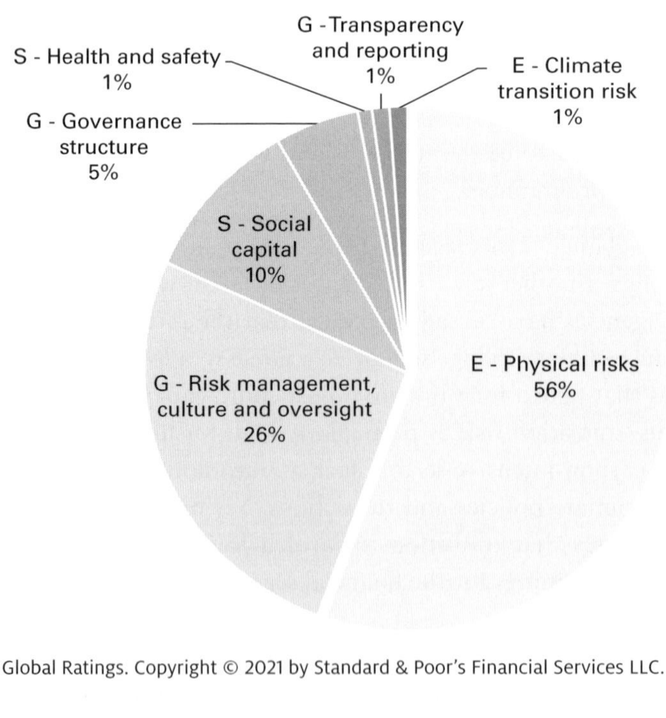

SOURCE S&P Global Ratings. Copyright © 2021 by Standard & Poor's Financial Services LLC. All rights reserved

consider the companies and individuals they do business with, such as brokers, cedants, policyholders and investee companies, which they refer to collectively as the 'value chain'. While this is insurance-specific, the rating process is applicable to other sectors.

4.5.8 Government and regulators

The role of governments is integral with regard to the management of climate change risk. This covers a complex and diverse range of influence but can include:

- Improving awareness and knowledge of the impacts of climate change risk (by financing research and the distribution of information/education to heighten awareness).
- Enacting policies that are in place that encourage a transition to clean energy (thus reducing the emissions side of the equation).
- Establishing an appropriate regulatory framework (by establishing laws, setting standards and appointing regulators) and ensuring that this is appropriately monitored and enforced.
- Providing the regulatory framework for insurance markets (which can cushion the impact of natural disasters through insurance markets or by making disaster insurance mandatory).
- Developing an infrastructure that supports stakeholders, which reaches across national, regional and local government but which is focused on the reduction of barriers that prevent the consideration of climate change risk management.
- Controlling the appropriation of funds (by offering subsidies and/or incentives) but also by cutting subsidies/support to polluters.
- Creating an environment for investment (via the tax system) and influencing positive behaviours via tax initiatives (an example being the charge for plastic bags in the UK, which overnight reduced the use of single-use plastic bags by 85%).
- Providing public services when there are gaps in provision by the private sector

Governments cannot be expected to manage climate change risk in isolation but they are a critical component and contribute positively by establishing robust foundations that can support and complement the initiatives undertaken by the other stakeholder groups.

4.5.8.1 REGULATORY OVERSIGHT

Organizations need to evaluate ongoing changes and trends in a combination of regulatory oversight (covering international and national laws) and climate-related regulatory frameworks.

Global regulatory forums have been established to support national prudential oversight bodies for climate change and the systemic risks posed. The key ones are TCFD, NGFS and CFRF, each of which is explained next.

4.5.8.2 TASK FORCE ON CLIMATE-RELATED FINANCIAL DISCLOSURES (TCFD)

Recognizing the risks that climate change may pose to the financial system, the Financial Stability Board (FSB) at the request of the G20 launched the industry-led Task Force on Climate-related Financial Disclosures (TCFD) to develop recommendations on climate-related financial disclosures. The TCFD has developed a framework to help public companies and other organizations more effectively disclose climate-related risks and opportunities through their existing reporting processes.[18]

The recommendations are structured around four main pillars: governance, strategy, risk management, and metrics and targets. The recommendations provide clear guidance for risk managers and boards and the requirements for reporting are discussed in detail in Chapter 12.

4.5.8.3 NETWORK FOR GREENING THE FINANCIAL SYSTEM (NGFS)

A group of central banks and supervisors formed the NGFS to exchange experiences, share best practices, and contribute to the development of environmental and climate risk management in the financial sector. They produce regular reports that guide key climate-related topics. A recent publication was on the macroeconomic and financial stability impacts of climate change and research priorities.[19]

4.5.8.4 THE PRA AND CLIMATE FINANCIAL RISK FORUM (CFRF)

At a country level, regulators work with industry to establish best practices for climate risk management, conduct surveys and field-test for examples of national requirements. In 2019, the UK's PRA and FCA established the Climate Financial Risk Forum (CFRF). On 29 June 2020, the CFRF published their guide to climate-related financial risk management.[20]

To embed climate risk management recommendations by the TCFD in financial decision-making, the PRA has become the first regulator to publish supervisory expectations over the management specifically for financial risks that include expectations for risk management:[21]

- Governance, where firms will be expected to embed fully the consideration of climate risks into governance frameworks, including at the board level, and assign responsibility for oversight of these risks to specific senior role holders.
- Risk management, where firms will need to consider climate change in line with their board-approved risk appetite.
- The regular use of scenario analysis to test strategic resilience.
- Developing and maintaining an appropriate disclosure of climate risks.

4.5.9 Communities and societies

Organizations need to understand the wider impacts and changes that climate change is bringing to communities and society, including the demands of activists. Global public concern increases year on year and can be expected to increase further as the physical effects become increasingly apparent.

In 2019, millions of people took to the streets uniting across time zones, cultures and generations to demand urgent action on the escalating ecological emergency. It should be expected that increased public engagement will drive action by elected representatives and governments. The Paris Agreement 'ratchet mechanism' will help enable this to be incorporated into global action plans pledged by individual countries, and reputational risks will increase for organizations whose public positions or lack of public positions don't align with these concerns or where their business activities don't align with public concerns.

New influential movements are forming such as Extinction Rebellion (abbreviated as XR), a global environmental movement with the stated aim of using non-violent civil disobedience to compel government action to avoid tipping points in the climate system and biodiversity loss. These environmental groups and movements aimed at forcing businesses and politicians to act on climate change are increasingly exerting pressure on governments and businesses to do more.

4.5.10 Competitors

Climate change affects almost all industries and thus their competitive landscape. Addressing climate risks is sometimes perceived by boards and senior management purely as a cost, or a trade-off with other priorities, but it is now generally recognized that companies that manage and mitigate their exposure to climate change risks while seeking new profit opportunities can generate a competitive advantage over rivals in a carbon-constrained future (where the profile and demands of other stakeholder groups have evolved and the market dynamic changes). It's not enough to do something; you have to do it better – and more quickly – than your competitors.[22]

Therefore, it is critical to evaluate the competitive landscape because this can influence the organization's risk profile particularly in areas such as ongoing and future product strategies. This has been seen across many industries but most notably in the automotive industry. Consumer concerns about national energy security, climate change, local air pollution and the cost of filling up at the pump have been shaping the competitive dynamics within the industry.

Companies in all sectors can reduce their emission intensity at little or no cost by accelerating the switch to renewable energy, improving energy and process efficiency in their operations, and leveraging their buying power to ensure that their suppliers decarbonize.

Companies with the technology and vision to provide products and services that address climate and other pressing issues will enjoy a competitive advantage. Additionally, companies that quantify their footprints send a strong message that they recognize the importance of climate change as a business risk and an opportunity.

Calculating the impact of climate risk on cash flows and the cost of capital is critical to understanding an organization's ability to compete in a carbon-constrained (reduced) future. These moves will help to future-proof businesses against growing external pressure from the public, regulators and investors.

One simple technique that organizations can use to assess their position is to map or plot their climate competitiveness against peers using two variables – positioning against risks and preparedness to seize opportunities. In doing so you are likely to uncover ideas on how to move to a position of competitive advantage.

4.6 Framework to prioritize climate stakeholders

In order to assist in assessing the stakeholders of the organization relative to each other and the action required (and by whom), we outline in Figure 4.7 a simple two-by-two matrix. This matrix can be used to map stakeholders in terms of priority to the organization (i.e. low/high) and influence or controllability by the organization (i.e. the influence/control the organization has over that stakeholder group).

This acknowledges that all stakeholders are important but recognizes that depending on a number of variables their relative importance will differ across organizations (i.e., variables could include the size of firm, the industry in which it operates, the ownership structure, the point in the business cycle and the regulatory environment). Stakeholders may move between these boxes depending on these variables over time.

FIGURE 4.7 Prioritization of climate stakeholders

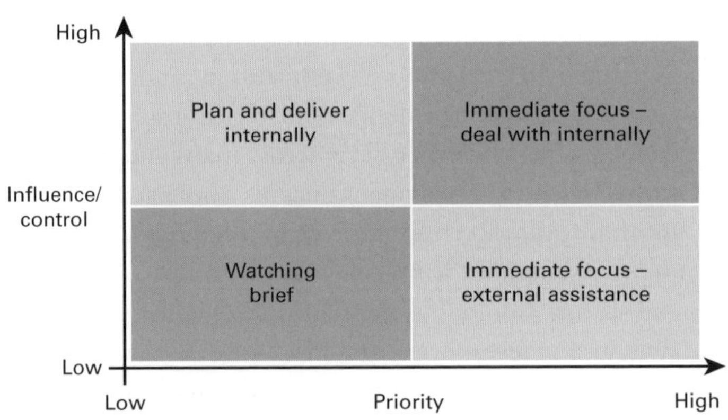

SOURCE © OneRisk Consulting. All rights reserved 2022

For example, a high-priority stakeholder over which a firm has more influence at a point in time could be employees that have developed an innovative new low-carbon product. In an ideal world, this could be dealt with immediately using in-house resources.

Alternatively, a high-priority stakeholder that the organization has less influence over could be a regulatory body or the actions of competitors. These would still require immediate focus but there needs to be recognition that the relationship dynamic and levels of information may differ and there may be instances where external expertise would be beneficial (examples being external legal counsel ahead of a significant regulatory change relating to climate change, or the use of external consultancy to understand changes in consumer demands within the wider competitive landscape).

A lower-priority stakeholder over which an organization has a higher degree of influence or control would be in the top left box where less immediate focus is required but where it can be dealt with in-house. An example of this could be 'employees', where there may be perceived scope for management to plan and deliver in order to maintain high employee engagement.

A lower-priority stakeholder over which there is less direct influence could be 'community/society'; if there are no particular issues at that particular point in time, it will be sufficient to maintain a watching brief and focus some resources on other stakeholder requirements. This is not to be complacent in any way; if any initiatives that the organization is involved with present a potential negative impact on the local community (e.g. the building of a nuclear power station or an inland wind farm) it can move around the matrix at an alarming pace.

Conclusion

This chapter has highlighted the need for organizations to develop a robust identification process, which is really important in respect of identifying wide-ranging climate risks, both threats and opportunities.

Organizations need to consider a variety of processes and techniques to identify and capture material climate risks. Risk identification should therefore be an ongoing process that can be supported through employees identifying and communicating risks to the risk function and through regular quarterly risk management committee and working group meetings.

An adequate risk identification and assessment process for climate risks should address key portfolios and geographic areas related to products and services of the organization but will need to be tailored depending on the size, nature and complexity of the organization involved.

The chapter has outlined a range of different approaches and the benefits and challenges of risk identification, with one of the main goals being to develop a climate 'risk radar' that maps out a climate risk taxonomy to an organization's risk categories.

As explained in detail in this chapter, stakeholder analysis should be considered as one of the key first steps in strategic planning activities and developing an overall climate strategy and ongoing implementation plans. Organizations therefore need to research and understand the internal and external expectations of key stakeholders such as regulators, and factor these into their risk management and decision-making processes.

Notes

1 P Moar. Accentuate the positive, *RMIA Yearbook 2016*, 2016. Risk Management Institute of Australasia

2 Airmic. Roads to Resilience, 2014, www.airmic.com/sites/default/files/technical-documents/Roads-to-Resilience-full-report.pdf (archived at https://perma.cc/QT5A-5MHA)

3 G Rubasundram. Fraud risk assessment: A tool for SME's to identify effective internal controls, *Research Journal of Finance and Accounting*, 2014, 5 (15), https://core.ac.uk/download/pdf/234630083.pdf (archived at https://perma.cc/68HM-UGFJ)

4 P Hopkin and C Thompson (2021) *Fundamentals of Risk Management*, 6th edn, Kogan Page, London

5 L W Smith. Stakeholder analysis: A pivotal practice of successful projects, 2000. Project Management Institute

6 ISO. ISO/DGUIDE 83: High level structure and identical text for management system standards and common core management system terms and definitions. www.iso.org/standard/81251.html (archived at https://perma.cc/JVQ7-9TK2)

7 ISO. ISO GUIDE 73:2009 Risk management – Vocabulary. https://www.iso.org/obp/ui/#iso:std:iso:guide:73:ed-1:v1:en (archived at https://perma.cc/R89P-ZCQ2)

8 L Fink. The Power of Capitalism, BlackRock, 2022, www.blackrock.com/corporate/investor-relations/larry-fink-ceo-letter (archived at https://perma.cc/U8PH-F99Y)

9 M Baig, quoted in A Mooney and P Temple-West. Climate change: asset managers join forces with the eco-warriors, *Financial Times*, 26 July 2020, www.ft.com/content/78167e0b-fdc5-461b-9d95-d8e068971364 (archived at https://perma.cc/2LZM-ANA7)

10 UNEPFI. Target Setting Protocol Second Edition, nd. www.unepfi.org/net-zero-alliance/resources/target-setting-protocol-second-edition/ (archived at https://perma.cc/UV6S-5TQM)

11 T Barrett. UK employees 'speaking up' on climate change in the workplace, *Environmental Journal*, 11 March 2020, https://environmentjournal.online/articles/uk-employees-speaking-up-on-climate-change-in-the-workplace/ (archived at https://perma.cc/Y4WC-5AAP)

12 S Sax. Employees are fighting for a new cause at work: the climate impact, *HuffPost*, 20 August 2020, https://www.huffingtonpost.co.uk/entry/employee-activism-climate-change_n_5ea04b1ac5b6a486d082480d (archived at https://perma.cc/H7CN-DKXT)

13 Freshfields Bruckhaus Deringer. Climate change and the workplace: What do global employers need to know? 15 November 2021, www.freshfields.com/en-gb/our-thinking/knowledge/briefing/2021/11/climate-change-and-the-workplace-what-do-global-employers-need-to-know/ (archived at https://perma.cc/9UEJ-MUZR)

14 ClimateWise. The ClimateWise Principles Independent Review 2021: The insurance industry pulling together, 2021. www.cisl.cam.ac.uk/files/cisl_climatewise_principles_2022.pdf (archived at https://perma.cc/G67G-QUSJ)

15 I Palmer. Six in ten consumers think UK businesses need to act now on climate change, Wrap, November 2021. https://wrap.org.uk/media-centre/press-releases/six-ten-consumers-think-uk-businesses-need-act-now-climate-change (archived at https://perma.cc/SFC9-MN4L)

16 Moody's. Environmental Heat Map, December 2020. https://esg.moodys.io/reports (archived at https://perma.cc/EH2A-XGVG)

17 S&P Global Ratings. Environmental, Social, And Governance Evaluation Analytical Approach, 2020. https://www.spglobal.com/_assets/documents/ratings/research/100048049.pdf (archived at https://perma.cc/MYW3-RN6C)

18 TCFD. Implementing the Recommendations of the Task Force on Climate-related Financial Disclosures, June 2017. https://assets.bbhub.io/company/sites/60/2020/10/FINAL-TCFD-Annex-Amended-121517.pdf (archived at https://perma.cc/DRR7-YJY4)

19 Network for Greening the Financial System. Technical document. The Macroeconomic and Financial Stability Impacts of Climate Change: Research Priorities, 2020. https://www.ngfs.net/sites/default/files/medias/documents/ngfs_research_priorities_final.pdf (archived at https://perma.cc/B66X-DARZ)

20 FCA. Climate Financial Risk Forum, 12 August 2109. www.fca.org.uk/transparency/climate-financial-risk-forum (archived at https://perma.cc/7B2F-RLPX)

21 Bank of England Prudential Regulation Authority. Enhancing banks' and insurers' approaches to managing the financial risks from climate change, 2019. www.bankofengland.co.uk/-/media/boe/files/prudential-regulation/supervisory-statement/2019/ss319 (archived at https://perma.cc/BB88-BCWY)

22 J Lash and F Wellington, Competitive advantage on a warming planet, *Harvard Business Review*, March 2007, https://hbr.org/2007/03/competitive-advantage-on-a-warming-planet (archived at https://perma.cc/BM77-7QEA)

5

Managing transition risks

This chapter explains in more depth the backdrop to why governments and regulators have been focusing on developing net zero targets and the role that organizations can play in reducing their own carbon footprints and meet net zero targets. The chapter also discusses the range of knock-on risks that organizations are facing as a consequence of transitioning to a lower-carbon or 'green' economy.

By focusing on how organizations can calculate, manage, mitigate and monitor their CO_2e emissions across emission types (commonly known as Scope 1–3, which are referred to later in the chapter), the reader will gain an understanding of how organizations can meet their net zero targets and support the wider societal and global goals.

The main learning outcomes from this chapter are to:

- Provide an overview of the main transition risks facing organizations, including the influence of global structural changes and risk drivers and specific industry vulnerabilities.
- Provide a global perspective on carbon emissions and mitigation strategies, and what government and regulators are doing to meet their net zero targets.
- Outline the main sources of greenhouse gas (GHG) emissions.
- Explain the emissions types and how organizations can seek to use or develop tools and techniques to measure carbon footprints (including Scope 1, 2 and 3 emissions), consider calculation tools, methodologies and the use of models, and outline the underlying data requirements (including the associated challenges).
- Illustrate and explain the main transition risks that organizations need to consider, highlighting a top-down approach from leading global drivers through to structural changes and risk drivers to a broad range of threats and opportunities.
- Outline a six-step risk management framework for calculating, managing and mitigating carbon emissions, including how to develop a carbon risk appetite strategy and reduction plan, how to calculate an organization's emissions, how to design mitigation strategies for reducing carbon emissions and the concept of 'carbon hierarchy' and control mechanisms.

Chapter 11 will provide further detailed insights into how organizations can integrate and manage their carbon emissions within specific business processes (such as investment strategy, third-party processes and supplier due diligence).

Introduction

Between 1950 and 2010 the global population almost trebled in size and the real-world GDP increased sevenfold. The effects of this dramatic intensification of human activity are clearly visible in an array of indicators that monitor the Earth's living systems.[1]

Since 1950 there has been an accompanying surge in ecological impacts, from the build-up of greenhouse gases in the atmosphere to ocean acidification and biodiversity loss.

Scientists state that to avoid dangerous climate change we need to keep concentration of CO_2 below 350 parts per million but we are now above 400 parts per million, which is pushing us towards a hotter, drier and more hostile climate, along with a rise in sea levels that threatens the future of islands and coastal cities worldwide.

'For over 60 years economic thinking told us that GDP growth was a good enough proxy for progress and that it looked like an ever-rising line. But this century calls for quite a different shape and direction of progress.... That calls for a profound shift in our metaphors: from "good is forward-and-up" to "good is in-balance".'[2] In summary, this can be referred to as sustainable development and the recognition that we all have a role to play.

Climate risk management is complex. There are a multitude of participants all with a range of important roles to play and which place a degree of reliance on the others to undertake their activities. These include multinational government organizations (i.e., the United Nations), national governments, the public sector (i.e., the civil services, lawmakers and regulators in each country), the private sector (across both small and large organizations) and the activities and behaviours of individuals.

One of the leading authorities on climate change research is the United Nations Intergovernmental Panel on Climate Change (IPCC) who released 'The Physical Science Basis' report in 2021, in which the UN chief has stated 'the climate crisis is a code red for humanity'.[3] The report states that human activity is changing the climate in unprecedented and sometimes irreversible ways. The landmark study warns of increasingly extreme heatwaves, droughts and flooding, and the key temperature limit of 1.5°C being broken in just over a decade.

This is the backdrop to why governments and regulators have particularly in recent years been focusing and increasing their efforts to develop and tackle climate change through setting net zero emissions targets. Organizations have their own role to play in supporting and meeting these global, regional and local targets by setting and reporting their own emissions targets.

Mark Carney, the former Governor of the Bank of England and now the United Nations Special Envoy for Climate Action and Finance, recently stated 'Managing climate-related financial risks requires that disclosure go beyond the static (a company's carbon footprint today) to the strategic (their plans to manage down their emissions). Risk management means assessing such forward-looking disclosures to judge the resilience of firms' strategies to the transition.'[4] Consequently, companies will continually need to adapt due to changes in legislation, technology and changing customer behaviours.

Stakeholder expectations are also shifting (this was detailed in Chapter 4) and customers and investors focus on corporate purpose, fulfilling regulatory requirements and pledging to meet emissions targets. It is becoming increasingly apparent that, as well as profit, environmental, social and governance (ESG) ratings are also going to be an important driver for stakeholders including lenders, pension funds, insurers, shareholders, regulators and, increasingly, consumers.

5.1 Global perspective on carbon emissions

The leading cause of climate change over the last half century is the increase in concentration of atmospheric greenhouse gas (GHG) emissions including carbon dioxide.

According to the UN Environment Programme (UNEP) report, global greenhouse gas emissions need to fall by 7.6 per cent each year between 2020 and 2030 to stay on track towards the 1.5°C temperature goal of the Paris Agreement and the world is not meeting these targets.

It is important that organizations understand the global impacts and ways that governments are seeking to tackle climate change through various mitigation strategies that then can, to some degree, be cascaded to organizations to mitigate climate change in meeting government targets. They key is that governments and organizations cannot do this independently as there is an explicit reliance by both sides to support each other. Governments can provide the rules, regulations and frameworks and coordinate the bigger initiatives; whilst organization's responsibility rest primarily at the implementation level.

Figure 5.1 provides a simple high-level illustration of the global problem of climate change as a global disrupter.

According to Swiss Re, global economic losses from natural catastrophe events in 2020 amounted to $190 billion of which $81 million were insured, the fifth highest on record. We explore the role of climate data and climate and catastrophe models in Chapter 7 in respect of the physical risks from climate change.

FIGURE 5.1 The great disrupter – global climate change

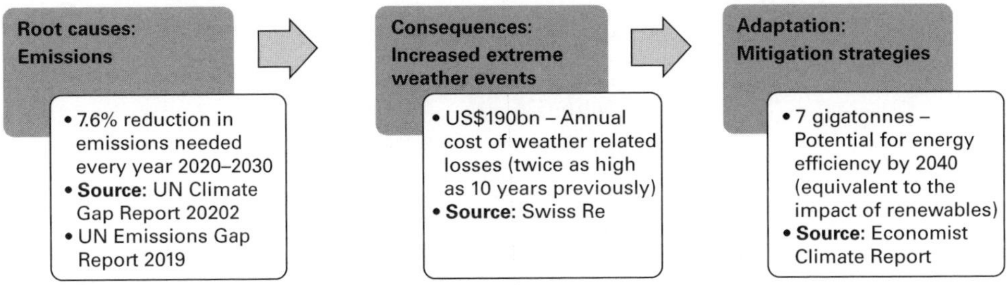

The Group Chief Economist of Swiss Re, Jerome Haegeli, recently stated that 'climate change is a systemic risk for the whole world. Unlike the Covid-19 crisis, it does not have an expiry date.'[5]

Figure 5.1 highlights the increasing cost of weather-related losses that are twice as high now as they were 10 years ago. The Swiss Re Institute stated in 2021 that 'Severe floods in Australia, ice storms in Texas, wildfires in California – the latest series of natural catastrophes point to a world increasingly at risk from extreme weather and climate change.'[6]

The report also points out that secondary perils have been rising steadily, driven by urban sprawl and climate change, and include localized weather events such as thunderstorms, flooding and wildfires, which are making certain parts of the world less habitable, more volatile (from a weather perspective) and which are pushing up insurance losses (which could mean some hazards will not be insurable or the premiums will be prohibitive).

As well as moving to renewable energy, most observers believe that if firms (as an example) can increase their energy efficiency by 10–20 per cent, that would be the equivalent of 7 gigatonnes of CO_2 by 2040 and have the same impact as a move to renewables. Nevertheless, this may not be achievable for all firms and there is realization that there will be discrepancies in approach across geographies and the respective wealth of nations.

5.2 Sources of greenhouse gas (GHG) emissions

This section provides further context and definitions in order to develop greater understanding about the sources of emissions and related metrics that can be developed to measure and monitor emissions. These metrics help to better understand the risk mitigation strategies that organizations can ultimately adopt across their own businesses and value chains through setting targets.

At a high level this can be broken down by types of greenhouse gases and the largest emitters by industry and by country.

FIGURE 5.2 Carbon emissions by gas

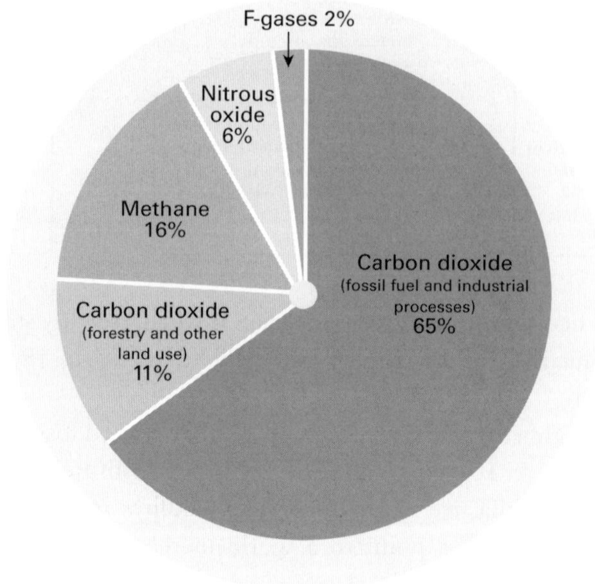

SOURCE IPCC (2014); US EPA

5.2.1 Types of GHGs

There are a number of different GHGs that are being emitted into the atmosphere and causing climate change through the greenhouse effect. The four main types of GHGs are:

1. **Carbon dioxide (CO_2)** – The most well-known of the GHGs (which is frequently used as a generic term when referring to the need for a 'carbon reduction strategy'). CO_2 relates to 76 per cent of all GHG emissions. This is due to it being generated when we burn fossil fuels to generate power or manufacture cement (and other common, large-scale activities).
2. **Methane (CH_4)** – This is generated by livestock (as well as other farming activities) and landfill decay. Methane makes up around 16 per cent of the GHGs.
3. **Nitrous oxide (N_2O)** – Generated through various agricultural activities, fossil fuel combustion and water treatment processes. Nitrous oxide makes up around 6 per cent of the GHGs.
4. **Fluorinated gases** – This is a range of gases (including hydrofluorocarbons, perfluorocarbons, sulphur hexafluoride and nitrogen trifluoride). These make up around 2 per cent of emissions but are the most potent from a global warming perspective.

Carbon emission targets on their own are not enough to curb temperature rising; they are part of the solution but a comprehensive transition plan needs to be developed across all types of greenhouse gases. In particular, focusing and cutting methane emissions, given its high impact, is very important for addressing future climate change. The Global Methane Pledge aiming to reduce methane emission by 30 per cent by 2030 is an example of a specific focus on particular gases.

5.2.2 CO_2 equivalent (CO_2e)

To aid measurement and comparability of carbon footprints, all emissions are converted into a single measure known as the 'carbon dioxide equivalent' which is written as 'CO_2e'. So, when people or companies simplify and declare 'our carbon footprint is X tonnes' or 'our carbon footprint is Y tonnes of CO_2' what they are actually referring to is CO_2e.

Comparisons are made possible by using CO_2 equivalent emissions via the notion of global warming potential (GWP): contribution to global warming over a fixed time horizon, say 100 years.

Using the GWP comparison, it is evident that although CO_2 is the most common GHG it is not the most powerful from a global warming perspective. One tonne of methane is estimated to be the equivalent of around 25 tonnes of CO_2 in terms of its impact as a greenhouse gas (but will remain in the atmosphere for a different period of time) and it is estimated that 1 tonne of hydrofluorocarbons (HFCs) is the equivalent to over 1,800 tonnes of CO_2. It is fair to assess that not all GHGs are equal and that is why when calculating the overall carbon footprint, it is important to consider GHGs in their entirety.

The pie charts in 5.3 are provided as context in relation to the breakdown of emissions by sector and geography in order to understand the sources of emissions and as a guide to where there is most scope for improvement.

5.3 Setting and achieving net zero targets – society's responses

To meet the global challenges that we face, the Paris Agreement set ambitious targets to cut emissions significantly year-on-year in order to reach net zero CO_2 emissions by 2050.

These drivers and expectations have led to a step change in momentum and action by governments and organizations worldwide. There is a recognition and realization that the management of climate change for the future is reliant on understanding the actions of the past and the present-day risks being faced. Some countries, such as the UK, have now embraced these targets and set national legal obligations to achieve net zero carbon emissions by 2050, which are being cascaded to organizations in both the

FIGURE 5.3 Global emissions by economic sector and by country

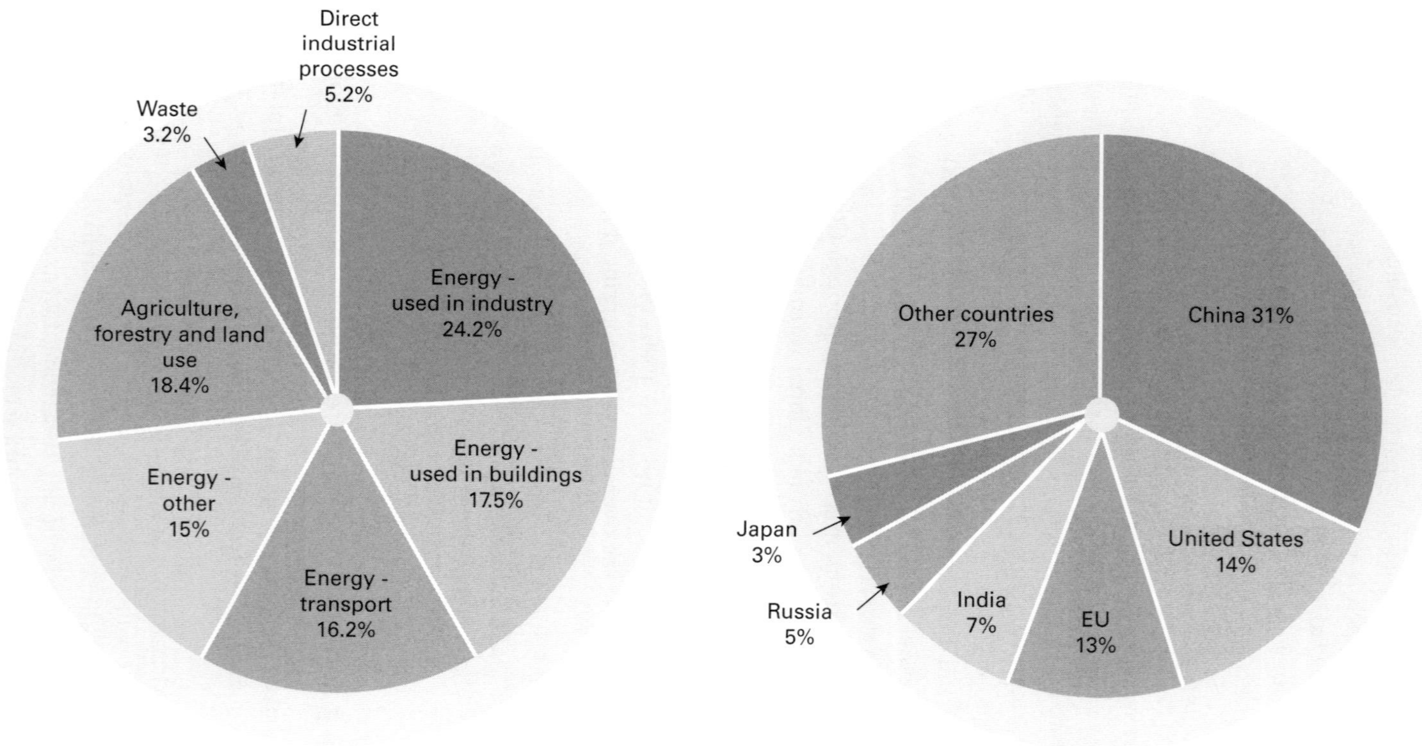

SOURCE OneRisk Consulting

public and private sectors. Many large multinational organizations such as Microsoft have made bold pledges, in Microsoft's case to become 'carbon negative' by 2030, and to remove all carbon emitted since the company was founded in 1974 by 2050.

They have set up a new $1 billion Climate Innovation Fund to stimulate and accelerate the development of carbon removal technology. In the energy sector, BP's boss Bernard Looney has pledged net zero emissions by 2050. In his words, 'the world's carbon budget is finite and running out fast'.[7]

To meet the targets, energy companies need to reduce existing production over time, develop technologies to capture carbon and invest more heavily in renewables (such as wind farms and solar power). They should see this as an opportunity to review their entire processes, the benefits of which could include: improved efficiency, enhanced profitability, reduced emissions and improved competitive positioning. A sample of organizational responses and targets are set out in Figure 1.10 in Chapter 1.

Other examples include associations such as the Association of British Insurers (ABI), which has set a net zero commitment for the sector of 2050, which is in line with the Paris Agreement. The UK's National Farmers Union (NFU), which represents the whole of the agricultural sector in England and Wales has set net zero greenhouse gas emissions targets by 2040 in its report,'Achieving Net Zero: Farming's 2040 goal'.

Many of these targets are high level and require further consideration of the granular details. The ABI for example refers to 'financed emissions' across insurers' investment and underwriting portfolios. They confirm that much of the wider thinking in this area has been developed primarily with investment/banking in mind and that its application to general insurance underwriting will need to be worked through.

Before describing a carbon risk framework that is often interchangeable with a sustainable risk framework it is important to clarify some of the prevailing carbon definitions.

5.3.1 The carbon budget

Carbon budget is an important concept and represents the total amount of carbon dioxide that can still be pumped into the atmosphere before a certain amount of warming is likely. For example, the IPCC says that 'for a 50% chance of limiting warming to 1.5°C by 2100, no more than 500bn tonnes of CO_2 can be emitted beyond 2020, equivalent to little more than a decade of emissions at current rates.'[8]

The IPCC estimates that approximately 75 per cent of the carbon budget has already been used if we want to limit the temperature by 2°C . This is illustrated in Figure 5.4.

FIGURE 5.4 The Remaining Carbon Budget to limit to 2°C

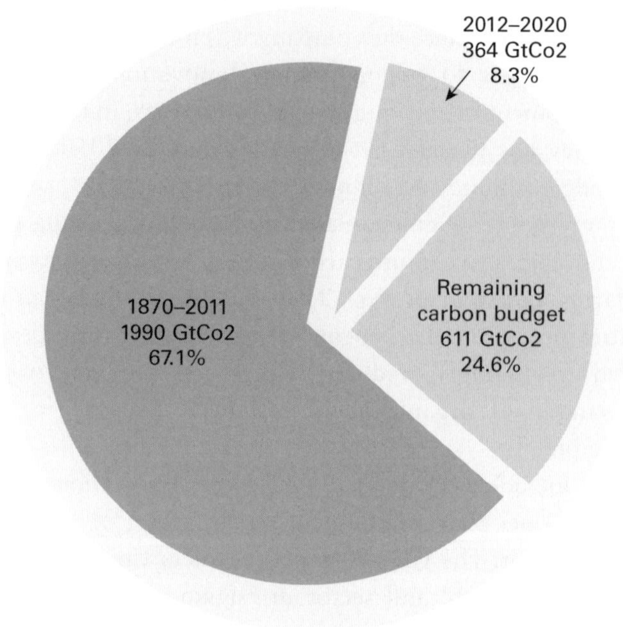

SOURCE One Risk Consulting

There are a number of additional definitions that are referenced in this chapter. These include net zero, carbon neutral/neutrality, carbon negative and climate positive.

5.3.2 The Greenhouse Gas Protocol – Scope 1, 2 and 3

When developing a climate risk framework (or sustainability framework), there is a need to understand the different types of emissions. The Greenhouse Gas Protocol, the most widely used international accounting tool for GHG emissions, classifies a company's direct and indirect emissions throughout the supply chain into three 'Scopes' that we will discuss in detail in this chapter.

CO_2e emissions can be broken down into emission types (commonly known as Scope 1–3) in order to understand the source. These are defined as:

Scope 1 – all direct emissions – The generation of GHGs directly from the activities of an organization, or under their control. This includes fuel combustion on site (i.e. gas boilers, generators or furnaces), the fleet of company vehicles and air-conditioning leaks.

Scope 2 – indirect emissions – These are indirect emissions from purchased or acquired electricity, steam, heat and cooling (although electricity will be the primary consideration for most businesses). Unlike Scope 1 emissions, Scope 2 are indirect emissions because the company is not directly creating the greenhouse gases by burning fossil fuels in this case (unless they are an energy company). Instead, they are indirect emissions caused by the purchase of electricity from the national grid. It is also worth noting that if any organization is using a 100 per cent renewable energy provider, their Scope 2 emissions can be recorded as zero.

Scope 3 – all other indirect emissions – These are indirect emissions. Scope 3 emissions occur in the value chain of the reporting company, including both downstream and upstream processes, and are the residual of all other emissions generated by an organization that aren't covered in Scopes 1 and 2 (and can be the largest emission group for some firms).

Scope 3 emissions are much more likely to evolve and develop and are much less clear cut. It may be a reason why most reporting is currently focusing just on Scopes 1 and 2.

5.4 Global drivers of change

There are a number of global drivers that are leading to structural changes across economies and industries and leading to what can be termed transition drivers. For ease of understanding it's important to distinguish drivers from risks, which are so often misrepresented or misunderstood.

The main change, as we have acknowledged, is the Paris Agreement, to cut emissions significantly year on year to reach net zero CO_2 emissions by 2050. The key question is how societies worldwide put in place the steps outlined under the agreed global action plan.

Climate change also poses a financial stability risk to the global financial system and as such, various national and international and industry bodies, driven by the Financial Stability Board (which represents the G20 countries), are working together to achieve long-term regulatory alignment. Although it is easy to feel overwhelmed by the complexity of the problem there are a range of solutions, including the need to replace fossil fuels with cleaner, renewable energy like wind and solar power that we will explore in more detail in this chapter.

5.4.1 Transition risks – structural changes and risk drivers

Transition risk is a broad risk type that affects organizations across all industries, and relates to a range of risks as a consequence of transitioning to a lower-carbon or 'green' economy. Factors that influence this include adjusting to climate-related developments in policy and regulation, emergence of disruptive technology or business models, shifting sentiment and societal preferences and evolving evidence, frameworks and legal interpretations.

Transition risk (which in some ways is forward-looking in nature, due to it being associated with the journey to low carbon) can be proactively managed. In comparison, the management of physical risks (which have wider impact that no one can manage in isolation), tend to be more reactive in nature and focused on minimizing the impacts.

Transition risks constitute a range of threats and opportunities and many of the risks can act as either a threat or an opportunity to an organization depending on how the risk is perceived and acted upon from a strategic or operational perspective.

5.4.2 Exposure and vulnerabilities of sectors and organizations

It is also important to be aware that economic sectors will be impacted differently by transition risk depending in part on the intensity of their emissions and ability to adapt their business strategies and models.

In the context of climate change, transition risk is the risk that organizations face through changing strategies, policies or investments by society and industry as they work in tandem to reduce reliance on carbon and the impacts of climate risk.

For example, some sectors are very energy intensive and there are very few economically viable low-carbon alternatives at present. These include sectors such as petrochemicals, aluminium, steel, cement and fertilizers, and extractive industries such as mining that provide the raw materials.

Organizations that are 'front-runners', that adjust to future structural changes and put sustainability at the heart of their strategies more rapidly, will be well positioned to reap the potential benefits that it will bring. These will include enhanced brand image, employee engagement, innovation, new sources of revenue, enhanced relationships with stakeholders and operational resilience.

Transition drivers arise primarily from transformations, namely in regulatory policy changes such as carbon taxes, technology advances and market shifts that include innovation in, for example, renewable energy. Recent government and regulatory changes in legislation and pressure for improved reporting and disclosures have also led to many new risks that organizations need to manage.

The main transition risks identified by global regulators were set out in the TCFD report in 2017.[9] Table 5.1 summarizes the main threats.

These are not specific risks but highlight strategic changes and risk drivers that organizations need to evaluate and understand in order to ascertain the impact across their risk profile.

5.4.2.1 RECOGNIZING OPPORTUNITIES

The focus of risk managers is often on identifying and managing the downside of these risks. However, what is equally important is for organizations to also grasp the

TABLE 5.1 Main transitional threats to organizations

Threats	Description
Policy risk	Risks as a result of energy efficiency requirements, carbon pricing mechanisms that increase the price of fossil fuels, or policies to encourage sustainable land use
Legal risk	The risk of litigation for failing to avoid or minimize adverse impacts on the climate, or failing to adapt to climate change
Technology risk	When a technology with a less damaging impact on the climate replaces a technology that is more damaging to the climate
Market sentiment risk	When the choices of consumers and business customers shift towards products and services that are less damaging to the climate. This may leave the owner of carbon-intensive assets with no alternative but to write down their value (potentially to write off their value) in what has been termed 'stranded assets'
Reputational risk	The difficulty of attracting and retaining customers, employees, business partners and investors if a company has a reputation for damaging the climate

SOURCE Climate Disclosure Standards Board

opportunities that transition risks present, particularly given the vast amount of investment and support from government and private businesses that are investing in new technologies, products and services.

The TCFD framework outlines the following opportunities linked to the perceived threats.

The TFCD report highlights the importance of innovation in helping organizations to improve efficiency across a range of new technologies including advances in LED lighting technology and industrial motor technology, retrofitting buildings, employing geothermal power, offering water usage and treatment solutions, and developing electric vehicles.

The use of clean energy sources (such as renewables) is increasing in part due to reducing costs and improved storage capabilities. Consequently, organizations that shift their energy usage towards low-emission energy sources should save on annual energy costs.

Organizations that innovate and develop new low-emission products and services should improve their competitive position and capitalize on shifting consumer and producer preferences. Organizations that proactively seek opportunities in new markets or types of assets may be able to diversify their activities and better position themselves for the transition to a lower-carbon economy.

The TFCD report states that:

> opportunities exist for organizations to access new markets through collaborating with governments, development banks, small-scale local entrepreneurs, and community groups

TABLE 5.2 Main transitional opportunities for organizations

Threats	Description
Resource efficiency	The opportunity to reduce operating costs by improving efficiency across an organization's production and distribution processes, buildings, machinery/appliances and transport/mobility – in particular in relation to energy efficiency but also including broader materials, water and waste management
Energy source	The opportunity to shift an organization's energy usage towards low-emission energy sources such as renewables could potentially save on annual energy costs
Products and services	Organizations that innovate and develop new low-emission products and services may improve their competitive position and capitalize on shifting consumer and producer preferences
Markets	Organizations that proactively seek opportunities in new markets or types of assets may be able to diversify their activities and better position themselves for the transition to a lower-carbon economy
Resilience	This is a general concept of climate resilience that involves organizations developing adaptive capacity to respond to climate change to better manage the associated risks and seize opportunities, including the ability to respond to transition risks and physical risks

SOURCE Climate Disclosure Standards Board

in developed and developing countries as they work to shift to a lower-carbon economy. New opportunities can also be captured through underwriting or financing green bonds and infrastructure (e.g., low-emission energy production, energy efficiency, grid connectivity, or transport networks).

5.4.3 Transitional drivers – options available for reducing emissions

The UN IPCC report issued in 2022 'Climate Change 2022: Impacts, Adaptation and Vulnerability' provides a list of options that focus on reducing emissions for both governments and organizations that will be discussed later in this chapter.[10]

To illustrate and explain the main transition risks that organizations need to consider, Figure 5.5 highlights a top-down approach from leading global drivers through to structural changes and risk drivers to a specific broad range of threats and opportunities. Organizations will ultimately need to agree on a set of transition risks (both threats and opportunities) that should be translated into specific transition scenarios and a list of these is provided in Table 5.3 to provide clarity on the process and to support the design of concrete mitigation strategies.

In 2017, an article from International Investment.net provided a useful definition of transition risk and what this means for companies which remains valid today: 'Transition

FIGURE 5.5 Transition drivers, threats and opportunities

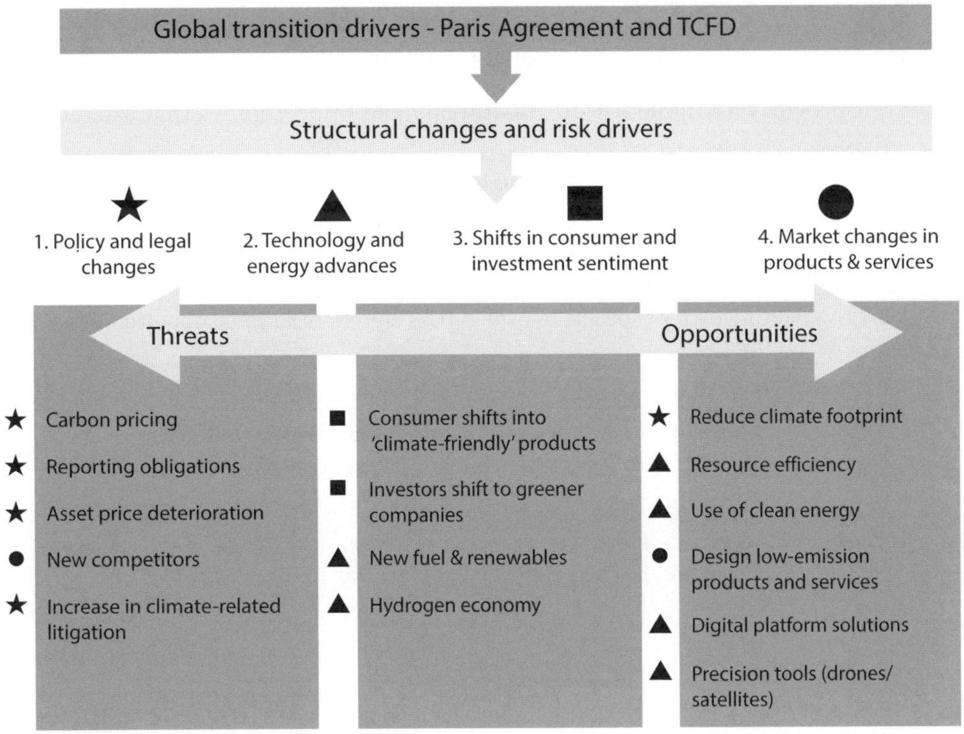

SOURCE © OneRisk Consulting. All rights reserved 2022

risks relate to the impacts and costs of policy, legal, technology and market changes that will be required to mitigate and adapt to climate change. In concrete terms this will result in a higher carbon price associated with carbon emissions.'[11]

Chapter 9 outlines some of the emerging or longer-term transition threats and opportunities in more detail including the growth in the hydrogen economy and increase in climate-related litigation.

Companies that fail to respond to the impacts of the transition to a lower-carbon economy face financial and reputational risks, potentially harming their credit ratings and share price. How they respond and adapt their business strategies and models will be critical, and there will be winners and losers. However, the consequences of a failure to transition are far greater.

Transition risks are therefore developing rapidly as governments support and subsidize low-carbon industries and regulate and tax high-carbon ones.

When it comes to shifting focus to address climate, broad transition risks might include:

- Changed land-use policies or water conservation practices impacting the agricultural sector

- The costs the energy industry faces in developing low-carbon technologies
- A reduction in the value of investments in carbon-heavy industries
- The requirements of additional regulation and reporting

Table 5.3 provides a sample list of risks/threats and opportunities that are relevant to many organizations.

The risks outlined (it is not an exhaustive list) highlight the interconnectedness of the risks and the opportunities. These will have operational, investment, financial

TABLE 5.3 An indicative list of specific transition risks and the associated opportunities

Threats (manage the downside)	Opportunities (strategic initiatives)
• Reduction in investment returns due to overexposure in sectors that are overpriced (stranded assets)	• Increase in investment in 'green' infrastructure spending
• Increase in operational costs due to stricter 'green' legislation to improve building efficiency	• Switch electricity use away from fossil fuels to renewables
• Failure to comply with TCFD disclosures including mandatory reporting requirements	• Use the data requirements for TCFD disclosure as a catalyst to improve your data management practices (from an analysis and efficiency perspective)
• Potential legal disputes due to accusations of 'greenwashing'	• Make a conscious decision to be a leader in your industry with regard to sustainability and adhere to (and help develop) higher industry standards
• Increase in carbon taxes for externalities such as pollution associated with fossil fuels	• Opportunity to reduce emissions (in order to minimize carbon taxes)
• Increase in the carbon pricing and approaches – the carbon price is the explicit price on GHG emissions, i.e., a price expressed as a value per tonne of carbon dioxide equivalent (tCO_2e).	• Introduce internal carbon pricing in order to prioritize internal investments and to instil a focus on innovation/carbon reduction
• Unsuccessful investment in new technology	• Successful investment in new technology that enhances operational efficiency and improves the cost base
• Increase in cost base of raw materials	• Opportunity to source raw materials from alternative providers, to reduce waste and/or find cheaper alternative inputs

(continued)

TABLE 5.3 (Continued)

Threats (manage the downside)	Opportunities (strategic initiatives)
• Lack of understanding of requirements at executive level	• Opportunity to develop a company-wide learning culture
• Lack of understanding of changing societal demands	• Design of product and marketing strategies to meet changing consumer demand for 'climate-friendly' products

SOURCE: Climate Disclosure Standards Board!]

and competitive consequences. Nevertheless, they are some of the items that should be at the forefront of the minds of management (and stakeholders) as they attempt to navigate the move towards a low-carbon economy.

Using Cambridge City Council again as an example, while acknowledging that climate change represents a range of challenges, the council did identify a number of opportunities to respond with greater impact. These included building on the increased public awareness and acceptance that climate change is occurring, sustaining the low-carbon impacts of changes in behaviour that arose during the Covid-19 lockdown, leveraging the increased appreciation of the green spaces, trees and other green infrastructure and undertaking initiatives to maintain lower levels of emissions from changes in travel arrangements.

5.5 Global mitigation concerns and options

The IPCC report 'Climate Change 2022 – Impacts, Adaptation and Vulnerability' provides a comprehensive list of options for how the world can help to stabilize the climate and avoid catastrophic global warming while fulfilling the commitments made in the 2015 Paris Agreement.[12]

The report provides an assessment of global emissions by 2050 that uses four different scenarios, with each scenario affecting the projected global GHG emissions by the year 2050.

The projected global GHG emissions data is based on assuming:

1. current trend from implemented policies
2. effects after high overshoot and then reducing the emission
3. immediate action taken after 2020 to limit temperature increase to 2°C
4. the consequence after limited or no overshoot after the limit of 1.5°C increase

The IPCC report highlights 45 different options for emission reductions across different categories. The IPCC analysis further provides the estimated cost (net lifetime cost) to achieve the goal of emission reduction for each specific sector and each sector's potential contribution to reduce the GHG emissions by the year 2030. This acts as a ranking of relative effectiveness that is helpful in terms of prioritization, which is focused on policy makers for government but is also very helpful for businesses.

Moreover, what is helpful is to see the potential and relative contribution of each option to reduce emissions. *The Economist* commented on the report and stated that 'Its 278 authors have gone to great pains to offer a smorgasbord of opportunities to reduce emissions and stabilise the climate, and to point out that not all are eye-wateringly expensive. There is just one catch. In order to meet Paris goals, humanity must order just about everything on the menu, and fast.'[13]

An organization can use Table 5.4 as a helpful guide to consider options for how its own organization and value chain can seek to reduce its own carbon emissions and build a more sustainable business. The options can help in looking at reducing organizations' carbon footprint as well as in the development of strategic options.

One of the most important and impactful solutions is 'fuel switching', which involves replacing inefficient fuels with cleaner and economical alternatives, such as substituting coal or kerosene for natural gas. Complemented by modern equipment upgrades, fuel switching is a simple approach to reducing energy consumption and costs for end users, while also curbing carbon emissions.

TABLE 5.4 IPCC report – most important mitigation options by industry sector

INDUSTRY SECTOR	MITIGATION OPTIONS
Energy	Wind energy Solar energy
AFOLU (Agriculture, Forestry and Other Land Use)	Carbon sequestration in agriculture Reduced conversion of forests and other ecosystems
Buildings	New buildings with high energy performance Efficient lighting, appliances and equipment
Transport	Electric light duty vehicles Shift to public transportation
Industry	Fuel switching (natural gas, bioenergy, H_2) Energy efficiency
Other	Reduce emission of fluorinated gas Reduce CH_4 emissions from solid waste

5.5.1 UK Government's green strategy

Governments have also been publishing some helpful reports in this regard and the UK Government issued an insightful booklet in November 2020, 'The Ten Point Plan for a Green Industrial Revolution: Building back better, supporting green jobs, and accelerating our path to net zero'.[14] The UK plan set out how the UK Government plans to mobilize £12 billion of government investment, and potentially three times as much from the private sector, to create and support up to 250,000 green jobs.

The plan covers a wide range of technologies, including a quadrupling of offshore wind capacity, accelerating the uptake of electric vehicles, expanding low-carbon hydrogen production and use, advancing nuclear power, and aiming to become a

FIGURE 5.6 The UK's Ten Point Plan for a Green Industrial Revolution

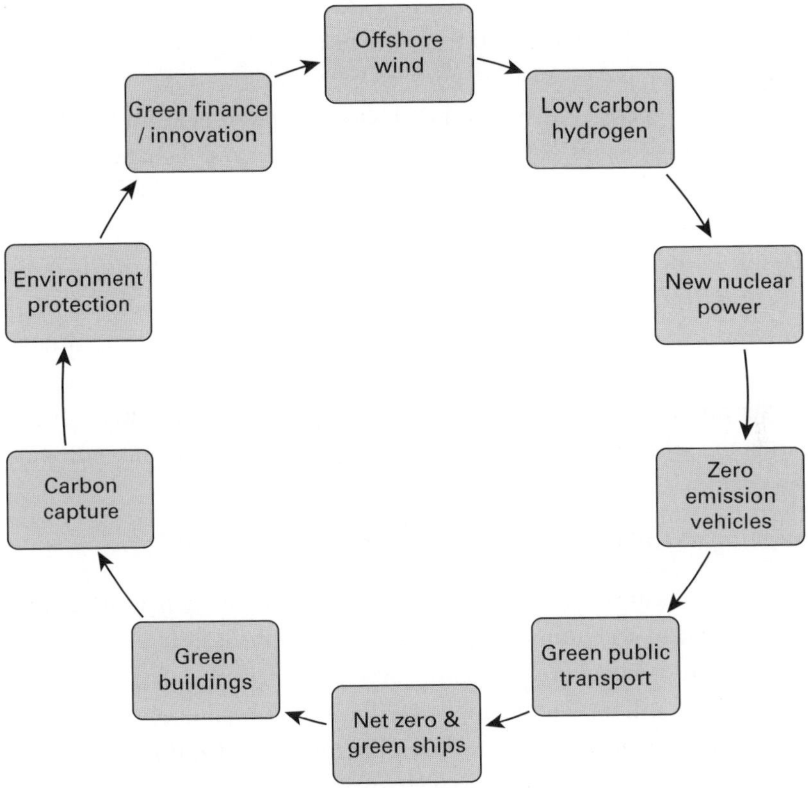

SOURCE The Ten Point Plan for a Green Industrial Revolution (HM Government)

world-leader in carbon capture and storage. The development of new technologies is explored further in Chapter 9.

The breadth of green technologies mentioned in the UK Government's Ten Point Plan illustrates the sheer complexity and size of the challenge ahead. While there is acknowledgement that there is no quick-fix solution to decarbonize the economy, instead the UK's future energy strategy will consist of a combination of low-carbon and renewable energy technologies, which complement each other to enable the targets to be met. At this stage, it remains unclear on the precise mixture of the components.

The Russian war with Ukraine has highlighted the dependency, particularly for Europe (including the UK) on Russian oil and gas. Russia is the second largest gas producer (17 per cent of global output in 2020) and at the time of writing the war is starting to impact on the international gas markets (which in turn impacts the UK). Consequently, this could act as a catalyst for investment in and the use of renewable energy (in the longer term) and also lead to a reduction in consumption (in the near term).

Greater energy efficiency is now a key focus of government. In risk management terminology it is a preventative control to restrict the use and demand for gas through, for example, greater house insulation and use of heat pumps and renewables.

In the UK, like many countries, there is increasing use of energy performance certificates in homes. With the rise in benchmarking, this heightened transparency highlights that 'If all homes that were band D were upgraded to band C [the most common band], the UK's total gas demand would be cut by 7%, and net imports by 15%.'[15]

Two other important and perhaps less well understood of the initiatives in the plan are investing in carbon capture, usage and storage and green finance and innovation.

5.5.2 Investing in carbon capture, usage and storage (CCUS)

CCUS technology captures carbon dioxide from power generation, low-carbon hydrogen production and industrial processes, and stores it deep underground where it cannot enter the atmosphere.

This technology will need to be applied globally, but no one country has yet developed a market-leading position in the development and utilization of this technology.

The UK's ambition is to capture 10Mt of carbon dioxide a year by 2030, the equivalent of 4 million cars' worth of annual emissions, by investing £1 billion to support the establishment of CCUS in four industrial clusters. The UK plans to store the captured carbon under the seabed in the North Sea.

5.5.3 *Green finance and innovation*

In order to support these ambitions, the UK Government is developing and investing in innovation, and new sources of finance are fundamental for further developing the green technologies for net zero. In July 2020 the UK Government published the UK Research and Development Roadmap and have committed to raising total R&D investment to 2.4 per cent of GDP by 2027.

The UK plan is to help bring down the cost of the net zero transition, nurture the development of better products and new business models, and influence consumer behaviour. Part of the country's ambition is to be the first country in the world to commercialize fusion energy technology, enabling low-carbon and continuous power generation. The UK is providing funding for the visionary STEP programme (Spherical Tokamak for Energy Production), which aims to build the world's first commercially viable fusion power plant in the UK by 2040.

To further help develop and support these initiatives the UK government has also launched the Green Jobs Taskforce, working in partnership with business, skills providers and unions, to help develop plans for new long-term good quality, green jobs by 2030 and advise what support is needed for people in transitioning industries. This is crucial and often overlooked as a key enabler as employees need to reskill and this aligns with improved awareness training for all staff.

5.6 Carbon/sustainability risk management framework

Many organizations are developing ways to ensure that their own carbon footprints can be measured and monitored to track progress. Most organizations are seeking to reduce their carbon footprint by implementing practices that reduce the environmental impact across their business.

Many organizations are also seeking to improve their emissions tracking and reporting infrastructure to put in place more comprehensive emissions reporting across their value chain in order to define a baseline, perform trend analysis and set targets to reduce its emissions.

With the intention of reducing the organization's carbon footprint, the steps required include obtaining the required emission data (relating to Scope 1, 2 and 3 emissions, i.e. both direct and indirect emissions) across all parts of the organization (note: this will not be without challenge) and determining the calculation methodology for deriving the emission figures.

5.6.1 *Stages for assessing and measuring emissions*

It is important to develop an overall framework for managing and mitigating the carbon emissions that are depicted in Figure 5.7. It is important to note that the main

FIGURE 5.7 Framework for calculating, managing and mitigating carbon emissions

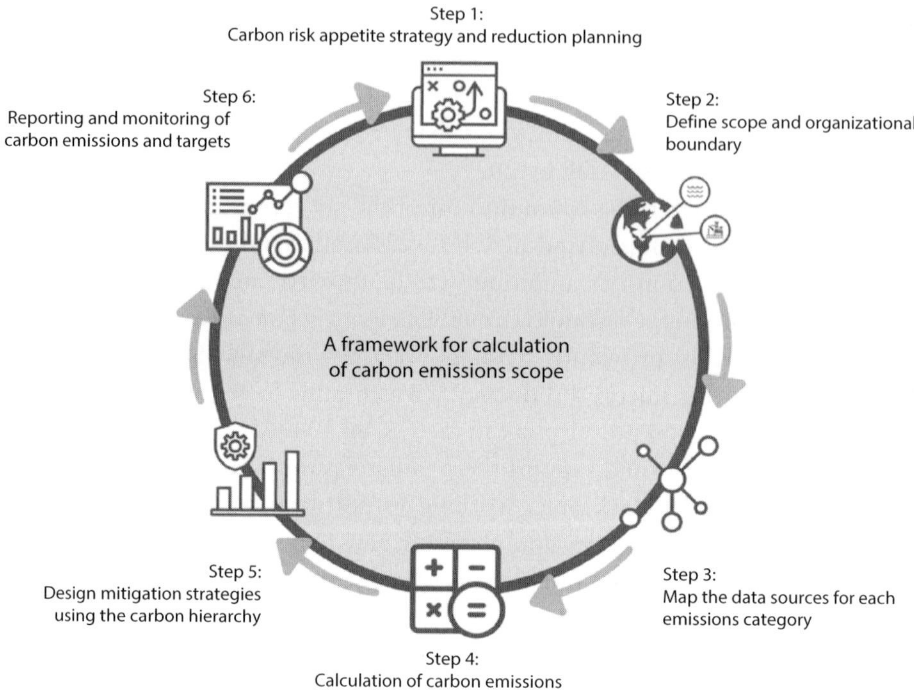

SOURCE © OneRisk Consulting. All rights reserved 2022

steps in the process are not necessarily sequential (with one stage needing to be complete before the next one can commence) but that they are complementary and make the framework stronger by working cohesively together. This requires organizations to continue to evolve and improve and reinforces the circularity of the process. It also facilitates the integration into the existing enterprise risk management (ERM) framework.

Notwithstanding the assessment and measurement of a company's emissions, it is an ongoing process and actions will need to be taken once measurement is complete and disclosures made in order to maintain minimum standards and to continue to improve.

The overall process is summarized in Figure 5.7.

There are a number of stages required to assess and measure the emissions from an organization. These are:

1 Carbon risk appetite strategy including net zero targets
2 Determine scope of what needs to be calculated (Scope 1, 2 and 3)
3 Identify the sources of the information required (i.e., the data inputs) to undertake the calculation; clarify the range of data characteristics (i.e., sources, structure, parameters, frequency)

4 Develop the calculation methodology (i.e. assumptions, simple versus advanced)

5 Ascertain the tools or models available to support the calculation (note: different tools will have differing data requirements)

6 Reporting and disclosure

Depending on the size of the organization and the complexity of the emissions, this may require the need to consider the most appropriate calculation methodology and tools/models to be used. Once the process of calculation is established, this then requires management identifying actions to reduce the emissions, on-going monitoring and reporting to various stakeholders (as appropriate).

5.6.1.1 STEP 1: CARBON RISK APPETITE STRATEGY AND REDUCTION PLANNING

Organizations need to develop their climate risk strategy and as part of that consider their carbon footprint and define the level of ambition, which was discussed in detail in Chapter 2.

Organizations are generally committed to reducing their global carbon footprint and implementing practices that reduce the environmental impact of their business, and integrating net zero targets within their long-term business strategy. Key questions to address include: what actions are being considered to support efforts to reduce GHG emissions across the value chain, such as with suppliers and customers?

An example from the public sector of developing a carbon risk appetite strategy is seen in Cambridge City Council's Climate Change Strategy 2021–2026.[16] The council worked with researchers from the University of Manchester's Tyndall Centre to set ambitious targets to reduce the council's direct carbon emissions from its corporate buildings (including swimming pools, office buildings, car parks, sheltered housing schemes, community centres, arts venues and the crematorium), its fleet vehicles (including vans, trucks and refuse vehicles), and business travel to net zero carbon emissions by 2030. This forms the basis for spending decisions and priorities with regard to all facets of the work undertaken by the council in the coming years.

It is important that the council's new climate change strategy shows ambition and leadership, however it recognizes its sphere of influence and the role that other organizations and individuals need to play. The council itself is only directly responsible for 1.1 per cent of carbon emissions in Cambridge, so it is working with central government, other tiers of local government, businesses, organizations and residents to reduce city-wide carbon emissions, including in the context of the Cambridgeshire & Peterborough Independent Commission on Climate's reports and the UK Government's work in preparation for the COP26 inter-governmental conference in December 2021. The importance of stakeholders is covered in Chapter 4.

Many organizations are also currently seeking to understand what 'net zero' means for their firm and set targets and metrics. This will require organizations

FIGURE 5.8 CO_2 reductions pathways in Cambridge proposed by the Tyndall Centre

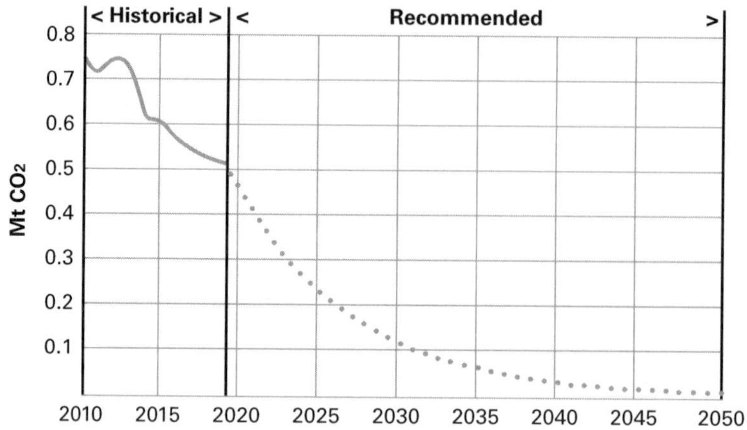

SOURCE Tyndall Centre, 2021, Setting Climate Commitments for Cambridge

reviewing their risk appetite strategy and guidelines in respect to climate change, including their position in respect to supporting wider government targets of achieving net zero emissions targets by 2050. This was discussed in Chapter 2.

Organizations are often seeking to set targets that relate to specific scopes. Some organizations, for example, are setting science-based targets for commitments to the achievement of net zero by 2025 on directly controlled emissions (Scopes 1 and 2) and then setting other targets for Scope 3 (with a later target date) once they have a better understanding of how they are going to achieve their targets. This ultimately means first measuring their carbon emissions, and then taking steps to reduce the emissions of their organization in the future.

The feedback from risk professionals with respect to risk appetite statements are that they are evolving, and according to Will Monelle, the CRO of Canopius, 'organizations need to set both realistic and achievable targets which will also help to avoid greenwashing', which we discuss further in Chapter 9. Organizations also need to develop key risk indicators to assist in measuring and monitoring their climate exposures on an ongoing basis and this is one of the most difficult areas for risk managers given the lack of data and agreed metrics.

5.6.1.2 STEP 2: DEFINE SCOPE AND ORGANIZATIONAL BOUNDARY

Organizations need to get a clear picture of their emissions through determining the quantity and geographic locations of both direct and indirect CO_2 emissions.

This will include defining what emissions are included in each option so that the organizations can understand the pros and cons. Organizations need to consider the emissions from owned, leased or directly controlled vehicles or equipment that use fossil fuels; emissions from the generation of purchased electricity, heat, and cooling; and emissions from waste and business travel.

5.6.1.3 STEP 3 MAP THE DATA SOURCES FOR EACH EMISSIONS CATEGORY

Calculate carbon: The basis for climate protection is always your carbon balance. All emissions are recorded in it, caused, for example, by:

- heating
- steam
- business trips
- employee approach
- paper consumption
- ... and other factors

The data is often captured and stored through cloud-based software. It can be used to map complex corporate structures, such as several locations at home and abroad.

5.6.1.4 STEP 4: CALCULATE AN ORGANIZATION'S CARBON FOOTPRINT

It is important to calculate carbon emissions in an accurate and conservative manner. The carbon balance shows which greenhouse gas emissions you can most easily reduce and which you can be avoid in the long term. A few examples include conversion to renewable electricity, video conferences instead of business trips, the use of rail instead of domestic flights, etc. Often these changes can lead to reductions in both operating costs and emissions.

FIGURE 5.9 Scope 1, 2 and 3 emissions

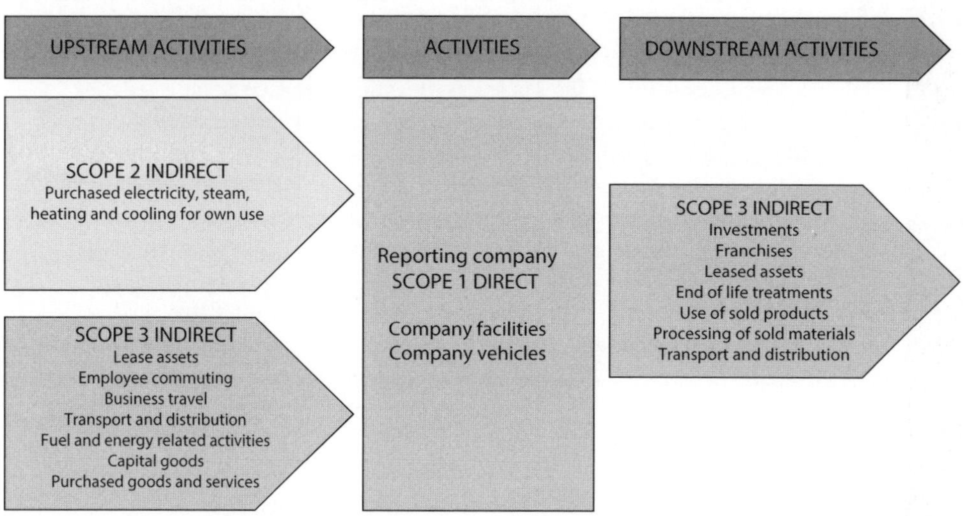

SOURCE The Greenhouse Gas Protocol (Corporate Value Chain (Scope 3) Accounting and Reporting Standard)

From a reporting perspective, which we discuss in more detail in Chapter 12, Scope 1 and 2 emissions are increasingly being reported by organizations. However, most companies are yet to include Scope 3 in their disclosures, although arguably these potentially have the largest impact.

Figure 5.9 illustrates the differences between the scope emissions, some of the main contributors and where in the production cycle they originate in the value chain.

5.6.1.5 STEP 5: DESIGN MITIGATION STRATEGIES

Mitigation strategies are complex and multidimensional and a range of actions will need to be undertaken simultaneously in order to reduce emissions (across Scope 1, 2

TABLE 5.5 Examples of actions that can be taken to reduce different emission types while addressing transition risk

		Scope emissions reduced		
		1. All direct emissions from activities under the control of the organization	2. Indirect emissions from purchased energy	3. Indirect emissions that occur in the wider value chain (both upstream and downstream)
Risk type addressed	Physical	i. Moving from high-risk area to a lower-risk area in premises that have more energy efficient boilers or require fewer air-conditioners	i. Moving from high-risk area to a lower risk area nearer to your customers (and thus requiring less energy)	i. Moving from high-risk area to a lower-risk area nearer to your suppliers
	Transition	i. Investment in technology to improve productivity ii. Replacing own transport fleet with EV iii. Utilizing internal carbon pricing in capital allocation decisions/ investment decisions (which provides a catalyst for reducing own emissions)	i. Introduction of working-from-home practices ii Undertaking renovations to existing premises to reduce energy consumption iii. Changing energy providers and selecting a more sustainable provider iv. Reviewing internal processes, looking for improvements, reducing waste and embracing the 'circular economy'	i. Selecting suppliers based on emissions ii. Consciously reducing business travel iii. Encouraging homeworkers to source electricity from sustainable providers iv. Investment managers actively engaging with investee companies to be more aggressive in meeting their emission targets v. Credit providers offering preferential rates to 'green' or more energy efficient initiatives vi. Reducing credit exposure to companies more sensitive to transition risk

and 3) and to mitigate against physical and transition risks. There is no 'silver bullet' to solve this issue once and for all; the key is that these actions complement and support each other, and collectively they can make a significant contribution to the reduction in emissions and the achievement of stated corporate emissions targets. Table 5.5 provides examples of this in a matrix that considers emission and risk types.

5.7. Carbon assessment process – use and availability of tools

There is a wide range of modelling tools available for companies to calculate their carbon footprint. Each model has different calculation methodologies, data requirements, degrees of integration with existing systems and will vary across industry sectors. However, as specific expertise is often required, many organizations are using niche external consultancies that have developed external expertise.

Before deciding on a model, the key is to assess the pros and cons of each and evaluate which one is the best fit for your organization.

A number of examples are provided below (it is not an exhaustive list but is provided for illustrative purposes). These range in complexity, data requirements and some will be more appropriate than others (depending on your organization size and relative maturity in this area).

Many organizations are using the Greenhouse Gas Protocol approach (ghgprotocol.org), which is the UK Government standard.

1 **Carbon Trust – SME Carbon Footprint Calculator**

This carbon footprint calculator is from the Carbon Trust (a UK-based global climate consultancy, which has been focused for 20+ years on pioneering decarbonization for businesses, governments and organizations around the world, with 300 sustainability experts including engineers, financiers and policy specialists). The calculator provided is publicly available on its website and is suitable for small- and medium-sized businesses.

The calculator is designed to help UK-based SMEs measure their corporate emission footprint following GHG Protocol guidance and includes direct emissions (Scope 1) from fuel and processes and Scope 2 emissions from purchased electricity for assets operated. It is not a definitive solution (due to it excluding Scope 3) but this is typical for SMEs and provides a reasonable basis for calculations at the outset of the calculation exercise.

Key data requirements for this tool are: fuel consumption (from sites and owned vehicles), energy consumption (based on utility bills/meter readings) and top-ups to air-conditioning, refrigeration and fire protection units (which contain fluorinated gases, and which are high CO_2e and contribute significantly to the carbon footprint).

This tool allows smaller firms to determine their carbon footprint (for Scope 1 and 2 emissions), to assess their energy use relative to firms in their chosen sector and it can assist in the building of a business case for introducing carbon-saving initiatives.

2 **Carbon Footprint**
Provides a free tool (which may be better for smaller, less complex businesses) looking to begin the process of calculating their carbon footprint.[17]

3 **GHG Protocol and Quantis Scope 3 Emissions calculator**
Due to the challenges of quantifying Scope 3 emissions, the GHG Protocol and Quantis have collaborated to provide a Scope 3 Evaluator tool in order to help calculate a comprehensive assessment of the Scope 3 carbon emissions.[18]

There are acknowledged limitations with the model and it is stressed that this tool has not been assured for adherence to Scope 3 standards, but it does nevertheless provide a tool to help develop an internal calculation approach. It provides a useful structure and also informs future efforts by highlighting the various data collection points across all of the key categories (as mentioned earlier in this chapter).

4 **Carbon Calculator – GOV.UK**
The MacKay Carbon Calculator is available on the UK Government website, and provides a model of the UK energy system that allows an organization to explore pathways to decarbonization, including net zero by 2050. It identifies a range of key factors that influence the overall carbon emissions of the economy and provides a range of options (with varying levels of ambition – and details of the actions required to meet those ambitions). Decisions can be made and ambitions revised and the contribution to meeting net zero targets is assessed. This will be a useful tool for organizations so that they can identify which changes in behaviour, transportation, building and energy usage will have most impact on emission levels.

5.8 The carbon hierarchy

The concept of carbon hierarchy provides a useful framework for understanding the prioritization of efforts to decarbonize and achieve absolute reductions in greenhouse gas emissions throughout global value chains.

Figure 5.10 illustrates the carbon hierarchy approach that outlines the most favoured options such as avoid (avoid activities that generate emissions) to the least favoured option of offset (offset remaining emissions that cannot be eliminated), the full hierarchy being avoid, reduce, replace, sequester and offset, which will be explained subsequently in further detail.

FIGURE 5.10 The carbon hierarchy

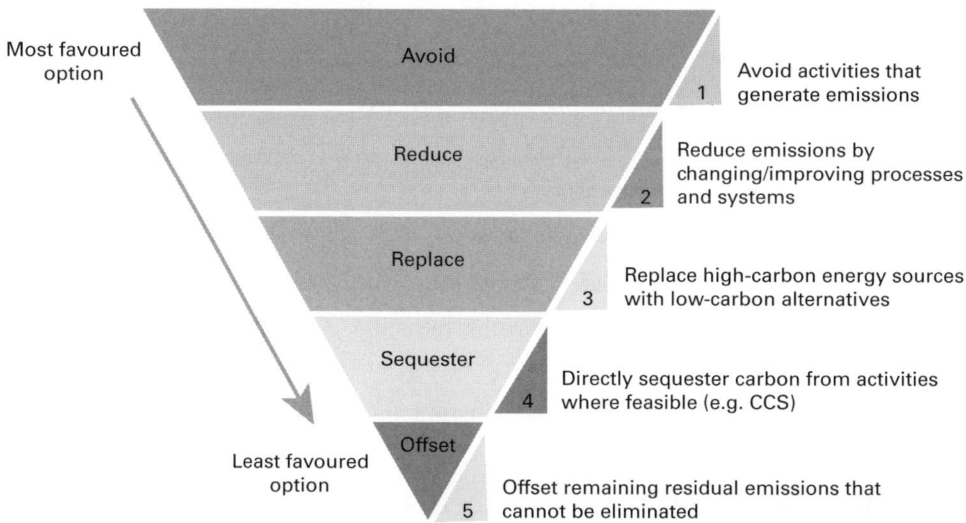

SOURCE University of Cambridge Institute for Sustainability Leadership, insurers in Paris-aligned climate transition: practical actions towards net zero underwriting

5.8.1 Avoid

In short, this option results in the cessation of an activity due to the volume of emissions it generates. This may not be an option in the short term – the ongoing burning of fossil fuels is an example of this. These activities are becoming increasingly unacceptable from a political and societal perspective; however, it is not always practicable for the activity to be stopped with immediate effect. This may be influenced by the interests of various stakeholder and lobby groups.

As an example, if the burning of fossil fuels was to be immediately banned, this would cause immediate energy shortfalls, substantially reduce the value of assets involved in certain activities, or push the activity underground, which could then lead to the advancement in technology or reductions in activity being hampered.

5.8.2 Reduce

To reduce their emissions, organizations need to review their business processes in order to understand where the emissions are generated and the level of those emissions. This then provides the opportunity to challenge and reconsider the processes in order to determine whether there are efficiency gains or where automation can reduce the carbon footprint.

Organizations can demonstrate their commitments by increasing the efficiencies of internal company operations and physical assets under the company's control and reducing their energy consumption.

Examples of mitigation options to reduce an organization's emissions include:

- Replacement of inefficient machinery with more efficient lower-emitting machinery
- Investigating options for reducing waste in production processes
- Utilizing by-products from the production process
- Reducing packaging (e.g. pasta packaging or removal of plastic around fruit and vegetables in French supermarkets)
- Replacing car fleets with electric vehicles
- Using renewable energy providers across all of your premises
- Encouraging working from home (thus reducing carbon footprint relating to commuting)
- Premises – improving insulation of existing buildings, replacing lighting with energy-efficient LED lighting options
- Promoting behavioural changes

5.8.3 Replace

As old infrastructure or machinery reaches end of life and as capital investment decisions are made, rather than replace like-for-like, companies will be looking to source replacements that help mitigate against climate risks relating to sustained higher emissions. This naturally facilitates a reduction in emissions.

This will be further augmented by the incorporation of carbon pricing into investment decision-making (where the internal cost of carbon is considered and feeds into the return-on-investment criteria). Examples are arising across a multitude of industries where new technologies are being introduced that reduce emissions while also improving operating efficiencies – these include heat pumps replacing gas or electric heating, development of hydrogen planes, delivery firms using electric vehicles or sails being added to container ships.

As companies look at the options for replacing infrastructure, an approach gaining favour is the establishment of an internal carbon price (ICP) (which is a theoretical price that companies can use to place a monetary value on each tonne of carbon emitted) in order to capture and put a monetary value on the costs/impacts of their activities in climate change terms. This approach allows for companies to more comprehensively consider the operational costs, the costs of compliance and adhering to future regulations as they make strategic decisions. In summary, the benefits of adopting such an approach are threefold:

1 to support decision making with regard to capital investments (and so project assessments explicitly evaluate climate change/carbon factors and disclose supporting assumptions)

2 to measure, model and manage the risks (both financial and regulatory) associated with existing and future government policies; and

3 to help identify risks and opportunities and to provide the chance to adapt strategy.

An alternative application of ICPs is when a company imposes a fee on each business per unit of emission. This money is then pooled and can be used to reward those that have the best emission reduction performance over a specified time. This approach incentivizes the reduction in emissions and promotes the investment in carbon-friendly initiatives (i.e operational efficiency initiatives, green projects or low-carbon product development) and reinforces a carbon reduction mindset.

As a consequence, ICP (or alternative approaches) are becoming more mainstream such that companies in more carbon-intensive sectors are likely to incorporate climate considerations into their capital investment and financial planning decisions.

In his 2022 Letter to CEOs, Larry Fink (CEO of Blackrock – the world's largest asset manager) reinforces this when he accepts that organizations cannot address climate change (and the associated risks) in isolation, that there is a need for governments to provide clear pathways and a consistent taxonomy for sustainability policy, regulation and disclosure across markets.[19] Governments must also support communities affected by the transition, help catalyse capital for the emerging markets, and invest in the innovation and technology that will be essential to decarbonizing the global economy.

With governments setting the parameters and regulators determining the accompanying framework(s), rules and principles, this provides the basis by which firms can operate in a coherent and efficient manner and highlights how the public and private sectors have complementary roles to play in the management of climate risk.

5.8.4 Sequester

Carbon sequestration is the process of capturing and storing atmospheric carbon dioxide. There are two main types of processes, namely geologic and biologic.

The US Geological Survey (USGS) defines carbon sequestration as Geologic carbon sequestration is the process of storing carbon dioxide (CO_2) in underground geologic formations. The CO_2 is usually pressurized until it becomes a liquid, and then it is injected into porous rock formations in geologic basins.

Biologic carbon sequestration refers to storage of atmospheric carbon in vegetation, soils, woody products, and aquatic environments. For example, by encouraging the growth of plants—particularly larger plants like trees—advocates of biologic sequestration hope to help remove CO_2 from the atmosphere.[20]

5.8.5 *Offset*

Once emissions have been measured and assessed (based on an approved carbon calculator), one of the options available is participation in carbon offset projects. Examples include:

- Certified emission reductions (CERs)
- Clean energy-verified carbon standard projects
- Tree-planting projects (where a number of trees are planted for every tonne of carbon)

As with the independent validation of any carbon footprint calculations, companies looking to offset their emissions will need to undertake due diligence on their offset partner and gain assurance that the provider selected is operating an accredited scheme and is undertaking what is required of them in an appropriate manner.

5.9 Monitoring and reporting carbon emissions and targets

In striving to meet their carbon net zero targets, organizations need to be able to measure and then monitor their emissions. One of the issues that organizations face is how to monitor emissions on a scale relative to the size of the business.

In monitoring and reporting of environmental performance there are many good guidance documents with one of the most comprehensive and insightful being from DEFRA which is part of the UK Government.

They set out two distinct types of targets:

- An absolute reduction target, which compares absolute figures in the target year to the base year
- An intensity target based on an appropriate normalizing factor (e.g. CO_2e emissions per full-time equivalent staff member)

Clearly an absolute target is designed to achieve actual reductions in environmental impact, and organizational growth needs to be decoupled from the environmental impact in order to achieve an absolute target. Whereas the DEFRA guidance points out that 'In contrast, an intensity target can drive resource efficiency and relative environmental impact, but the total resource use/impact may actually increase even if an intensity target has been reached due to increases in organizational activity e.g. production'.[21] These targets both have a role to play and their relative importance may vary over time.

In the private sector investors are starting to develop and use carbon footprint analysis to understand the exposure of companies to the potential effects of carbon pricing and as a simple proxy for gauging climate-related transition risks, both as a standalone tool and in combination with a carbon target, as part of an investment strategy. The assessment and monitoring of an organization's carbon footprint becomes more and more important.

5.9.1 Independent assurance of GHG emissions reported

Organizations globally will be collecting and using emissions data in order to quantify their emissions across their entire value chain and so that they can manage and report their climate risk exposure/GHG emission. This will in turn influence carbon-related costs, their corporate reputation and determine whether they need to undertake any offset activities. Consequently, in order to avoid detriment, organizations will be looking to independent bodies to validate and provide independent assurance with regard to the GHG emissions reported.

In the UK, the QAS (formerly known as the Quality Assurance Scheme) is a not-for-profit organization that provides independent verification of carbon emission calculation methodologies (which are subject to audit standards). This accreditation enables organizations to participate in carbon offsetting projects or carbon retirement (as per carbon emission permits – which can be retired at appropriate carbon registries).

In summary, by following a structured and incremental approach (similar to the one outlined above), companies can both reduce their emissions and reap other associated benefits. The key is to determine the full range of sources of the organization's emissions, make informed calculations and then identify options for reducing your emissions (across Scopes 1, 2 and 3). Depending on your business, the industry in which you operate and the operating model, this will influence the size of your reductions and from which Scope savings can be made.

CASE STUDY 1
Cornish Mutual

Here is an example of the process followed by Cornish Mutual (a British insurer) for carbon reduction and how it measures the full carbon impact of its operations across its organization as accurately as possible.

Carbon reduction

Cornish Mutual has explained that, in part through internal climate change training, it has generated a range of ideas for areas that it considers it can most easily target to reduce its footprint, and that it continuously seeks to engage staff by discussing how they can help the organization with its mission to become net zero. Specific considerations are around commuting behaviour, office energy-saving approaches and how it can engage with its members and supply chain to become greener. Some of the examples that it is considering are quite generic so many other organizations could consider them too, as outlined here:

- Continue to replace internal and supplier face-to-face meetings with video conferencing where appropriate (balancing this with the need to maintain a strong culture and relationships within the business) and minimize foreign travel.
- Choose smaller, hybrid or electric hire cars to reduce emissions. Avoid or combine car-based journeys and replace journeys with video conferencing. Choose rail journeys where possible.
- Continue the staff commuter survey and incentivize car sharing, and active travel.
- Explore electric car leasing and installing electric car charging stations in the main offices.
- Consider replacing the gas used in the air-conditioning system.
- Consider improving insulation and auditing hot water and heating settings on office buildings.
- Migrate customers to paperless transactions.
- Consider purchasing only recycled office supplies and paper, reducing the amount of paper sent out and encouraging members to recycle anything that is sent.
- Consider water-saving devices in bathrooms and install water meters.

FIGURE 5.11 Cornish Mutual – example of carbon emissions

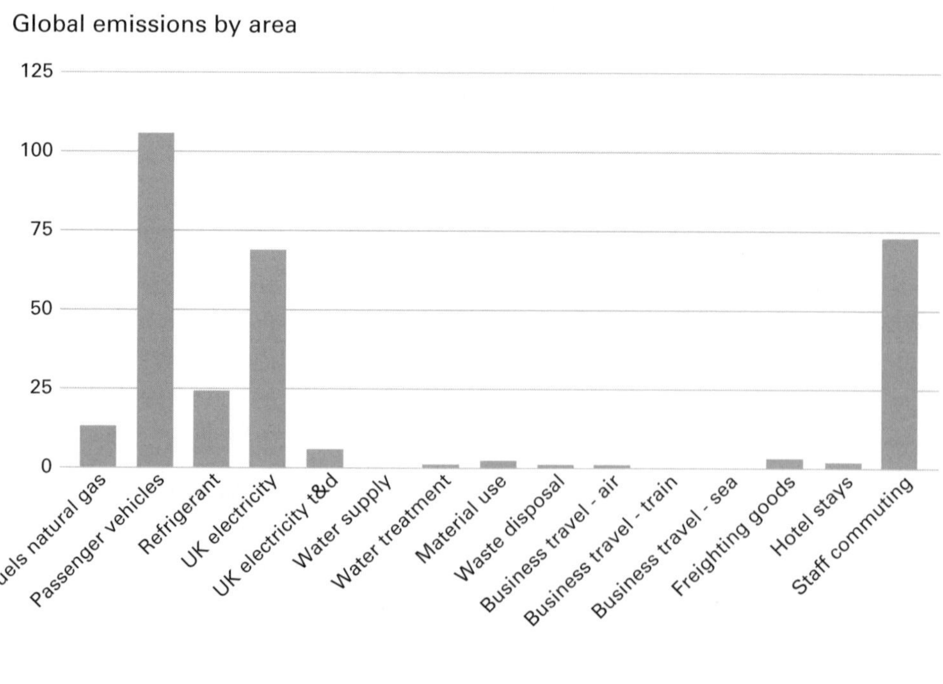

Measurement

- Cornish Mutual has included Scope 3 data where it is available and is considering whether it can (or how it can) integrate customer and supplier information into its carbon footprint assessment going forward.
- The example provided by Cornish Mutual highlights how companies can provide a breakdown of its carbon footprint by area.

It has stated that it hopes to recognize some of the benefits from the Covid-19 pandemic such as reduced commuting and business travel in its plans for reducing its emissions, but will also be conducting an office energy audit and considering software solutions for better monitoring of fleet vehicle miles and emissions.

CASE STUDY 2

Cambridge City Council – monitoring of carbon emissions

The Department for Business, Energy & Industrial Strategy in the UK (by combining the data from UK's greenhouse gas inventory) has developed a basis to monitor emissions that uses per capita emissions, which is shown in Figure 5.12. In the example shown for Cambridge City Council, you can see how the per capita emissions have reduced by 38 per cent over the same period in Cambridge, from 6.6 $ktCO_2$ to 4.1 $ktCO_2$. On an absolute scale the total carbon emissions reduced by 33 per cent from 779.7$ktCO_2$ to 521.5 $ktCO_2$ over the same period.

Both measures (total terms and per capita) are equally applicable within the private sector. Organizations need to continue to endeavour to meet reductions in both metrics. To focus on one risks a focus on the wrong thing if the organization (be that a firm or a city council) is undergoing a period of growth or a contraction. Notwithstanding this, the per capita metric may provide a suitable benchmark for comparison with appropriate peer groups.

The reduction in emissions from Cambridge (and other cities) in more recent years has been driven primarily by the reduced use of coal in electricity generation and the increased use of renewable energy generation at a national level. By 2019, 48.5 per cent of electricity in the national grid was generated from zero-carbon sources (wind, solar, hydro and nuclear), and this share is expected to increase further given planned investments in North Sea offshore wind and the Government's commitment to turn off all UK coal-fired power stations by 2024.

FIGURE 5.12 Carbon emissions in Cambridge 2005–2018 ($ktCO_2$) per capita and in absolute terms

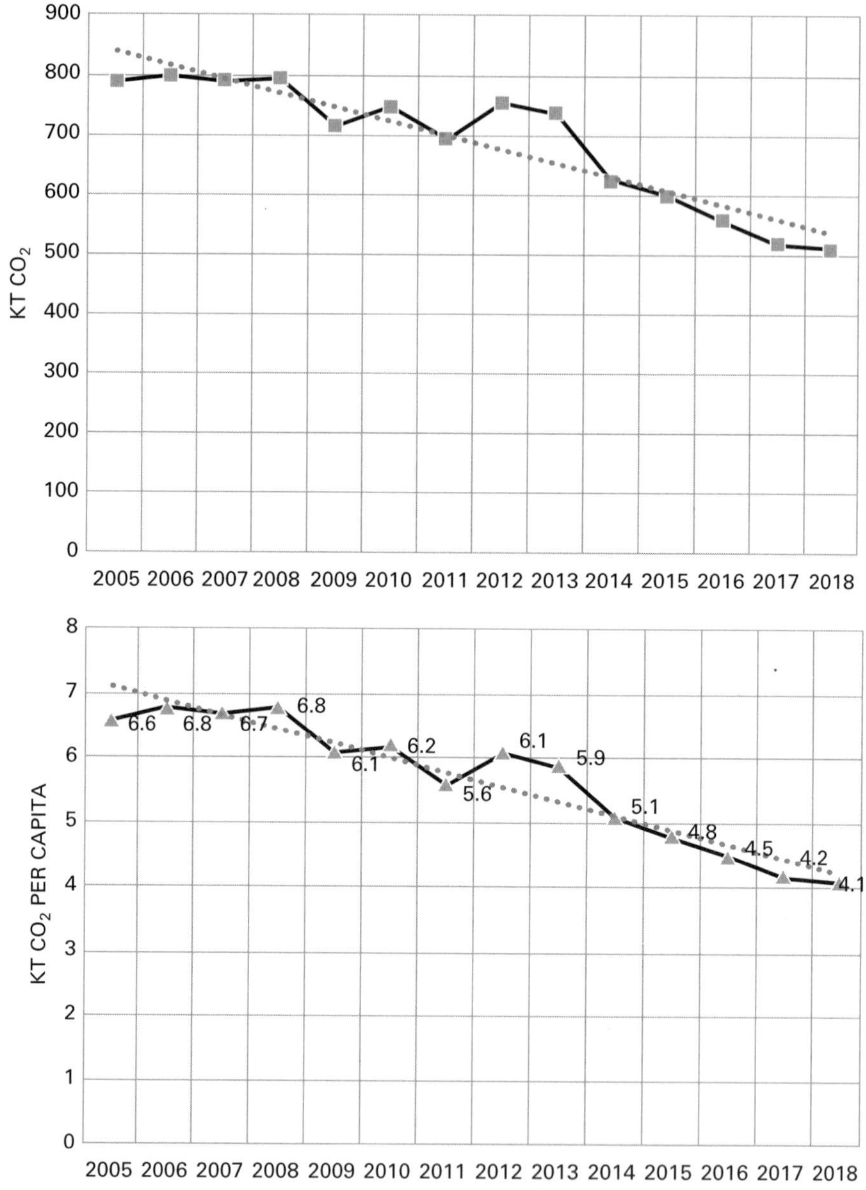

SOURCE Cambridge City Council[22]

5.10 Setting milestones of progress

Organizations need to consider how they set milestones for progress, which can be done annually or on a periodic basis incrementally (e.g. 3- or 5-year time horizons). As the scientific evidence on greenhouse gas emissions progresses (and best practice evolves) and as regulatory expectations increase, organizations can seek to provide their risk committees with an annual update on their progress.

It is often helpful to develop a realistic operational carbon footprint that can be plotted over time, including a comparison to highlight against a worst-case scenario if the organization takes no action on reductions.

Conclusion

This chapter has outlined the main sources of greenhouse gas (GHG) emissions and the main transition risks that organizations need to consider, highlighting a top-down approach from leading global drivers through structural changes and risk drivers to a broad range of threats and opportunities.

Stakeholder expectations are shifting as regulators, customers and investors, etc focus on corporate purpose, fulfilling regulatory requirements and pledging to meet emissions targets in line with the Paris Agreement, and providing a global perspective on carbon emissions and mitigation strategies for how government and regulators are going to meet their net zero targets.

The chapter has focused on explaining the emissions types and how organizations can seek to use or develop the six-step risk management framework for calculating, managing and mitigating carbon emissions across the entire value chain in order to reduce their carbon emissions and build a more sustainable organization.

The chapter has highlighted the need for organizations to assess the tools or models available to calculate their emissions and then to develop a strategic plan that should follow a structured and incremental approach to reduce their emissions and reap other associated benefits.

In summary, the chapter has highlighted the importance of developing a carbon risk appetite strategy and reduction plan and to design mitigation strategies for reducing carbon emissions through the concept of 'carbon hierarchy' and control mechanisms, and to consider how they set milestones for progress that can provide a basis for project planning and enable ongoing improvements, which will have environmental and commercial benefits to organizations.

Notes

1 K Raworth (2017) *Doughnut Economics: Seven ways to think like a 21st-century economist*, Random House Business, London
2 K Raworth (2017) *Doughnut Economics: Seven ways to think like a 21st-century economist*, Random House Business, London
3 IPCC. IPCC Sixth Assessment Report: The Physical Science Basis, 9 August 2021. https://www.ipcc.ch/report/ar6/wg1/ (archived at https://perma.cc/CA6F-CZR7)
4 M Carney. Memo to the Financial Stability Board on supporting the transition to net zero carbon emissions. PIIE, December 15 2020. www.piie.com/blogs/realtime-economic-issues-watch/memo-financial-stability-board-supporting-transition-net-zero (archived at https://perma.cc/Z627-LHSY)
5 L Bevere and A Weigel. sigma 1/2021 – Natural catastrophes in 2020, Swiss Re Institute, 30 March 2021, www.swissre.com/institute/research/sigma-research/sigma-2021-01.html (archived at https://perma.cc/7RVY-9GFJ)
6 Swiss Re Group. In 5 charts: natural catastrophes in a changing climate, 30 March 2021, www.swissre.com/risk-knowledge/mitigating-climate-risk/sigma-in-5-charts.html (archived at https://perma.cc/AF7F-4SFH)
7 BP. BP sets ambition for net zero by 2050, fundamentally changing organisation to deliver, 12 February 2020, www.bp.com/en/global/corporate/news-and-insights/press-releases/bernard-looney-announces-new-ambition-for-bp.html (archived at https://perma.cc/B8HG-MKCE)
8 The Economist. The latest IPCC report argues that stabilising the climate will require fast action, 9 April 2022, www.economist.com/science-and-technology/2022/04/09/the-latest-ipcc-report-argues-that-stabilising-the-climate-will-require-fast-action (archived at https://perma.cc/28MC-5MWP)
9 TCFD. Final Report: Recommendations of the Task Force on Climate-related Financial Disclosures, June 2017. https://assets.bbhub.io/company/sites/60/2020/10/FINAL-2017-TCFD-Report-11052018.pdf (archived at https://perma.cc/J4JK-3GL8)
10 IPCC. Climate Change 2022: Impacts, Adaptation and Vulnerability, 2022. www.ipcc.ch/report/ar6/wg2/ (archived at https://perma.cc/QS7Q-LQF9)
11 J Boyd. Understanding climate risk: how carbon footprinting can help, *International Investment*, 10 November 2017, www.internationalinvestment.net/internationalinvestment/opinion/3719969/understanding-climate-risk-carbon-footprinting-help (archived at https://perma.cc/A6KA-N7Q9)
12 IPCC. Climate Change 2022: Impacts, Adaptation and Vulnerability, 2022. https://www.ipcc.ch/report/ar6/wg2/ (archived at https://perma.cc/U7F5-JWEP)
13 The Economist. The latest IPCC report argues that stabilising the climate will require fast action, 9th April 2022, https://www.economist.com/science-and-technology/2022/04/09/the-latest-ipcc-report-argues-that-stabilising-the-climate-will-require-fast-action (archived at https://perma.cc/24E4-E5XB)
14 HM Government. The Ten Point Plan for a Green Industrial Revolution, November 2020. https://assets.publishing.service.gov.uk/government/uploads/system/uploads/attachment_data/file/936567/10_POINT_PLAN_BOOKLET.pdf (archived at https://perma.cc/QC65-AZDC)

15 J Ralston. Ukraine conflict and impacts on UK energy. Energy & Climate Intelligence Unit, 2022. https://eciu.net/analysis/briefings/uk-energy-policies-and-prices/briefing-ukraine-conflict-and-impacts-on-uk-energy (archived at https://perma.cc/W32N-MFQB)

16 Cambridge City Council. Climate Change Strategy 2021–2026, nd. www.cambridge.gov.uk/media/9581/climate-change-strategy-2021-2026.pdf

17 Carbon Footprint. Business Calculators, nd. www.carbonfootprint.com/small_business_calculator.html (archived at https://perma.cc/V7F7-LQ9Z)

18 Quantis. Greenhouse Gas Protocol, nd. https://quantis-suite.com/Scope-3-Evaluator/ (archived at https://perma.cc/ZAS2-WY7V)

19 L Fink. Letter to CEOs: The power of capitalism, BlackRock, 2022, www.blackrock.com/corporate/investor-relations/larry-fink-ceo-letter (archived at https://perma.cc/H87A-V43A)

20 USGS. What is carbon sequestration? nd. www.usgs.gov/faqs/what-carbon-sequestration (archived at https://perma.cc/LFA7-TBRR)

21 Gov.uk. Environmental reporting guidelines: including streamlined energy and carbon reporting guidance, March 2019, www.gov.uk/government/publications/environmental-reporting-guidelines-including-mandatory-greenhouse-gas-emissions-reporting-guidance (archived at https://perma.cc/PSJ4-MNAS)

22 Cambridge City Council. Climate Change Strategy 2021–2026. www.cambridge.gov.uk/media/9581/climate-change-strategy-2021-2026.pdf (archived at https://perma.cc/VG8P-JA3L)

6

Building climate resilience

This chapter will cover how organizations can build improved resilience from an operational, financial and strategic perspective in respect to climate change. This is mainly driven by increased uncertainty as future weather patterns can no longer be expected to reflect the past and organizations will need to be more agile and resilient to these ongoing changes.

Climate resilience is the ability to anticipate, prepare for and respond to hazardous events, trends or disturbances related to climate. So, in this chapter we will be focusing on the physical impacts of climate change and how organizations can improve their resilience to their impact.

The main learning outcomes from this chapter are to:

- Understand the main types of resilience that can be used to build climate resilience covering operational, financial and strategic
- Appreciate the variety of acute and chronic physical climate risks that can impact upon different industry sectors
- Explain how specific risk management tools and techniques can help organizations to improve their resilience
- Appreciate the importance and use of a bow tie analysis to help improve risk controls across different profiles to assess the impact of a climate event on the organization
- Understand how to integrate climate change into existing control processes, especially business continuity management, supply chain risk management and insurance procurement
- Understand the concept of compounded or connected extreme events, highlighting the fact that climate change can be connected and cause other extreme events such as blackouts

The chapter will focus primarily on how organizations need to build both operational and financial resilience with respect to climate change and provide examples of some of the tools and techniques, as well as discussing some specific controls that can help build improved resilience. This is supplemented through some practical and insightful industry case studies.

Introduction

'Most of the world's homes, businesses, and infrastructure were built to meet the needs for a 20th Century climate. As the effects of climate change accelerate, the need to prepare for the more intense events of tomorrow becomes more urgent with each passing day.'[1]

The business case for building resilience to the changing climate can be made primarily in terms of avoiding unexpected costs, managing risks and making the most of opportunities, although the focus is on the former. Organizations will ultimately need to improve their control environment by designing improved risk mitigation plans.

The reasons for this include the fact that weather events can be very costly with regard to lives, money, security, internal morale and reputation. Good risk management practices should allow for early recognition of threats so as to empower the organization to classify and highlight the risks. The organization can then deal with the threats in an effective and timely way.

In the context of disaster risk reduction, the UN defines resilience as 'the ability of a system, community or society exposed to hazards to resist, absorb, accommodate, adapt to, transform and recover from the effects of a hazard in a timely and efficient manner, including through the preservation and restoration of its essential basic structures and functions through risk management.'[2]

This chapter explores in detail the growing importance of risk management as a way to help build a more resilient organization. Risk management often achieves this through the promotion and facilitation of improved communication between employees, management board and stakeholders concerning how the threats are being managed.

The changing climatic conditions are leading to a wide range of threats. It is important for organizations to recognize and assess the associated volatility of physical risks. Understanding these threats can also present opportunities with a positive impact on business performance.

There is general consensus that physical risks of climate change that are associated with natural events, such as storms or floods, can inflict both direct damage and indirect impacts to businesses. We can generally split these into two main risk types:

- Acute – extreme weather events – floods, windstorms, wildfires, etc
- Chronic – changing climate conditions/patterns – droughts, heatwaves, coastal erosion, etc

This split is very important in the context of building resilience as organizations will need to develop different approaches and solutions for each type of physical risk.

While no one has yet discovered how to play God, there are a range of both preventive and reactive risk management controls and solutions that can be developed to reduce the impact on business. These are often referred to as pre- and post-loss mitigation strategies, such as business continuity plans and insurance, which seek to protect income affected by unfavourable weather conditions.

Another consideration is that while identifying and assessing climate change risks for most organizations, these may change depending on their respective geographical locations. Companies with global operations therefore need to assess their risk profile across each territory and region of their respective activities.

6.1 Key climate drivers and industry impacts

In building resilience, it is important to recognize the specific changes to the risk profile that an organization is evaluating. The next chapter discusses climate data sources, their use and the challenges in providing climate forecasting and projections.

A good example is from DEFRA that highlights some of the main climate conditions or key drivers of risks in the UK that organizations should take into consideration when building improved resilience.[3]

Changes in annual/seasonal averages

- Higher average temperatures, particularly in summer and winter
- Changes in seasonal rainfall patterns
- Rising sea levels

Changes in extremes

- More very hot days and heatwaves
- More intense downpours of rain
- Higher-intensity storms

6.1.1 Physical weather risks and climate change

Many industries are at risk of the effects of normal weather fluctuations, as well as the acute and chronic types of physical risks that were outlined earlier.

Table 6.1 summarizes some of the key industries and the reasons why they have exposure to different climate risks. The table provides details of the risk event and impact on the industry concerned and provides a basis for an organization to develop climate scenarios that can be assessed and mitigated (covered further in Chapter 10). Perhaps surprisingly, even organizations involved in producing new types of renewable forms of energy, such as solar and wind, are themselves vulnerable to physical climate risks, such as hail and lack of wind respectively.

The analysis highlights the range of physical climate risks and the fact that organizations need to carefully consider both acute and chronic types, which can also be classified as catastrophic and non-catastrophic types of exposures.

TABLE 6.1 Identification of physical climate risks and impacts by industry

Industry	Generic climate threats (cause)	Risk event	Impact/consequence
Construction	Precipitation or snowfall	**Operational** – disruption in construction **Financial** – potential delays in completion	**Regulatory and legal** – delays in completion lead to fines and penalties
Agriculture/agrochemical	Extreme temperatures and heat stress	**Operational** – significant loss of quantity and quality of milk for dairy farmers from livestock	**Financial** – reduction in revenues from sales
Gas utility	Mild winter	**Operational** – reduction in demand for gas	**Financial** – reduced earnings and profitability
Restaurant/hospitality	Precipitation	**Operational** – reduced demand for outdoor seating **Financial** – damage of outdoor furnishing and decor	**Financial** – reduced earnings; additional expense on refurbishing and repairs
Food/beverage	Cooler summer	**Operational** – reduced demand for cold beverages	**Financial** – loss of revenue due to sales reduction and futile stock on product expiration **Strategic** – lack of storage capacity for additional unsold stock
Retail companies	Precipitation	**Operational** – reduced store traffic	**Financial** – reduced earnings overall and profitability on season collection
Natural gas	Precipitation	**Operational** – obstruction of gas pipeline (e.g. due to precipitation-led mudslide)	**Operational** – delay in completion of project **Reputational** – inefficiency towards supplier commitments

(continued)

TABLE 6.1 (Continued)

Industry	Generic climate threats (cause)	Risk event	Impact/consequence
Renewable – hydro	Drought	**Operational** – reduced volume and flow of water	**Operational** – reduced generation of electricity **Financial** – scarcity of generated electricity for sales
Renewable – solar	Hail	**Operational** – disruption in functionality and efficiency **Financial** – destruction of solar panels	**Financial** – loss of revenue from sales and damage of asset
Renewable – wind	Critical low wind	**Operational** – turbines unable to rotate fast enough	**Operational** – reduced power output

SOURCE

6.2 Building climate resilience

When building operational resilience, developing pre- and post-loss event operational controls is important in the context of reducing the severity or financial impact of physical risks due to climate change.

It is important to first understand the context of what is meant by resilience and then to consider what controls can be designed to help organizations improve their resilience to climate change physical risks. Resilience can be grouped into different areas of focus. This chapter will focus on three broad categories, namely operational, financial and strategic resilience.

6.2.1 Operational resilience

The primary objective of operational resilience is the ability of the organization to continue to deliver critical operations, i.e. products and services, throughout a disruption. Operational resilience is really linked to the ability of an organization to prevent, adapt, respond to, recover and learn from operational disruptions.

A business service is defined as 'a service that an organization provides to an external end user'. It is deemed 'important' if its disruption would materially impact an organization's (financial or operational) viability, cause significant harm to customers or impact a firm's ability to deliver the board's approved strategy.

Regulators' expectations also extend to the fact that building operational resilience is necessary to protect the wider society and consumers. Financial regulators, for example, state that 'Operational resilience is also about changing your organization's mindset. Instead of thinking about operational disruption as something that could happen, firms should assume it will happen. This shift in attitude should propel your organization to make operational resilience a priority and will help to drive cultural change within the industry.'[4]

The key components or control mechanisms that will be covered in this chapter include:

- Business continuity and crisis management
- Supply chain risk management

6.2.2 *Financial resilience*

Financial resilience is the ability of an organization to withstand events that affect its capital structure, liquidity, revenue and assets.

Organizations can design pre- and post-loss controls that they can use through risk financing mechanisms. This will be either pre-financing of losses from climate events or through insurance and hedging strategies. Both arrangements will seek to reduce volatility of earnings that can in turn help to provide other financial benefits and targets, such as:

- Stronger credit ratings
- Lower cost of debt
- Improved access to funding

Furthermore, eliminating or reducing the uncertainty generated by different non-core risks allows management to concentrate on executing core business strategies. Physical risk from climate change is mainly linked to the uncertainty in cash flow and earnings caused by volumetric risk (which is variability in supply and/or demand caused primarily by variability in the climate conditions).

With growing awareness of the impact of weather risk due to, for example, temperature changes and associated volatility, stakeholders and analysts can view physical risks from climate change as a non-core operating risk that needs to be addressed through the use of insurance or other risk financial techniques such as hedging instruments.

As awareness of climate risk increases among shareholders, chief executives are no longer able to use the climate as an excuse for lower profits. As a result, a growing number of companies are developing risk financing solutions to hedge specific exposures. In section 6.7 we expand on some of the risk financing mechanisms available for companies, including the use of captive insurance companies and of innovative solutions such as parametric or index solutions.

The key components or control mechanisms that will be covered in this chapter include:

- Risk financing
- Strategic insurance risk gap analysis
- Financial planning and capital management

6.2.3 Strategic resilience

Strategic resilience considers the implications of the strategic and organizational choices a firm has to make, and the potential implications for long-term stability.

One of the most important techniques is to develop an emerging risk management framework (outlined in Chapter 8) and using tools and techniques such as horizon scanning. Emerging risks are those that you can see approaching but are not yet sufficiently clear to enable a formal impact and likelihood risk assessment. However, the key is to understand emerging risks as best as possible. Consider monitoring them to ensure they don't arise unexpectedly and consider any possible cost-effective actions that can be taken now to prepare for when the risk materializes.

The emerging risk management framework should feed into strategic and operational planning processes to support strategic decisions that need to be made and consider the funding of any mitigating actions or steps needed. From a climate change perspective this is likely to centre on the potential for customers' needs or markets to change due to climatic changes or transitional influences, geographical footprint, supply chain transformation over time and/or access to capital, especially for those impacted by transition. The following example helps to illustrate the importance of developing strategic resilience.

The key components or control mechanisms that will be covered in this chapter include:

- Emerging risk management framework
- Strategic planning

GLOBAL EXAMPLE

The wine industry

A pre-emptive example of how physical risks relating to climate change are being managed can be evidenced by the impact that projected temperature increases will have on wine producers.

As temperatures rise these impact grape yields and the taste of the wine. This will mean that at a point in the future, large swathes of land in certain parts of the world may become too hot to produce wine. One of the consequences of this (and how we witness horizon scanning in response to this emerging risk) is the purchase of land for wine production in Belgium, northern Germany and England by French wine producers (e.g. Taittinger – one of France's most prestigious champagne producers – buying 120 acres of grapes near Canterbury in south-east England).[5] In the southern hemisphere we are witnessing Tasmania developing as a wine producer. This is an example of climate change risk management being applied in a sector that has existed for thousands of years, and which is requiring all aspects of the value chain be reassessed.

6.2.3.1 EMERGING INNOVATIVE OPPORTUNITIES TO GAIN COMPETITIVE ADVANTAGE

There is a growing realization that for many physical risks, such as flooding and wildfires, organizations can gain competitive advantage by developing new innovative customer communications. The case study below sees a property insurer use technology to alert the customer to increased surface flooding so they can take action, the benefits being the customer can take action to 'de-risk' their own risks while reducing losses to the insurer.

CASE STUDY

Acies MGU & Previsico – flood warning service – alert systems embedded within insurance policies

Background

In England, the surface water flood risk puts over 3 million properties at risk, which is even more than the risk from river and sea combined that affects 2.4 million properties collectively.

Currently, there aren't enough credible and reliable weather forecast technologies that can prevent the damage and loss caused to buildings, stocks, contents and business interruption due to surface water flooding. The greater delay in responding to flood damage increases the insurance claims settlement process as well as the financial risk to small and medium enterprises (SMEs).

Action taken

Flood forecasting systems are valuable and essential for flood risk management. The solution was to design and provide a customized surface water flooding alert system to provide a pre-warning of impending flood within 24 hours to the specific location via an email or directly to mobiles, which allows businesses to act in a timely manner to reduce the impact of losses.

FIGURE 6.1 Flood warning service

SOURCE Acies

Results

The use of the alert system has been embedded within the insurance policy for the customer to provide real-time flood warnings. The SMEs receive personalized warnings in their immediate areas allowing them to take action to protect their premises from flood water.

The use of technology and data insights in this case study addresses the current gaps in flood forecasting in surface water and ordinary watercourse flooding while improving the warning systems accuracy, which in turn reduces false alarms.

The overall benefits are that the alert system allows the 'de-risking' of the risk for customers and for the insurance companies to reduce losses.

6.3 Developing a climate resilience framework

Figure 6.2 provides a broad outline of a climate resilience framework that can be used to improve resilience across operational, financial and strategic dimensions.

The framework helps to explain the main controls that organizations should seek to develop and the associated tools and techniques. Some of the traditional controls for building operational risk will be covered in this chapter, such as the use of business continuity planning and insurance.

6.3.1 Stress and scenario planning

A number of tools are available within the risk manager's 'toolkit', to enable them to assess and control risks facing an organization.

One of the most important tools for building climate resilience is stress and scenario testing, which is covered in Chapter 10. However, it is important to note the importance of stress testing and scenario analysis to climate resilience both in understanding the nature of potential events and the steps needed to build operational, financial or strategic resilience. The techniques vary slightly but the principles apply equally across all three. Operational resilience relies on stress testing to challenge the impact tolerance assessments. Financial resilience relies on it to test sensitivities to

FIGURE 6.2 Climate resilience framework

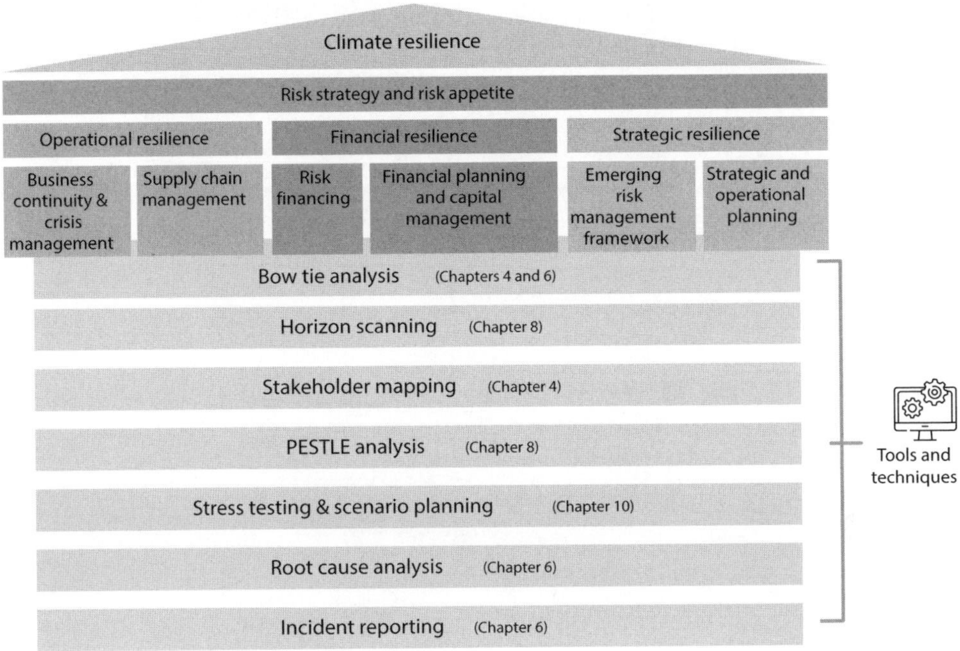

SOURCE © OneRisk Consulting. All rights reserved, 2022

key financial shocks. Strategic resilience utilizes the technique to 'war game' future scenarios.

6.3.2 Use of the bow tie analysis

One of the best risk management tools is the bow tie analysis, which helps to document, monitor and communicate the risk environment of an undesirable event such as acute climate physical risk. The use of the tool also helps to draw the attention of controls in the prevention and mitigation of negative risk events. For climate change, it can be used to assess a specific event across different risk categories in the risk profile.

It is particularly useful in assessing not only root causes, but also possible outcomes, and provides a basis for debate regarding key controls that could be implemented. Bow tie analysis is also a simple and effective tool for communicating risk assessment results to employees at all levels.

The bow tie itself is formed of five key components:

1 **The event** –the centre of the bow tie describes the risk event that an organization could face.

2 **Causes** – the root cause of the event, which could include earlier catalyst events.

FIGURE 6.3 Bow tie analysis – flood event for a bank

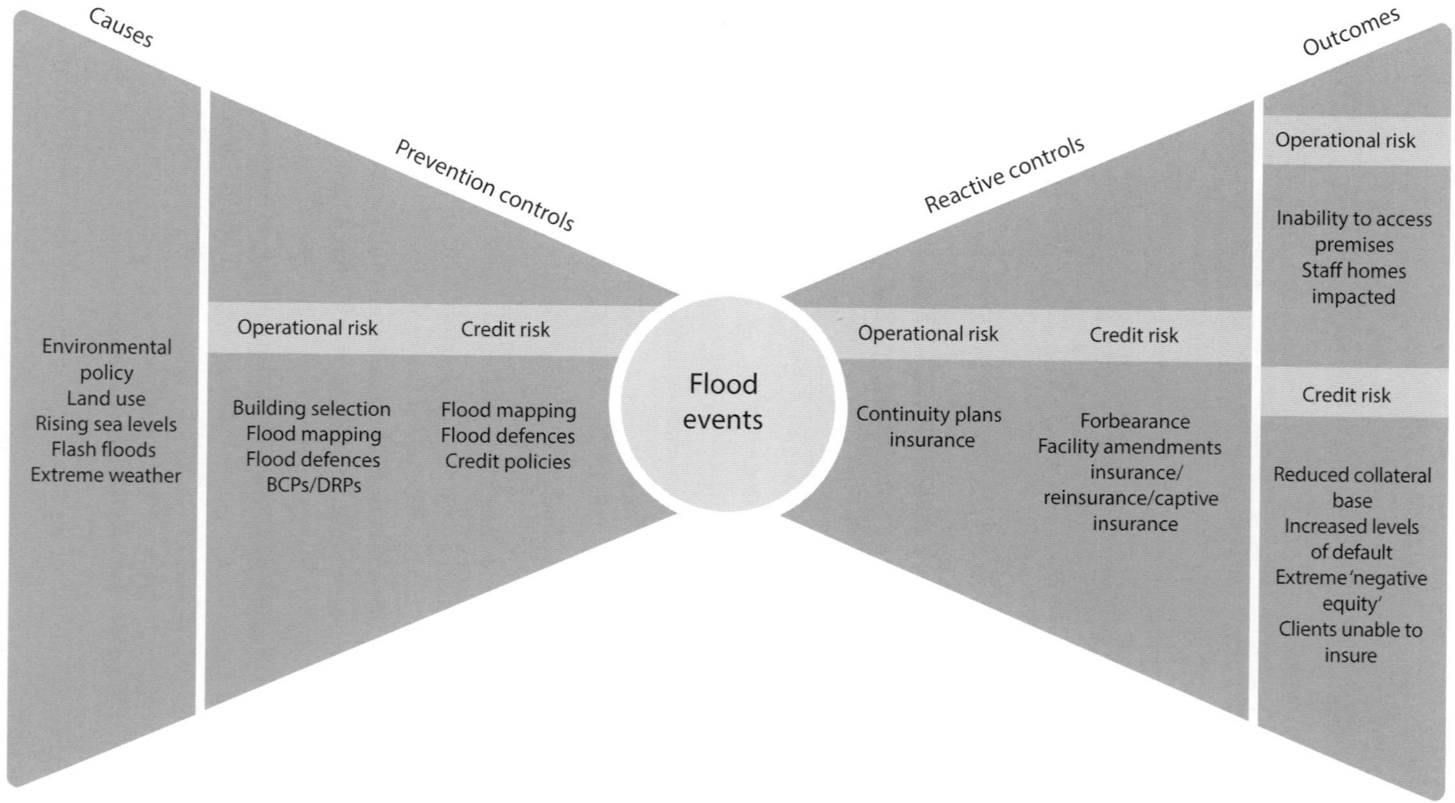

SOURCE

3 **Outcomes** – the eventual results of an event materializing.

4 **Prevention controls** – controls that an organization could use to stop the event from occurring.

5 **Reactive controls** – actions to be taken should the event materialize, to minimize or mitigate possible outcomes.

By working through these steps, and accounting for varying teams' views and perspectives, a full picture of the event can be gained. Figure 6.3 is an example of how the bow tie can be applied to the physical effects of climate change, from the perspective of a flood event for a bank, which in this case would have most impact on the operational and credit risk profile.

The main objective of the tool is to help evaluate whether the existing controls are effective in meeting the organization's target risk appetite for the specific climate scenario.

The outputs of any bow tie process should be assessed against the overarching risk appetite of an organization. For example, while an event could cause negative consequences for a business, it may be that controls are either too expensive or the residual risk level is deemed small enough that 'no action' is deemed to be the best approach. Above all, the bow tie acts as a tool for debating the best approach, rather than necessarily providing a miracle answer.

A specific industry case study using the bow tie analysis is provided below from Southern Water plc in the UK. Southern Water UK define resilience as 'the ability of a water source to cope with and/or recover from lack of rain to continue providing the same water quality while protecting the environment'. One of the main climate-related risks linked to meeting this operational objective is different levels of 'droughts' and the case study below highlights how the utility company is adapting business processes and developing ongoing mitigation stages and plans.

CASE STUDY

Southern Water[6]

Building operational resilience for a future drought event

Background

According to the UK Climate Change Risk Assessment 2017 Evidence Report, the risk of shortages in the public water supply stands within the top six areas of climate risks in the UK.[7] In this context, we define resilience as the ability of a water source to cope with and/or recover from lack of rain to continue providing the same water quality while protecting the environment.

Risk identification process

The main causes of a drought are:

- Absence of or reduced rainfall particularly during winter. Aquifers are an important characteristic of South East England, considering the recharge period given.
- High water demand, in the spirit that there is great need to balance demand against supply to satisfy customer needs.
- Climate change alters large-scale atmospheric circulation patterns, which can shift storm tracks off their typical paths. Rising temperatures make wet regions wetter and dry regions drier.

Categorize the risk

Drought vulnerability assessment: The company carried out a high-level screening against a set of criteria to identify water resource zones that are 'drought vulnerable'. Furthermore, Southern Water has identified various stages of droughts that may have different duration, intensity and geographical extent.

The main risks identified across our risk profile are as follows:

- **Operational risk** – Uncertainty about a company's operations, including delivery of its products or services.
- **Strategic risk** – Risks that pose a threat to a company's ability to set and execute its overall strategy.
- **Environmental and legal risk** – Uncertainty related to lawsuits or the freedom to operate. Potential environmental liabilities or the impact of changes in the environment.

Assumptions

- The higher the drought severity, the higher the cost in relation to our drought response.
- Our drought response will rely on:
  - How we reduce leakage
  - How we encourage customers to reduce water use
  - How we implement restrictions on water use when necessary
  - How we maintain water supplies during the drought
  - How we ensured our water sources are protected
  - How we monitor and mitigate for any impacts upon the environment
- Preventative barriers are more likely to alleviate the drought's symptoms rather than fully mitigate it with respect to climate change.

FIGURE 6.4 Drought event – bow tie analysis

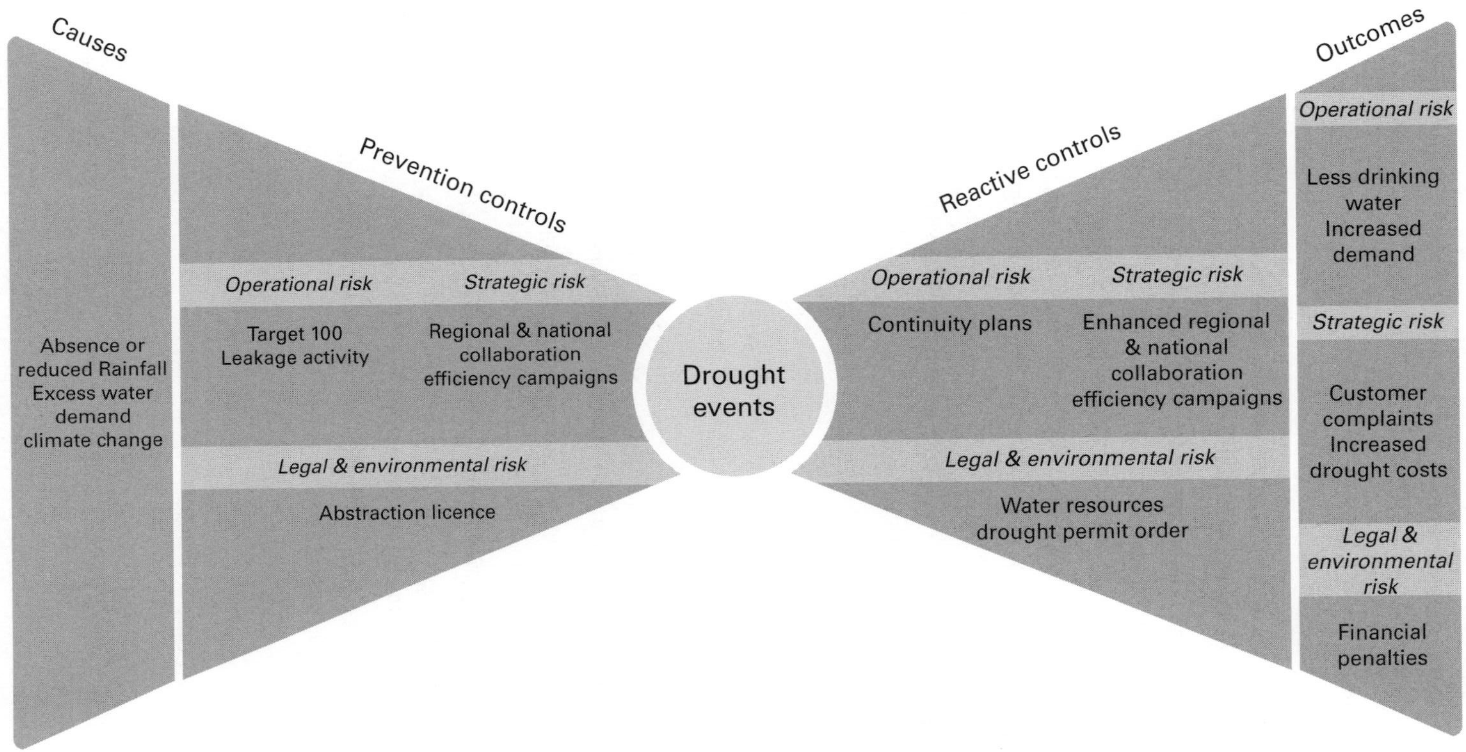

SOURCE

Mitigation plans to improve resilience

Southern Water has developed or is in the process of developing/optimizing mitigation plans to reduce the impact of a drought to meet our objectives:

- If the drought is severe in some areas, we will consider imposing water restrictions in order to reduce demand.
- Depending on the drought severity, we have developed a robust planning procedure to anticipate drought events and protect our resources.
- The company intends to undertake proactive and reactive water efficiency campaigns to raise public awareness that can be carried out using a variety of ways and media. The key message is to encourage customers to consume less water during a dry period.
- Active member of the Water Resources South East (WRSE), in order to facilitate dry weather meetings, which focus on the risk of potential drought events and regional collaboration (e.g. joint communications).
- The company has a number of supply agreements with neighbouring water companies that include imports and exports.

Next steps/ongoing steps

- We plan to be less reliant on drought permits and orders, in accordance with our regulator, to ensure greater resilience to droughts and reduce our impact on the environment (Regional Plan Development, 2040).
- From a demand management perspective, we have committed to reducing leakage by 15 per cent over Asset Management Plan7 (2020–2025) and by 50 per cent by 2050.
- By implementing our 'Target 100' plan, we pledge to help our customers reduce their personal consumption to an average of 100 litres per day by 2040.
- Leakage may increase during a drought – a result of soil drying out, resulting in ground movement and different pipe work movement. Additional leakage detection and repair sources are needed to ensure that leakage won't be increased during a drought event.
- Water Resources Management Plans (WRMP) to protect and sustain water sources and promote water network interconnectivity.

6.3.3 Impact on property assets

As already outlined, one of the major issues impacting both governments and organizations is the protection of property from physical risk and developing greater resilience to, for example, flood events. More intense physical risk events impact on residential and commercial properties or infrastructure.

In terms of building resilience it is essential to limit damage potential and protect assets in the future. Even in the most developed parts of the world there remains a critical need to retrofit properties that reside in known high-risk locations.

Other solutions being developed are more stringent building code requirements in addition to further growing insurance take-up where gaps exist.

6.4 Climate resilience guidance and frameworks

From an enterprise risk perspective in managing and mitigating physical risks and in the context of climate change (and any other strategic risk), organizations need to embrace a helicopter view across the whole risk profile of the organization.

Before explaining a formal process that organizations can adopt it is important to recognize how governments are addressing the problem from a more long-term perspective in project planning.

6.4.1 Government guidance in respect of climate resilience

For risk professionals it is important to recognize that governments have been providing some excellent guidance on how to build resilience against climate change in the context of their policies, programmes and projects.

The Department for Environment, Food and Rural Affairs (DEFRA) in the UK has provided guidance specifically addressing climate change. Its report sets out to provide analysts and policymakers with information on how to design adaption measures in respect of climate risks and challenges to improve resilience in, for example, infrastructure projects.

One of the most important and helpful guides in the context of building resilience is the Green Book issued by HM Treasury in 2020 on how to appraise policies, programmes and projects.[8]

Within the report, Section 5.49 sets out good risk management practice guidance on the appraisal, monitoring and evaluation of projects that include the need for how specific risks may be avoided, minimized or managed. They recommend, for example, that a risk register is created and maintained through implementation and owned by those responsible for operational delivery.

One of the insights that governments use is 'optimum bias', which is in effect a built-in contingency that helps to reduce false expectations, for example that a larger project could have been delivered at a lower cost. It also includes an appendix entitled 'Uncertainty, Optimism Bias and Risk' in which it outlines real option analysis and illustrates a proposal for investing in infrastructure protecting against the impacts of river flooding due to climate change, which was undertaken by the

FIGURE 6.5 UK Government guidance on climate integration to improve resilience

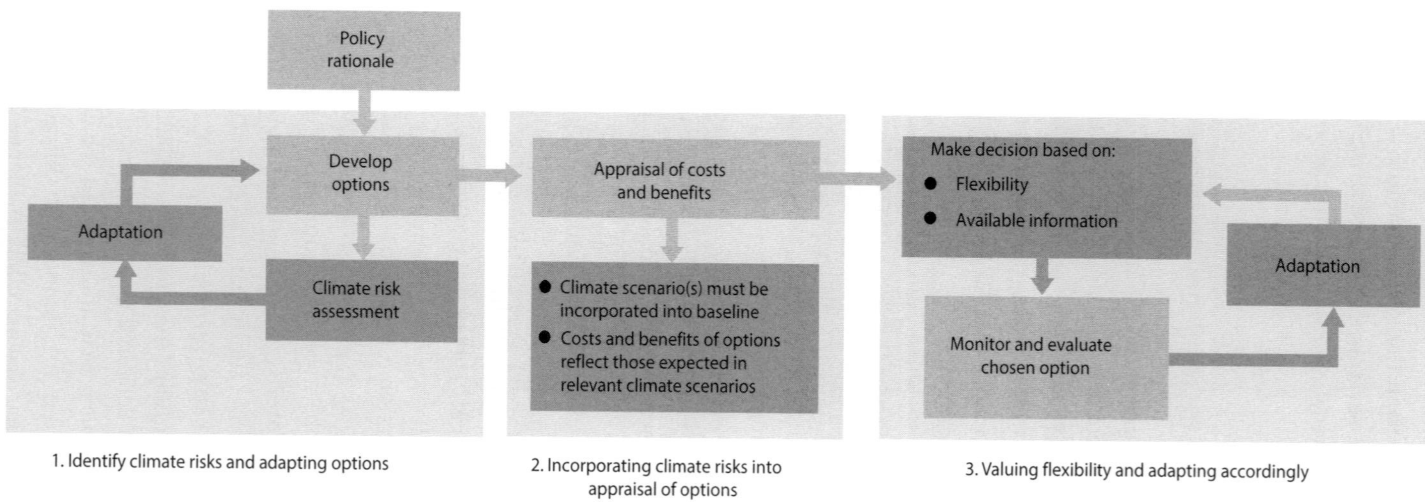

SOURCE DEFRA – Supplementary Green Book Guidance (2020)

Department for Environment, Food and Rural Affairs. The details of the assessment are set out in the Green Book (2022) – Guidance.[9]

Its approach to climate resilience appraisal builds on the Green Book approach and helps to ensure that decisions are resilient to future climate change risks. The process is summarized in Figure 6.5.

This approach can be adapted to all organizations as they consider the threats to their existence from physical risks.

6.5 Organizational climate resilience process

In terms of developing a generic high-level strategic process to build increased resilience for climate change, it is important that risk professionals within their respective organizations develop a methodology like the four-step process described below and in Figure 6.6 that can be adopted for any areas of risk, but can be tailored for the assessment of physical risks.

FIGURE 6.6 Climate resilience framework process

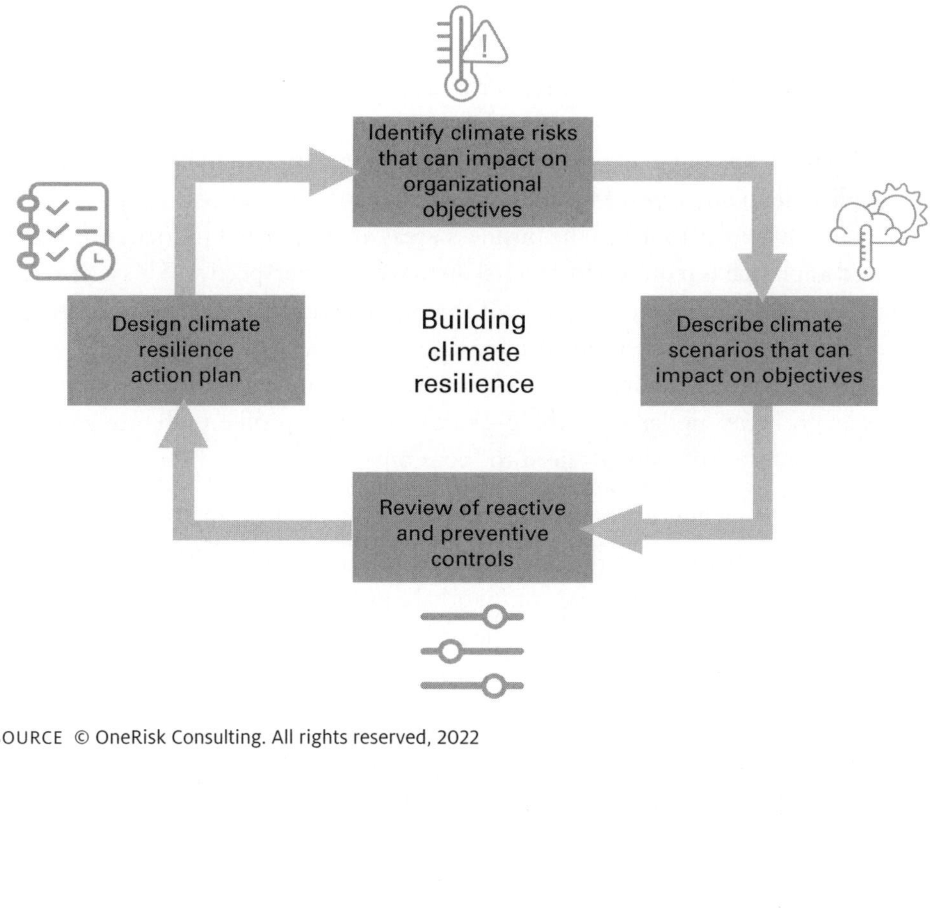

SOURCE

1 Identify climate risks that can impact on an organization's objectives (e.g. KPIs and risk tolerance levels).
2 Build out climate scenario descriptions that relate to physical climate risks.
3 Review the reactive and preventive controls environment through an assessment of available risk mitigation techniques that can improve resilience.
4 Design a formalized climate resilience action plan.

6.5.1 *Identify climate risks that can impact on organizational objectives*

Organizations should first identify the physical climate risks that impact on meeting their objectives, including key performance indicators (KPIs). These are typically articulated as causes that can impact on the risk profile, which will be primarily on the operational and/or financial risk profile across specific business activities and processes.

The overall objective of the process will be to assess the existing control environment and either identify any gaps in either existing controls or see whether new controls and mitigation plans can be developed to build improved resilience in the organization.

There are some helpful climate physical tools that can be used to help, such as the climate impact assessment tool (BACILAT) developed by the environmental agency and used by the UK Climate Impacts Programme (UKCIP), which is based at the Environmental Change Institute at the University of Oxford.[10]

Its framework sets out a set of six generic business functions and has been designed to be applicable to any type of business or sector.

Whilst it is a helpful tool and the business areas are important to focus on, a more structured approach is required from a risk management perspective. This is provided through understanding the risk profile of the organization and the related activities and objectives, and ultimately identifying climate scenarios that could prevent the organization from meeting its objectives, or indeed enhancing its objectives.

In order to better understand the organization's risk profile there are generally two areas that risk professionals need to focus on:

- Review of existing internal documentation including business and risk information.
- Understanding the risk profile and business activities and developing risk questionnaires, structured interviews and workshops that will assist in identifying the climate threats that will impinge on the organization meeting its key performance and thus from achieving its overall organizational goals and objectives.

In developing key performance indicators and tolerance levels it is important to note due to climate change some of the existing metrics will need to be recalibrated or new ones developed as part of the wider design of a climate risk appetite strategy, which we covered in Chapter 2.

The impacts are the ones that should align with the organization's own risk assessment criteria, which can be developed through workshops in developing climate scenarios that we will discuss in Chapter 10.

6.5.1.1 MAPPING THE RISK PROFILE TO BUSINESS ACTIVITIES

As part of this first phase it is helpful to map out climate threats that could impact on the specific business processes and risk assessment criteria (RAC) or KPIs.

Ultimately it is important to map out how physical risk impacts on the existing risk profile and how that can be developed and matured over time. This approach helps to identify the key areas of focus and prioritize those that are most likely to be impacted by physical climate risks. This is equally applicable to transition risks but we will focus our discussion on physical risks.

The main output of this review process should integrate into internal business and risk information gathered, such as prevailing risk registers, and then be supplemented by expert judgement and feedback and discussion through risk questionnaires, structured interview and workshops. This will help to build a list of risks and threats aligned to specific divisional or departmental risk assessment criteria or KPIs.

TABLE 6.2 Example of physical risk from a water and electricity utility company

Risk category	Business activity	Relevant risk assessment criteria or KPI	Risk event of concern	Generic climate threats (cause)
Operational	Supply of desalinated water network	Revenue service disruption, health and safety, environment, corporate objectives and reputation	Partial or complete outage of water production	Algal bloom
Financial	GL and statutory reporting results (profit and loss)	RAC – revenue, absolute deviation from approved budgeted revenues	Seasonal temperature volatility (against expectation/budget)	Seasonal volatility
Operational	Customer demand forecasting	Revenue, service disruption	Failure to accurately forecast future water and electricity demand may result in insufficient or excess capacity	Underlying forecast factors incorrectly estimated – including trends in weather-related factors

(continued)

TABLE 6.2 (Continued)

Risk category	Business activity	Relevant risk assessment criteria or KPI	Risk event of concern	Generic climate threats (cause)
Operational	Business continuity management/ crisis management	Reputation	Lack of formal internal crisis management plan	Lack of formalized documented and communicated crisis management policy
Operational	Project management	Revenue, service disruption, corporate objectives and reputation	Inventory shortage to meet project requirements	Natural catastrophe event such as major flooding

SOURCE

Some specific examples that organizations need to consider are highlighted in Table 6.2, which comes from the utility sector. Many of the examples are generic and can be applicable to many other industry sectors.

6.5.2 Build out climate scenario descriptions that relate to physical climate risks

Having identified the physical risks and threats it is important to then build out specific 'scenarios of concern'. According the BSI Group report, as we have discussed it is important to:

- Understand the timescales of relevant decisions
- Use information about the future rather than the past[11]

Risk managers can support the process by assessing the risk of each threat or benefit and considering how far into the climate future it is necessary to look or predict. This will depend on the lifetime of decisions associated with it. For example, when assessing threats or benefits associated with large-scale fixed assets or long-term contracts it will be important to assess their likelihood by thinking about what the climate will be like at the end of their life. In addition, it is important to remember that the climate is not the only thing that is changing. Any changes to other external or internal factors, such as changes in locations or technologies, should also be considered.

TABLE 6.3 Climate scenario descriptions

Department	Generic climate threats (cause)	Scenario description
Water and civil	Algal bloom	Natural process due to change in weather conditions, e.g. temperature/climate change leads to algae blocking the intake of water to desalination plant causing partial or complete outage
Finance	Seasonal volatility	'Mild summer' leads to reduced temperatures that are directly correlated to reduced demand and revenues
Power and planning	Underlying forecast factors incorrectly estimated – including trends in weather-related factors	Due to lack of planning, inability to determine trends and causations between consumer demand and supply for extreme weather factors including a mild summer
Marketing and corporate communications	Area-wide flood event	Area-wide flood event that leads to financial losses to businesses within the vicinity, and damage and loss of assets that lead to service disruption and reputational damage
Distribution	Natural catastrophe event such as major flood event	A global flood event impacts the global supply chain and as a result leads to delaying the supply of key inventory, e.g. transformers for installation at project site

SOURCE

6.5.3. Review of reactive and preventive controls

Having developed a set of physical risk climate scenarios that can impact upon the objectives of the organization, the next step is to review the current control environment and risk mitigation options available.

One of the fundamental roles of a risk manager is to identify and assess critical risks and then develop appropriate risk controls that help to move risks from an inherent risk perspective (assuming no controls) to a target level of risk or risk appetite as set out in Figure 6.7 below. At a high level, a traditional approach could be used such as the 4Ts of risk management: tolerate, treat, transfer and terminate.

It is important to understand the different types of controls that can be utilized. A control is a measure or action that should seek to modify the risk, either through reducing its likelihood, severity or both. Controls should already exist and can include:

- Policies
- Practices

FIGURE 6.7 Review of risk mitigation options

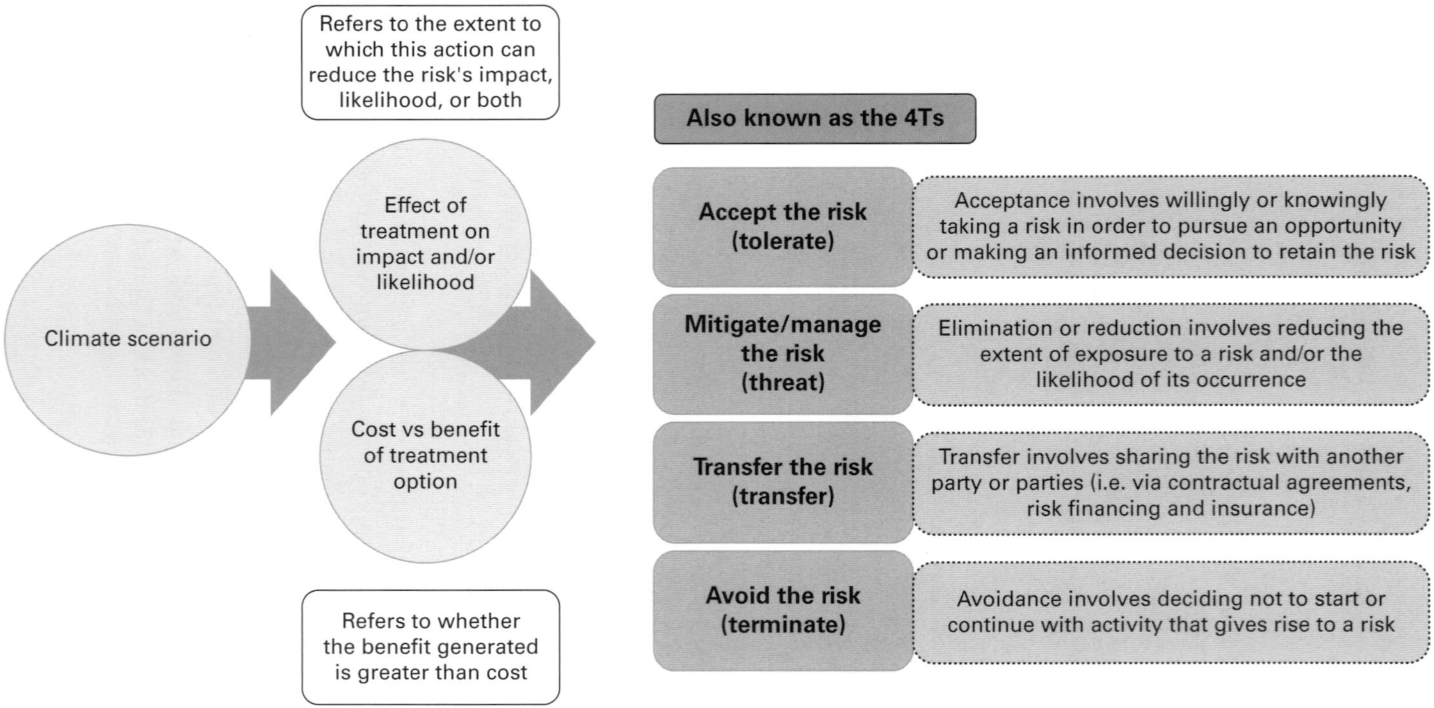

SOURCE

- Processes
- Technologies
- Methods
- Devices

Organizations should therefore either seek to improve the existing control environment or introduce new controls to help align the risk to an acceptable level to meet the risk appetite or target score of the board.

6.5.4. Design risk mitigation strategies

Developing risk mitigation plans and improving the control environment is critical and organizations need to align them with stakeholder expectations and then align them with their strategic objectives, core operations and processes.

As shown in Figure 6.5, organizations should seek to evaluate and develop risk mitigation plans that need to:

1. Reduce the impact and/or likelihood of the climate scenario of concern.
2. Ensure the long-term benefits of implementing the control or risk mitigation initiative are greater than its cost. It is important to consider conducting cost/benefit analysis to optimize the risk and reward trade off.

The risk mitigation plans should be formalized as part of ongoing climate change plans in line with risk appetite strategy, as discussed in Chapter 2.

6.6 Specific risk management controls to improve operational climate resilience

As discussed in section 6.2.1 two of the main of the operational resilience components include business continuity and crisis management, and supply chain risk management.

6.6.1 Integration of climate change into business continuity management

One of the most important controls with respect to developing operational resilience is business continuity management (BCM). In the context of climate change risk, this requires management to give consideration to how the business can continue to operate in the face of a major weather event (which can be direct, or indirect via disruption to the wider supply chain). This risk can present both financial and operational challenges for organizations.

One of the most important elements of BCM is to identify mission-critical systems, ensure they can still operate during a business disruption and make sure that the plans are tested on a regular basis.

It is important to recognize that the challenge of initializing a business continuity process and preparing for a business disruption is daunting, and it is important to seek external advice often, particularly with respect to independent evaluation.

The options available to organizations are to:

1 Reduce the likelihood of a physical risk disruption
2 Reduce the period of disruption
3 Reduce the impact of a disruption

This will result in a range of specific actions to change either the likelihood, impact or both and will involve a combination of changing location (or increasing the security of the physical infrastructure), utilizing technology, developing operational arrangements (with suppliers or similar firms) or building flexibility (or additional capacity) into existing processes.

Organizations should seek to integrate specific actions into the existing BCM plans. These actions can be simplified into a four-step process as shown in Figure 6.8.

Organizations should follow the four key steps outlined in Figure 6.8:

1 Identify their important business services by considering how disruption to the business services they provide can have impacts beyond their own commercial interests.

FIGURE 6.8 Business continuity process

SOURCE © OneRisk Consulting.

2 Set a tolerance for disruption for each important business service (an impact tolerance).
3 Ensure they can continue to deliver their important business services and are able to remain within their impact tolerances during severe but realistic scenarios.
4 Conduct the exercise programme with a broad set of stakeholders to help test the procedures that can be used to assess the level of preparedness.

Therefore, in respect of climate change threats it will be important that organizations review and revise the business continuity policy and strategy. This will involve revisiting and updating the business impact analyses (BIAs). It will also require the organizations to review the wider supply chains (and those of partners, suppliers and third-party providers) in order to identify weaknesses. Integration into the supply chain risk management is discussed in section 6.6.2 below.

EXAMPLE

Climate change and data centres

Many organizations are concerned about the location of their data centres, for example in current or future flood zones.

In terms of implementing improved controls to build greater resilience to future floods, an organization should consider relocating its data centre to a new location that is less prone to flooding. Other related controls include installing uninterrupted power supply (UPS) at the new location or having a real-time back-up of data in the cloud, so that even if the adverse outcome was to occur, the impact would be minimized. The reduction in impact and likelihood will depend on the investment made to improve the control environment.

6.6.1.1 CRISIS MANAGEMENT

As well as effective planning for an event it is essential to build out a plan for how to respond in a crisis. This could involve the governance around an event (who is involved, at what level and when), the communication plans for various stakeholders and any pre-determined steps around how to walk through the crisis from start to finish. War gaming and scenario planning may help inform knowledge and understanding of how to respond in a crisis. Any learnings from these exercises should feed into an updated crisis management plan.

Tone and drive from the top will be key as well as a good understanding of the plan across the senior executive team. Acting as one unit and moving in the same direction at the same time will simplify the response enormously.

For the more extreme shocks that relate directly to your organization, the public communications made during the crisis can make a significant difference to the way the customer perceives the company and its reputation moving forward. Even if the right actions are taken, if these are poorly communicated the customer may not recognize the strength in the response.

In climate change terms, responding to a weather or natural catastrophic event is likely to be industry wide, although a failure to plan can sometimes turn an industry-wide shock into a company-specific crisis. The longer-term 'slow burn' risks are not likely to trip an individual company up unless there is a lack of recognition that a crisis is happening.

GLOBAL EXAMPLE

Lessons learnt from Hurricane or 'Superstorm' Sandy, 2012

Hurricane Sandy is an interesting example that can be associated with climate change. The hurricane called 'Superstorm Sandy' caused an estimated $70 billion in damage and killed 233 people across eight countries. It flooded downtown Manhattan and caused major disruption to transportation.

Organizations spend a lot of senior management time and money creating their business continuity plans. In this example, however, many of the plans did not respond adequately as they had not factored in such an extreme event. It was more difficult to find alternative office space to accommodate staff than the plans envisaged and there were associated issues with IT connectivity.

GLOBAL EXAMPLE

Hurricane Katrina, 2005

Hurricane Katrina in 2005 was the third most intense US storm at the time, but the costliest with total property damage that was estimated at $108 billion. The event helped to change the way businesses and governments manage disasters arising from natural catastrophe events and climate change.

The event highlighted the important of crisis management in building operational resilience.

The main reason why the storm caused so much destruction along the Gulf Coast from central Florida to Texas was due to the storm surge and levee failure. The hurricane surge forces breached protective levees in New Orleans and resulted in catastrophic flooding in the City and 1.3 million residents of the greater New Orleans metropolitan area were evacuated. The main causes and consequences are illustrated in Figure 6.9.

FIGURE 6.9 2005: Katrina – common causes and impact on ERM

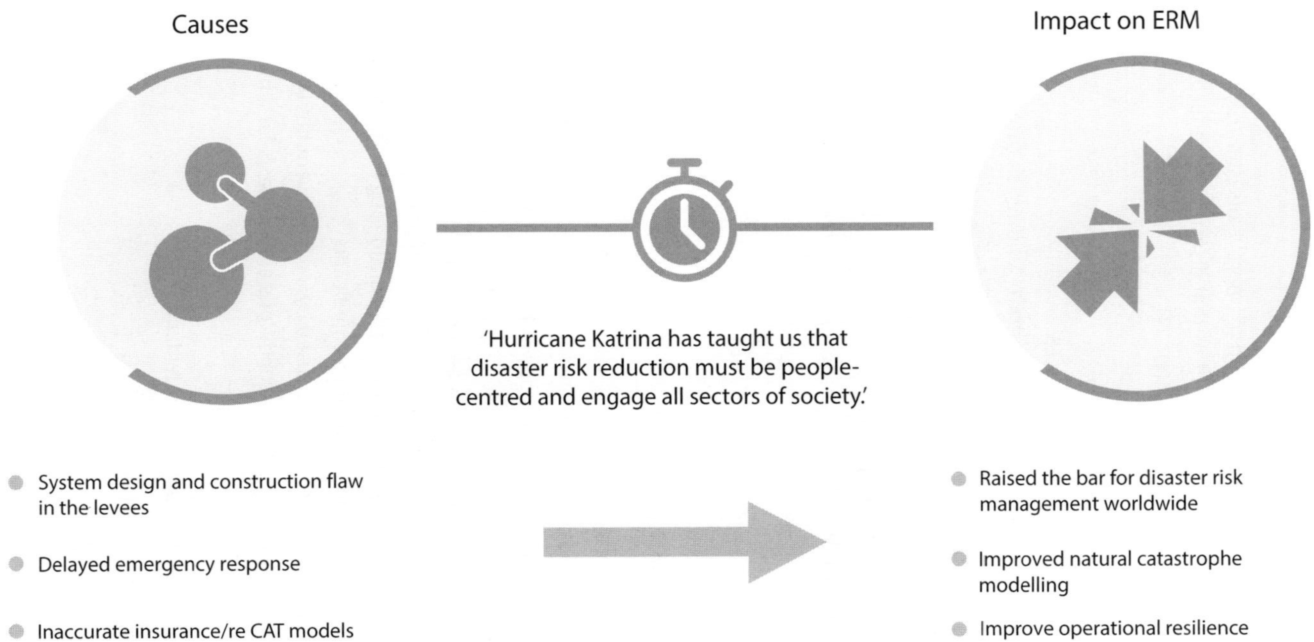

SOURCE © OneRisk Consulting. All rights reserved, 2022

Criticism focused on the delayed response to the flooding of New Orleans, and the subsequent state of chaos. The emergency evacuation order was left until 19 hours before landfall, which led to the deaths of hundreds of people who could not find any way out of the city.

This incident ultimately led to the need to improve disaster risk management worldwide. Hurricane Katrina has taught us that disaster risk reduction must be people-centred and engage all sectors of society.

6.6.1.2 MANAGING CONNECTED EXTREMES

An emerging topic in the discussion of climate change is the concept of compounded or connected extremes. We explore this here as it is relevant when considering the risks across the various approaches to climate resilience.

Combinations of extreme events are often termed 'connected', to convey the complexity of interacting physical and societal mechanisms that cause their impacts to be amplified relative to the impacts from those same events occurring separately.

EXAMPLE

Climate change and blackouts

One of the major risks facing many organizations, particularly the power industry sector, is 'blackout' with an outage of say, more than 10 hours, which can be perceived to be a 'catastrophic event'. While short-term power blackouts are experienced frequently on a local or regional level around the world (e.g. caused by natural catastrophe events like storms, floods or heatwaves), societies are not familiar with large-scale, long-lasting, disruptive power blackouts. Traditional scenarios assume blackouts for only a few days and losses seem to be moderate, but if we are considering longer-lasting blackouts, the impact on society and economy might be significant.

Typically, power blackouts are not caused by a single event but by a combination of several deficiencies. The following preconditions are the basis for a higher power-outage risk:

- High grid utilization or high power demand
- High power plant utilization
- Multiple power line failures
- Defects due to material ageing

FIGURE 6.10 Causes of blackouts

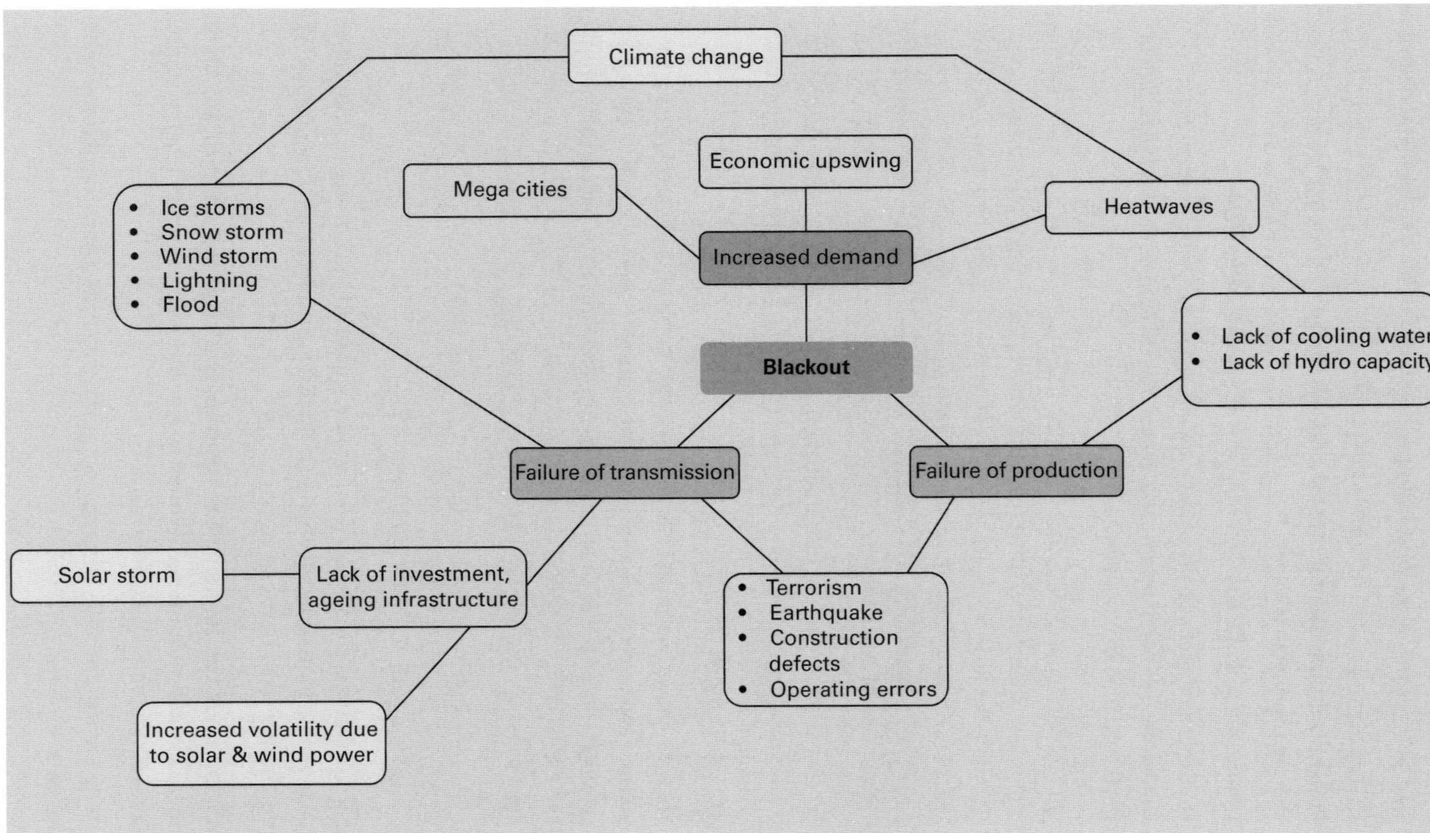

SOURCE OneRisk Consulting

If the following events occur in combination with the above-mentioned conditions there is a very high likelihood of a power blackout occurring that can be linked to climate change, such as:

- Power plant shutdown for revision or due to supply failures (e.g. cooling water shortage during heat waves)
- Unforeseen simultaneous interruptions of several power plants
- Sudden simultaneous high power demand (e.g. simultaneous usage of air conditioners during hot summers, power line collapse or electrical equipment breakdown due to natural hazards)

Figure 6.10 flags how climate change can be a key factor in this and how connected extremes can add to the existing risks and amplify the impact. The challenge now is not only limiting the further impact people have on the atmosphere but also adapting to and tackling the extremes we are already facing.

Consequences of blackouts

Direct costs of blackouts are lost production, idle labour and facilities, damage to electronic data, spoiled food and damaged products, damage to equipment, or customer refunds. Indirect costs are looting, accidental injuries, legal costs or loss of water supply. In general, indirect costs exceed direct ones by up to five times.

The well-known 'Northeast blackout of 2003' in the US and Canada that affected 55 million people seems to have caused the highest economic loss ever during an outage, with an estimated total cost between $4billion and $8 billion. But even short blackouts, which occur several times during a year in the EU, add up to an annual economic loss of between $104 billion and $164 billion.

6.6.2 Supply chain risk management

Interruptions to supply chains are regular and costly occurrences. Climate change is likely to make managing global supply disruptions more challenging. The main climate change risks that can impact supply chain include:

- An increase in the frequency, magnitude and scope of acute supply chain disruptions. This will require companies to invest more time and money in their supply chain risk management programmes.
- It will create chronic changes to supply chains that companies will need to adapt to.
- It will create new types of risks that have not typically been addressed by supply chain risk management programmes.

In seeking to improve supply chain resilience to manage climate change risks it is important to incorporate climate change risks as part of the supply chain risk management strategy. The main risks that organizations need to address include:

- Lack of available supply
- Delay of supply
- Lower quality of supply
- Increased cost of production

The consequences can lead to serious repercussions for an organization's reputation, cash flow and revenue.

In terms of solutions The Sustainability Consortium in conjunction with HSBC state in their report that 'a company has two strategies to enhance supply chain resilience: bridging and buffering. Bridging strategies enhance the capability of a supplier to withstand risk events and recover more quickly from a disruption... Buffering strategies protect the company from inevitable supplier failures and supply disruptions.'[12]

In terms of specific mitigation strategies:

- **Bridging strategies** – Bridging strategies should seek to engage in collaborative planning and control with suppliers, providing suppliers with financial support and developing strong supplier relationships.
- **Buffering strategies** – Companies can use inventory buffers, lead time buffers, capacity buffers, liability buffers and cost buffers to make their supply chain more resilient. A supply chain organization can also intentionally work to develop the culture, processes and discipline of a high-reliability organization to provide the foundation for a resilient supply chain. Attention to climate change risks will not only make the company's supply chain more resilient but may make the company more attractive to its employees, customers and investors.
- **De-risking the supply chain** – With respect to concentration of exposure, consider de-risking the supply chain by re-engineering where possible, managing risk and assessing the role of contracts and agreements as a tool for risk management. This can include removing dependencies on sole suppliers or multiple suppliers based in the same geographical region.

6.6.2.1 INTERCONNECTED SECONDARY RISKS FOR SUPPLY CHAINS

An emerging topic in the discussion of climate change is the concept of compounded or connected extremes. Much has been written on the concerns around multiple large-scale disasters happening concurrently that put major strain on governmental agencies, emergency managers and the insurance industry in responding to these events in real-time.

What have become more prevalent are the secondary or tertiary effects seen across the commercial sector. The most obvious effects to the commercial sector due to climate change come via the global supply chain. Many of these effects have already been observed and are likely to occur with increased frequency if strategic planning is not done to limit disruptions in the future. There are multiple components to how supply chains can be disrupted by climate change:

1. More intense events damage critical infrastructure to minimize shipping avenues
2. Direct damage to manufacturing facilities or equipment
3. Reduction in employee productivity
4. Increased market prices for labour, energy and logistics (such as transport)

6.6.2.2 GLOBAL EVENTS IMPACTING SUPPLY CHAINS – THAILAND FLOODS 2011

In Thailand, floods in 2011 resulted in a total of 815 deaths and 13.6 million people being affected. 65 of Thailand's 76 provinces were declared flood disaster zones, and over 20,000 square kilometres (7,700 square miles) of farmland was damaged.[13]

The World Bank estimated $46.5 billion in economic damages and losses due to flooding, as of 1 December 2011.[14] Most of this was due to the manufacturing industry, as seven major industrial estates were inundated by water as much as 3 metres (10 feet) deep during the floods.[15] Disruptions to manufacturing supply chains affected regional automobile production and caused a global shortage of hard disk drives, which lasted throughout 2012.

The World Bank's estimate for this disaster meant at the time that it ranked as the world's fourth costliest disaster as of 2011, surpassed only by the 2011 Tōhoku earthquake and tsunami in Japan, the Great Hanshin earthquake in 1995 Hurricane Katrina in 2005.[16]

The Thailand floods helped propel flood risk to the top of the policy and business agenda in Asia and other parts of the world. It has provided more focus on enhancing relevant infrastructure, expertise and data capabilities.

6.6.2.3 ALIGNMENT WITH FINANCIAL RESILIENCE

Section 6.7 provides more details of how an organization can develop financial resilience. In managing supply chain risks it is important to recognize that an organization can also improve existing supply chain processes and procurement operations through risk transfer solutions.

Organizations should consider traditional and non-traditional solutions such as self-insurance through captive insurance company and innovative insurance solutions such as parametric or index solutions that can provide protection against business interruption and contingent business interruption exposures.

CASE STUDY

Skyline Partners: Heat stress solution for livestock

Hot summers have negative impacts on dairy herds and, in aggregate, on the short- and long-term output of the dairy industry. This problem is worsening not only due to global average temperature increases, but also due to intensive selection for production among dairy herds in temperate climates.[17]

In conjunction with SCOR and ITK, Skyline Partners have developed a parametric product that aims at mitigating this ever-growing concern, thanks to a specifically designed heat stress index, taking the best of the scientific literature on the matter.

This innovative parametric insurance solution allows farmers and companies involved in the dairy supply chain to protect themselves against all economic losses related to heat stress, including:

- Milk yield loss
- Quality losses due to loss in protein and fat content impacting price
- Increase in operating costs such as additive feed and ventilation, etc

Moreover, it can also provide protection against intangibles such as loss of reputation and long-term health-related losses through protection against short-term (lower production, reduced quality) and long-term (chronic effects on animal health) perils of heat stress.

The solution involves the automatic collection of third-party weather data at a granular level, and a calibration of the triggers to align with farming practices and their estimated economic losses. The compensation for farmers is triggered at the end of the season, where applicable.

FIGURE 6.11 INSDEX visual data

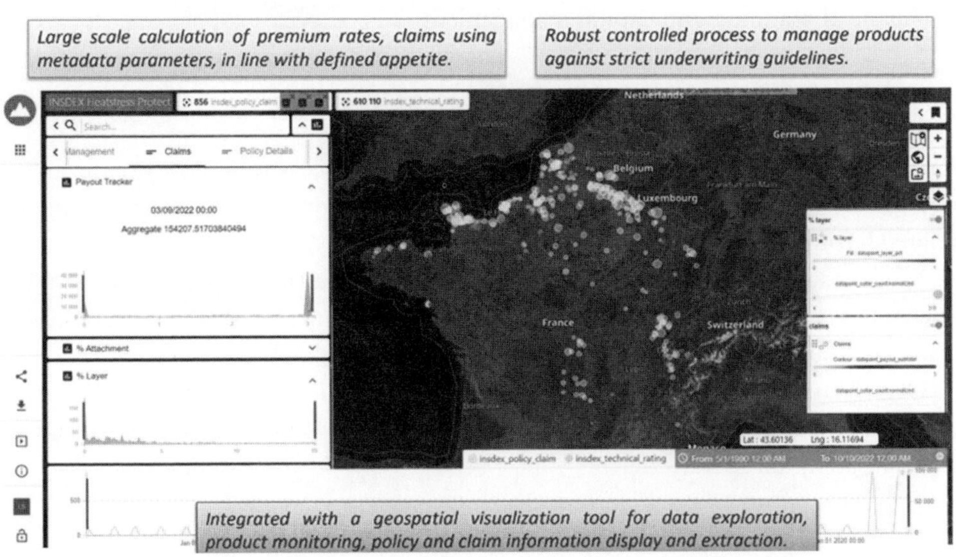

Both the terms of the guarantee and the compensations are automatically calculated using Skyline Partners' INSDEX® parametric calculation engine, allowing for at-scale deployment while preserving the local link between conditions and payout for individual farms.

6.6.3 Incident reporting

Reflecting and learning from an incident or event after it has occurred is essential to building a resilient organization. Utilizing the experience to build understanding, skills and capabilities should significantly enhance the ability of the firm to respond to future events. The key to understanding an incident is some form of root cause analysis using techniques like the bow tie approach described earlier. If properly executed and considered the responses to one incident may well improve control over several other similar incidents. The art is to be open to the underlying root causes and aim to avoid overly defensive responses or creating any sense of blame for an event. To run an effective root cause analysis requires everyone to be open to discuss the event with as little emotion as possible. The success is to define strategies to avoid such incidents in the future.

6.7. Building financial resilience

As discussed in section 6.2.2, key components or control mechanisms that are covered in this chapter include:

- Risk financing
- Strategic insurance risk gap analysis
- Financial planning and capital management

6.7.1 Risk financing

Financing of risk using an insurance company is a process that most organizations undertake and insurance is a useful tool for dealing with the financing of climate-related hazard risks such as flood, to protect property.

While insurance provides a near perfect hedge against the financial effect of a loss covered by a policy, by protecting a policyholder's balance sheet and its revenues, it also brings an additional contingent risk – the credit risk of the insurers.

Organizations need to optimize their risk transfer decisions between risk retention and risk transfer in terms of cost of risk and volatility, for example to contain external premium spend.

Consequently risk-financing programmes should consider the following features, which will vary dependent on the size and risks faced by the organization.

- Local policy deductibles sufficient to energize subsidiaries in risk management matters but not large enough to threaten stability or demotivate local management.
- Establishing a self-retained layer commensurate with the consolidated organization's risk appetite/tolerance.
- Establishing a captive insurance company that bridges the gap between the risk tolerance of subsidiaries and the attachment point of insurance with third-party insurers. Captives can play a key role in building up surplus funds to pay for more catastrophic risks such as hurricanes, as they help organizations reduce cash flow volatility and decrease budget uncertainty.

The next chapter discusses how climate data can be used to model and finance climate risks, including some innovative new solutions using parametric index and financial hedging solutions.

6.7.2 Strategic insurance risk gap analysis

Section 6.5 set out the importance of building out climate scenario descriptions that relate to physical climate risks.

Once the threats and scenarios have been identified a risk mapping exercise can be undertaken to both existing insurance coverage and against alternative or new coverage. The main objective of the exercise is to determine whether there are any gaps in coverage when mapped against the business processes and activities of the organization.

The focus of the deliverables is to align the core activities of each area of the business with the coverage availability.

This strategic exercise or internal project should ideally be undertaken with support from technical insurance experts to review the insurability of the scenarios. The review should take into consideration:

- Existing insurance policies
- Potential coverage extensions
- Alternative insurance policies including new insurance products

Once the insurability options are exhausted, the scenarios are considered uninsurable and alternative risk mitigation solutions are then required. This process allows an organization to support the justification for buying insurance, including new types of insurance, and a better understanding of the financial and reputational benefits of risk transfer. This process can also support:

- Ability to assess the impact of an event across multiple jurisdictions and business functions

- Improving the internal risk registers
- Improved communication and leverage of the ERM internal function

The methodology can be used to focus on specific areas of risk such as supply chain risks.

Typically, it is best to undertake this process using a gap analysis comparing the risks against coverage availability across the businesses and develop an RAG status that will lead to recommendations to the organization with regard to prioritizing its cost of risk spend.

Ultimately this process is an important risk management tool that can help assess and understand what risks are insured, uninsured and uninsurable. It addresses the question of mapping the risks aligned to an organization's insurance policies and against the threats in the organization and therefore is very effective in the context of climate change risk.

6.7.3 Financial planning and capital management

Financial planning and capital management ensures the organization has the cash and capital needed to support both the short-term liquidity demands of the business plus any longer-term capital demands that may be placed on the business. Ensuring this is in place increases flexibility in the event of a resilience demand, ensuring the predicted/known liabilities can be met. This is particularly important where you have customers dependent on the cash being available to support them, like financial services, or where the business is dependent on a functioning supply chain.

These activities may utilize a wide range of the tools listed within this chapter and some covered elsewhere. Understanding your climate resilience abilities will help, as will using stress and scenario testing to draw out the key sensitivities. Formal capital modelling is employed within financial services and so a form of modelling may be useful for your organization. In financial services this is all about modelling the future assets and liabilities so the right funds are available at the right time in line with expected customer demands.

Many regulators of financial services companies have issued rules on capital management and operational resilience.

The primary resilience mechanism utilized by the financial regulators is to set capital rules that are risk-based and run specific scenarios to test firms' own resilience and the financial markets' resilience. Solvency II regulations are in place for insurers and BASEL III regulations for banks, which provide detailed guidance for managing the solvency of the organization. Annual stress testing is run by the regulator with scenarios specific to each industry. The UK regulators recently ran their Climate Biennial Exploratory Stress Test (CBES). Other financial regulators are running similar tests. These tests have been insightful into the ramifications of climate change on asset values and how physical risks may manifest. Their design can be a helpful source for others consider the design of their own climate resilience tests.

One key part of Solvency II is the Own Risk and Capital Assessment (ORSA) process. This regulatory driven process defines how the evaluation of risk in the capital planning process is performed. It results in a formal report that brings together the understanding of the risks facing the organization and how the capital assessment ensures adequate coverage of these risks. The process and reporting are a useful part of presenting the current and future status of how the organization is improving its control environment to provide greater resilience to climate change. Climate change risk needs to be a key consideration within this process, either being considered as a 'stand-alone' risk or integrated into the organization's existing principal risks as appropriate.

Conclusion

Organizations are increasingly hard-pressed to remain agile in today's environment and need to understand both their current and possible future risk exposures, including the influence of climate change. It is increasingly important to anticipate key events from emerging trends, constantly adapt to change and rapidly bounce back from adversity.

It is important to first understand the context of what is meant by resilience to the organization and then to consider what existing or new risk mitigation plans can be designed to help improve resilience to climate change.

It is clear that management need to prepare better for global systemic events and have fully prepared agile contingency plans in place for such events.

Businesses ultimately need to understand their exposure to climate conditions and translate these to specific scenarios that can have an impact on the business from an operational, financial or strategic perspective. It is important to consider the range of scenarios and articulate them.

As companies deal with physical changes and a transition to a more sustainable business, they need to align the impacts of climate change to balance sheet solutions that can reduce volatility. Climate change requires a forward-looking approach and the assessment of the 'more intangible' transition risks.

This chapter has highlighted the need for risk management to be more fully integrated into the DNA of the business, elevated as a critical process that supports both strategy and financial planning.

Notes

1 Aon. 2021 Weather, Climate and Catastrophe Insight, 2021. www.aon.com/weather-climate-catastrophe/index.html (archived at https://perma.cc/357W-JCWL)

2 United Nations General Assembly. Report of the open-ended intergovernmental expert working group on indicators and terminology relating to disaster risk reduction, 2016. www.preventionweb.net/files/50683_oiewgreportenglish.pdf (archived at https://perma.cc/W2AL-KMW7)

3 J M Murphy et al. UK Climate Projections Science Report: Climate change projections, 2009. http://cedadocs.ceda.ac.uk/1320/1/climate_projections_full_report.pdf (archived at https://perma.cc/F4HQ-FRVR)

4 P Walsh. Operational and technological resilience, Treliant, 23 March 2022, www.treliant.com/knowledge-center/operational-and-technological-resilience/ (archived at https://perma.cc/6D9M-C3VK)

5 Abacela. SOU professor says climate change impacts wine-making, Abacela.com, 29 January 2022, www.abacela.com/blog/SOU-professor-says-climate-change-impacts-wine-making (archived at https://perma.cc/944L-FBAS)

6 Thanasis Chasapis, Southern Water

7 HM Government. UK Climate Change Risk Assessment 2017, January 2017. https://assets.publishing.service.gov.uk/government/uploads/system/uploads/attachment_data/file/584281/uk-climate-change-risk-assess-2017.pdf (archived at https://perma.cc/XWB9-N6XL)

8 HM Treasury. The Green Book: Central Government Guidance on appraisal and evaluation, 2022. https://assets.publishing.service.gov.uk/government/uploads/system/uploads/attachment_data/file/1063330/Green_Book_2022.pdf (archived at https://perma.cc/6M97-CJNX)

9 GOV.UK. Guidance: The Green Book. 2022. www.gov.uk/government/publications/the-green-book-appraisal-and-evaluation-in-central-governent/the-green-book-2020#a5-uncertainty-optimism-bias-and-risk (archived at https://perma.cc/K665-B867)

10 Climate Just. BACLIAT, nd. www.climatejust.org.uk/resources/bacliat (archived at https://perma.cc/ZG47-HL2T)

11 BSI Group. Adapting to Climate Change using your Business Continuity Management System, Smart Guide, nd. www.bsigroup.com/localfiles/en-gb/iso-22301/resources/bsi-sustainability-report-adapting-to-climate-change-using-your-business-continuity-management-system-uk-en.pdf (archived at https://perma.cc/449U-C35E)

12 C Slay and K Dooley. Improving Supply Chain Resilience to Manage Climate Change Risks, 2020. The Sustainability Consortium/HSBC. https://sustainabilityconsortium.org/download/35952/ (archived at https://perma.cc/AZZ7-G7V4)

13 Wikipedia. 2011 Thailand floods. https://en.wikipedia.org/wiki/2011_Thailand_floods#cite_note-EOC_report_17_Jan-1 (archived at https://perma.cc/FT3V-QCTH)

14 The World Bank. The World Bank supports Thailand's post-floods recovery effort, 13 December 2011, www.worldbank.org/en/news/feature/2011/12/13/world-bank-supports-thailands-post-floods-recovery-effort (archived at https://perma.cc/23Z4-TAL4)

15 S Mydans. Thai Prime Minister to take command of flood control efforts, New York Times, 21 October 2011, www.nytimes.com/2011/10/22/world/asia/bangkok-opens-floodgates-as-government-response-is-criticized.html#:~:text=BANGKOK%20%E2%80%94%20Prime%20Minister%20Yingluck%20Shinawatra (archived at https://perma.cc/6GHD-8ULD)

16 Accuweather. Top 5 most expensive natural disasters in history, Accuweather.com, 30 March 2011, www.accuweather.com/en/weather-news/top-5-most-expensive-natural-disasters-in-history/192022 (archived at https://perma.cc/A4UJ-NCG4)

17 O Ravagnolo, I Misztal and G Hoogenboom (2000). Genetic component of heat stress in dairy cattle, development of heat index function, *Journal of Dairy Science*, 2000, 83 (9), pp 2120–5. doi:10.3168/jds.S0022-0302(00)75094-6 (archived at https://perma.cc/LL9U-3JV3)

7

Climate physical risks – data sources, uses and challenges

In this chapter we will provide an overview of climate risk data sources and how they are used to help organizations and businesses in climate-related risk management, with a focus on the opportunities and challenges of how the data and data tools/models can be best used in a changing climate.

The main learning outcomes from this chapter are to:

- Provide an understanding of the climate data value chain in the context of how physical data inputs such as data from weather stations and satellites are used in various tools to support business uses and decision making
- Outline the evolution of climate data, meteorology and climate models focusing on the use of weather stations and satellite data that can be used to determine trends and help predict the future changes of the Earth's climate system
- Understand the importance of the concept of 'climatological normals', which is an important method of identifying changes in global, regional or local climate patterns
- Outline the main global climate data providers (governmental, academic and private) such as NASA and NOAA that provide 'open data' sources
- Appreciate the main uses of climate data including weather forecasting and longer-term climate projections, catastrophe risk modelling and design of index-based insurance solutions
- Provide an overview of how companies are developing historical databases and event sets to help to improve forecasting through techniques such as reanalysis and loss development

With respect to the application of climate data, Chapter 6 provides more practical insights and risk management guidance on how organizations can build and improve resilience to physical threats from climate change.

Chapter 10 provides a more in-depth review of how organizations can design future climate stress and scenario tests to support strategic decisions and business planning.

Introduction

Weather and climate are essential to our own lives and human civilization. In many situations, people tend to mix up these two concepts. It is important to distinguish between them when it comes to risk management. According to the World Meteorological Society, 'The difference between weather and climate is a measure of time. Weather is what conditions of the atmosphere are over a short period of time, and climate is how the atmosphere "behaves" over relatively long periods of time.'[1] In other words, weather is the current atmospheric conditions, which includes parameters such as temperature, rainfall, wind and humidity. Climate is the usual weather conditions based on many years of averaged weather data for a location.

In the context of managing climate change physical risks there will be a range of data requirements for organizations to source, and in this chapter, we will be focusing primarily on climate hazard parameters such as temperature, rainfall and wind. Clearly the data needs to be aligned with the business purpose and use, and for many organizations this is to assist in understanding the current and future projections of mean and volatility of climate statistics to support projections of future demand or supply of products or services.

7.1 Applications of weather and climate data

Weather and climate data are used in a wide range of applications, from public finance, assets management (such as electricity grids and infrastructure) and transport systems, to emergency response, and so on. Weather data are mostly used for short-term planning and emergency responses to specific weather-related risks, e.g. flood events. Climate data are used for longer-term impacts, for example sea-level rise and higher frequency of wind storms in specific areas due to climate change. 'Both private and public sector decision-makers need accessible, credible and relevant climate information to increase resilience to the more intense and frequent weather extremes scientists foresee as a potential consequence of climate change.'[2]

Past assumptions about how the weather and climate will act no longer hold true, which means our ability to make decisions is challenging. Poor decisions can lead to greater risk to property and lives. Risk practitioners need to be aware of the availability and accessibility of climate risk related data within and outside their organizations and understand how to best use the data they can obtain to support improved decision-making for their risk management practices.

7.1.1 Climate data and model risk

One of the common risks that companies are facing is model risk. Most organizations will be aware of the risk of natural catastrophes in the locations in which they operate, as they rely on catastrophe modelling to feed their risk management decision-making.

Most catastrophe (CAT) models are based primarily on historical hazard event sets, not compatible with climate change scenarios. Although a wide range of future hazard event sets are simulated in CAT models, they are more useful for short-term analysis and predictions. They have less applicability when considering longer terms, such as 10–15 years from now, where careful adjustments are needed. Model risk can lead to risk managers being unaware of the likelihood of losses and allow unacceptable concentration of risk to build up.

To avoid this problem, risk managers need to consider:

- What data is available?
- What is it appropriate for?
- Which time period is it appropriate for?
- What should it not be used for?
- What is the veracity of the data?

7.1.2 Evolution of ERM best practices and use of climate data

Enterprise risk management (ERM) as a process today is largely a result of evolution. It has developed incrementally either as a reaction to events or as a result of regulation. Included in this evolution of best practice standards is the assessment and monitoring of both man-made and natural catastrophe events.

In chapter 6, we discussed Hurricane Katrina which was the third most intense US Storm. This impact changed the way businesses and governments manage disasters arising from natural catastrophe events and climate change.[3] The importance of having assessable climate data became a much higher priority.

The insurance industry used catastrophic risk models long before Hurricane Katrina, but Katrina challenged the standards of these models.

Specific learnings from Katrina from a data and modelling perspective were that Katrina as an event challenged the standards and performance of these prevailing models. It called into question the quality of exposure data, how the models were used and their suitability for various business applications. It has ultimately led to improvements in the development, use and interpretation of catastrophe models. The importance of having accessible climate data subsequently became a much higher priority.

Katrina also paved the way for enhancements in the way storm surge and flooding in general is modelled. There is also now much closer scrutiny of the assumptions and science behind natural catastrophic risk models, resulting in better-informed decisions. There is also a greater emphasis on understanding and assessing the 'knock on effects' and interconnectedness of risks following major events that was discussed in more detail in Chapter 6.

However, there is a word of caution here in relation to climate change. Capturing climate data is seen as a significant challenge and models need to develop to capture the changing risk landscape caused by climate change. Model risk is an important consideration for organizations that develop the models and for those that rely on and use models for decision making. These concerns and limitations are explained in more detail in later sections of this chapter.

7.2 Climate data and global projections

One of the main issues facing local, regional and national governments, as well as businesses, is that it is important to factor in climate changes, for example temperature rises, to derive best estimate projections of the future. One of the techniques to do this is to detrend data sets through the use of econometric modelling techniques.

Although we tend to focus on the aggregate impacts of change it is important to better understand the changes in terms of both frequency and severity of climate-related events and the underlying distribution and associated data that can support this understanding.

The importance of climate data and projections were mentioned throughout COP26 to indicate the impact of future global temperatures. The latest climate projections are shown in Figure 7.1.[4] The most comprehensive projections come from the IPCC reports.[5]

Figure 7.1 illustrates the potential timeframes of global warming (April 2022 experts' prediction), a 1.5°C temperature rise is anticipated to happen between 2030 and the early 2050s.

Organizations need to carefully consider the impact of the changing average temperatures and associated volatility and the various knock-on effects. Chapter 9 provides detailed insights into some of the emerging physical climate risk such as extended wildfire seasons, prolonged heatwaves and a discussion on potential future climate 'tipping points'.

FIGURE 7.1 Global temperature projections for reaching 1.5°C

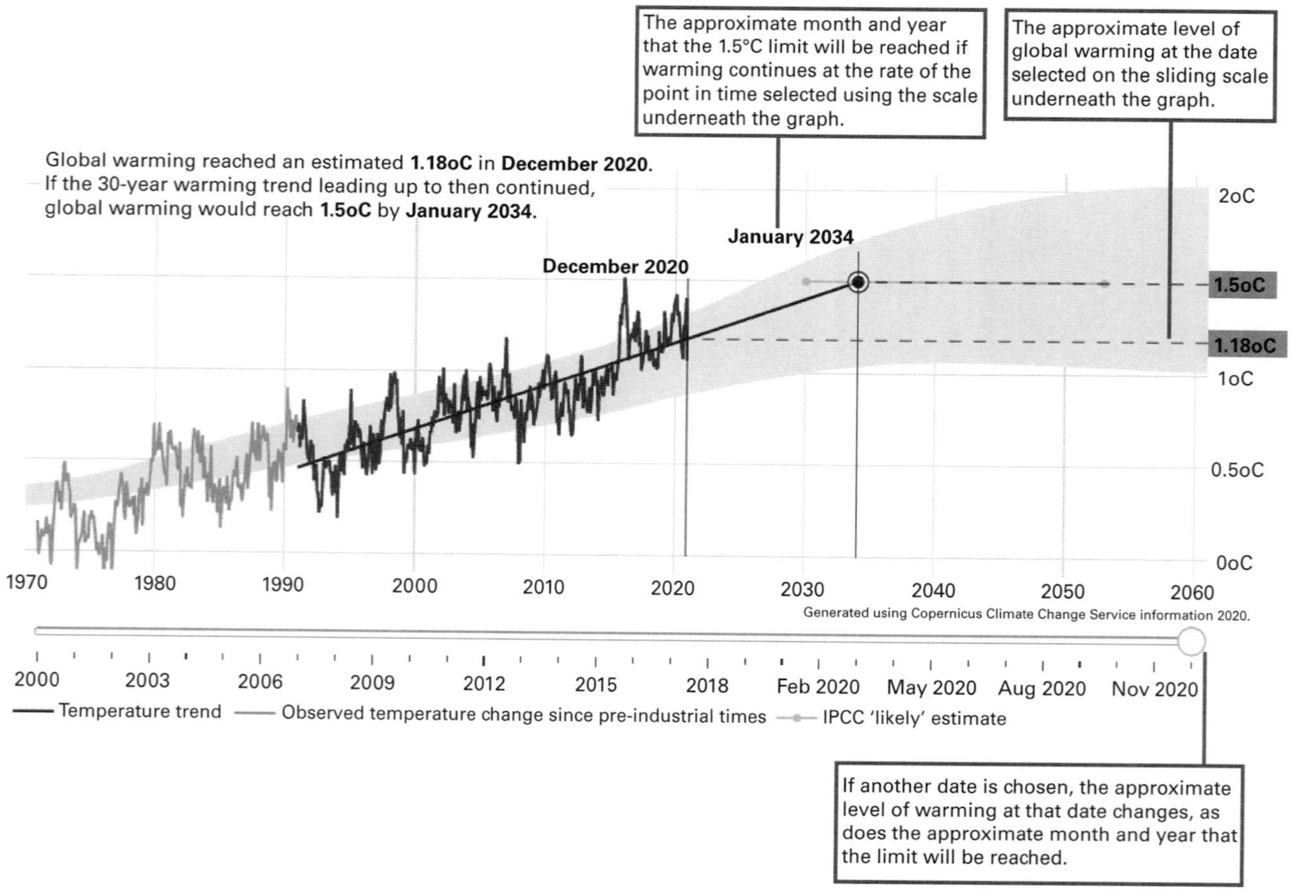

SOURCE Illustration from Copernicus Climate Change Services

7.2.1 UK Met Office – UK Climate Projections 2018 (UKCP18)

There are many sources of climate data and projections. One of the best sources is the UK Climate Projections (UKCP) 2018.[6] The UKCP18 produced by Defra and the Met Office provides the most up-to-date assessment of how the UK climate may change in the future. It forecasts that temperatures and rainfall are likely to increase in the future due to greenhouse gas emitted by human activities. The information available consists of historical observations and future projections for the UK, covering both its land and marine environments. The marine projections, for example, include updated projections of time-average sea level rise around the UK coastline, and new projections of extreme water levels, including storm surges and tides. The UKCP have been developed to support government, businesses and other interested parties to assess the challenges and opportunities that they face from a changing climate. The general climate change trends projected over UK land for the 21st century in UKCP18 is broadly consistent with earlier projections (UKCP09) showing an increased chance of warmer, wetter winters and hotter, drier summers along with an increase in the frequency and intensity of extremes.

Data modellers typically run several thousand future weather simulations, stochastically generating predictions under low, medium and high emissions scenarios, to give a range of estimates. The outputs show the present day, and three different climate scenarios in three future epochs as follows:

- Present-day flood risk
- 2020s – low (RCP 2.6), medium (RCP 6.0) and high (RCP 8.5) emissions scenarios
- 2050s – low (RCP 2.6), medium (RCP 6.0) and high (RCP 8.5) emissions scenarios
- 2080s – low (RCP 2.6), medium (RCP 6.0) and high (RCP 8.5) emissions scenarios

IPCC scenarios based on 'representative concentration pathways' (RCPs) are examples of physical climate change scenarios adopted by the IPCC in its fifth assessment report (AR5).[7] The model results are frequently 'downscaled' to derive potential local-level changes in climate, which are then used to generate scenarios of impacts from climate change (first-order impacts such as flooding or drought, second-order impacts such as loss of crop production and third-order impacts such as famine). RCPs are discussed more in the context of design climate stress and scenarios tests in Chapter 10.

The importance of this type of information is that modelling firms are able to take the information and project low, medium and high emission scenarios, for example for flood models, to support the incremental impacts of climate change. These can then be superimposed on an organization's asset portfolio. This is important when finance is required for an asset. We will discuss this further through use of an example of UK flood modelling using flood-mapping techniques.

Before we discuss the main uses of climate data it is important to recognize how historical natural catastrophe events have helped to shape the risk management profession and enterprise risk management practices. The learning outcomes from them have helped to enhance the use of improved climate data.

Businesses ultimately need to understand their exposure to climate conditions and obtain a range of exposure-related data (e.g. asset valuations across their portfolios, and areas of land where they are exposed to climate risks such as wildfire or heatwaves).

7.3 Evolution of climate data, meteorology and climate models

Climate data and associated climate models and forecasting have evolved significantly in recent decades primarily with the introduction of Earth observation data from satellites in the 1960s.

The first era of meteorological observations started around 1600 when Galileo Galilei constructed a thermoscope. However, as there was no standard measurement at the time they were of little use until the work of Daniel Gabriel Fahrenheit and Anders Celsius in the 18th century.

Figure 7.2 below provides a high-level summary of the evolution of climate data, models and forecasting capabilities.

FIGURE 7.2 Evolution of climate data, models and forecasting capabilities

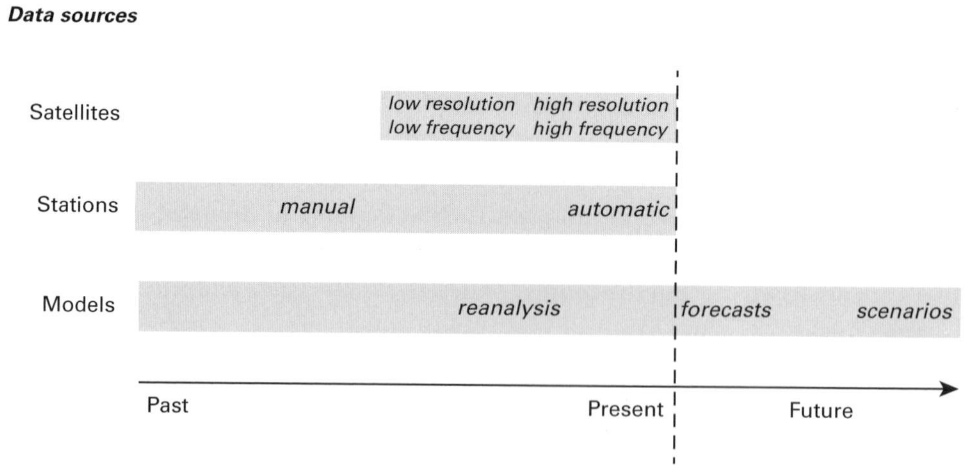

•shading = certainty

7.3.1 *Weather stations*

The Met Office was founded in 1854 under the leadership of Robert FitzRoy. Given his naval background FitzRoy understood the importance of the weather to the lives of those at sea. The Met Office started to collect daily weather data in 1860 at set locations, known as stations, around the British and Irish coasts and sent to the Meteorological Office in London by the new telegraph system, the cutting-edge technology of its day.

This information consisted of pressure, temperature, wind direction and force, cloud amount, weather conditions, for example rain, thunder, fog and sea disturbance for each location.[8] The observations were collated into Daily Weather Reports and these, renamed the Daily Weather Summary from 1980, form the longest continuous series of data in the National Meteorological Archive.

Interestingly, in recent years these early weather observations in the UK from the 1800s have been digitized using a crowdsourced solution led by Reading University though Ed Hawkins.

Weather stations have advanced considerably and are now automated. As defined by Bertrand D Tanner, 'An automated weather station is an integrated system of components that are used to measure, record, and often transmit weather parameters such as temperature, wind speed and direction, solar radiation, and precipitation. Weather stations are used on land and sea for a variety of operational and research purposes.'[9]

7.3.1.1 THE TECHNOLOGY OF WEATHER STATIONS

It is easy to visualize weather data being measured at a weather station where a traditional mercury bulb thermometer measures the temperature of the air, a barometer measures the air pressure, an anemometer measures wind speed and direction, and a rain gauge measures the amount of rainfall.

The technology of weather stations has evolved from requiring human observers to regularly check the instruments and note the readings to current automatic weather stations where the data is continually logged by computer. Alas, the network of such weather stations is not uniform and of a high enough density to allow for a comprehensive view of weather and climate. Globally, there is a paucity of stations in developing countries and where there is a high density currently, that has not always been the case so we have less confidence looking further back in time.

These shortcomings of station observations means that we have to rely on alternative technologies to provide historical data on climate variables across much of the world.

7.3.2 *Weather satellites*

The first successful weather satellite, TIROS-1 (Television Infrared Observation Satellite), was launched on 1 April 1960 from Cape Canaveral, Florida by the

National Aeronautics and Space Administration (NASA) with the participation of the US Army Signal Research and Development Lab, RCA, the US Weather Bureau and the US Naval Photographic Center.

During its 78-day mission, it relayed thousands of pictures showing the structure of large-scale cloud regimes, and proved that satellites can provide useful surveillance of global weather conditions from space. TIROS paved the way for the Nimbus program, whose technology and findings are the heritage of most of the Earth-observing satellites NASA and NOAA (National Oceanic and Atmospheric Administration) that have launched since then. These provide data sources that we will explain in more depth later.

A major breakthrough for these technologies occurred with the satellite era in the late 1970s. For the first time, we had access to sensing technologies that could span wide geographic areas, regularly, and at a fine enough resolution to be able to provide local information. The technology and capabilities have advanced to the extent that today there are coordinated missions providing high-quality, high-resolution data, as well as private enterprises sending satellites into space to measure the Earth's atmosphere.

7.3.3 Models of Earth's climate system

Computer models that solve mathematical equations to predict the future of the Earth's climate are called climate models, and consist of three main types:

- Earth balance models (EBMs)
- Earth models of intermediate complexity (EMICs)
- General circulation models (GCMs)

Climate scientists around the world are contributing to simulation models of the future climate. Their aim is to produce critical information to assist decision makers struggling to plan effectively for the future, but much of their output remains beyond the understanding of end users, thus cannot be integrated into policies. However, the WMO-led Global Framework for Climate Services (GFCS) and its partners are advancing the production of tailored local, regional and national climate information services for users in both public and private sectors.

Through the use of satellites, climate models have evolved that use computers to simulate the Earth's climate system, including the atmosphere, ocean, land and ice. They can be used to recreate the past climate or predict the future climate.

Climate modelling is to some extent just an extension of weather forecasting but focusing on changes over decades rather than hours.

Climate models separate the Earth's ocean, surface and atmosphere into three-dimensional grids of cells in order to solve the equations of motion, fluid dynamics, physics and thermodynamics that govern the evolution of the climate systems. As computing power has increased the grid length (i.e. resolution) has reduced resulting in a more granular simulation, which is particularly beneficial for considering climate impacts which are mostly felt at the local scale.

7.4 The climate data value chain

The climate data value chain is a process of data generation, collection and use, from identifying data needs to its application and potential reuse. Along the process, data value increases. The climate data value chain has five major stages: primary data collection, tools application, actionable information, knowledge and outcomes.

It explains how physical data inputs, for example data from weather stations, are analysed and used in various tools (e.g. catastrophe models), to support business uses. Following this value chain can bring benefits for organizations, such as increasing their shareholder value and meeting stakeholder expectations. Figure 7.3 provides an overview of a climate data value chain.

Figure 7.3 highlights the data value chain from obtaining primary data, through the use of tools that provide actionable information. This leads to knowledge and business uses, which in turn provides outcomes and benefits though improved decision-making. There are many examples of models being used to assess the impact

FIGURE 7.3 Climate data value chain – five key stages

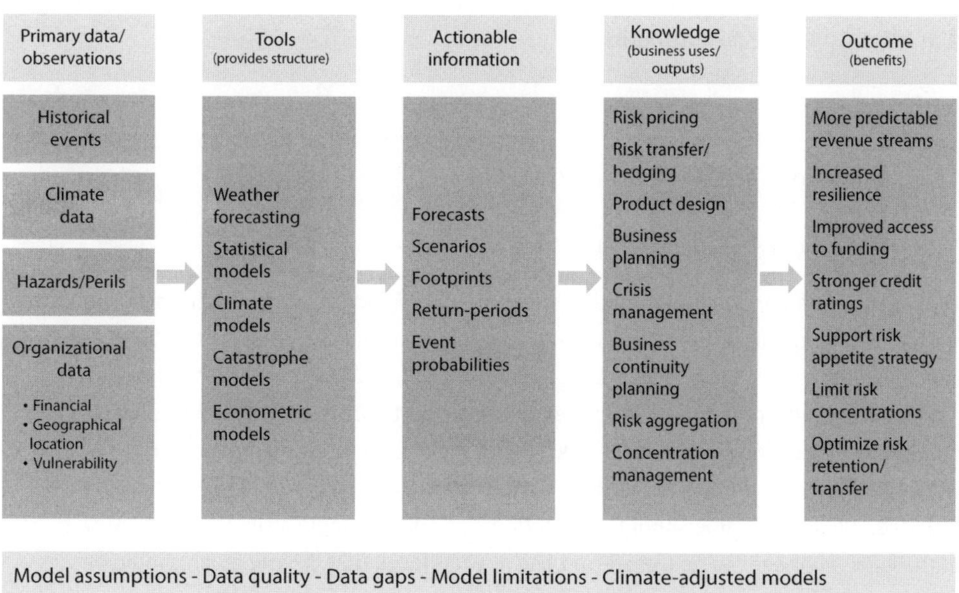

SOURCE © OneRisk Consulting. All rights reserved, 2022

of climate change without providing clear explanation of how the outputs can be used for specific decision-making. We cover this in more detail through various case studies. The list of outcomes is a helpful guide to explain why organizations are undertaking climate risk modelling.

The availability of relevant and high-quality climate data is linked to the evolution of improved ERM and has been an area of focus for organizations for decades. One of the main uses of obtaining data, which still holds true today, is to assist in pricing insurance and capital market solutions to hedge climate risks. This was discussed in the last chapter.

One of the main uses has been the improvement of the calibration and validation of catastrophic risk models. The use of improved quality data to improve their accuracy has led to better disaster risk management and recovery, which we will also explore more in this chapter.

To illustrate the five stages of the value chain, an anonymized case study is provided that explains how an organization can seek to utilize climate data to ultimately improve access to funds and smooth its revenue streams through designing a hedging strategy. The tool used is econometric modelling which is able to produce forecasts of projected revenue aligned to a climate index that could be hedged in the capital markets using underlying temperature data.

It outlines how the climate data value chain can be applied in practice from using primary climate data that can be used to support an organization in building greater financial resilience to climate change. The project highlights some of the key principles that organizations should consider in the context of designing a hedging strategy that aligns with its risk appetite.

CASE STUDY

Hedging a mild winter for a utility company

Background and research problem

The organization had identified that seasonal volatility in temperature, specifically a 'mild winter', was one of their top risks as it impacted on their revenue and profitability. It also had knock-on effects on sales targets that could negatively impact on performance incentives.

The project attempted to address the following questions: How should the company quantify its risk exposure to climate risk? Would they benefit from hedging the risk? What would be the most appropriate hedging solution to the company?' Other considerations included: What time frame should the solution cover, for example a single season? How much of the exposure needs to be transferred and at what level; that is, how much should be retained?

Stage 1: Primary data

The climate data used in the case study was as follows:

- **Daily temperature data** – The organization had its own primary climate data sets from weather stations. The data provided in this case by the utility company was daily temperature data that was based on a composite weather variable (CWV) that the company had developed, which was a function of actual daily temperature, wind speed, effective temperature and seasonal normal effective temperature. The data was provided for over 70 years for over 20 weather stations across the UK.
- **Heating degree days (HDD)** – Heating degree days were provided by an external consultancy specifically in capital market solutions to help price the risk transfer solution against a specified (HDD) index.

Additional exposure information and organizational data included the following:

- **Annual demand and revenue data** – Demand data was provided by the company, which was broken down into load bands aligned to business customers, primarily small and large. The company also provided revenue data.

Through interviews and discussions it was agreed to structure a solution for the period November to March, often termed the 'winter' period in the UK, reflecting the most volatile months in temperature.

In terms of exposure the most volatility was derived from 'small' or household customers and so it was agreed to develop a solution for household customers only.

Stage 2: Tools applied – quantitative analysis and econometric modelling

As well as structured interviews one of the main aspects of the project was to analyse the data sets provided. Given the fact that there was over 70 years' worth of temperature data, a good sample size was provided to assess both the mean and volatility (standard deviation) of temperature for each month. This is shown in Figure 7.4.

From Figure 7.4 we note:

- December appears to have the highest volatility and July the lowest.
- The volatility per month appears higher for the period from October through to April, i.e. around the winter period.

One of the main aspects of the analysis was to use econometric modelling techniques, using software to develop a dynamic regression model to assess the relationship between temperature and demand. This is the equivalent of assessing the relationship between temperature and revenue. The main quantitative analysis included a number of statistical procedures using hypothesis testing, including correlation analysis.

A regression model was developed for a specific data set and detrended to take account of climate change, which would allow the model to predict future revenue more accurately. Some

FIGURE 7.4 Mean and standard deviation for each month (illustrative purposes)

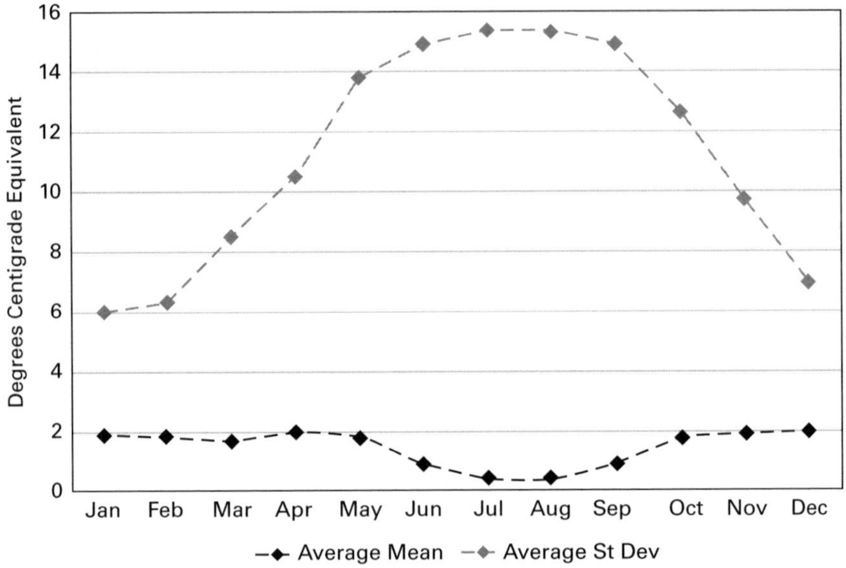

TABLE 7.1 Likelihood and amount of potential lost revenue in future years

Probability Scenario percentile	Likelihood Once in:	Revenue reduction (Volatility measure)	Percentage of revenue
<1%	20,000 years	£50,000,000	20.0%
1%	100 years	£30,000,000	12.0%
2%	50 years	£25,000,000	10.0%
5%	20 years	£20,000,000	8.0%
10%	10 years	£16,000,000	6.0%
20%	5 years	£10,000,000	4.0%

observations included the fact that price is assumed to be fixed, therefore inelastic. There was a statistically significant correlation between temperature volatility and demand.

Stage 3: Actionable information – forecast of revenue reduction

The dynamic regression model outputs were able to predict revenue from the underlying HDD and therefore match the loss of revenue for the company. A simulation model was used to run 20,000 iterations of the likely future HDD index, providing a solid basis upon which to understand the likelihood and amount of potential lost revenue in future years. This is shown in Table 7.1.

The forecast provided some important outputs:

- The worst-case scenario generates a loss of £50 million per annum.
- The likely revenue volatility over a 10-year horizon is more likely to be between £10 million and £16 million (1 in 5 years and 1 in 10 years forecasts).
- The volatility represents up to 20 per cent of small customer revenue during a winter period.

Observation: The level of impact of temperature volatility and climate change was far higher than the company had realized.

Stage 4: Knowledge – business uses – risk transfer solution

The typical winter period as used within the capital markets, namely November to March, has a significantly higher volatility in terms of temperature than over an annual period. This has important repercussions in terms of developing a risk financing solution, as the company needed not to hedge the annual exposure but concentrate on a winter period. In fact, the winter period represented over 80 per cent of the annual volatility and therefore a risk financial structure was developed to hedge the risk in line with the company's risk appetite.

In terms of risk transfer solution, the recommendation was to adopt a symmetrical strategy that was to hedge only the downside in line with the company's risk appetite strategy. The most cost-effective strategy for most companies is to retain a layer of risk within the

FIGURE 7.5 Illustrative impact of a put option strategy on revenues

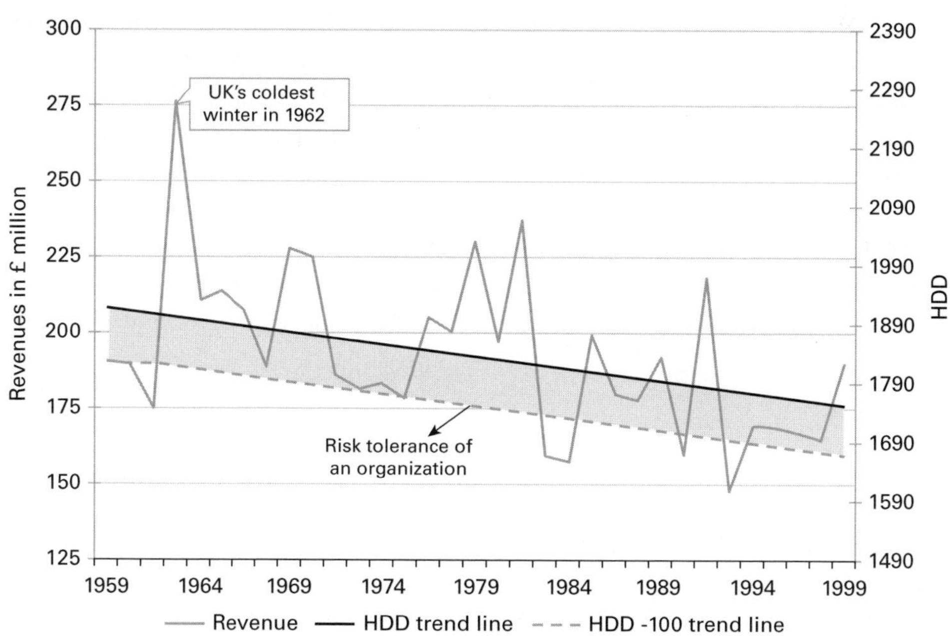

company's risk tolerance and then hedge a layer of risk that would take out the historical peaks.

Quotations were provided for a number of options from the capital markets. Figure 7.5 illustrates the main output of the case study. The dotted line represents the company's risk tolerance (or maximum amount of acceptable volatility) to help smooth its revenue, which equated to 100 HDDs. This was used to set the level of risk transfer to stricture the solution through a put option.

In producing the output, primary consideration had been given to developing a derivative 'put' option solution rather than insurance. However, there are a number of alternatives that the company could have considered, including the use of its own captive insurance company and other derivatives instruments including swaps.

Stage 5: Outcomes – more predictable revenue streams

Alternative option and pricing terms were provided to the company and a historical analysis of the potential payments was illustrated to highlight the value of the structure if the company had purchased the put option, illustrating the strategic benefits of smoothing cash-flow volatility and other associate benefits.

The overriding conclusion at the time of the case study was that the company should give serious consideration to the establishment of a risk-financing solution to hedge its weather exposures due to temperature volatility.

There is now a relatively mature weather risk market and these products can create a more predictable earnings stream, providing lenders with greater comfort and investors with greater returns. Implementing weather risk management techniques is about financial responsibility and it is universally acknowledged that strong results from beneficial weather patterns are not rewarded by the same amount that poor results are punished. Guarding against a mild winter, in particular, would allow the company to focus on its core business.

The use of index (now commonly termed parametric) insurance solutions is growing fast and details are provided in Section 7.9. They are a powerful financial tool, based on the same approach as the case study but that can cover a wider range of risks.

7.5 Main climate data variables, data types and availability

When we think of climate data, we tend to think of those that link to physical risks and hazards. Climate data is a measured parameter or variable that is collected and recorded at weather stations. Short-term climate data is used for weather forecasts whereas a record of climate data over a longer period can be used to build up a picture of climate. The climate data helps to specify the climate of a region and may be used to build up a picture of seasons and determine longer term climate activity.

The most common climate variables include:

- Temperature
- Precipitation (rainfall, snow)
- Wind speed
- Sea-level rise

Other climate variables include pressure, humidity, sunlight and other phenomena such as fog, frost and ice/hail storms. The examples above can be extended to other variables of interest such as changes in glaciers/icecaps, etc.

It is important to use past data that can be used to extrapolate to forecast the future, with the caveat that climate future trends need to be captured in those forecasts. Organizations should seek to use different types of data such as daily, monthly and seasonal data that can be used for decision making.

It is important to provide a brief overview of the evolution of climate data that is based on the development of meteorology and climate science.

The main types of climate data that we have today comes from three main sources:

- Weather station data
- Earth observation data
- Climate projections

Before we discuss these climate data types it is important to provide an overview of the evolution of meteorology and how climate data has developed and is being used.

7.5.1 Other types of climate data

Climate data in the context of managing and mitigating physical risks for organizations should encompass a much broader set of data infrastructure to help manage their exposures. Some of the other main categories include the following:

- Asset-level data (location data, asset-specific area, land surface dynamics)
- Geospatial data (land usage, elevation)
- Environmental data

Climate data that is required for catastrophe models is outlined later, in section 7.8.

7.5.2 Climate data availability and data platforms

There are an increasing number of data platforms available now, providing a good source of climate data. Some organizations have been working on open, transparent data platforms to help provide environmental, climate change and catastrophe risk information to business and wider society, which encourages collaboration and crossover around data and services.

It is also important to distinguish different types of data with respect to sourcing of information types. Figure 7.6 provides a high-level summary of open data, shared data and closed data types.

- **Open data** – This can be used by anyone for any purpose for free.
- **Shared data** – Can be licensed by a data owner for conditional usage by another party. Its users are also most often in the private sector. Data licensing is done on one-to-one contract basis and is often complex.
- **Closed data** – Is not shared outside an organization and may only be used by a single legal owner.

7.5.3 Climatological normal – research provided by Aon Impact Forecasting

An important method of identifying changes in global, regional or local weather/ climate patterns is found in what are known as 'climatological normals'.

Put simply, 'normals' are an average that is computed based on 30 years of daily weather readings. They serve as a point of reference to the climatology of a specific location and are used as a benchmark against present-day weather.

FIGURE 7.6 Open, shared and closed data sources

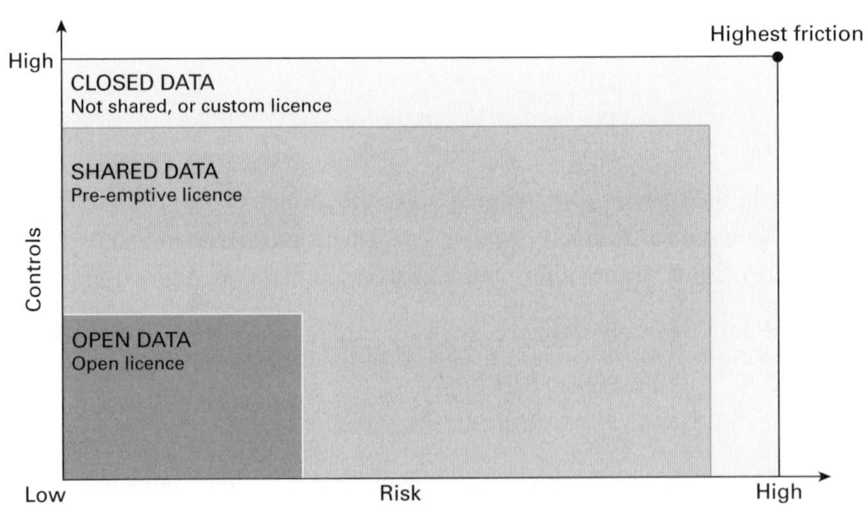

SOURCE IcebreakerOne.org

The World Meteorological Organization (WMO) defines the climatological standard normal as the most recent 30-year period that is updated with the conclusion of every decade. The most recent WMO 30-year baseline – 1991 to 2020 – was enacted in 2021.

Governmental agencies are requested by the WMO to implement and use the current baseline to affirm consistent points of comparison around the world. For modern historical reference periods, the WMO retains the 1961–1990 period as a standard reference for modern-era climate change assessments. The main challenge using the 1961–1990 baseline for climate change is that it does not account for changes to temperature and precipitation since the start of the Industrial Revolution (1850–1900).

Using the 1850–1900 baseline provides a more robust view of how the global climate has accelerated rates of change since carbon dioxide emissions from human activity have dramatically increased. Looking at changes between the two most recent baselines (1981–2010 and 1991–2020) provides useful guidance on how quickly the climate is evolving. It helps identify areas showing climate change effects at a faster or slower pace. In many locations, the rates of change are increasing notably with each passing decade. This highlights the urgency of passing meaningful legislation and developing investment strategic planning to slow down climate change and improve mitigation/adaptation practices.

Decadal changes to climate normals vary by geographical region, season and time frame. Though as already mentioned, some of the more recent trends in normals indicate an accelerated rate of change in the warming of average temperatures.

A NOAA study of the global climate in 2020 found that combined land and ocean temperatures have increased at an average rate of 0.08°C (0.13°F) per decade since 1880. However, this rate of increase has more than doubled to 0.18°C (0.32°F) since 1981.

While extreme heat continues to set new maximum temperature records in recent years, it may come as a surprise to realize that the biggest driver in global warming has resulted from a significant shift in minimum temperatures. This means temperatures are not cooling as much overnight as they did in the past. This is particularly concerning during the warm season, as it inhibits the ability of people and 'stuff' to cool down overnight, putting vulnerable populations at a greater risk for heat-related stress and illness.

Care should be taken when considering regions with dry baseline conditions; relatively small absolute changes appear as large percentage changes here. For example, the Sahara region and the Arabian Peninsula are two areas with the highest observed 'relative' change between climate normals. Figures 7.7 and 7.8 both show climate change impacts that are in relatively good agreement with the long-term climate projections released in the IPCC's Sixth Assessment Report (AR6).

FIGURE 7.7 Global climate impacts of annual average temperature

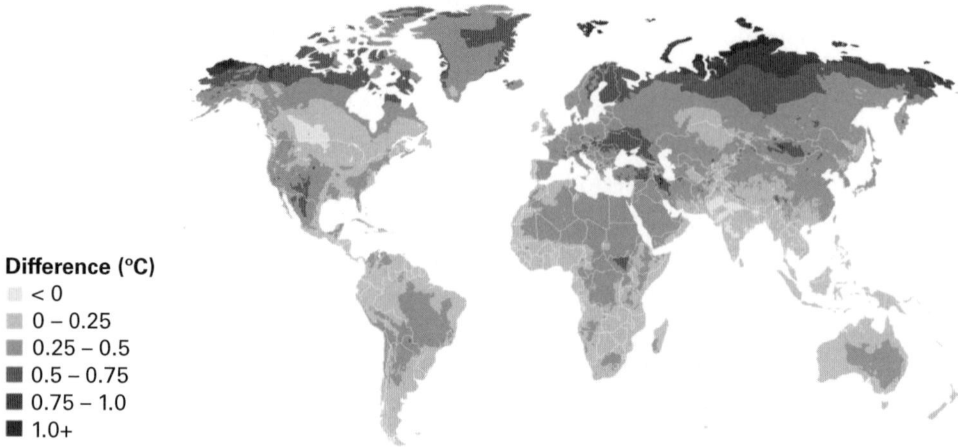

SOURCE Data: ERA5/Copernicus/ECMWF. Graphic: Aon (Catastrophe Insight)

FIGURE 7.8 Global climate impacts of annual precipitation

SOURCE Data: ERA5/Copernicus/ECMWF. Graphic: Aon (Catastrophe Insight)

7.6 Climate data sources

There is a plethora of sources for climate risk data and information. National meteorological agencies, such as the UK Met Office and the National Ocean and Atmospheric Administration (NOAA) in the US, collect weather observations. These run weather and climate models and are, therefore, the primary source of data availability. However, the data is typically provided in raw, un-processed formats and so can be difficult to access and make use of for the non-technical end user. Therefore, data platforms and private enterprises exist and offer easier access to a range of data, in some instances for a commercial fee. Two examples are given below.

EXAMPLE 1

ERA5

The core mission of the European Centre for Medium-Range Weather Forecasts (ECMWF) is to:

- Produce numerical weather forecasts and monitor the Earth system
- Carry out scientific and technical research to improve forecast skill
- Maintain an archive of meteorological data

As part of the Copernicus programme, ECMWF provides access to their fifth-generation reanalysis product, ERA5, which includes hourly estimates of a large number of atmospheric, land and oceanic climate variables. The data cover the Earth on a 30km grid and resolve the atmosphere using 137 levels from the surface up to a height of 80km. ERA5 includes information about uncertainties for all variables at reduced spatial and temporal resolutions.

EXAMPLE 2

Oasis Hub

The Oasis Hub was launched in June 2017 as an aggregator of catastrophe, extreme weather and environmental risk data, tools and services. An example is given in Table 7.2, which highlights commercial data that is available to model various global flood scenarios. There is consistency in methodology that is being applied by aligning, for example, the scenarios with future RCP scenarios. Representative concentration pathway (RCP) is a greenhouse gas concentration (not emissions) trajectory adopted by the Intergovernmental Panel on Climate Change. Four pathways have been selected for climate modelling, which describe different climate futures. The four RCPs are labelled after a possible range of radiative forcing values in the year 2100 relative to pre-industrial values (+2.6, +4.5, +6.0 and +8.5).

TABLE 7.2 Global flood modelling scenarios and commercial data availability via Oasis Hub

Flood					
Commercial Data					
Name	Res.	Scenarios	Release	Processing	Extent
American Flood Hazard	10m	RCP4.5 (2035–2050)	Mid 2020	2–3 Month	USA

(continued)

TABLE 7.2 (Continued)

Flood					
Commercial Data					
Name	Res.	Scenarios	Release	Processing	Extent
Global Flood Hazard Model	90m	RCP4.5 (8.5)	Late 2020	2–3 Month	Global
Climate Indicators & Full CAT model	30m	RCP 2.6/ RCP4.5/RCP8.5	AOR	2–3 Month	Global
Global Storm Surge Model	1.5km	Historical (1979–2018) & RCP 2.6, RCP 4.5 (2070–2100) & RCP 8.5 (2040–2070)	Available		Global
Central & Eastern European Flood Model	Up to 5m	RCP 2.6, 4.5 & 8.5	Requires processing	2–3 Month	Central Europe (Global on req.)
UK Flood	5m	RCP4.5 /RCP8.5/ UKCP18	Available	3–6 Month	UK
European flood hazard risk	25m	All RCPs	On req.	TBC	Europe

SOURCE Oasis Hub

7.6.1 Climate data gaps and reanalysis

Climate model reanalysis is a great solution for filling in gaps in our observation systems while also being able to retrospectively extrapolate to past dates. Reanalysis is a technique of running state-of-the-art weather simulation models for past years and using mathematical data assimilation methods to ensure that the model outputs are consistent with true observations. However, they cannot magic data out of nowhere and so their quality is still dependent on the quality and availability of the true observations that are assimilated.

Models are also useful for providing data on weather variables that have a devastating impact on humanity but the short observational record does not provide us with enough of a sample to make confident risk-based decisions. The most obvious examples are for atmospheric disturbances such as wind storms, tropical cyclones and hurricanes. Here, use of historical information only would provide a precise but overly confident view of the risk (i.e., is the strongest storm recorded in a 50-year historical time series really a 1-in-50-year event?). This shortcoming has led to the development of catastrophe models which, when provided with a set of external conditions, can simulate atmospheric conditions thousands of times.

An obvious shortcoming of using historical data is that it is difficult to make inferences about future climate from it. If you need to understand the origination's exposure to a certain weather variable/event over the next 5–10 years then you need to ask:

- What data should I use?
- How should I use it and what are the limitations?

Climate models are used to provide data on future climates but are typically considered scenarios rather than forecasts because they rely on assumptions about how key climate drivers (e.g. how greenhouse gas concentrations will vary in the coming years). Considering the more immediate timescale, there are seasonal forecast models projected for several months that give an indication of whether we can expect major anomalies.

Equally, from a risk perspective a thorough analysis of historical data for a location will likely give a good indication of expected variability, and trends to date.

7.7 Climate data modelling tools and techniques

It is important for organizations to understand the impact of climate variables in terms of historical variability and future trends.

There are a range of modelling tools that can use climate data, and the use of econometric modelling was discussed in the earlier case study. The following section covers some of the most important modelling techniques:

- Weather forecasting and projections (used by industry sectors)
- Catastrophe risk modelling (used by the insurance sector)
- Parametric climate index solutions
- Climate scenario analysis (will be discussed specifically in Chapter 10)

7.7.1 Weather forecasting and projections

Weather forecasting and climate predictions are central to an understanding of near- and long-term climate events and associated risk and contingency planning. Weather forecasting focuses on shorter-maturity weather events while climate prediction centres on longer-term phenomena. Weather forecasting accuracy has improved considerably over the past few decades. However, it is important to understand the limitations.

FIGURE 7.9 Time and event spectrum of weather forecasting

Forecast category	Time horizon	Typical event
'Nowcast'	<2 hours	Tornado strike
Very short-range forecast	12 hours	Severe storm
Short-range forecast	12–72 hours	Developing cold front
Medium-range forecast	3–10 days	Developing high/low pressure zone
Extended-range climate forecast	1 month	Anticipated rain shortfall
Long-range climate forecast	Season/1–2 years	Deviations in regional temperature range
Climate prediction	2+ years	Developing global warming patterns

SOURCE Element Re – Weather Risk Management

For example, forecasts of droughts are generally better than predicting extreme wind gusts. The location where a tropical cyclone makes landfall can sometimes be predicted days in advance, but sometimes the forecast is not accurate. The exchange of basic observational data is critical for improved weather forecasts and climate services.

Weather forecasting is typically divided into several distinct stages. Very short-term weather forecasting spans 0–12 hours; long-term climate forecasts extend into the seasonal and inter-annual periods. Figure 7.9 provides a good summary of the time and event spectrum of weather forecasting.

EXAMPLE

NOAA – weather forecasting

The National Oceanic and Atmospheric Administration's (NOAA) National Weather Service Forecast Offices and National Centers for Environmental Prediction evaluate the latest observational and numerical data to disseminate outlooks, watches and warnings.

The organization has for over 50 years used climate and related environmental data to provide data services to a range of stakeholders, including the fishing industry.

Weather and climate forecasting services help in areas such as forecasting impending weather hazards such as extreme rainfall, tornadoes, high winds and extreme temperatures. These are provided all year round and the information is critical to resilience building, national security, and the protection of life and property

Challenges and opportunities in weather forecasting

One of the greatest challenges of weather forecasting according to NOAA is the need to improve precipitation forecasts across timescales. As we shift from 'day-to-day' weather to longer-term climate patterns, there is a critical need for improved projections of how the climate will change on more granular, regional scales and over the next several decades.

More accurate climate projections will work to better inform regional and local adaptation and resiliency planning for infrastructure, natural resource management, food production, finance, national security and other sectors.

NOAA is focused, for example, on improving fire weather forecasting as wildfires are influenced by the weather and climate, and equally the weather and climate are influenced by wildfires. One of the key challenges is to be able to improve short-term predictions of fire behaviour and the longer-term modelling of interactions between climate variability, climate change and the likelihood of hazardous wildfire conditions.

7.8 Catastrophe risk modelling

Catastrophe modelling firms were founded in the late 1980s and have developed quite sophisticated approaches, from a single statistical model to more calibrated probabilistic models. The focus has been to build models for earthquake, hurricane and flood models across specific jurisdictions with the latter obviously linked to climate change.

The importance of climate change is that it exposes the future assumptions that lie behind physical catastrophe risk models. This can change the accuracy of predicting catastrophe risk, particularly if the frequency and severity of catastrophic events such as hurricanes, tornadoes, floods, wildfires and windstorms, and other natural disasters continue to increase.

7.8.1 Catastrophe model components

Catastrophe models require substantial amounts of data for model construction and validation, and the main components are set out in Figure 7.10.

FIGURE 7.10 Catastrophe model components – example flood model

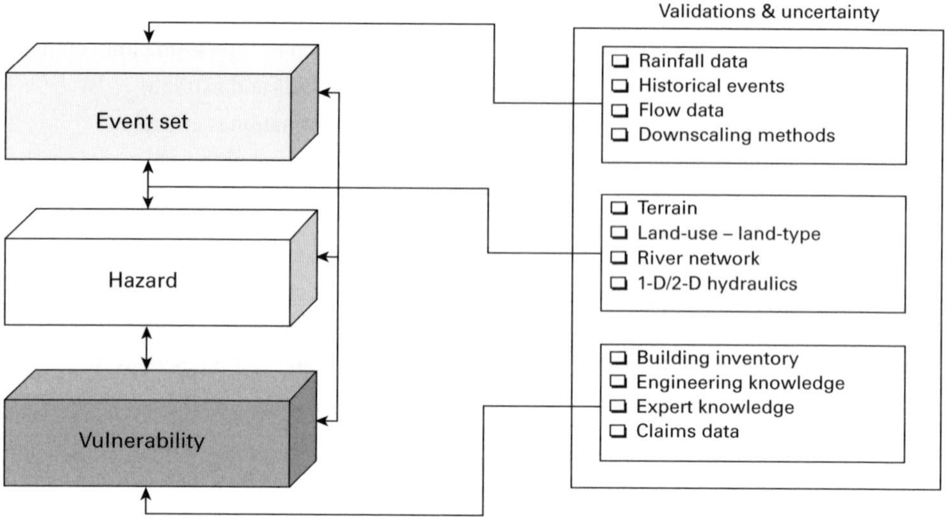

SOURCE OneRisk Consulting

7.8.2 Catastrophe modelling data requirements

Catastrophe models need organizational data inputs as outlined in Figure 7.10. Like most models that rely on the accuracy of the data input, the main organizational input information required includes the following:

- Location
- Types of risk – commercial, residential
- Sums insured by building, contents, loss of profits
- Line of business
- Geographical location – geocode
- Perils, windstorm, flood
- Construction, occupancy, height, age
- Insurance conditions– deductible/limits

7.8.3 Data challenges

For climate events such as flood and windstorm models, these require details such as property location data and other related data linked to construction, occupancy, protection and exposure (COPE). Specific information to improve the models' outputs include construction (age, height, method/material), occupancy and size (floor area). Typically catastrophe models will provide the data inputs that are of most importance. If there is missing information assumptions will have to be made for the models.

The process of geocoding risk locations introduces additional challenges. This often requires the translation of address information into a precise latitude and longitude, for which there are a multitude of approaches that can result in different outcomes.

The concern for risk managers is to recognize the importance of providing accurate data and also to understand how the data assumptions drive the results that in turn would lead to different decisions, such as risk transfer decisions, being made in the organization.

Data issues can lead to under- or over-estimates in the outputs and therefore it is important to focus on providing complete datasets and agree acceptable levels of granularity.

7.8.4 Model vendor providers

There are a number of catastrophe modelling providers listed below, many of which provide products and services to the property and casualty insurance, reinsurance and financial markets globally:

- RMS
- AIR
- EQECAT
- ERN
- EigenPrism
- Aon Impact Forecasting
- Oasis

Proprietary models have also been designed by global insurance brokers such as Willis Towers Watson, Aon and Marsh.

These can be for general or client-specific use, or be part of an integrated catastrophe modelling platform.

The current trend for large organizations is to consider the results from several different models to take into account the different approaches and methodology across vendors and their level of expertise with the specific peril and/or territory.

Some of the main perils that insurers and vendors are focusing on in terms of current and ongoing research include the following:

- Cyclones/typhoons/hurricanes
- Storm surge

- Flooding
- Severe convective storms
- Wildfires
- Extratropical storms

The main focus by the industry has generally been to utilize internal and external sources of information including the most recent climate change assessment reports published by the Intergovernmental Panel on Climate Change (IPCC) as well as peer-reviewed scientific literature that supports the IPCC's view.

Vendors are also seeking to redesign their models to adjust for alternative time horizons and representative concentration pathways (RCPs) to assess the impacts and uncertainties associated with different climate change scenarios.

This helps to shape the degree to which they can then modify their overall view of the risk due to climate change. Most large (re)insurers have a comprehensive methodology for calculating their exposures to climate-related peril risk. This typically would include near-term, intermediate and long-term perspectives on the evolving nature of climate change.

In respect of model risk, insurers plan to update their catastrophe models to accommodate the changing climate, which will often include a road map to consider new and emerging risks such as wildfires and other perils/regions that may need to be incorporated into existing models. We discuss emerging physical risk in Chapter 9.

From a risk perspective, since natural catastrophe related risk exposures are generally underwritten and renewed annually, it affords an opportunity for the insurance industry to regularly re-underwrite and re-price exposures.

7.8.5 Catastrophe modelling outputs and interpretation

Model outputs from catastrophe models will often provide gross and net losses after (re)insurance at different return periods. The outputs will typically provide both occurrence exceedance probability (OEP) and aggregate exceedance probability (AEP) outputs, which represent individual loss and aggregate loss amounts in a single year.

Examples for windstorm and flood outputs are shown in Tables 7.3 and 7.4.

Many organizations use a 1-in-100 or 1-in-200 return period as a base to set risk appetite on a net loss basis for exposures to catastrophe losses (discussed in Chapter 2).

It is important to recognize that the results are often opaque. Understanding the specific loss scenario is challenging; for example, what scenarios *are* a 1-in-100-year event for the organization? Risk managers should seek to understand and interpret

TABLE 7.3 Example catastrophe modelling outputs – windstorm

Windstorm	Gross aggregate	Net aggregate	Gross single loss	Net single loss
10	4,728,000	3,000,000	3,500,000	2,250,000
50	18,000,000	4,500,000	1,600,000	3,000,000
200	43,50,0000	7,000,000	40,000,00	3,250,000
500	63,000,000	9,300,000	60,000,000	3,500,000
1000	77,000,000	1,650,0000	75,000,000	1,500,000
Annual Avg Loss	2,400,000	1,300,000	2,500,000	1,500,000

TABLE 7.4 Example catastrophe modelling outputs – flood

Flood	Gross aggregate	Net aggregate	Gross single loss	Net single loss
10	3,00,000	2,500,000	2,500,000	1,880,000
50	9,00,000	7,300,000	7,300,000	2,600,000
200	18,500,000	16,200,000	16,200,000	3,150,000
500	25,500,000	21,500,000	21,500,000	3,300,000
1000	30,000,000	28,600,000	28,600,000	3,500,000
Annual Avg Loss	1,350,000	1,350,000	1,350,000	900,000

the results and, for example, look to calibrate the results against historical loss events. One technique is to simply look at the largest historical losses, estimate return period for those events and compare them against the model outputs.

Key questions to ask with respect to the tables shown:

- What specific scenario(s) are driving, say, the 1-in-10 and extreme 1-in-200 flood and windstorm events?
- What are the differences in the assumptions that derive the variance in the loss estimates?
- What internal data help to improve the modelled outputs?

It is also important to consider individual loss events of most concern and also multiple events in the same year. Organizations can also seek to supplement the analysis with use of bespoke scenarios, which are covered in Chapter 10.

In terms of uses, it is important to recognize the need to develop appropriate risk management controls to manage the risks, including ongoing management actions and contingency plans.

7.8.6 Climate model risk – research from S&P

Reinsurers have increased their efforts to incorporate climate change in their decision-making process, particularly in risk management, exposure management and pricing.

However, this is still nascent across the industry, and many companies are facing difficulties in implementing climate change considerations robustly. Their scenario analysis suggests that reinsurers' estimates of their exposure to natural catastrophe risk – and therefore physical climate risk – could be underestimated significantly, which could lead to some insolvencies in the future.[10]

While not their base case, this scenario illustrates significant potential for volatility in earnings and capital. Unmodelled risks and the inherent difficulties in attributing extreme events to climate change create the risk that climate change may not be fully reflected in catastrophe modelling, particularly in the short term.

7.9 Parametric index solutions

The last chapter provided an outline of how organizations can build financial resilience to climate change. This section provides details of a growing development of use of parametric or index solutions that can help to transfer risk for specific climate-related hazards.

The parametric market has existed for around 20 years, with an initial major focus on weather risks. However, it is immature with only a few experienced niche providers, risk carriers and buyers (utilities, energy companies, governments) transacting 'over-the-counter' derivatives or large (re)insurance transactions.

With the rise of new datasets, satellites and Internet of Things (IOT) sensors, parametric or index-based insurance solutions are expanding fast and becoming an alternative or, in many cases, the only option to transfer risks to provide organizations with improved resilience. It works particularly well where traditional insurance struggles, such as non-physical property damage related losses.

7.9.1 Parametric insurance vs traditional indemnity insurance

A traditional loss or liability contract insures a policyholder against financial loss, usually within a 12-month period. If a loss occurs, the insurance company is notified, and the loss will be 'adjusted' according to the terms of the policy. Any compensatory payout is determined on an indemnity basis.

Parametric policies are in general for 12 months but can be structured on a multi-year basis: renewable energy products can be for up to 10 years, and natural disaster products up to 3–5 years.

These solutions cover the probability of a defined index exceeding a given loss-correlated trigger (rather than requiring a specific financial loss). They pay out if the index goes beyond the limits that have already been specified. The contract dispenses with the requirement for assessment, adjustment or proving any related expenses.

7.9.2 Structuring a parametric solution

To function in a way that meets a policyholder's requirements, a parametric solution should meet particular criteria (see Figure 7.11):

1. The index and trigger on which the policy hinges should be clearly defined; to construct a parametric solution dependent on the occurrence of a hurricane, policyholder and insurer need an agreed and objective definition of 'hurricane'.
2. The index on which the policy hinges should be objectively measurable; like the above, if a policy is structured to pay out upon a certain amount of rainfall, a method and geography of observation should be agreed upon. Usually this will rely on independent third-party data and monitoring.

FIGURE 7.11 Risk financing solution structuring process

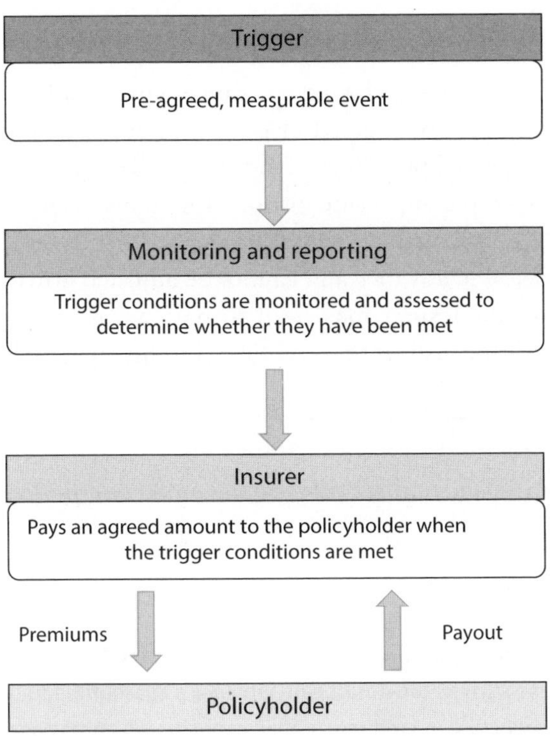

SOURCE OneRisk Consulting

A well-structured parametric solution should:

- Be flexible for the policyholder: the level of optionality in definition of index, trigger, modes of measurement and payout structure allows for bespoke, tailored solutions.
- Provide a seamless transition from event to payout: in obviating the need for loss assessment and potential points of disagreement over loss incurred, parametric solutions allow for faster and smoother realization of payouts based on verifiable and clear-cut triggers.
- Expand insurability: parametric solutions may be appropriate in many cases where traditional insurance is unavailable or prohibitively expensive.

It is worth noting that a trigger need not be a single event or peril; many solutions involve a series of marginal triggers with associated payouts at each threshold. Therefore, trigger points may be based on an accumulation of chronic conditions over a given time frame such as total amount of rainfall or average temperature over one year or say, a summer or winter seasonal period.

The index should also, of course, be independent of the actions of either the insurer or the policyholder – if the index can be influenced by either party, it ceases to be a fair and objective benchmark on which to base a policy.

7.9.3 Payment of claims

When the index diverges from the agreed range, coverage kicks in and payout is determined according to a pre-agreed mechanism. However, premiums for a parametric policy tend to exceed premiums associated with a traditional insurance policy. This is mostly in order to compensate insurers for commensurate benefits offered to policyholders by these policies.

The payout is agreed in advance and cannot be adjusted downwards as a result of loss assessment, and the insurer may need to pay out a range of highly covariant policies almost simultaneously, if they are linked to highly correlated indices.

CASE STUDY

Skyline Partners: Hurricane natural catastrophe protection for loan defaults in the Caribbean

Background

Natural disasters and loan defaults are strongly correlated particularly for financial institutions in highly exposed areas such as the Caribbean, which are susceptible to hurricanes. This is compounded by the reduction in credit insurance capacity, which has been driven by factors such as the Covid-19 crisis.

The Jamaican Co-operative Credit Union League (JCCUL) is relied upon for loans by 100,000 smallholder farmers to cover the cost of essentials, such as seeds, day-old chicks and farming equipment. Farming is the main source of income for around 18 per cent of the Jamaican population. Adverse weather events could lead to farmers being unable to repay their loans, putting the JCCUL's ability to continue to offer financial support at risk.

Actions taken

A collaboration between Howden, the international insurance broker, Skyline Partners and Munich Re has developed a product that protects the JCCUL against non-repayment of micro-loans by farmers in the event of extreme weather.

The insurance product, which is based on a parametric trigger, replaces funds lost as a result of farmers defaulting on loans in the event of an extreme hurricane. This is designed to trigger for the full limit when the hurricane wind field of category 3 and above covers the whole of Jamaica.

The methodology has been developed through dividing Jamaica into tiles to ensure that they are able to accurately pay out the areas that have been affected. The policy also provides protection for hurricanes where the eye doesn't directly hit the island but payment will still be made for any of the resulting hurricane winds (cat 1+) hitting Jamaica (based on the hurricane wind field hitting the various tiles across Jamaica).

Results

The solution comes with dedicated risk visualization software to monitor events to assist the client with the risk awareness and the settlement of claims in line with the policy terms. The tool comes with history of hurricanes since 1850, as well as 10,000 years of simulated (also termed synthetic) storms. This type of solution can be tailored for other natural catastrophe perils, including earthquakes, flood, wildfire and winter storms anywhere in the world.

Parametric solutions offer new ways of protecting against risks that are otherwise not sufficiently covered, and the market is growing significantly.

FIGURE 7.12 Illustration of hurricane wind path in the Caribbean

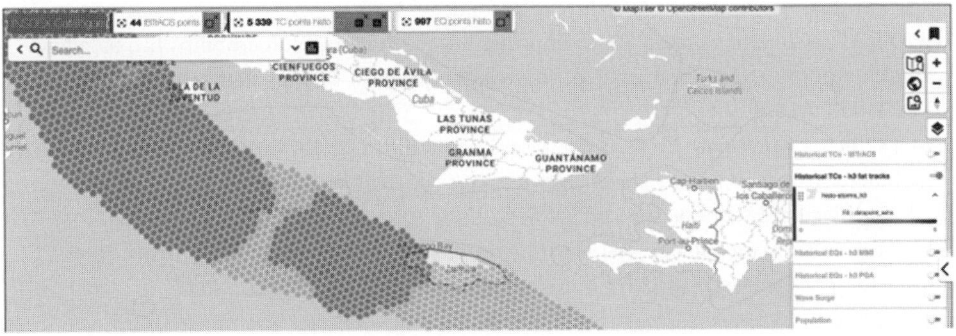

Conclusion

In this chapter we have seen that organizations have always been aware of the weather and, in the longer term, have assumed that the climate in the locations in which they operate will be largely static. This is now changing and the climate in those areas is changing; sometimes beneficially, often with increased threat of damage to life and property.

Over time society has collected many datasets around the weather and what the climate (or the longer-term weather pattern) was in the past. Clearly, climate change is affecting the ability to use these past records to forecast the future. In order to do that, use must be made of models and forecasts, which technology can provide in the form of satellite data, automatic and more detailed weather records, and processing capability to enable multiple iterations of possible outcomes.

From these models we can develop insights into the possible future climate and plan accordingly. This is where we can introduce risk management processes such as mitigating potential losses, avoiding then by relocating, or transferring the financial effects of loss through hedging strategies.

Notes

1 R Gutro. NASA – what's the difference between weather and climate? NASA, 1 February 2005, https://www.nasa.gov/mission_pages/noaa-n/climate/climate_weather.html (archived at https://perma.cc/C5L9-BCKJ)

2 K Bell-Pasht and D Krechowicz. Why does access to good climate data matter? World Meteorological Organization, 2015, https://public.wmo.int/en/resources/bulletin/why-does-access-good-climate-data-matter (archived at https://perma.cc/A4DA-BA38)

3 R Marsooli and N Lin. Numerical modeling of historical storm tides and waves and their interactions along the U.S. East and Gulf Coasts, *Journal of Geophysical Research: Oceans*, 2018, 123 (5), pp 3844–74, doi:10.1029/2017jc013434 (archived at https://perma.cc/D9KR-EFLK)

4 Copernicus Climate Change Services. Global temperature trend monitor, nd. https://cds.climate.copernicus.eu/apps/c3s/app-c3s-global-temperature-trend-monitor?month:float=3&year:float=2022 (archived at https://perma.cc/B2YU-JT92)

5 IPCC. AR6 Climate Change 2022: Impacts, Adaptation and Vulnerability. https://www.ipcc.ch/report/sixth-assessment-report-working-group-ii/ (archived at https://perma.cc/EK7T-VZDA)

6 Met Office. UK Climate Projections: Headline Findings, 2019. https://www.metoffice.gov.uk/binaries/content/assets/metofficegovuk/pdf/research/ukcp/ukcp-headline-findings-v2.pdf (archived at https://perma.cc/FK2W-B747)

7 IPCC. AR5 Climate Change 2014: Mitigation of Climate Change, 2014. https://www.ipcc.ch/report/ar5/wg3/ (archived at https://perma.cc/3EKJ-STMQ)

8 Met Office. Robert FitzRoy and the early Met Office, https://www.metoffice.gov.uk/research/library-and-archive/archive-hidden-treasures/robert-fitzroy (archived at https://perma.cc/MY5Z-RM5E)

9 B D Tanner. Automated weather stations, *Remote Sensing Reviews*, 2009, 5 (1), pp 73–98, doi:10.1080/02757259009532123 (archived at https://perma.cc/MU6F-U6UR)

10 S&P Global Ratings. Global reinsurers grapple with climate change risks, 23 September 2021, https://www.spglobal.com/ratings/en/research/articles/210923-global-reinsurers-grapple-with-climate-change-risks-12116706 (archived at https://perma.cc/KA9A-4GWN)

8

Designing an effective emerging climate risk management process

This chapter will cover the role and design of an emerging risk management process, a key element in the toolkit of the risk function and very important in managing climate-related risks.

The main leaning outcomes from this chapter are to:

- Define and explain the characteristics of emerging risks.
- Explain the process and benefits of having a formal emerging risk management process to support the identification of risk by serving as an early warning system.
- Provide an overview of some of the risk management tools and techniques that can be used to manage emerging risks, focusing on horizon scanning.
- Guide on how to prioritize and make assessments.
- Highlight the challenges in managing emerging risks.
- Discuss treatment options.
- Provide examples of how good reporting can influence senior executive decision-making.

While this chapter focuses on designing an emerging risk management framework that can incorporate climate change, in the next chapter we will explain specific emerging climate trends, issues and challenges, providing details of some specific physical and transition examples as well as interconnected risks.

Introduction

Emerging risk management has become a critical component of enterprise risk management (ERM) in supporting an organization's understanding of its future risk profile, for an organization to have an early warning system in place to improve its

FIGURE 8.1 Examples of emerging risks

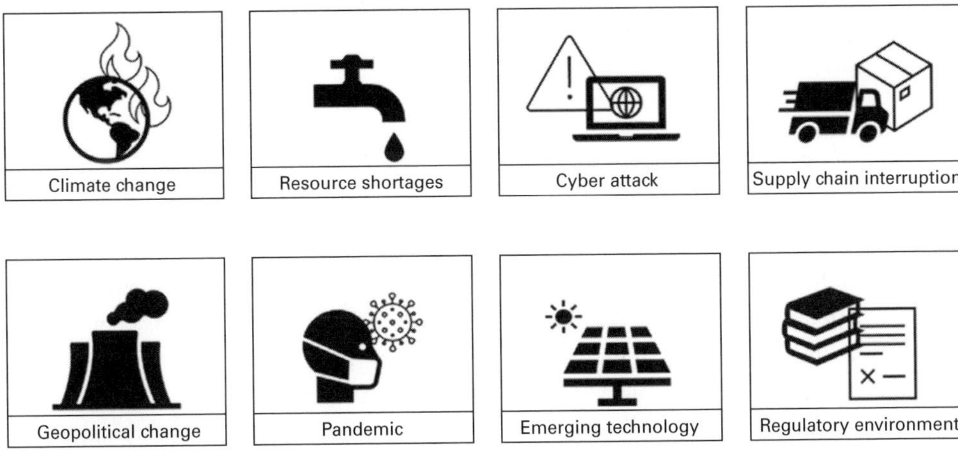

SOURCE OneRisk Consulting

resilience, and to identify any derailers of its corporate strategy. The key word here is 'future' and it can be argued that one of the most important roles of risk managers is to help anticipate the future, to avoid surprises (such as unanticipated earnings volatility) and to prepare for future changes in business strategy in line with the organization's changing risk profile.

Emerging risks can originate from a multitude of sources, are driven by a range of factors and can have both financial and non-financial impacts. They are typically difficult to predict and not fully understood. Figure 8.1 highlights some of the prevailing emerging risk that most organizations have on their emerging risk radars.

If we were to take the quote from Donald Rumsfeld, '… there are known knowns; there are things we know we know. We also know there are known unknowns; that is to say we know there are some things we do not know. But there are also unknown unknowns – the ones we don't know we don't know.'

In risk management parlance, black swans are the 'unknown unknowns' (i.e., risks that may not be on anyone's radar), whereas grey swans are the 'known unknowns' (i.e., risks that may not be well known or fully understood). The art of emerging risk management aims to help organizations manage these black and grey swan events (as and when they occur), while recognizing that the risk may not manifest itself in the precise way originally predicted but possibly in a variant of the emerging risk identified. The essential point here is risk managers need to support their organizations by raising awareness of emerging issues and trends.

Organizations, the ecosystem in which they operate and the risks that need to be managed are becoming increasingly interconnected. Decision makers often have limited time to think about risk on the horizon and so risk managers need to develop a process so that they can pick up the warning signals (while ignoring unnecessary 'noise') that can help translate the emerging issues, and provide improved risk information that can change the focus of management, while also providing advice and guidance on appropriate options.

8.1 Forecasting and the role of risk management

This forward-looking predictive aspect of risk management is well-defined as:

> We are all forecasters. When we think about changing jobs, getting married, buying a home, making an investment, launching a product, or retiring, we decide based on how we expect the future will unfold.... But when big events happen – markets crash, wars loom, leaders tremble – we run to the experts, those in the know.
>
> These experts are often risk managers or chief risk officers of organizations and this is one of the main areas in which risk management creates value.[1]

This illustrates how the identification of future/emerging risks is an area where risk management professionals can add value by collaborating with and enabling management to scan the horizon and to consider what extraneous factors can destabilize the business and prevent it from achieving its strategic objectives.

With respect to climate change, one of the most critical aspects of forecasting is the projection of global temperature, often referred to now as 'future climate pathways', which will be discussed next.

8.1.1 Climate forecasts – United Nations Intergovernmental Panel on Climate Change (IPCC)

The leading authority on climate predictions is the Intergovernmental Panel on Climate Change (IPCC). In July 2001, the IPCC, comprising hundreds of the world's top climate scientists, published a report stating that the planet is warming faster than they had previously predicted, as a result of industrial pollution, and that the human consequences are likely to be catastrophic.

The IPCC's most recent report, issued in 2022, predicts that increases in global mean temperature will range from 1–3°C above 1990 levels, which can lead to beneficial impacts in some regions but primarily harmful ones in others. Net annual costs will increase over time as global temperatures increase. The report, 'Climate Change 2022: Impacts, Adaptation and Vulnerability' provides details of global impacts.[2]

The report states that:

> risks are projected for the near-term (2021–2040), the mid (2041–2060) and long term (2081–2100), at different global warming levels and for pathways that overshoot 1.5°C

global warming level for multiple decades. Complex risks result from multiple climate hazards occurring concurrently, and from multiple risks interacting, compounding overall risk and resulting in risks transmitting through interconnected systems and across regions.

Many climate models attempt to project increases in global mean surface air temperature (SAT) continuing over the 21st century, driven mainly by increases in anthropogenic greenhouse gas concentrations, with the warming proportional to the associated radiative forcing.[3] Climate models were discussed in Chapter 6 and climate pathways and projections will be discussed in detail in the climate scenario section in Chapter 10.

From a risk management perspective, the important issue here is to recognize the fact that these examples represent three alternative but discrete future states or outcomes of the future macro environment. In making projections risk managers need to support the business by making best estimates through, for example, assessing weighted averages of the outcomes that can be accomplished by assigning probabilities to each forecasted future state.

This will ultimately assist in future strategic planning and in a range of business decisions such as improvements to financial reporting (covered in Chapter 12) by making sure, for example, that organizations hold sufficient capital and reserves to account for the impending future levels of anticipated volatility.

8.2 Emerging risk definitions

There are differing views within risk management circles as to the definition of emerging risks. Some simplified views on emerging risks are that they represent 'new risks' or 'events that have not yet happened'. This is true to a point but not entirely accurate.

Some key words that stand out from the many definitions that we cite include unexpected/shock event and trends/changing risk factors. Emerging risk management does not necessarily mean a specific scenario or event but also a trend that is linked to a specific risk. If we take climate change as an example, it is different because it is a known risk that is changing and continually evolving, and it also has a velocity or speed, which we will discuss in more detail later in this chapter.

Leading risk management definitions include one from RIMS (the Risk Management Society, based in the United States):

- Emerging risks are those issues that have not manifested themselves sufficiently to be managed using the tools commonly applied to more developed exposures. They are 'those risks an organization has not yet recognized or those which are known to exist but are not well understood'.[4]

ORIC International states that emerging risks are:

- A material, previously unconsidered or changing risk factor that has the potential to significantly alter the firm's risk profile.

Many definitions have evolved from the insurance industry, given the importance to the industry of managing emerging risks. Munich Reinsurance uses the following definition:

- Emerging risks are either new or developing or changing risks. They include trends as well as potential shock events and are characterized by a high degree of uncertainty in terms of occurrence probability and loss amounts, and with a substantial potential impact on the company's insurance lines and balance sheet.

The following considerations are helpful in establishing whether a risk is emerging or not:[5]

- A risk that did not exist before appears as a result of the emergence of a new technology or a change in lifestyle and/or mode of production.
- The existence of a risk that previously was undetectable is brought to the surface thanks to breakthroughs in scientific knowledge.
- An issue is transformed into a new risk as a result of changes in the perception of society.

A good overall summary of emerging risks comes from Swiss Re: 'We define emerging risks as newly developing or changing risks that are difficult to quantify and could have a major impact on society and industry.'

Swiss Re note in their 2021 SONAR Report that 'New risks do not emerge during times of crisis alone. To regularly profile and think through new or changing risks, and their associated uncertainties, helps build societal preparedness for the future.'[6]

8.2.1 Emerging risk definitions – climate change and global warming

In risk management it is important to make sure that risks are well articulated and this is often a key challenge for risk professionals.

An example of this is that when people refer to climate change they mainly mean global warming, which is more specific in nature (i.e. it refers to a long-term rise in the average temperature of the Earth's climate system). Global warming more specifically relates to worldwide surface temperature increases, while climate change is any regional or global statistically identifiable persistent change in the state of climate which lasts for decades or longer, including warming or cooling.[7] Climate change is somewhat anomalous when talking about emerging risks (and in many ways similar to cyber risk). To some extent it is now an existing risk but simultaneously it is an emerging risk that continues to evolve (with an increasing number of disparate drivers and outcomes) and consequently it presents a challenge with regard to managing it. Any loss event data that may be relevant can be rapidly obsolete due to technological and process changes within firms (which inhibit comparability between the present and the past).

8.3 Traits and characteristics of emerging risks

One of the main characteristics of emerging risks is that they are difficult to identify and assess. This is due to the fact that they may appear slowly, may not be fully understood and have dependencies; conventional approaches may not be effective, are typically outside the organization's control and may not have arisen before.

The main characteristics of risks that are well suited for managing in an emerging risk framework or risk register using horizon scanning are typically those that are:

- Highly uncertain – either in outcomes or timing or both.
- Typically external – they arise from outside of the organization.
- Wide breadth – impacting on multiple organizations, industries or even geographic areas.
- Foreseeable – horizon scanning is not about predicting the future.
- Longer term – stretch beyond traditional business planning cycles.

If these characteristics are present, it is then possible to drill down on these emerging risks when applying them in an organizational context. Emerging risks possess a variety of additional (and more specific) traits that differ from traditional existing risks. These may make it more challenging to convince senior management to focus attention and resource on them when there are finite resources, the full nature of the risk is not defined (or understood) and the risk can feel abstract in a world where value is attached to facts and supporting data.

Figure 8.2 illustrates some of the key traits.

Climate change as an ongoing emerging risk has historically had most of these traits and that is mainly why it is a very complex risk to manage and mitigate.

At an IRM SIG event in 2020, in discussing climate change risk Giorgis Hadzilacos from the PRA stated 'As an industry it is not the first time we have dealt with a complex problem – asbestos, cyber, GDPR are some examples from the recent past. Take a complex problem and break it down and communicate it to your stakeholders – it can gain traction and become more manageable.'[8]

There are some broad categories of emerging risks that are also helpful to consider when an organization undertakes a horizon scan, which we explain later in this

FIGURE 8.2 Emerging risk traits

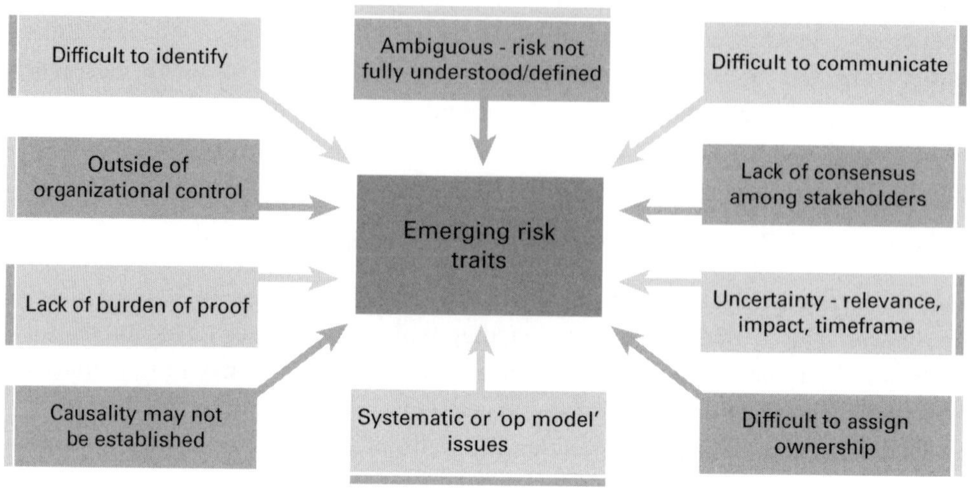

SOURCE © Onerisk consulting. All rights reserved, 2022

chapter. As mentioned previously, it is important to note that emerging risks can be both new and/or developing risks.

Additionally, it is also important to focus on areas that can be considered as threats and opportunities to the organization.

Threats: What is coming over the horizon that could adversely affect your future commercial or other success?

Opportunities: What does the information gathered suggest might be a new direction for you to take that would give you an advantage in the future marketplace?

One of the critical issues for risk practitioners is to consider the opportunities and threats as they communicate the risk and raise awareness, which we now explore in more detail.

8.4 The role of a formal emerging risk management process

With a successful ERM framework that includes an emerging risk process, organizations can learn to anticipate and successfully manage critical risks that have not yet occurred or manifested themselves. By recognizing and responding to uncertainties before they erupt, organizations can help to avoid losses, improve allocation of resources and stay ahead of competitors. Some of the main reasons that emerging risk management is important include the following:

- Establishes a process to uncover the unknown or poorly understood threats to the business
- Brings stakeholders together to facilitate consensus and prioritization of risks
- Serves as an early warning system in order not to catch an insurer by surprise
- Addresses a multitude of possible threats and opportunities aligned to changing risk profile
- Leverages emerging risk processes for competitive advantage
- Aids operational resilience by encouraging contingency planning
- Reduces uncertainty in business results

Enterprise risk management, therefore, needs to be able to develop a process that is comprehensive and integrated within the organization. The main objective of having a formal emerging risk management process is to ensure that risks that could impact the organization's future are identified on a forward-looking basis so that they can be appropriately tracked and treated. The trick is to know how to minimize the shocks and manage the risks in order to profit from them.

What differentiates the management of emerging risks is primarily the time frame within which organizations should develop formal mechanisms to identify, assess, evaluate and treat emerging risks. This may include the need for a separate emerging risk register, with associated risk owners, separately from existing 'managed' risks. Emerging risks often lead to the need for more research to assist in making more informed decisions with respect to business planning and strategy.

In developing a formal emerging risk process, it is important for organizations to capture emerging risk information that is relevant in the context of the risk profile of the organization. This could include (but is not limited to):

- Risk categorization
- Legal entity
- Time horizon
- Weak and strong signals

These important factors will be covered later in the chapter.

8.5 Uses and benefits of emerging risk management

Managing emerging risks can support a range of business processes, which we will explore in more detail through the book.

Emerging risk management can play a major role in supporting and challenging the business in understanding both risk accumulations such as geographical and market sector, and also in calculating the impact or financial consequences at different confidence levels/return periods.

This understanding is becoming more and more critical in strategic decision-making such as risk pricing in transactions and in determining what risk exposures to accept and transfer.

The following is a list of some of the benefits of having a formal emerging risk management process:

- Alignment of emerging risk management with strategic planning
- Challenging corporate strategic plans
- Enhancing risk reporting
- Improved risk maturity and risk culture
- Improved credit rating – emerging risk is one of the five pillars for S&P's ERM rating assessments
- As an input into risk appetite statements
- Capital setting and allocation
- Better understanding of risk aggregation and concentration risks across business units and geographies
- Supports stress and scenario analyses (which improves the process for capital reserves)
- Improved risk-based decision-making
- Improved management information
- Product development – opportunity risk management
- Improves crisis management and business continuity plans
- Improved operational and financial resilience

The Institute of Actuaries focus on firms needing to understand their vulnerability to highly uncertain tail risks. Interestingly it states that its emerging risk management process can enhance the risk culture of a firm, as it can alert decision makers to potentially inconvenient truths and provide a framework to enable firms to base their business strategies and risk mitigation activities on a range of forecasts rather than a single best-estimate projected result or an average of stochastic results. It is worth adding that by enhancing the risk culture, this enables organizations:

- To deepen the understanding of the driving forces affecting future development of a policy or strategic plan
- To identify gaps in understanding and bring into focus new areas of research required to understand emerging risks better

- To build consensus among a range of stakeholders about the issues and to develop options on how to tackle them
- To identify and make explicit some of the difficult policy choices and trade-offs that may need to be made in the future
- To create a new strategy (or revise the existing strategy) so that it is resilient by being more adaptable to changing external conditions

8.6 Key objectives of developing a framework for managing emerging risks

One of the main developments in enterprise risk management, particularly since the global financial crisis, has been for larger organizations to develop a formal stand-alone process for managing emerging risks. There is widespread consensus that emerging risk management provides an early-warning system in order to prevent organizations being caught by surprise and helps focus more on external risks.

The ability to support such an approach will naturally depend on the size and profitability of organizations, the industries and markets in which they operate, the relative risk maturity of their firm, the risk appetite and the resources that can be allocated to it. Nevertheless, it is an important forward-looking component of the risk management toolkit. It can provide a competitive advantage and allow an organization to take advantage of opportunities that arise when emerging risks do materialize. An effective enterprise risk management framework should seek to contribute to the identification and management of emerging risks and to meet the following key objectives:

- The early identification of potential threats and opportunities, allowing more timely analytics and potential treatment
- More dynamic and ongoing management of the full risk register and the addition of new risks as and when appropriate
- Continued strengthening of the risk culture and awareness of the organization's risk profile through ongoing discussions about potential emerging risks

8.6.1 Emerging risk identification and sources of information

Risk professionals should first seek to identify inputs and sources of emerging risks (including relevant climate risks) from a broad diaspora of sources. Specifically, these can include:

- Review of industry journals and articles
- Industry publications

- Research surveys/questionnaires
- Structured interviews (with internal and external stakeholders)
- Working groups and workshops
- Internal and external loss events and near misses
- External emerging risk publications
- Regulatory updates
- Thought-leadership papers from the consultancy firms
- Annual emerging risk reports from global think tanks
- External vendors that provide AI and analytics
- Industry conferences
- Professional trade bodies (e.g. Institute of Internal Auditors, ACCA, CFA, CISI, IRM)
- Stakeholder mapping

External publications are a great source for identifying emerging risk themes, with a comprehensive source being the Global Risks Report published by the World Economic Forum. It includes a list of the top risks and the trends that drive them. Partnering with risk institutions and universities can provide valuable insights for understanding emerging risks.

Internal and external industry loss data is a good source of information to understand underlying trends and causes of losses. However, probably the most effective approach for identifying emerging risks is through internal brainstorming and workshops that identify specific threats and scenarios.

Swiss Re identifies emerging risks by gathering input and feedback from underwriters, client managers, risk experts and others across the company, and also from external experts and research institutions. However, a similar approach can be adopted with the relevant experts from the sector in which you are operating.

ACCOUNTABILITY FOR MANAGING EMERGING RISKS

Boards and committees throughout an organization are ultimately responsible for reviewing and reporting on emerging risks and providing oversight of any proposed management and mitigation plans. The risk management function should seek to maintain an emerging risk register and undertake separate reporting of the risks. Chapter 3 provides more details of governance through a best practice case study.

8.7 Current risk management guidance and standards

There is currently no formal guidance on how to manage emerging risks within the traditional enterprise risk management (ERM) standards that we covered briefly in Chapter 1. However, managing emerging risks now forms a critical component of ERM. Although sometimes difficult to define explicitly, the management of them needs to be considered in the here and now, and planning must be undertaken for those that will happen in the future, such as a regulatory change, and also for those that may not happen at all, which may form part of a business continuity plan.

Standard and Poor's (the rating agency) as part of its ERM evaluation criteria, has enterprise risk emerging risk management as one of its five key criteria within the evaluation of risk exposure management. It states:

> We evaluate [the] ability to determine the likelihood, impact or severity, and velocity of the risk (speed of potential change), as well as its ability and willingness to mitigate the risk such that it does not significantly affect the company or its ability to opportunistically take advantage of the risk (level of preparedness if those emerging risks materialize)'.[9]

Climate change risk (and the various emerging derivatives of it) is increasing in profile and is becoming recognized as integral to the success of organizations and their strategic plans. Failure to manage these risks in a systematic, structured and forward-looking way will hamper the execution of strategic plans and may contribute to the failure to identify any strategic derailers. That is not to say this is an easy discipline to master; there are challenges in doing this well and we will cover these now.

8.7.1 Emerging risk management challenges

Emerging risk management has many challenges. These include finite time and resources, determining ownership and accountability, the complexity and nature of emerging risks and the issues with categorization.

Black swans, in terms of the events, are by definition impossible to predict; for example, the global pandemic, which no one saw coming, is an event that is still emerging and the ERM function can play an important role in mitigating the ongoing impact. Emerging risks generally have a high degree of uncertainty due in part to few statistical benchmarks.

This is also linked to the Cassandra 'syndrome' or 'dilemma', where valid warnings or concerns are raised but dismissed or disbelieved. The financial crisis was a good example where the banks, governments and rating agencies refused to acknowledge the emerging problem. Climate change is now an ongoing example where scientists have been providing repeated warnings to governments over the last decades but they have been very slow to act and heed the warnings.

However, some emerging risks, such as changing climate legislation, are going to happen so it is important to be prepared. By developing a range of scenarios and knock-on effects companies can improve their crisis management and business continuity plans.

It is a challenge but it is important, particularly in respect of climate change, to create a sense of urgency to attract the attention of stakeholders. Gaining consensus from various stakeholders is difficult and hampers the ability to make decisions (due to a lack of precision with regard to the threats and scenarios that need to be captured and modelled – this is also affected by interconnectedness). There is often confusion around the root cause. ERM facilitation through brainstorming is a useful tool to reach consensus and is one of the best ways to highlight the value of the function in support of improved decision-making.

Looking at some of the challenges in turn, we will provide some additional detail on the challenges faced.

8.7.1.1 TIME AND RESOURCES

Most risk functions and business owners don't have the time and resources to adequately assess the emerging risk exposures. This is partly due to the perception that emerging risks are remote and never going to happen. The risk function can do some of the heavy lifting in researching the risks prior to raising them with the business and also when supporting senior management.

8.7.1.2 OWNERSHIP AND ACCOUNTABILITY

It is often difficult to agree ownership and accountability because emerging risks can cut across a range of stakeholders and costs can be prohibitive to managing and mitigating the risks. Again, the priority is to agree ownership and accountability for risks, which we cover in Chapter 3 under governance.

8.7.1.3 EMERGING RISK CATEGORIZATION

To capture emerging risks, it is important to develop a framework to categorize them in terms of risk types. There is increasing consensus to using PESTEL as a global basis to categorize macro emerging risks. Alternatively, they could just be aligned to the prevailing risk categories within the risk framework.

The Global Risks Report categorization The Global Risks Report published by the World Economic Forum uses five risk categories. These are:

- Economic risks
- Technological risks
- Social risks

- Geopolitical risks
- Environmental risks

These are used to form a basis for identifying themes, prioritizing actions and for coordinating responses.

Swiss Re Institute – SONAR report categorization Another of the leading publications on emerging risks is from the Swiss Re Institute, who since 2013 have developed their SONAR report that focuses on global emerging risk themes and trends.

By identifying and monitoring macro trends it helps understanding of the risk landscape of the future. Based on internal surveys and workshops, Swiss Re curate a set of macro trends deemed to be of high importance for the reinsurance sector in the next decade.

They categorize macro risks into four main headings (which are similar to PESTEL) but highlight the fact that companies should seek to develop their own risk categorization:

a Demographic and social environment
b Political and economic environment
c Technological and natural environment
d Competitive and business environment

What is of particular interest in their 2021 report is that there are a few emerging risks that relate to climate change that impact across a number of the nine emerging risk themes and six emerging trends that they spotlight, although they don't have a specific category for either environmental or climate risk. The emerging risk themes outlined are based on early signals collected over the course of a year. Relevant trends and themes identified include:

Climate risk trends

1. Mass migration and urbanization (links to a in the SONAR categories above)
2. Low-yield environment and risk of inflation (links to b)
3. Addressing the physical risk of climate change (links to c)
4. Transition to a low-carbon economy (links to c)
5. Rising importance of biodiversity and ecosystem services (BES) (links to c)
6. Data as an asset (links to c)
7. Increasing digital customer interaction (links to d)
8. Increasingly litigious environment (links to d)
9. Rising importance of ESG (links to d)

The importance of these global trends is that they identify a trend from a long-term pattern that is currently taking place and that could contribute to amplifying global risks and/or altering the relationships between them.

We will explore some of these specific climate risk related trends and challenges in the next chapter.

Alignment to the risk profile categories Alternatively, organizations can seek to develop their own internal risk categories and have related risk policies. They can seek to review and design their own ways to categorize aligning risks tailored to their needs. Here is an example set of generic categories that are commonly used that can be expanded to suit the organization's risk profile:

- Strategic
- Financial
- Operational
- Regulatory

8.8 Emerging risk tools and techniques

The most traditional management technique used by organizations and taught at business schools is the use of SWOT and PESTLE. Organizations should use this process to better understand the threats and opportunities from emerging risks and to assist in making more informed decisions with respect to strategic and business planning.

The most important developments in emerging risk management in recent years have been the development of more formal tools and techniques that help identify and assess emerging risks, which are becoming critical components of the toolbox for risk practitioners in addressing how to identify and assess new and evolving risks. These tools and techniques can be applied to emerging risk management and can assist key stakeholders to identify emerging risks, focusing 'deep-dive' analysis and as a powerful tool in emerging risk workshops when looking to build out consensus on emerging threats and opportunities.

The risk function should not be operating in isolation and needs to work collaboratively with experts across the organization including risk champions, who act as listening posts in the business.

One good technique is to send out a risk questionnaire and follow up with workshops across all business areas. Use of external experts to help facilitate the workshops is also very helpful.

Partnering with risk institutions and universities is another way to understand emerging risks (good examples, among many others, are the Willis Research Network and ClimateWise). Internal and external industry loss data is an additional source of information to help understand the underlying trends.

8.8.1 Horizon scanning and stress and scenario testing

In terms of specific approaches that can help risk managers, there are two main techniques that many organizations are using and that are advocated by stakeholders (such as regulators) to both capture and quantify emerging risk:

1. Horizon scanning
2. Stress and scenario testing

Stress and scenario testing (SST) frameworks have been a huge revolution in ERM since the financial crisis. In Chapter 10 we shall provide an in-depth look at how organizations should design an SST framework and develop climate scenarios highlighting different methodologies. It is important, at this point, to highlight the importance of distinguishing between:

- **Scenario (analyses) planning** – Looking at possible future states on the basis of different starting states.
- **Stress testing** – Testing how the organization copes in the face of a range of potential situations.

There are also other techniques that we won't be covering in detail, such as:

- **Forecasting** – Using qualitative and quantitative techniques, including historical data and statistics, individual and collective judgement, and environmental monitoring.
- **Driver mapping** – Using analytical tools such as STEEPLE (societal, technological, economic, environmental, political, legal, ethical) to consider a wide range of future risks. The main difference from PESTLE is the inclusion of ethical considerations and a focus on social/demographic as opposed to sociocultural drivers.
- **Trend analysis** – using mathematical techniques on historical data to predict future trends.

Let's take a closer look at horizon scanning.

8.8.1.1 HORIZON SCANNING

Horizon scanning is a formal process to help to explore what the future might look like, to understand uncertainties better and to analyse whether the organization is adequately prepared for potential opportunities and threats.

The horizon effectively adds another dimension by capturing when the event may (or may not, of course) appear on the horizon.

The Institute of Risk Management published a guide on horizon scanning in 2018, which serves as a good reference. As stated in the guide:[10]

> [H]orizon scanning can be a good technique for people to look at complexity, challenge assumptions and review multiple ways that events could unfurl, in order to increase the

resilience and reliability of their organizations. It is not about trying to predict the future but rather to review options so that evidence-based decisions can be made

The IRM guide refers to the UK Government paper on futures, which, in the opinion of the IRM Innovation SIG, comprises best practice to follow if undertaking a detailed horizon scanning exercise. The UK Futures document describes a three horizons model, shown in Figure 8.3, which is now being commonly used by practitioners as a basis to map out their future climate change risks and opportunities:

- Horizon 1: where you are currently taking action
- Horizon 2: visible trends for strategic consideration
- Horizon 3: little trend information today but planning needed

In developing an emerging risk management process an organization should seek to develop a stand-alone process to ensure emerging risks are identified and assessed on a forward-looking basis so that they can be appropriately tracked, prioritized and treated.

To implement a horizon scanning approach within an organization is an iterative approach that involves the identification of key stakeholders, communication of the approach and the objectives, research, reporting, debate and challenge, and then monitoring and reviewing (in order to determine priorities at any given point in time).

Assessing climate risks over different time horizons It is a natural extension of the horizon scanning approach to apply it to a specific subset of emerging risks (in this instance climate risk); however, the consideration of time horizons is not without challenges. One of the most challenging aspects to assessing the impact of climate

FIGURE 8.3 Horizon scanning – three horizons model

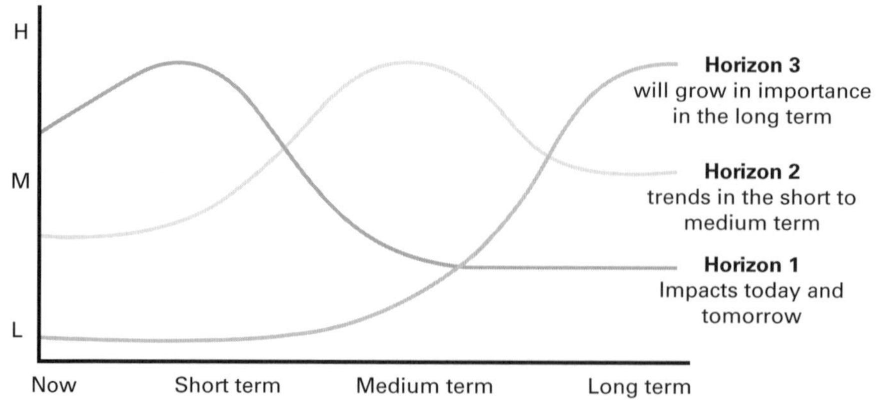

SOURCE Future Toolkits, Waverley Consultants (Open Source)

change is the time horizon and it is important to distinguish between existing risks that will change over time due to climate change, and new emerging climate risks that may impact the organization in the future.

One of the most complex aspects of climate scenario analysis is to understand the incremental impacts over time. Climate change in respect of physical risks, for example, is expected to lead to an increase in the frequency and severity of 'acute' weather-related events, such as floods and droughts, as well as longer-term 'chronic' shifts in climate, such as increases in average temperatures and sea-level rise.

Mark Carney, in his famous Lloyds of London address in 2015, stated that 'Climate change is the Tragedy of the Horizon' and that 'once climate change becomes a defining issue for financial stability, it may already be too late'.[11]

When identifying risks one main consideration is therefore the use of different time horizons or time frames over which the risk could crystallize and thus the window to respond and adapt. The design of climate scenarios is discussed in Chapter 10, including tools and techniques that can model different time horizons.

Regulators, such as the PRA, provide comprehensive guidance and explain that the scenario analysis should include short-term assessments, covering the existing planning horizon and longer-term assessments of a firm's exposures based on its current business model.

The Climate Financial Risk Forum scenario guide issued in June 2020 helps to explain the requirements of scenario assessment by stating that 'This requires leveraging historical data and providing a forward-looking assessment over an extended time horizon, whilst also evaluating the likelihood that extreme climate-related events will become more frequent and severe.'[12]

Emerging risk assessment – an extra dimension Traditional risk assessment criteria enable the risks to be assessed in respect of the consequence (or impact/severity) based on agreed upon risk appetite level and likelihood (probability) of occurrence.

As discussed, one of the main objectives of managing emerging risks is to identify and assess them on a forward-looking basis so they can be appropriately tracked and treated, and thus risk managers need to consider a third key criterion, which is speed or time to impact.

Speed refers to the time it takes for an emerging risk event to manifest itself or, in other words, the time anticipated for such an emerging risk to impact the group/entity.

Speed should not be used as a proxy for when action should be taken, as some emerging risks may require an action plan that is implemented well in advance of the risk crystallizing.

8.9 Emerging risk management process

Organizations (as mentioned previously) need to develop a formal process that should include both internal and external scanning for the identification of risks over alternative time horizons.

As a central function, the risk management function should seek to collate information about trends and events in both an internal and external context by adopting 'always on' sensing that monitors changes in the firm's strategic assets, systems, culture and knowledge, etc.

Perhaps the most important step to identify emerging risks is to conduct detailed research through a 'deep-dive' exercise (which is particularly helpful for climate change given its complexity).

Figure 8.4 provides a high-level overview of the formal emerging risk management process that organizations should seek to develop.

The process highlights an assessment process that we will expand on in the next section from the point of identifying new emerging risks, through the prioritization stage (and determining the levels of analysis to be undertaken) to the categorization stage and then how they will be reported and monitored going forward.

These are therefore the things more likely to unexpectedly and adversely affect a firm in the future, which we can be aware of but may perhaps miss if they have not been considered. Figure 8.4 outlines a flexible approach that looks at new emerging risks (or extensions of already identified emerging risks), and categorizes and prioritizes these risks (and determines the additional analysis required). Depending on the outcomes, weak signals can be tracked via an emerging risk tracker on a SharePoint site or an intranet that only the risk and compliance team have access to. Emerging risks once evaluated can be added to either the emerging risk register or the watch list, according to the following criteria:

Emerging risk register: This listing is to comprise those emerging risks that are judged as having a higher than 25 per cent potential of crystallizing into a risk that should ultimately be added to the risk register. The emerging risk register is to be subject to a quantitative oversight and monitoring regime overseen by the management risk committee (MRC) and other local committees as appropriate.

Watch list: This is to comprise those emerging risks that are judged as having a lower than 25 per cent potential of crystallizing into risk that should be added to the risk register, or where the emerging risk is assessed as having a low impact on a time horizon greater than three years. The watch list is to be subject to an annual monitoring regime overseen by the MRC and other local committees as appropriate.

They can also become part of the existing risk reporting if it is considered that the risk has emerged and that there are sufficient indicators to enable management to

FIGURE 8.4 Emerging risk management process

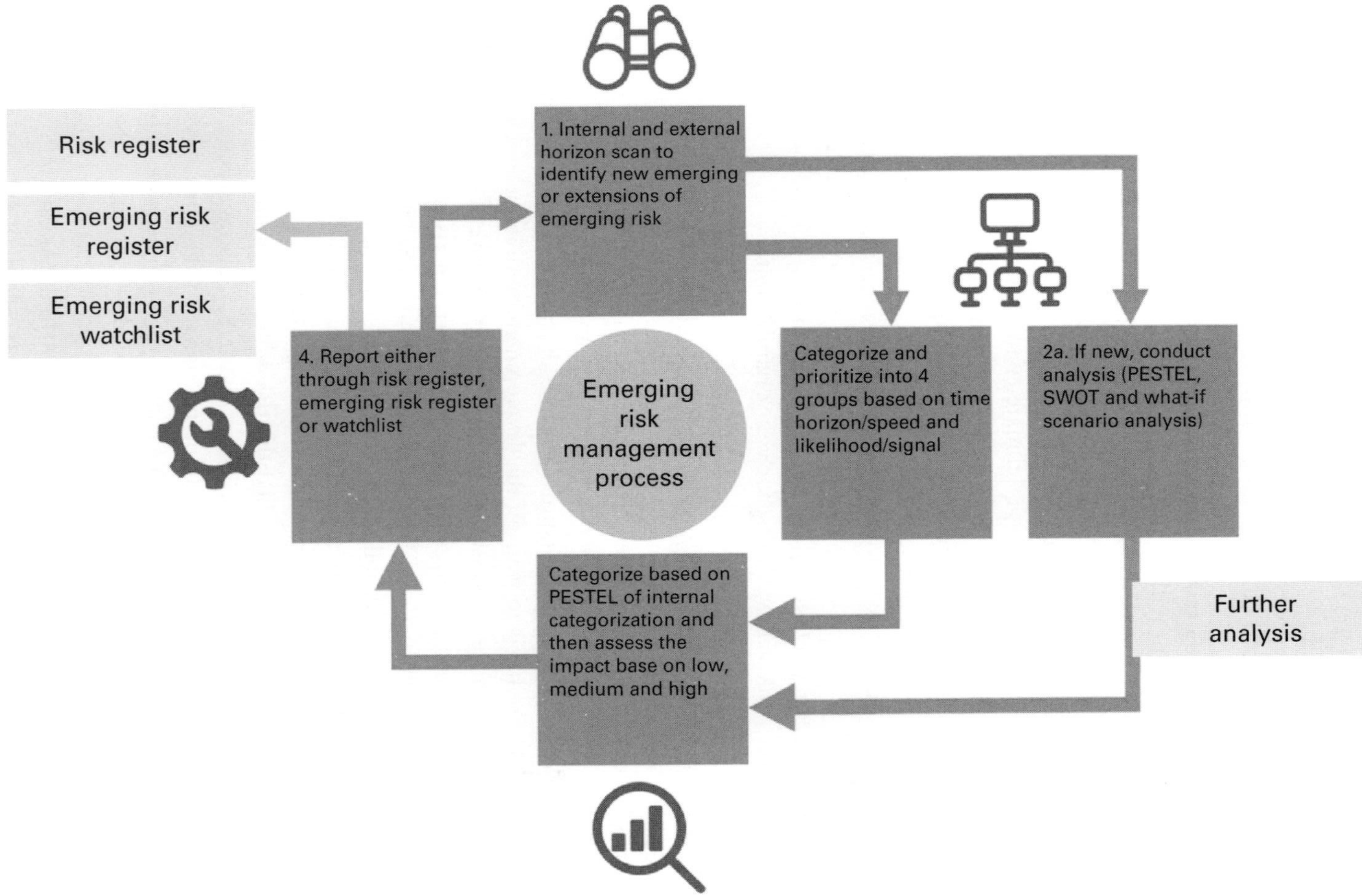

SOURCE

form an ongoing assessment of the risk. These could include management information, key risk/performance/control indicators and loss event data (both internal and external).

8.9.1 Emerging risk assessment – an alternative approach

The IRM Charities SIG outlined a flexible approach to emerging risk assessment in 2018, which is relevant with regard to this chapter.

The assessment approach chosen is likely to differ due to both the size and risk maturity of the organization, which in turn relate to the internal resources available, and leadership and management preferences.

This means that when looking at climate change as an example for an international wildlife charity, this risk's proximity is immediate as the climate crisis is already impacting on species survival. However, for a national health charity, the impact of this risk might not be felt for a few years. In the advanced approach, you can assess the concepts of proximity and velocity using simple scales and definitions (e.g. 'fast or slow' for velocity, 'near or far' for proximity) or more complex scales (e.g. very fast, fast, slow, very slow, etc.). Consequently, it is important to choose the scale that you think will work best for your organization.

8.9.2 Evaluation and prioritization of emerging risks

Emerging risks can be expected to move between the emerging risk register, the watch list or an entity/entities risk register (as and when additional information becomes available to better quantify the overall impact on the business). Not all emerging risks are likely to warrant the development of an immediate risk treatment strategy, however in certain instances it may be appropriate to develop a risk treatment plan in the near term given that some emerging risks may require longer adaptation/treatment periods. Where treatment plans are developed a project lead should be assigned responsibility for completing; this may be the emerging risk owner (ERO) but in all instances the ERO will have overall responsibility for monitoring and reporting on progress of the treatment plan.

Once an emerging risk is identified the risk function should then assess the risk using an assessment process like the one in Figure 8.5, distinguishing between time horizon and/or speed, and likelihood and/or 'signal'. The figure illustrates how an initial prioritization decision of emerging climate risks can be made in order to determine relative priorities and how these can be treated (depending on the assessment).

8.9.2.1 VELOCITY AND SPEED OF RISKS – 'STRONG' AND 'WEAK' SIGNALS

The key is identifying whether something is a 'weak signal' or not, that is, whether it is something that is expected to impact an organization (i.e., a 'strong signal') or if it

FIGURE 8.5 Emerging climate risk evaluation and prioritization

Emerging risk prioritization	Time horizon and/or 'speed'	Likelihood and/or 'signal': Low/weak	Likelihood and/or 'signal': High/strong
	Near-term/fast	Medium risk - monitor and focus on the connections to existing risks and impacts on business resilience Add to 'emerging risk register' and revisit in three months	High priority - requires immediate active management Add to 'risk register' as: (1) New risk; and (2) Consider impacts on and other existing risks
	Long-term/slow	Low risk Add to 'emerging risk watchlist' and revisit in 12 months	High risk - undertake: • SWOT and PESTLE analysis; • Deep-drive review • Develop insights (market, legal and regulatory) Add to 'emerging risk register' and revisit every three months

SOURCE

is something that currently isn't expected to have an impact but that could in the future (i.e., a 'weak signal'). These are normally things that are occurring in:

- **Other geographical markets** – e.g. regulation change in Europe or the United States that the United Kingdom could possibly look to replicate in the future or demand changes in those areas leading to new business models or practices that again may be replicated in the United Kingdom.
- **Other industries** – e.g. something happening in the energy sector that could be replicated in the insurance sector in the future (an example of this being pricing fairness).
- **Other regulatory bodies** – e.g. something happening with a regulator that does not yet have a direct impact on the insurance sector but that could be replicated in the future.

Recent events provide an example of an emerging risk that has arisen at a great velocity. In January 2022, most political and economic commentators would have said that there was no expectation of a war unfolding in Ukraine; by the end of March 2022, this unexpected emerging risk (which may have been on an emerging risk tracker as a generic 'political instability risk') had materialized and become a real risk, fast-tracked to the main risk register. Another example for most organizations was the global Covid-19 pandemic, where companies were underprepared.

Emerging risks are expected to move between the emerging risk register, the watch list or an entities risk register as and when additional information becomes available to better quantify the overall impact on the business. Not all emerging risks are likely to warrant the development of an immediate risk treatment strategy. However, in certain circumstances it may be appropriate to develop a risk treatment plan in the near term given that some emerging risks may require longer adaptation/treatment periods. Where treatment plans are developed a project lead will be assigned responsibility for completing; this may be the ERO but in all instances the ERO will have the overall responsibility for monitoring and reporting on progress of the treatment plan.

8.9.2.2 EMERGING RISK TREATMENT

In 2021, the IRM's Charities SIG released a practitioner guidance paper entitled 'How to assess and treat emerging risks', which outlines how the treatment of emerging risks should involve considering options such as using the 4Ts approach (see Chapter 6).

Given the paucity of information around some emerging risks, you could choose to monitor how the risk develops, then modify and adjust your organizational plans and priorities to respond to the risk. For example, reduced resources may require you to accelerate the delivery of services using technological solutions rather than face-to-face methods of service delivery.

8.9.3 Emerging risk evaluation – governance process

It is important to assign ownership for managing the ongoing monitoring of and reporting on emerging risks. One approach is to assign accountability to an emerging risk owner (ERO) within the business. Ideally quarterly updates should be provided and documented. Risk management should help facilitate the collection and consolidation of the emerging risk register and watch list and report to management and/or board committees as appropriate. From time to time, deep-dive analysis should be developed on an ad hoc basis.

The ERO is normally responsible for ensuring that any actions (e.g. undertaking deeper-dive workshops) arising from the local committees' oversight are performed on a timely basis.

The risk management function should seek to ensure that emerging risk assessments, along with the current status of any associated actions are appropriately included within the risk reports and other associated risk-based reporting presented to committees, boards and/or other stakeholders. Emerging risks should be linked to the design and inputs during stress and scenario testing that are discussed in Chapter 10.

If the assessment suggests that the risk can be adequately assessed in accordance with the ERM framework then the emerging risk should be considered to be moved to the existing risk registers.

It is helpful to have a separate emerging risk register to document the initial analysis and ongoing updates within the organization's internal risk management system.

8.9.3.1 EMERGING RISK ASSESSMENT CRITERIA – IMPACT ASSESSMENT

The next step in the process should be to assess the overall impact of an emerging risk as an indicator of the potential financial, reputational and/or regulatory effect on the organization.

One of the main approaches that is typically used is to assign qualitative assessment from low to high, subject to incremental increases (i.e., minor, moderate and severe or low, medium and high).

Swiss Re use the following definitions in their SONAR analysis:

High, medium, low

- **High/Severe** – Potentially high financial, reputational and/or regulatory impact or significant stakeholder concern.
- **Medium/Moderate** – Potentially medium financial, reputational and/or regulatory impact or moderate stakeholder concern.
- **Low/Minor** – Potentially low financial, reputational and/or regulatory impact, or low stakeholder concern. Therefore, concern is minimal and hence no action is required – can be accommodated within the existing control environment.

Time horizon – speed (time to impact)

- **0–3 years – near term** – The emerging risk can be expected to occur within a three-year time horizon.
- **+3 years – mid term/long term** – The emerging risk can be expected to occur within a greater than three-year time horizon.
- **TBA likelihood** – This indicates the probability of the risk crystallizing. It is assessed in two categories (<25 per cent chance of occurring, and >25 per cent chance of occurring).

8.10 Emerging climate risk reporting

Emerging risk reporting can come in many forms. Due to the breadth of the emerging risk universe, it can be high-level and generic or distilled down to specific granular-level risks applicable to individual parts of a business or product line. The variety of reporting available affords risk managers the chance to adapt to the needs of their senior management/boards and to enable them a way to determine relative urgency and impacts, so that finite resources can be allocated accordingly.

The key is that the risks are well articulated (and categorized), that there is senior management ownership, that the assessment considers time horizons (i.e., urgency), the velocity/speed of the risk occurring, the relative potential impacts and that it enables senior management to make informed prioritization decisions and that mitigating actions are tracked and monitored to completion.

8.10.1 Overall risk visualization – emerging risk radar

Organizations should also seek to develop a stand-alone emerging risk radar visualization of climate change emerging risks. Many organizations use an output that uses specific time periods that are typically broken down into four or five PESTEL risk categories.

Figure 8.6 makes the distinction between physical risks and transition risks but also considers these with much longer time horizons. This is a useful depiction of how different underlying causes can have differing time frames and impacts when considered with regard to physical or transition risks.

8.10.2 Emerging climate risk radar – mapping of business decisions

Another way of presenting emerging risk information is to map the risk to business decisions that align with the future climate strategic plan. This can help the risk manager to present the range of emerging climate threats and opportunities internally at senior risk management and board risk committees, based on a high-level initial evaluation that can act as a good basis for discussion and to agree areas that need to be assessed further in terms of better understanding the impact on the organization. Some threats and opportunities will be difficult to model but still important to contextualize in terms of initial impact and velocity.

The approach maps out the risk and opportunities against a specific business decision, which in turn is evaluated against an initial intuitive qualitative materiality assessment of low, medium or high impact. This is not a straightforward exercise but it can really help to filter out the most important areas, which the organization should then take to the next stage of analysis (a more detailed risk assessment process and design of scenarios, which we cover in Chapter 10).

Figure 8.7 highlights the types of output that will be very helpful to risk managers to articulate regular updates to management. This will help with prioritizing resources to undertake more detailed research and 'deep dives'. Analysis of climate scenarios can be used as a dynamic reporting tool that can be updated to integrate with both new climate threats and opportunities, or changes in the perceived threats or opportunity level. As already discussed, the horizon effectively adds another

FIGURE 8.6 Initial emerging climate risk framework – physical and transition risks

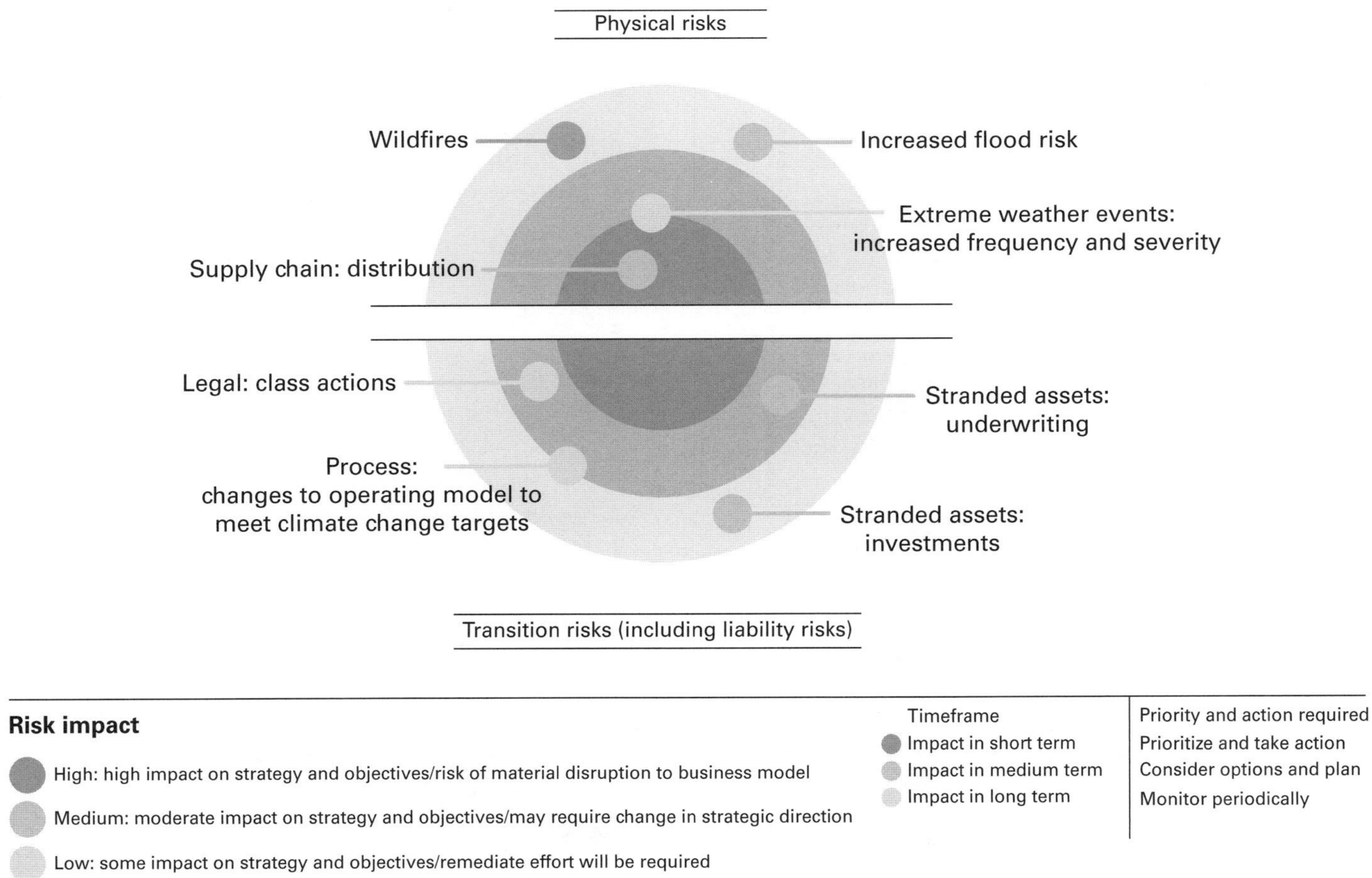

SOURCE

FIGURE 8.7 Initial emerging climate risk framework – mapping to business decisions over alternative time horizons

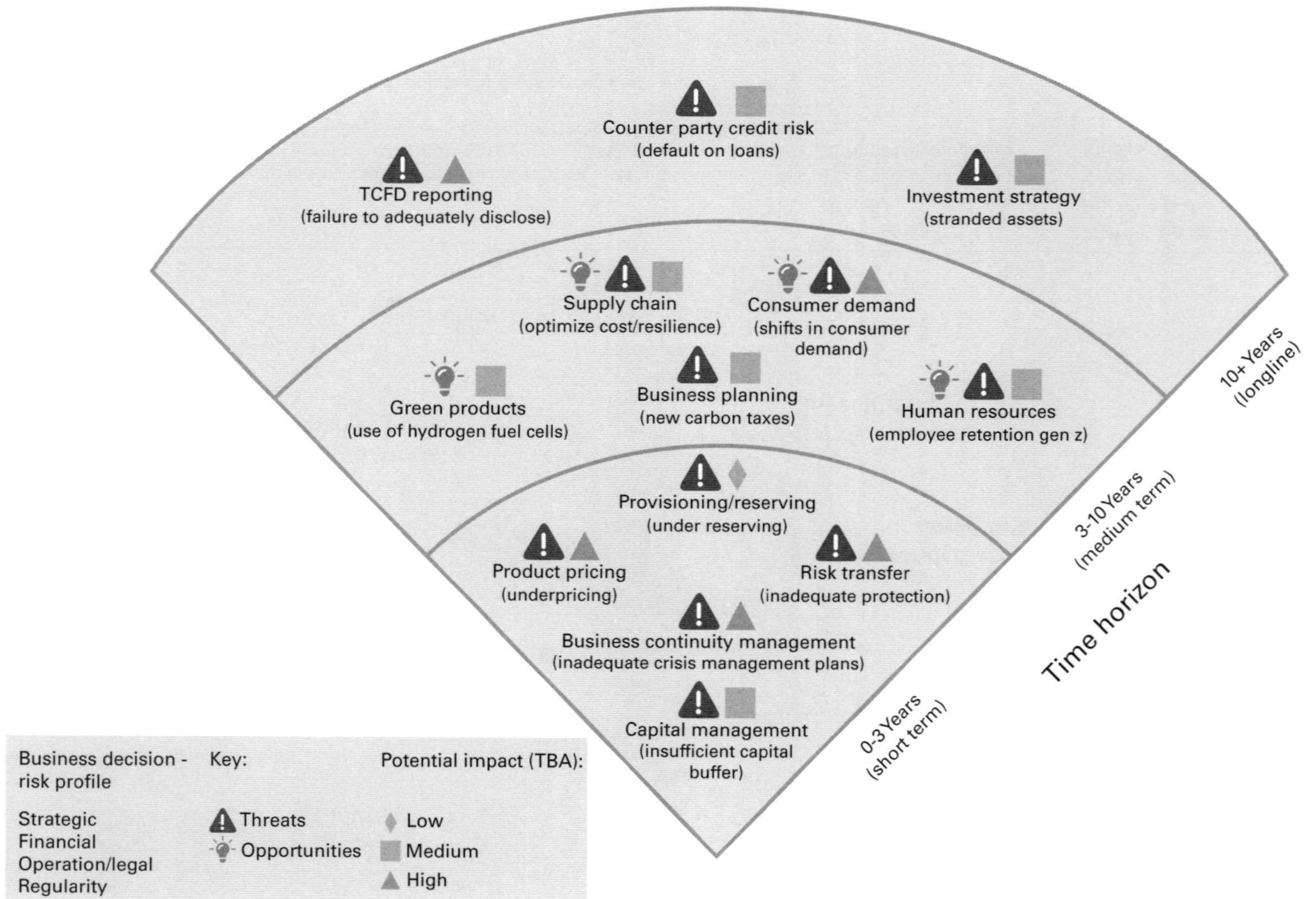

dimension by capturing when the event is predicted to happen on the horizon (which is typically chosen with respect to set periods, i.e., short, medium and long term).

8.10.3 Frequency and nature of reporting

Depending on whether you manage the emerging risk process through your normal risk management reporting cycle, as a stand-alone exercise or as part of another process (e.g. strategic and business planning), this will determine the frequency and nature of the reporting to be provided. Options for reporting when you manage emerging risk through your normal risk management cycle include:

- Integrating emerging risks into your normal risk report, with or without special indicators or commentary to identify and draw attention to certain risks as 'emerging'.
- Carving out a separate section in your normal risk reports (e.g. a stand-alone appendix) to identify and draw attention to emerging risks. This could be in the form of a summary 'watch list' to ensure risks are on the radar without providing too much detail.
- Creating a separate stand-alone risk report focused on emerging risk, with a fuller analysis and commentary than the summary 'watch list' approach.

This aligns with the prioritization section earlier in this chapter where, depending on the assessment of the emerging risk, it would be incorporated into the existing risk reporting, be part of the emerging risk register or be monitored on a periodic basis on the 'watch list'.

Conclusion

In this chapter we have explained the process and benefits of having a formal emerging risk management process to support the identification of climate risks by serving as an early warning system, and it is clearly important to leverage both internal and external informational resources across multiple functions to support the development and implementation of a robust process.

Emerging risks by their nature are ambiguous and it is impossible to quantify impacts and likelihoods with any degree of certainty. Nevertheless, it is critical that emerging risks are identified, assessed, managed and reported on if an organization wants to build and maintain resilience in the face of uncertainty.

Climate risk is a subset of emerging risk but its effects can be felt in all aspects of what an organization does across its value chain (i.e. operational processes, operational resilience, sourcing of materials, emissions, client demands and expectations, product design, adherence to regulatory requirements, selection of partners or service providers) and consequently needs to be embedded within existing risk management practices so that it is an integral part of how the organization is run.

In the next chapter we will provide more specific details of climate change-related emerging risks, both threats and opportunities.

Notes

1. P E Tetlock and D Gardner (2015) *Superforecasting: The art and science of prediction*, Crown Publishers, New York
2. IPCC. Climate Change 2022: Impacts, Adaptation, and Vulnerability, Contribution of Working Group II to the Sixth Assessment Report of the Intergovernmental Panel on Climate Change. Eds H.-O. Pörtner et al, 2022, Cambridge University Press
3. G A Meehl et al (2007) Global Climate Projections. In eds S Solomon et al, Climate Change 2007: The physical science basis, Contribution of Working Group I to the Fourth Assessment Report of the Intergovernmental Panel on Climate Change, Cambridge University Press, Cambridge and New York. www.ipcc.ch/site/assets/uploads/2018/02/ar4-wg1-chapter10-1.pdf (archived at https://perma.cc/PS8U-VDYV)
4. RIMS. Emerging Risks and Enterprise Risk Management, RIMS, 2010. www.rims.org/resources/risk-knowledge/white-paper/emerging-risks-and-enterprise-risk-management (archived at https://perma.cc/8HJH-KJ4W)
5. A Barr and C Raimbault (2012) *Emerging Risks: A strategic management guide*, Routledge, Abingdon
6. Swiss Re. Swiss Re SONAR: New emerging risk insights, 2021. www.swissre.com/dam/jcr:5a8d21b6-3dff-4178-9f10-525850e7b3db/swiss-re-institute-sonar-report-2021-final.pdf (archived at https://perma.cc/TZY5-K5GU)
7. P U Zacharia, T M Najmudeen and L Wilson. Climate change impacts on Indian marine fisheries and adaptation strategies. In *Training Manual on Advances in Marine Fisheries in India*. eprints.cmfri.org.in (archived at https://perma.cc/KH9R-952F). Available at: http://eprints.cmfri.org.in/14038/ (archived at https://perma.cc/6MUE-MRJB)
8. M Massey et al. Climate Change Risk Management Guidance: IRM Climate Change Special Interest Group Report, Institute of Risk Management. www.theirmindia.org/uploads/thought-leadership/publications/climate-change-risk-management-guidance-report.pdf (archived at https://perma.cc/ST4S-RSMQ)
9. S&P Global Ratings. Enterprise risk management evaluation framework, 22 July 2019, www.spglobal.com/ratings/en/research/articles/190722-enterprise-risk-management-evaluation-framework-11070561 (archived at https://perma.cc/9P5Y-53DF)
10. Institute of Risk Management. Horizon Scanning: A Practitioner's Guide, nd. www.theirm.org/media/7340/horizon-scanning_final2.pdf (archived at https://perma.cc/DME9-MFVD)

11 Bank of England. Breaking the Tragedy of the Horizon -climate change and financial stability, 2015, www.bankofengland.co.uk/-/media/boe/files/speech/2015/breaking-the-tragedy-of-the-horizon-climate-change-and-financial-stability.pdf (archived at https://perma.cc/5KFN-LGW6)

12 CFRF. Climate Financial Risk Forum Guide 2020: Scenario analysis chapter, 2020. www.fca.org.uk/publication/corporate/climate-financial-risk-forum-guide-2020-scenario-analysis-chapter.pdf (archived at https://perma.cc/SGC6-ZSMG)

9

Emerging climate trends, issues and challenges

This chapter will cover some of the main emerging climate trends, issues and challenges related to climate change across physical, transition and liability risks.

The main learning outcomes from this chapter are to:

- Understand the main global macro and micro trends relating to climate change including the outcomes of future environmental global risks from the World Economic Forum's global survey.
- Recognize the increasing importance of understanding the impacts of physical emerging risks such as heatwaves, wildfires and 'tipping points' and how organizations can seek to mitigate them.
- Explore the emerging transition risks including 'greenwashing' and examine the different approaches than can lead to critical damage to an organization and its brand.
- Provide an overview of how new technologies can help businesses to change their business models and practices to support their own and the wider society's net zero strategies.
- Recognize the growing emerging liability risks through a range of specific litigation cases and the important impact on the reputation of an organization.

Introduction

In the last chapter we discussed the importance of developing a formal emerging risk management framework to support an organization to understand its future risk profile and for organizations to have an early warning system in place to improve their resilience.

In this chapter we will cover some of the main emerging climate trends, issues and challenges relating to climate change, including climate global trends and risks on both a macro and micro economic level, affecting countries, regions, organizations and people.

The chapter will provide an overview and some more detailed insights into specific emerging risks emanating from physical, transition and liability risks. Specific physical emerging risks will include both acute and chronic risks covering extended wildfire seasons, and prolonged heatwaves, as well as climate tipping points.

In looking into transition risks some of the emerging concerns such as 'greenwashing' will be explored in more detail, as well as explaining how emerging technologies are supporting the drive to meet net zero targets and can provide competitor advantage to organizations that act as first movers. In the last section, the latest insights into emerging climate change litigation highlight how litigation is a key driver of change that is supporting the climate agenda through providing some recent and ongoing legal court cases.

9.1 Global macro trends

Economic challenges flowing from both the Covid-19 pandemic and the war in Ukraine are persisting and will continue beyond 2022 with market risks such as financial market volatility and interest rate uncertainty being a major area of focus in the years ahead. Human capital risks will continue as organizations need to verify their work-from-home policies that seek to maintain staff retention rates

Global regulatory changes and policies outlined in Chapter 1 will ultimately cascade down to organizations in helping to meet the various targets, goals and expectations.

Geopolitical tensions and nation-first postures will also complicate climate action. Brazil, for example, joined the other 140 countries responsible for 91 per cent of the Earth's forests in endorsing the Glasgow Leaders' Declaration on Forests and Land Use, even as deforestation in the Amazon accelerated to a 15-year high in 2021.

The economic crisis created by the Covid-19 pandemic risks and the ongoing Ukraine war are also delaying efforts to tackle climate change by encouraging countries to prioritize short-term measures to restore economic growth, regardless of their impact on the climate, over pursuing green transitions.

Societal concerns have now mobilized under the new banner of 'ESG reporting'. Thanks to scrutiny through higher standards of audit, greater transparency in risk reporting, news media reporting of corporate abuses, and increased mobilization by citizens in social media spaces, the general visibility of organizational misconduct has raised public expectations of better future controls.

Some of these drivers are bringing about a significant change in the way organizations operate and provide a platform for a more 'purpose driven' organization that is explored in more detail in this chapter.

9.1.1 Global Risks Report – World Economic Forum

It is important to remember that climate change is a set of global trends. One of the best publications on emerging risks is the Global Risks Report published by the World Economic Forum. The report provides an oversight on global risks that are broken down between the five key categories.

Their 2021 report stated that a shift towards greener economies cannot be delayed until the shocks of the Covid-19 pandemic subside. These global risks and trends in turn are leading to other knock-on effects in socio-economic development, human health, migration and food security. The report clearly implies that organizations need to understand the direct and indirect effects of climate change and their interaction.

Climate change continues to be perceived as an existential threat to humanity and in the latest Global Risks Report (2022) respondents rated 'climate action failure' as the risk with potential to inflict the most damage at a global scale over the next decade.

The report states that:

> over a 10-year horizon, the health of the planet dominates concerns: environmental risks are perceived to be the five of the top 10 most critical long-term threats to the world as well as the most potentially damaging to people and planet, with "climate action failure", "extreme weather", and "biodiversity loss" ranking as the top three most severe risks.[1]

The report provides some specific examples of global impacts including droughts, fires, floods, resource scarcity and species loss. The results of its survey of the global risks over the next decade are shown in Table 9.1 below.

TABLE 9.1 Global Risks Report 2022 survey – the most severe global risks over the next decade

Rank	Type	Risk
1	Environmental	Climate action failure
2	Environmental	Extreme weather
3	Environmental	Biodiversity loss
4	Societal	Social cohesion erosion
5	Societal	Livelihood crisis
6	Societal	Infectious diseases
7	Environmental	Human environmental damage
8	Environmental	Natural resource crisis
9	Economic	Debt crisis
10	Geopolitical	Geo-economic confrontation

SOURCE World Economic Forum Global Risks Perception Survey 2021–2022

The Global Risks Report highlights the increasing concern in respect to 'climate action failure'. It reveals the respondents' lack of faith in the world's ability to contain climate change, not least because of the societal fractures and economic risks that have deepened in recent months.

Before discussing some of the more recent emerging risk themes and trends it is important to emphasize that it is vital not to get complacent in identifying emerging risks and trends. The point here is that organizations can easily dismiss risks that are now in 'fashion'. For example, financial risks facing the world are still critical as we look at the global growth outlook and rising debt levels that are now becoming an increasing concern due to the Ukraine war – so global risks can shift very quickly. The main macroeconomic impacts that are already being felt across the world are increasingly higher inflation expectations, fuelled primarily by elevated commodity prices.

9.1.2 Global economic climate trend and consequences

Climate change will have an impact on the economy and this needs to be factored into new and emerging trends. For example, it is likely that the supply of both finished and intermediate goods will be affected through property damage to premises from flood, wind or heat, which disrupts production processes. In addition, interruption of energy supplies and disruption of global supply chains will probably impact the way manufactured goods are distributed.

At the primary end of production, in agriculture, this sector will be most exposed to flood, heat and drought changes, which will reduce crop yields and disturb the way pricing has previously been established. Increased incidence of pests and weeds, and reduced availability of water and groundwater will probably lead to reduced supplies, which will increase prices for consumers. This will in turn widen inequalities in society without governmental intervention, since food is a basic consumable taking a higher percentage of the income of the poorest in society.

Further down the production line, infrastructure will also be at risk from, for example, flooding. Transport and energy infrastructure will in all likelihood need to have significant upgrades if the lights are to stay on and people can still get to work.

Our modern 'hyper-connected' world will find itself exposed in data centres, which need increased cooling against higher temperatures or need to cater for greater instability in fixed interconnections (fibre optics). For example, sub-sea cabling, which enables rapid transfer of data across the globe, may be at risk from sea-level rise.

The potential impact on human health needs to be considered also. Deaths from heat spikes will be worse in cities, increased heat and humidity will cause more waterborne disease, vulnerable populations, such as the elderly and low-income communities, will be visibly more at risk and as these concerns become more evident the impact on mental health will be aggravated.

If these dystopian images seem far-fetched, consideration will at least need to be given to impacts on more prosaic activities in the daily life of the population in first-world economies: tourism will be affected as established ski resorts suffer from lack of snow, island resorts could disappear as water levels rise and water sports will be affected through more intense algae blooms.

9.1.2.1 EMERGING TRENDS IN BUSINESS AND THE FINANCIAL MARKETS

Climate change, as is commonly known, has a range of impacts across the globe that will threaten the bottom lines of businesses in a variety of ways. The frequency and intensity of extreme weather can damage factories, supply-chain operations and other infrastructure, and disrupt transport. Increase in drought conditions will make water more expensive, which will likely affect the cost of raw materials and production.

Climate volatility may force companies to deal with uncertainty in the price of resources for production, energy, transport and insurance. And some products could become obsolete or lose their market, such as equipment related to coal mining, or wood-burning stoves releasing carbon and particulates.

New regulations such as carbon pricing and subsidies that favour a competitor may also affect a business's bottom line. A company's reputation could suffer if it's seen as doing something that hurts the environment. Investors and stakeholders are increasingly worried about the potential for 'stranded assets' – those that become prematurely obsolete or fall out of favour and must be recorded as a loss using 'mark to market' principles of accounting. This includes fossil fuels that many believe should stay in the ground or real estate in a newly designated flood plain. Clearly this move away from a carbon economy will impact financial structures that presupposed continuing revenue from the fossil fuel industry.

9.1.3 Climate change and opportunity

Climate change also presents business opportunities. The Carbon Disclosure Project reported that 225 of the world's 500 biggest companies believe climate change could generate over $2.1 trillion in new business prospects.[2]

There will be more opportunity in clean energy, resilient and green buildings, and energy efficiency. Hybrid and electric vehicle production and the electric public transit sector are expected to grow. Construction of green infrastructure and more resilient coastal infrastructure could create many new jobs. Carbon capture, sequestration and uses of captured CO_2 present opportunities, especially if these are coupled with public policy such as tax incentives.

A newly warming world with less sea ice in the Arctic should provide new trade routes that will cut time and cost of global shipping.

There will be opportunities to develop more efficient goods and services such as cooling technologies to help transform the energy use so that AC units consume less power. Other new scientific techniques should help develop drought resistance and vertical farming.

Opportunities will become available to both keep people alive and keep them in check. There is likely to be increased demand for drugs to fight existing and new diseases, such as zoonotic disease, as regions of biodiversity collapse. What has been described above may also give rise to civil unrest as the reality of a world with scarce resources becomes clearer. The opportunities for private security and military equipment manufacturers will be much greater.

9.1.4 What businesses can do to protect themselves

How much climate change will hurt the economy depends on what measures organizations take to adapt to and prepare for it.

'There's a groundswell towards the view that any companies that fail to study their exposure to extreme weather and fail to disclose the types of vulnerabilities, including indirect ones, are going to have a hard time in the future.'[3] Businesses need to scrutinize their operations carefully. Their plans need to take into account the new landscape that will emerge; more electric vehicles will mean garage and car repairers will need to address the services they supply.

Asset managers are already scrutinizing their portfolios to assess if they are exposed to coastal properties, the agricultural sector or carbon-intensive operations. The sustainable investment market has continued to grow and evolve globally. While each region's approach to sustainable investment is slightly different, some trends have had a global reach. Every region again saw a rise in ESG integration and sustainability themed investing.[4] With BlackRock's announcement of its commitment to sustainable investment those numbers will have increased exponentially.

9.2 Physical risks – emerging trends

Extended wildfire seasons and prolonged heatwaves are two of the major trends that we have seen. Wildfires in California and Australia have been in the news for the last few years but in 2021 there were many intense wildfires across some previously unaffected regions of the world including southern Europe and Siberia. In August 2021 wildfires broke out in the Mediterranean, where the Greek Prime Minister described them as the country's 'greatest ecological disaster in decades'. One of the main related concerns is that in some countries, such as India, the summer heat is starting earlier and is more intense for longer periods of time.

In 2022 extreme flood also hit certain countries and regions that included Spain and parts of eastern Australia. In a period of just six days Brisbane saw almost 80 per cent of its annual rainfall pour down. Sydney recorded more than its average rainfall for the year in a little over three months.

In a BBC report it was stated that with respect to 2022: 'In the Southern Hemisphere, Argentina, Uruguay, Paraguay and Brazil all saw an historic heatwave in January, and many areas reported their hottest day on record. In the same month, Onslow in Western Australia hit 50.7C, the joint-highest temperature ever reliably recorded in the Southern Hemisphere.'[5]

The continued extreme weather events such as heatwaves increase healthcare services' strain on water, energy and transportation resulting in power shortages and even blackouts. Indirect impacts on food and livelihood security impact people who lose their crops or livestock due to extreme heat. Interconnected extreme events that can be attributed to climate change are discussed in more detail in Chapter 6 in terms of techniques that can assist in building greater resilience to physical risks.

9.2.1 Specific physical emerging risks and opportunities

This section provides specific examples and more details of the physical risks. Some of the main emerging threats as well as opportunities split between acute and chronic risks are shown in Figure 9.1.

FIGURE 9.1 Physical emerging risks and opportunities

Key physical risks	Emerging threats	Emerging opportunities
 Acute: extreme weather events	• Extended wildfire seasons • Prolonged heatwaves • Surface water flooding (localized flooding) • Interconnected extreme events, e.g. blackouts	• Development of risk adaptation solutions • Predictive alert/communication services to customers • Sustainable and resilient insurance/risk transfer solutions
 Chronic: changing weather patterns and rising mean temperatures and sea levels	• Droughts • Tipping points e.g. permafrost thawing • Reduced water availability • Biodiversity loss	

SOURCE OneRisk Consulting.

To highlight some of the emerging trends, this chapter focuses on providing more detail of some of the specific emerging threats and opportunities outlined in Figure 9.1:

1 Acute risk – extended wildfire seasons
2 Acute risk – prolonged heatwaves
3 Chronic risk – climate tipping points

Chapter 6 provided more insights into the some of the opportunities for improved resilience against physical risks, including interconnected extreme events such as blackouts that can be caused by climate change.

9.2.2 Acute physical risks – extended wildfire seasons

One of the main threats that is often linked to global warming is wildfire. Wildfires are not new and in fact in some regions the frequency is reducing, due to improved risk management practices. High temperatures and drier conditions are, however, creating ideal conditions for wildfires that are becoming increasingly extreme in terms of intensity due in part to the effects of climate change.

2016 and 2020 have been the warmest years on record to date and new scientific evidence points to a lengthening in the average time of fire seasons.[6,7] Therefore, climate change is a cause of the growing scale of wildfire events in different regions of the world even in regions where fires have historically happened only rarely.

One of the other major concerns in respect of wildfires is that they release more carbon into the atmosphere, which exacerbates the problem by effectively turning carbon sinks into carbon sources.

Since the mid-1980s, earlier snowmelt and associated warming has also been associated with an increase in length and severity of the wildfire season in the Western United States.[8] A 2015 study indicates that the increase in fire risk in California may be attributable to human-induced climate change.[9] A study of alluvial sediment deposits going back over 8,000 years found warmer climate periods experienced severe droughts and stand-replacing fires and concluded climate was such a powerful influence on wildfire that trying to recreate resettlement forest structure is likely impossible in a warmer future.

It is important to note that the intensity of wildfires is also linked to other socio-economic trends such as population density and movement of people to underdeveloped natural areas (the so-called 'wildland–urban interface') and sub-optimal fire management strategies that may have led to an increasing availability of natural biomass fuels.[10]

In summary, climate change is leading to drought conditions with enhanced conditions for fire, namely high temperatures, low humidity and strong winds. In many areas this is leading to more intense and frequent wildfire, which in turn is leading to greater loss of property and lives.

9.2.2.1 ROOT CAUSES – IGNITION SOURCES OF A FIRE

In managing risks, it is always important to understand the underlying root causes of loss events. In Chapter 6 we provide an overview of developing processes for discovering the root causes of problems in order to identify appropriate solutions, including post-loss incident reporting and use of bow tie analysis.

Stages of a wildfire are outlined in Figure 9.2. The process is taken from an RMS report that provides more detail and insights.[11] Typically, after ignition fire spreads by wind through available fuels. Then the actual damage from wildfire comes from radiant heat (flames), embers (burning chunks of fuel) and smoke. The fourth stage is ignition of structures.

The next stage of the wildfire in terms of damage will be linked to what is called 'urban configuration', when the fire reaches a neighbourhood. The last stage is the smoke damage, which can lead to business interruption risks as businesses may need to close for evaluation and related damages.

Further insights are provided next that help to explain the root causes in more detail.

Stage 1: Wildfire ignition There are many ignition types that are important to understand in the context of developing risk management improvements to prevent wildfires from happening in the first place. These can be split between natural and man-made and are set out in Figure 9.3. According to the RMS report, 'wildfire ignitions often occur in proximity to humans – in towns or along roads.'

Stage 4: Sources of ignition for structures The RMS report provides the three main sources of ignition for structures stemming from the wildfire hazard:

i Direct – flame in direct contact with a structure or accumulated embers on a structure;

ii Indirect – flying embers ignite materials close to a home; and

iii Radiant heat – heat from the fire causes materials to ignite.

The two examples above highlight the complexity of understanding the root causes, in this case the ignition sources, both for the wildfire and for properties that can be impacted.

FIGURE 9.2 Stages of a wildfire

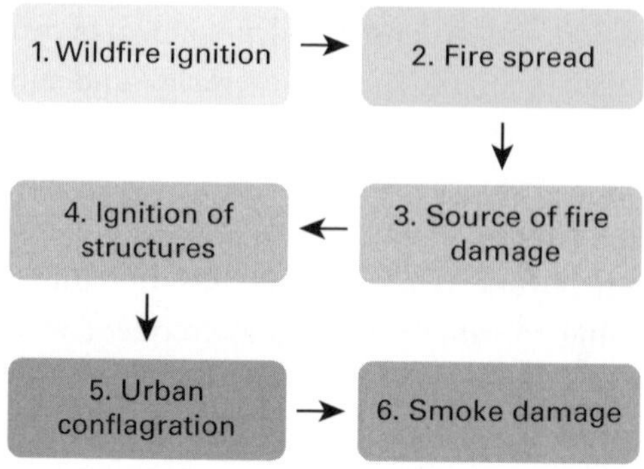

FIGURE 9.3 Stage 1:Wildfire ignition

Major cause	Specific cause	Climate change impact
Natural	Dry climate	Yes
	Lightning	No
	Volcanic eruption	No
Man-made	Arson	No
	Discarding cigarettes	No
	Power line - ARC	No
	Sparks from equipment	No
	Camp fires	No

SOURCE OneRisk Consulting. All rights reserved, 2022

BACKGROUND RESEARCH AND EVIDENCE FOR BUILDING BUSINESS CASES

When building a case to management about an emerging risk issue (discussed in detail in Chapter 8) it is very helpful to provide examples and undertake research on the subject.

In respect of wildfires many organizations will be susceptible to property and related losses that are linked to, for example, their building locations and vulnerabilities.

It is important that organizations seek to undertake background research and collate evidence on example historical losses and trends relevant to their risk profile or footprint that will ultimately lead to better decision-making in risk control measures, whether that's pre- or post-loss mitigation. In the context of climate change this can help to support the design of future climate scenarios outlined in Chapter 10, use of natural catastrophe models that we discuss in more detail in Chapter 7 and in building resilience that we discuss in detail in Chapter 6.

Historical global loss information and trends

Wildfires have increased in prominence from a financial loss and humanitarian perspective around the world in recent years. The United States, Australia, Portugal, Greece, Spain, Brazil and Russia – among many others – reported significant and historic fire activity in the past decade alone.

Here are some of the recent examples in the last few years.

Australian bushfires 2019

Australia's average temperatures have increased by 1.44°C since 1910, with 2019 being the hottest year on record.[12] In 2019 Australia suffered its largest drought and against this backdrop several climate drivers aligned to create conditions conducive to fire (high temperatures, low humidity and strong winds). This led to large destructive blazes spreading rapidly through dry vegetation in drought-affected lands.

North America including California 2021

Wildfires burned across western parts of North America for a significant period from the end of June to late August. The worst affected areas included several provinces in Canada, as well as California and the states in the Pacific Northwest of the United States. Among the fires was also the largest recorded fire in Californian state history, dubbed the Dixie Fire after the road in which it started. The Dixie Fire managed to burn through almost a million acres, before it was finally contained.[13]

No region of the world has seen more dramatic impacts of worsening fire conditions and resultant damage than the state of California in the United States. While large fires have been recorded in California for more than 100 years, there is a noticeable shift in the seasonality of fire events, the intensity of the fires themselves, and surface conditions fuelling the more unusual activity.

A 2018 study sponsored by the California Natural Resources Agency estimated that the average acres burned annually in the California Sierra Foothills could significantly increase in the coming decades.[14] Such increased acreage burnt could increase the number of postal codes 'at risk' by mid-century.

Mediterranean 2021

Many countries around the eastern and central Mediterranean suffered several days of high-intensity wildfires in summer months, leading to high concentrations of fire particle matter and degraded air quality. The particularly dry and hot conditions throughout the summer months provided the ideal environment for intense and long-lasting wildfires.

Turkey was the worst hit in July, with data showing daily fire intensity at very high levels that were well above average for the region. Other countries also affected by the devastating wildfires included Greece, Italy, Albania, North Macedonia, Algeria and Tunisia.

9.2.2.2 IMPACT OF WILDFIRES ON THE ENVIRONMENT AND CO_2 LEVELS

One of the related concerns about wildfires is the fact that wildfires can also have an effect on climate change itself, increasing the amount of carbon released into the atmosphere and inhibiting vegetation growth, which affects overall carbon uptake by plants. The Copernicus Atmosphere Monitoring Service (CAMS) keeps track of global wildfires and their emissions.

The fires in North America in 2021 released estimated total carbon emissions of approximately 83 megatonnes into the atmosphere.[15] The high intensity and persistence of the wildfire emissions could be seen in CAMS global forecasts as a large plume of smoke that crossed the North Atlantic and, mixing with wildfires from Siberia, reached western parts of the British Isles and northwest Europe in late August before travelling across large parts of Europe.

Therefore, it is important that decision makers have access to current, accurate information on atmospheric conditions, such as that produced by CAMS, so they can take the necessary steps to protect people from the effects of degraded air quality and smoke pollution

9.2.2.3 GROWING SCALE OF INSURED GLOBAL WILDFIRE LOSSES

According to Swiss Re, in 2020, wildfires triggered the third highest annual insured losses from this peril ever, after record seasons in 2017 and 2018. It states that from its analysis 'over 2016–2020, almost a quarter of all secondary peril insurance losses worldwide can be attributed to wildfire'.[16]

Most of the losses were in California. In recent years, annual losses from wildfire have been rising rapidly. This is unprecedented: before 2016, the share of this peril in losses averaged just above 3 per cent and rarely exceeded 5–10 per cent (see Figure 9.4). Rating agencies for insurers have had to reassess their risk appetites and as a result their pricing for these risks, which also suggests that reinsurance capital providers will be likely to do the same. The number of acres burned in 2018 was, for example, nearly double that seen in 2017, the rating agency notes.

According to Aon's report, 'Prior to 2015, the world recorded just four years in which aggregated wildfire-related insured losses had topped $2 billion (2021 USD).'[17] The report states that there have been 21 individual billion-dollar insured fires globally with 16 of these occurring since 2015, and all but two of those events were in the United States. The peak insurance industry loss years have totalled $18 billion (2017), $17 billion (2018) and $14 billion (2020).

FIGURE 9.4 Increasing trend in global insured losses from wildfires

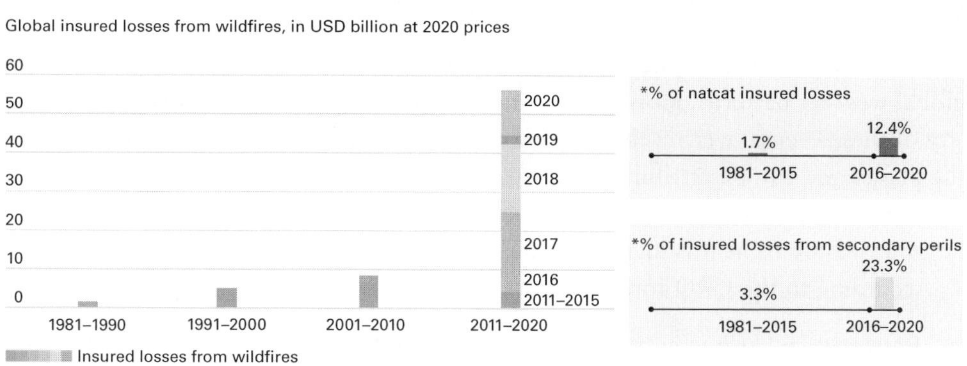

SOURCE Swiss Re Institute

One of the most important issues for an organization to recognize is that the insurance industry ultimately needs to make profits and the insurance market is now seeking to either increase its prices; reduce capacity; pull out of providing markets or seek to develop new innovative solutions.

This may lead to significant increases in premiums or unavailability of coverage and organizations to covers such as their property insurance covers, unless there are improved risk management practices.

9.2.2.4 RISK MITIGATION OPTIONS AND MEASURES

As climate change makes wildfire activity more challenging in the future, it is essential for strategic planning to include mitigation measures for homes and businesses that insist on living in these high-risk areas. This could include:[18]

- Enforcing or mandating defensible space between vegetation and a structure
- Installing fire-resistant or less-flammable material for roofing, siding and/or decking
- Maximizing distance between properties
- Vastly improved wildfire risk mapping
- Enhancing infrastructure to improve evacuation and firefighting efforts

Mitigating wildfire risk can involve several activities, including: enhanced building codes; land-use planning; environmental regulation; enhanced infrastructure; adoption of wildfire sensors; fire-resistant individual property modifications; and community-wide abatement.

Understanding the relative value of each of these mitigation measures is critical towards their implementation.

Businesses have started to respond to the need for more homeowner risk reduction activities to take place as well as improved communication strategies.

9.2.3 Acute physical risks – prolonged heatwaves

'Extreme heat events do occur within natural climate variations due to changes in global weather patterns. However, the increase in the frequency, duration, and intensity of these events over recent decades is clearly linked to the observed warming of the planet and can be attributed to human activity.'[19]

Many all-time or monthly extreme heat records continue to be broken and population exposure to heat is increasing due to climate change.

According to the CRO forums report:[20]

> Heatwaves are likely to increase, particularly in mid-latitudes on land, with the increase in peak temperatures being 2-3 times higher than global average increase. The strongest

change is found in Central and Eastern North America, Central and Southern Europe, the Mediterranean, Western and Central Asia, and Southern Africa. These regions all have a strong soil-moisture-temperature coupling leading to increased dryness.

9.2.3.1 HISTORICAL GLOBAL LOSS INFORMATION AND TRENDS

One of the most extraordinary and powerful heatwaves ever experienced by North America hit the west coast in June 2021. This was caused by what meteorologists called a 'dome of high pressure'. The heatwave extended from California – worsening the drought even as the first wildfires of the season began – and extended all the way up to Canada, where temperatures rose up to 121.28°F (49.6°C), shattering all previous records. 'This is the beginning of a permanent emergency', the Governor of Washington state said.

According to NOAA this was a 1-in-1,000-year occurrence; or having a 0.1 per cent chance of happening in any given year. A weather station in Lytton, British Columbia set a new Canadian national heat record on three consecutive days: peaking at 121°F (49.6°C) on 29 June 2021. The next day, 90 per cent of the village of Lytton was destroyed by a major wildfire. This highlights the linkage and connectiveness that can be drawn from the previous section in this chapter on wildfires.

9.2.3.2 IMPACTS OF EXTREME HEAT

As many as 1.2 billion people around the world could face heat stress conditions by 2100 if current levels of global warming continue, according to a study from Rutgers University in the United States. That is at least four times more than those affected today.

Heat stress will be a major challenge in less-affluent countries where more vulnerable populations handle more dangerous jobs. The UN cites that accumulated direct and indirect losses due to heat stress could reach $2.4 trillion by 2030 if nothing is done to mitigate climate change risk.

Heatwaves, or heat and hot weather that can last for several days, can have a significant impact on society, including a rise in heat-related deaths.

Heatwaves are among the most dangerous of natural hazards, but rarely receive adequate attention because their death tolls and destruction are not always immediately obvious. From 1998 to 2017, more than 166,000 people died due to heatwaves, including more than 70,000 who died during the 2003 heatwave in Europe.

The number of extremely hot days every year when the temperature reaches 50°C has doubled since the 1980s according to a global BBC analysis.[21] They also now happen in more areas of the world than before, presenting unprecedented challenges to human health and to how we live.

While the effects of heat may be exacerbated in cities, due to the urban heat island (UHI) effect, the livelihoods and wellbeing of non-urban communities can also be severely disrupted during and after periods of unusually hot weather.

Heatwaves can burden health and emergency services and also increase strain on water, energy and transportation resulting in power shortages or even blackouts. Food and livelihood security may also be strained if people lose their crops or livestock due to extreme heat.[22] Extreme events, including a discussion on blackouts, were discussed in Chapter 6.

People are also facing difficult choices as the landscape around them changes, as extreme heat makes drought and wildfires more likely.

9.2.3.3 SPECIFIC IMPACTS ON THE AGRICULTURAL SECTOR

Heatwaves can also cause heat stress in both animals and plants and have a negative impact on food production. Extreme periods of high temperature are particularly harmful for crop production if they occur when the plants are flowering – if this single, critical stage is disrupted, there may be no seeds at all.

Temperature is a key factor in plant growth and development. Along with the levels of light, carbon dioxide, air humidity, water and nutrients, temperature influences plant growth and ultimately crop yields. Hot summers also have a negative impact on, for example, dairy herds and, on aggregate, the short- and long-term output of the dairy industry. This problem could be worsening not only due to global average temperature increases, but also due to intensive selection for production among dairy herds in temperate climates.[23]

Some insurers are developing a specialist parametric product that can be used to design unique heat stress indices to provide protection for farmers. They can be used for intangible risks such as loss of reputation and long-term health-related losses through protection against short-term (lower production, reduced quality) and long-term (chronic effects on animal health) perils of heat stress.

Chapter 6 provides more specific details of new financial risk transfer solutions that can build resilience to climate-related perils such as heat stress.

Higher night-time temperatures may increase respiration at night, causing declines in yield (e.g. rice) and flowering or reproduction (e.g. beans). Most crops can tolerate higher daytime temperatures during vegetative growth, with photosynthesis reaching an optimum at between 20°C and 30°C.[24]

In Aon's report referred to earlier, in the US in 2021 it stated that 'The physical and financial toll due to prolonged drought and above-average temperatures left a major strain on the agricultural and agribusiness sectors as direct economic losses were anticipated to exceed $9 billion.'

9.2.4 Physical tipping points

One of the greatest concerns and emerging threats in relation to physical risks is the concept of tipping points, the threats of abrupt irreversible climate changes, which were introduced by the Intergovernmental Panel on Climate Change (IPCC) in their report in 2018.[25]

Evidence is mounting that tipping points such as the loss of the Amazon rainforest or the West Antarctic ice sheet could be more likely than was previously thought, and according to many scientists and economists would have significant impacts on biophysical systems, which could lead to long-term irreversible changes across the world.

According to Dr James Hansen, Climate Science, Awareness and Solutions Program, Earth Institute, Columbia University 'Tipping points are so dangerous because if you pass them, the climate is out of humanity's control: if an ice-sheet disintegrates and starts to slide into the ocean, there's nothing we can do about that.'

Table 9.2 highlights some of the main tipping points concerns and potential impacts on the planet. These highlight the need for organizations to conduct research into future climate scenarios in a wider and deeper context in order to assess the impact on their business.

TABLE 9.2 Examples of the main global climate tipping points and potential impacts

Tipping point concern	Potential impact on the planet
Reduction of northern hemisphere spring snow cover	Decreases the albedo effect and amplifies regional warming, as is already seen in higher latitudes
Arctic winter sea ice	It is linked to potential changes in thermohaline circulation (Gulf Stream and jet stream included) and rising sea levels.
Greenland sea ice loss	It is linked to weather anomalies in North America and Europe with potential to change thermohaline circulation linked to the Gulf Stream.
Ice sheet dynamics (Greenland and West-Antarctica)	Raising sea levels over the long term and potentially slowing down Atlantic thermohaline circulation
Permafrost thawing	Releasing CO_2 (under aerobic conditions) and/or methane (under anaerobic conditions). Note that IPCC have 'high confidence' permafrost will thaw and release carbon but 'low confidence' in how much will be emitted how soon
El Niño – Southern Oscillation (ENSO)	Increasing and changing in amplitude, changing patterns of hurricanes, precipitation and drought.
Collapsing marine ecosystems and dissolving coral reefs	Impacting fishing, biodiversity and coastal protection from storms or storm surges

(continued)

TABLE 9.2 (Continued)

Tipping point concern	Potential impact on the planet
Dying boreal forests and Amazon rainforest due to heat stress	Reducing rainfall and wildfire, thereby reducing CO_2 uptake
Reduced West African monsoon	Increased risk of drought and a greening of the Sahel
Interference in Indian summer monsoon	Increasing drought frequency
Prolonged SW North American droughts	Leading to desertification, as is already being experienced

SOURCE CRO Forum. The heat is on: Insurability and resilience in a changing climate emerging risk initiative – position paper[26]

9.3 Transition risks – high-level overview

Transition risks relating to the consequence of transitioning to a lower carbon or 'green' economy are resulting in a range of both global risks and opportunities facing organizations, which were covered in detail in Chapter 5.

To illustrate and explain the main transition risks that organizations need to consider, Figure 5.5 highlighted a top-down approach from leading global drivers through to structural changes and risk drivers to a broad range of specific threats and opportunities. Many of these are long-term emerging trends.

These include carbon emissions targets and plans, investment in green infrastructure, greenwashing, 'green' energy inflation, organizations' purpose, global flow of information, digital platforms and changing societal expectations.

9.3.1 Corporate pledges and climate-related financial disclosures

Perhaps the most important trends in recent years have been the increasing number of corporate pledges and climate-related financial disclosures. Climate change awareness and adaptation and wider ESG criteria are increasingly valued by shareholders including investors, employees and customers. We are continuing to see record numbers of corporate pledges, especially net zero targets on mitigating climate change, which is raising the bar for corporate governance.

The growing focus on climate change also extends to corporate disclosure, and there has been significant progress on this front with improvement in global flow of information and continued regulatory pressure that is leading some countries to introduce mandatory climate and wider ESG-related reporting. Continued global activism will also contribute to capturing global attention. Climate reporting and disclosure are covered in Chapter 12.

There has been a marked increase in global sustainable investment. The global Sustainability Investment Alliance's latest investment review shows that global sustainable investment now tops $25 trillion – up 15 per cent in two years – and in total equates to 36 per cent of all professionally managed assets. More than 70 asset managers, including BlackRock and Vanguard, have also recently signed a pledge with the New Zero Investors Initiative, which has been formed to help achieve net zero greenhouse gas emissions by 2050.

Changing societal expectations are leading to the increasing demand for sustainable products, as consumers want to purchase products that they view as sustainable across the entire value chain. Consumers are increasingly changing their consumption habits so that they don't negatively affect the environment and many are fearful of the overall impact of climate change. Unfortunately, this is also leading to a major risk issue, namely 'greenwashing'. This is primarily a marketing tactic where consumers or investors are misled into believing that an organization or brand is sustainable. Section 9.4 provides more detail around the emerging risks of greenwashing.

As the world begins to decarbonize, new market opportunities are available for organizations to create products and services for a low-carbon world that uses less energy and natural resources, emits fewer greenhouse gases and can help mitigate climate damage and regenerate natural systems. On the flip side there are opportunities to help organizations improve resilience, which in turn is leading to product innovation such as the electric and hydrogen economies and a range of new technologies.

9.3.2 Impact of wider societal issues

Overall, organizations are continuing to realize that modifying existing internal business activities to address climate change and wider social issues can protect the reputation of the organization in the long run.

People constantly adjust how they make sense of the world; perspectives change as a result of age and in response to changing surroundings ('social proof'). An important reference point for this 'mental modelling' process is the demographic with which one is associated giving a good indication of social and geopolitical awareness.

The change in outlook is also defined by the inequity between generations. Millennials are materially worse off than their previous generations through being saddled with tuition fees and unaffordable housing, and suffer living on a degraded planet through their parents' appetite for burning fossil fuels. The heart of their new outlook is less about concern for material wealth, more about seeking out a socially purposeful way of living – and challenging any organizations that fail to support this.

One of the important issues linked to this is that many Millennials are joining climate action groups such as the Climate Coalition, who are striving to make sure the public voice is heard and whose goals are focused on striving for cleaner and greener future. These organizations are putting pressure on governments around to world to take greater action and are themselves changing the mindsets of individuals, and this in turn is creating the need for organizational changes.

The global flow of information is significantly helping to raise the awareness of ecological and social crises around the world. The global and local activism that we saw in 2021 including 'Insulate', which blocked the M25 in England, has captured global attention and galvanized opinions.

9.3.3 Governments and regulators

Government and regulators are now stepping in to push further change, faster and with more consistency across the economy than the market alone could do. Europe is taking the lead on climate-related financial disclosures, and other jurisdictions are following suit, including the United States.

This has led to sustainability issues becoming core considerations in business. To be able to distinguish between companies, and investment opportunities, investors need high-quality, comparable data, and this is driving the call for global sustainability standards and the regulatory interest in mandatory climate reporting.

To highlight some of the emerging trends, the next section focuses on providing more detail of some of the specific emerging threats and opportunities.

9.4 Climate and ESG reporting and 'greenwashing'

Prompted by the global climate crisis all too clearly evident during recent years' news reports of corporate abuses and ecological emergencies – such as wildfires, flash floods, melting glaciers, islands disappearing under rising seas and heat-driven human migrations – there has been a public call for greater business transparency in reporting potential social and environmental harms. Investors and members of the public (including, of course, organizations' own staff) openly call on organized interests to report transparently how their activities affect the societies, and natural world, that they operate in.

An increasingly sharp strain of public criticism from public, NGO and media observers is focused on the claims made by businesses that make a highly-publicized virtue of conducting themselves well with regard to their social and environmental responsibilities. Where these claims have been shown to be unproven or unprovable, critics use the term 'greenwashing' to describe such misleading information. These critics now include a growing number of regulators who have shown a willingness to impose swift and severe penalties on organizations that indulge in greenwashing.

The critics are united in calling for business interests, in particular, to demonstrate how in practice they really do adhere to claims of probity. To be effective and credible, this proof is seen as requiring broadly agreed, comparable and easy-to-read reporting standards capable of decoding (making plain sense of) any organization's claims. By popular agreement, such proof is required under three broad category headings: environmental responsibility, social responsibility and good governance, collectively abbreviated to the term 'ESG reporting'.

Regulators, and in particular, financial and professional conduct regulators, have responded vigorously to these public concerns. Many, if not all, are working to assess, publish and roll out new standards.

Conduct regulators are concerned, for example, that asset managers are overstating ESG assets, which could lead to a 'green valuation bubble' and subsequent crash as and when the bubble bursts. New EU rules from the Sustainable Finance Disclosure Regulation (SFDR) will soon address this concern by forcing firms to disclose how environmentally sustainable their activities are. Asset managers will soon have to evaluate and transparently report how their funds fulfil universal standards of environmental, social and governance (ESG) responsibility.

Other jurisdictions, including the United States and United Kingdom, have yet to produce equivalent standards. However, the Securities and Exchange Commission, the US securities regulator, set up a task force in 2021 in its enforcement division to identify misconduct in ESG claims. Its first action was to collaborate with the German banking regulator BaFin to challenge Deutsche Bank's asset management subsidiary on their statement of environmental credentials.[27]

FINANCIAL CONDUCT REGULATORS LEAD THE CHARGE

In financial markets, the new regime of 'behavioural regulation' – aimed at preventing both financial and non-financial misconduct – has stepped up quickly to challenge a range of businesses.

Asset managers have been charged with 'overstating ESG assets'. The regulators' concern is that inflated claims to 'green asset' values could in turn inflate a valuation bubble, creating preconditions for a subsequent crash as the bubble bursts.

9.4.1 Universal standards for ESG: no time soon

At the Glasgow COP26 World Climate Conference in 2021, world leaders were outnumbered by representatives of the financial sector who presented a commercial version of the agenda for change; this asserted that financial incentives work faster than central government initiatives to achieve change, so financial markets should lead ESG standard-setting. This commercial intervention at a world leaders' event indicates how seriously institutional investors are committed to driving public policy recognition of an 'ESG agenda'.

Simultaneously with COP26, 168 asset managers from 28 countries, with a collective $17 trillion of assets under management, announced the Carbon Disclosure Project (CDP) aimed at standardizing corporate indicators for climate and social impact reporting. As a statement of intent, CDP called out over 1,000 brands, including such 'stars' as Alibaba, Amazon, Berkshire Hathaway, Chipotle, Facebook, Roche and Tesla. CDP's analysis announced that 'the tide was turning against companies that don't respond to investor demands for better disclosures of environmental risks'.[28] Specific concerns were raised in respect of the world's banks, insurers and asset managers. It also noted that (in mid-2021) more than half of all major financial brands had not yet produced any plausible evidence of a commitment to disinvest from global climate change activities.

The financial sector's response was a 'net-zero pledge' in November 2021: a coalition representing $130 trillion of funds committed to 'a virtuous cycle of innovation and investment for Net Zero' climate impact.[29]

New global standards of ESG and green finance reporting are proposed, though not yet fully developed or generally adopted. Examples are outlined in the following sections.

9.4.2 New 'anti-greenwashing' rules

Much of the early action is among the financial market community. Parallel pro-ESG anti-greenwashing initiatives are being cheered on by regulators (on grounds of 'social goods') and institutional investors (on grounds of 'protecting business resilience and long-term value').

In the EU, a suite of Sustainable Finance Disclosure Regulation (SFDR) is addressing this concern. SFDR will compel businesses to disclose how environmentally sustainable their activities are. For example, under SFDR Article 8, asset managers can claim a 'light green' or the higher 'dark green' status, depending on how far they 'actively promote environmental or social characteristics' of funds under their management. Other jurisdictions such as the United States and United Kingdom may be expected to produce similar or even equivalent standards.

9.4.3 Example forms of 'greenwashing'

The following activities give a warning sign that 'ESG misconduct' (greenwashing) is occurring:

- **Misdirection** – Where firms cynically divert public attention away from, say, a polluting activity, by running high-profile programmes of 'public good works'. They market a forceful message about social awareness or renewable energy, for example, while still investing in carbon-producing technologies.
- **Loose 'commitment'** – Announcing an intention or plan to comply, or conform to standard, that lacks any timescale or calibration. (Example: India announced its intention to 'phase down' rather than 'phase out' coal use by 2070.)[30]
- **Covert lobbying** – Setting up and funding 'pseudo-science' research groups who are briefed to blur the edges of any science debate around public policy, or the true extent of social harms resulting from certain products, investments or employment practices. This technique has been used, for example, by fossil fuel companies to cast doubt on the extent of global warming. (Example: Edelman called out for undeclared pro-fossil fuel lobbying for ExxonMobil.)[31]

It is important for organizations' risk managers to be aware of the desire among staff generally to be part of an enterprise that promotes an ESG-positive agenda. Ignoring this could quickly harm business value, eroding the retention rate of employees and degrading the quality of available human talent. For a firm *not* to acknowledge this agenda may even present an existential threat.

This leads to the forecast that in the near future risk managers must be aware of the reputational impact of explosions of public outrage as leaked disclosures overtake the efforts of regulators to focus firms' attention on genuine ESG initiatives.

9.5 Emerging technologies to meet net zero targets

The IRM's energy and renewables group stated in its 2022 Risk Prediction report 'Whether the economy recovers or fails, expect to see continuing investment in advanced and emerging technologies which support the impetus for Net Zero and the low carbon economy.'

There are four main areas of transition risk that were highlighted in Figure 5.5 (in Chapter 5) and one of the main types is technology risks, which is a now a major way that organizations can seek to reduce their carbon footprint and meet their emissions targets.

Technology risks can generally be categorized as either:

1. Substitution or replacement of existing technology/machinery across the value chain.

2 Substitution or replacement of existing products and services with lower emissions options.
3 Unsuccessful investment in new technologies.

Examples of mitigation options that are aligned to the use of new technologies to reduce an organization's emissions include the following:

- Replacement of inefficient machinery with more efficient lower-emitting machinery
- Renewable energy – procuring energy from Renewable Energy Guarantee of Origin (REGO) backed sources (which is independently verified)
- Investigating options for reducing waste in production processes
- Utilizing by-products from the production process
- Reduction of packaging for products (e.g. one example is the removal of plastic around fruit and vegetables in French supermarkets)
- Replacing car fleets with electric vehicles
- Using renewable energy providers across all of your premises
- Premises – improving insulation of existing buildings or replacing lighting with energy-efficient LED lighting options

Some specific examples of potential long-term solutions are highlighted in Table 9.3.

TABLE 9.3 Sustainable technologies that are supporting the drive to net zero

Emerging technological innovations and concepts	Description and objective	Example
Carbon capture and storage	A process to capture CO_2 from the air and permanently bury it underground in geological formation.	A machine traps and then heats CO_2 to a high temperature, then mixes it with water and pumps it underground. Thus eventually, by natural mineralization, it automatically mixes with basalt rock and turns into stone permanently. Technology example – bioenergy with carbon capture and storage (BECCS).

(continued)

TABLE 9.3 (Continued)

Emerging technological innovations and concepts	Description and objective	Example
Fusion reactor	Fusion reactors are devices that produce electricity from heat generated by nuclear fusion reactions. This process results in release of helium, thus it is completely harmless to the environment and produces clean energy like the Sun.	A machine called a tokamak that heats the light-weight elements like hydrogen atoms and releases helium, which results in release of large amount of energy.
Electric vehicle (EV)	Vehicles that run on rechargeable batteries that are powered by electricity are termed EVs. EVs do not emit any GHG in the air.	EVs become a part of every industrial sector to reduce their carbon footprint by utilizing them for supply chain or commuting, etc.
Biomass	Biomass is referred to as and includes woods, plants, animals or waste. The energy from these organisms or waste can be burnt to create heat or converted into electricity. It generates far fewer air emissions than fossil fuels and reduces the amount of waste sent to landfills.[32]	Sustainable aviation fuel is a fuel produced from biomass. Biomass energy is utilized for heating, cooking, etc.
Smart glass technology	Smart glass is an energy-efficient glass that can be used in buildings. During summer, the glass blocks any heating wavelength and during winter the glass allows sunlight to aid heating.	Electrochromic glass windows use electricity to change the tint and reflectiveness of the glass.[33]
Unmanned aerial vehicle (UAV)	UAVs can carry cameras (for video and still pictures) and sensors (including radiation sensors and weather sensors).	Farmers can use UAVs to monitor the health of crops and detect damage done by drought, floods, hailstorms. Researchers can use UAVs underwater to measure ocean heat.[34]
Digital monitoring solutions	Digital innovations that analyse the energy and water usage pattern, provide energy wastage information, track energy usage performance and identify inefficient operations without requiring an expert. They help in reducing energy wastage thereby reducing the cost of energy for the company.	Energy management solutions are being developed by several companies to monitor the required aspects to reduce their carbon footprint.

9.5.1 Hydrogen economy – fossil fuel alternatives

New technologies curbing the carbon emissions to drive decarbonization are being developed as substitutes for fossil fuels. This will be a major emerging trend and opportunity for organizations in their respective markets.

Section 301 (2) of the Energy Policy Act, 1992, states that hydrogen is an alternative fuel.[35] Hydrogen produced by the process of electrolysis is clean and usage of hydrogen in various devices/equipment results in emission of water, which is environmentally friendly.

It is pertinent to note the growing recognition of hydrogen in various industrial sectors like transportation, shipping, utilities/energy, aviation, etc.

Many companies are replacing their traditional technologies with hydrogen technology to reduce their carbon footprint and overall GHG reduction since hydrogen is a clean substitute for fossil fuels.

According to the International Energy Agency (IEA), in its report produced at the request of the Government of Japan under its G20 presidency, clean hydrogen is currently enjoying unprecedented political and business momentum, with the number of policies and projects around the world expanding rapidly.[36]

9.5.1.1 'GREEN' HYDROGEN

There is a growing demand for hydrogen that is produced with renewables. Green hydrogen is the hydrogen produced without jeopardizing the climate change, as there are other types that are less carbon-friendly such as grey and blue hydrogen.

Green hydrogen is the only type produced in a climate-neutral manner, and it is also easy to store and transport, making it critical to reaching net zero by 2050.[37] It can help to achieve net-zero carbon dioxide (CO_2) emissions in energy-intensive, hard-to-decarbonize sectors like steel, chemicals, long-haul transport, shipping and aviation.[38] Hydrogen is a gas at normal temperature and pressure, and condenses and forms into liquid at extreme cool temperatures.

The current main drawbacks are that the production process is expensive and complex and will require increased future investment in R&D to support efficiencies in the production prices to help reduce the cost. It is pertinent to note that the Green Hydrogen Catapult, a United Nations initiative to bring down the cost of green hydrogen, announced that it is almost doubling its goal for green electrolysers from 25 gigawatts to 45 gigawatts by 2027.[39]

9.5.1.2 SPECIFIC USES TO REDUCE CARBON EMISSIONS

Table 9.4 provides a summary of the main uses of hydrogen that will help to reduce carbon emissions in industry settings.

Substituting green hydrogen for fossil fuel is a favourable option for organizations to consider. Green hydrogen can be advantageous to every industrial sector because of its versatility.

TABLE 9.4 Hydrogen economy – main uses and challenges

Type of hydrogen	Technology	Sector	Description/main use	Challenges
Hydrogen gas	Hydrogen-fired boiler	Utilities/Energy	A hydrogen-fired-boiler is a home heating technology that is currently replacing natural gas boilers. These boilers are key to decarbonizing home heating and hot water since the by-product of burning hydrogen gas is water and it is therefore a carbon-free fuel source. Using hydrogen is also beneficial for energy systems because it offers one of the most attractive means of providing large-scale energy storage	
Hydrogen liquid (fuel)	Hydrogen aircraft	Aviation	Hydrogen-fuelled aircraft are gradually developing and in progress to improve further. The benefit is that hydrogen packs a lot of energy per unit of mass, i.e. three times more than conventional jet fuel, and more than a hundred times that of lithium-ion batteries	The energy density of liquid hydrogen is only about a quarter of that of jet fuel, so it requires storage tanks four times the size[40]
	Hydrogen car	Transportation	Hydrogen-fuelled vehicles do not need charging – they have fuel tanks like petrol/diesel vehicles. Hydrogen fuel is made from the process of electrolysis from water and thus the vehicle's tailpipe emission is water, which is harmless, making it a zero-emission vehicle	High cost
	Hydrogen ship	Shipping	Hydrogen fuel is an alternative to bunker fuel (diesel, etc) to power the marine boat/vessel. The newly introduced ships contain a hybrid-engine for the boat/vessel that allows it to be powered by conventional fuel as well as hydrogen fuel. Thus, this innovation certainly leads to powering the ship with zero emissions with hydrogen fuel	Does not work in existing engines; requires a new engine/ship that can facilitate the usage of hydrogen fuel

Many organizations consider utilizing hydrogen-fuelled vehicles because they emit water, which is an environmentally friendly emission and thus it reduces the overall carbon footprint of the organization.

Aircrafts and ships can be fuelled by hydrogen too and various companies have already commenced its development, setting it to be a long-term investment strategy, which eventually adheres to the policies that are formed to mitigate climate change.

Hydrogen is not only limited to usage by industries, but also can be utilized in products and equipment used for residential purposes. Boilers that are installed in homes for heating can be fuelled by hydrogen instead of natural gas and it has the same efficiency as natural gas. Hydrogen is gradually evolving to be a valuable and sustainable option to be used in technologies by organizations to support their business strategies and reduce their carbon footprint.

9.6 Liability risks – emerging climate change litigation

It is generally agreed within the legal fraternity that the field of corporate accountability, human rights, the environment or future climate litigation are areas that will develop at great speed in coming years as climate change continues to 'bite' and science allows the attribution of responsibility more clearly.

Climate change litigation has gained momentum since the adoption of the Paris Agreement in 2015, increasing in volume, scope and geographical coverage. Of the 1727 cases documented worldwide between 1986 and 2020, more than half have been brought since 2015. The majority of these cases are in the United States, where some of the biggest oil and gas companies are embroiled in legal disputes with cities and states over the industry's role in global warming.

Awareness of climate risks and the growing perception that courts can be a forum to advance climate goals are two main drivers of climate change litigation. New developments in attribution science, where the relationship between emissions and climate change-related impacts is quantified, have also encouraged efforts to attribute emissions to specific companies.

As climate change litigation grows, its complexity does also. Another legal approach has gained considerable traction especially in Europe: lawsuits against governments and corporations, seeking injunctions ordering alignment with the Paris Agreement. These are increasing the risk that states and corporations can be found negligent in their duty to protect the public from the harmful effects of climate change.

FIGURE 9.5 Historical legal cases shaping the climate agenda

Class action Exxon 2015	Legal case against Pacific Gas & Electric 2018	Legal case against Shell in 26 may 2021
Class action for compensation	*Corporate failure*	*Failure to mitigate GHG emissions*
Two states have launched fraud investigations into Exxon over climate change and sued (one went to trial in 2019, and the attorney general lost.) Nine cities and counties, from New York to San Francisco, have sued major fossil fuel companies, seeking compensation for climate change damages	A California utility has pleaded guilty to the deaths of 84 people in a wildfire, the deadliest US corporate crime ever successfully prosecuted	On 26 May 2021, the Hague District Court ordered Royal Dutch Shell plc (Shell) to reduce its worldwide CO_2 emissions by 45% by 2030 (compared to 2019 levels)

SOURCE OneRisk Consulting

9.6.1 Legal cases are shaping the climate change agenda

Major climate-related events are shaping the climate agenda and helping to improve risk management practices. Figure 9.5 highlights three important but different legal cases that highlight the growing trends in litigation.

9.6.1.1 CLASS ACTION LAWSUITS AGAINST POLLUTERS

In the first case, two US states have launched fraud investigations into Exxon over climate change and sued. The litigation, reinforced by science, has the potential to reshape the way the world thinks about energy production and the consequences of global warming.

Two specific examples of ongoing actions against Exxon are summarized below.

RAMIREZ V EXXONMOBIL CORP – LAWSUIT FILED: 2016

A man who invested in Exxon stock during 2016 filed a securities fraud class action against Exxon and three Exxon officers in the federal court for the Northern District of Texas. The action was filed on behalf of purchasers of Exxon common stock between 19 February 2016 and 27 October 2016. The complaint alleged that Exxon's public statements during that period were materially false and misleading because they failed to disclose that internally generated reports concerning climate change recognized the environmental risks caused by global warming and climate change; that due to risk associated with climate change Exxon would not be able to extract existing hydrocarbon reserves it claimed to have; and that Exxon had used an inaccurate price of carbon to calculate the value of certain oil and gas prospects. The complaint alleged that as a result of positive statements Exxon made during the class period, the common stock price was artificially inflated, and that Exxon's release of its third-quarter financial results on 28 October 2016, in which it disclosed it might have to write down 20 per cent of its oil and gas assets, resulted in the stock price falling by more than $2 per share.

COMMONWEALTH V EXXONMOBIL

10/10/2019: Letter sent to Exxon Mobil Corporation by the Massachusetts Office of the Attorney General providing notice that the Attorney General intended to commence an enforcement action against ExxonMobil – asserting that Exxon systematically and intentionally misled investors and consumers about climate change by failing to disclose climate change risks, misrepresenting its business practices related to use of proxy costs of carbon, misleadingly advertising its products, failing to disclose its products' impacts on climate change, and engaging in greenwashing campaigns – and thereafter launched enforcement action. (Challenged by Exxon.)

These two cases highlight the growing concerns in respect of historical and ongoing public statements provided by organizations that are alleged to have provided false and misleading information that is material in respect to some specific concerns, such as the potential to both artificially inflate the stock price and impact the cost of carbon for their products

9.6.1.2 LITIGATION FOR NEGLIGENCE

The second case relates to the Californian wildfires in 2018, which led to the corporate failure of the Pacific Gas and Electric Company (P&GE) due to litigation for negligence – now a key risk for many organizations to consider.

The proceeding against PG&E was for neglecting its infrastructure, which caused the deadliest and most destructive '2018 Camp Fire' because of its faulty equipment. PG&E admitted that it did not properly maintain the power line, which ignited in a forested area known for strong winds.[41] This event resulted in loss of lives of 85 people and destroyed more than 18,000 buildings, including 14,000 homes. The CEO of PG&E pleaded guilty and agreed to pay $25.5 billion for losses from the

2018 fire, and a maximum fine of $3.5 million for its crimes in addition to $500,000 for the cost of the investigation.[42]

9.6.1.3 SHAREHOLDER LITIGATION TO REDUCE GHG EMISSIONS – STANDARDS OF CARE

The third and most recent case is Shell – highlighting the need for leading energy companies to cut their emissions due to increased stakeholder litigation.

Standards of care are also evolving, increasing the risk that states and corporations can be found negligent in their duty to protect the public from the harmful effects of climate change. These trends have led to a number of new legal cases including the District Court in The Hague ruling in May 2021 that Shell must reduce its global net carbon emissions by 45 per cent by the end of 2030 from 2019 levels.

Insurers are increasingly concerned about the impacts on state financial lines classes of business including directors' and officers' insurance policies, and considering ways to adapt to increased litigation through, for example, more improved pricing and reserving practices. On a broader note, many companies that we speak to, including banks, are increasingly concerned about the cost and availability of future insurance to protect their business.

Conclusion

As can be seen from this review, while it is easy to view climate change risk through the lens of the growing physical effects of a warming planet, and the inevitable natural catastrophes that will arise with the impact of a changing climate – heat spikes, flooding, windstorms, etc – risk management needs to address the wider aspects of transition and legal risk too. Categorizing risk into these three broad areas is a key consideration in bringing the risk into manageable realms.

In this chapter we have reviewed some aspects of the physical damage that will inevitably occur as the climate changes. These physical risks are broadly capable of being forecast and having some element of mitigation provided for, whether that be through reconfiguration of premises to enhance resilience or a wholesale relocation to premises that offer greater protection against the likely forecasts.

The second area of risk that we have reviewed is that associated with the transition to a decarbonized world. Some of these risks are known but many more will emerge as the world changes. Here it is important to view risk management in its broadest context and to assess the opportunities that change will deliver, as well as the threats.

Risk management in the 21st century has always been about more than anticipating threats. What distinguishes risk management now from the past is the way in which it embraces risk to spot opportunities and focus on the ways to best exploit them. The changes that will take place in all human activity as we get to grips more with climate change will throw up myriad opportunities. The risk manager's role will include the rapid identification and exploitation of those opportunities as they emerge as well as offering mitigation to the inevitable threats.

Finally, we reviewed the area of legal risk. This is likely to become the most rapidly growing area of risk over the next few years. There is hearsay among the legal profession that climate issues could provide a more lucrative opportunity than tobacco or asbestos did in the last century.

As societal attitudes change some form of retrospective liability may be inevitable, especially as sources of funding will be required to implement the changes required. That funding may be through finding guilt in those parties that caused more carbon release and planetary damage. The courts, as representatives of society, may see their duty to impose penalties where there were none previously. This might be seen as expropriation by current generations but viewed from the perspective of Millennials could be seen as justice.

Notes

1 World Economic Forum. The Global Risks Report 2022, 17th Edition, 2022. www3.weforum.org/docs/WEF_The_Global_Risks_Report_2022.pdf (archived at https://perma.cc/X5B8-6REK)

2 N Bartlett and T Coleman. Major Risk or Rosy Opportunity: Are companies ready for climate change? CDP Worldwide, 2019. https://cdn.cdp.net/cdp-production/cms/reports/documents/000/004/588/original/CDP_Climate_Change_report_2019.pdf?1562321876 (archived at https://perma.cc/R9AU-GHLP)

3 R Cho. How climate change impacts the economy, State of the Planet, 2019, https://news.climate.columbia.edu/2019/06/20/climate-change-economy-impacts/?cv=1 (archived at https://perma.cc/572V-SLKY)

4 Global Sustainable Investment Alliance. 2018 Global Sustainable Investment Review, 2018. www.gsi-alliance.org/wp-content/uploads/2019/03/GSIR_Review2018.3.28.pdf (archived at https://perma.cc/55YW-QKYC)

5 M Taylor. Extreme weather: what is it and how is it connected to climate change? BBC News, 9 August 2021, www.bbc.co.uk/news/science-environment-58073295 (archived at https://perma.cc/7VQ6-6XFR)

6 Copernicus. Copernicus: 2020 warmest year on record for Europe; globally, 2020 ties with 2016 for warmest year recorded, Copernicus, 8 January 2021, https://climate.copernicus.eu/copernicus-2020-warmest-year-record-europe-globally-2020-ties-2016-warmest-year-recorded (archived at https://perma.cc/E26Q-7H85)

7 M Goss, D L Swain, J T Abatzoglou, A Sarhadi, C Kolden, A P Williams and N S Diffenbaugh. Climate change is increasing the risk of extreme autumn wildfire conditions across California, *Environmental Research Letters*, 2020, 15 (9), doi:10.1088/1748-9326/ab83a7 (archived at https://perma.cc/3JFJ-ZNDB)

8 A L Westerling, H G Hidalgo, D R Cayan and T W Swetnam. Warming and earlier spring increase Western U.S. forest wildfire activity, *Science*, 2006, 313 (5789), pp. 940–943, doi:10.1126/science.1128834 (archived at https://perma.cc/3BXS-C4RX)

9 M L Corrieri, N C Roy, K N Rose-Davison and C J Roy. Wildfire associated health risks impacting farmers and ranchers, *Journal of Agromedicine*, 2019, 24 (2), pp 129–32, doi:10.1080/1059924x.2019.1581494 (archived at https://perma.cc/EB58-SPYR)

10 C Kolden. Wildfires: count lives and homes, not hectares burnt, *Nature*, 2020, 586 (7827), p 9, doi:10.1038/d41586-020-02740-4 (archived at https://perma.cc/KJ5R-UWMR)

11 RMS. Application of wildfire mitigation to insured property exposure, RMS, nd. www.rms.com/offer/wildfire-mitigation (archived at https://perma.cc/M6ER-MB8V)

12 CSIRO. State of the Climate 2020. CSIRO, 2020. www.csiro.au/en/research/environmental-impacts/climate-change/state-of-the-climate (archived at https://perma.cc/Q2JD-GRR6)

13 H Smith. The Dixie fire threatened to pass 1 million acres, then was stopped in its tracks. Here's how, *Los Angeles Times*, 26 September 2021. www.latimes.com/california/story/2021-09-26/dixie-fire-stopped-just-shy-of-1-million-acres-heres-how (archived at https://perma.cc/Y844-SGPU)

14 Aon. Wildfire Risk in the United States: How climate change and other variables are enhancing the risk, Aon, 2021. http://thoughtleadership.aon.com/Documents/20211012-us-wildfire.pdf (archived at https://perma.cc/7DNL-QPRV)

15 Copernicus. Copernicus: 2021 saw widespread wildfire devastation and new regional emission records broken, Copernicus, 6 December 2021, https://atmosphere.copernicus.eu/copernicus-2021-saw-widespread-wildfire-devastation-and-new-regional-emission-records-broken (archived at https://perma.cc/A6X4-EBVU)

16 Swiss Re Institute. sigma 1/2021 - Natural catastrophes in 2020, Swiss Re, 2021, www.swissre.com/institute/research/sigma-research/sigma-2021-01.html (archived at https://perma.cc/5V8L-5ZWT)

17 Aon. 2021 Weather, Climate and Catastrophe Insight, Aon, 2021, www.aon.com/weather-climate-catastrophe/index.html (archived at https://perma.cc/4YFG-M969)

18 Aon. Real-Time Climate Change, Aon, nd, http://thoughtleadership.aon.com/Documents/20211027-real-time-climate-change.pdf (archived at https://perma.cc/46YP-LL39)

19 Met Office. UK and global extreme events – heatwaves, Met Office, nd, www.metoffice.gov.uk/research/climate/understanding-climate/uk-and-global-extreme-events-heatwaves (archived at https://perma.cc/B4VC-NNA5)

20 CRO Forum. The heat is on: Insurability and resilience in a changing climate emerging risk initiative - position paper, nd. www.thecroforum.org/wp-content/uploads/2019/01/CROF-ERI-2019-The-heat-is-on-Position-paper-1.pdf (archived at https://perma.cc/NNM8-RCMM)

21 B Dale and N Stylianou. Climate change: world now sees twice as many days over 50C, BBC News, 13 September 2021, www.bbc.co.uk/news/science-environment-58494641 (archived at https://perma.cc/DH4M-KKMM)

22 WHO. Heatwaves, World Health Organization, 2022. www.who.int/health-topics/heatwaves#tab=tab_1 (archived at https://perma.cc/KR4G-77P6)

23 O Ravagnolo, I Misztal and G Hoogenboom. Genetic component of heat stress in dairy cattle, development of heat index function, *Journal of Dairy Science*, 2000, 83 (9), pp 2120–25, https://doi.org/10.3168/jds.s0022-0302(00)75094-6 (archived at https://perma.cc/7NHC-CEB4)

24 A Wahid, S Gelani, M Ashraf and M Foolad. Heat tolerance in plants: an overview, *Environmental and Experimental Botany*, 2007, 61 (3), pp 199–223, https://doi.org/10.1016/j.envexpbot.2007.05.011 (archived at https://perma.cc/GP2A-VQHS)

25 IPCC. Global Warming of 1.5°C, 2018. www.ipcc.ch/sr15/ (archived at https://perma.cc/J5TP-7ZW2)

26 CRO Forum. The heat is on: Insurability and resilience in a changing climate emerging risk initiative - position paper, nd. www.thecroforum.org/wp-content/uploads/2019/01/CROF-ERI-2019-The-heat-is-on-Position-paper-1.pdf (archived at https://perma.cc/NNM8-RCMM)

27 T Quinson. Regulators intensify ESG scrutiny as greenwashing explodes, Bloomberg UK, 1 September 2021, www.bloomberg.com/news/articles/2021-09-01/regulatory-scrutiny-of-esg-greenwashing-is-intensifying#xj4y7vzkg (archived at https://perma.cc/NS66-S7UB)

28 C Flood. Heavyweight investors demand more disclosure of environmental risks, *Financial Times*, 21 June 2021, www.ft.com/content/7d23ef7f-33ba-4466-b2f1-2a5dfeba1e33 (archived at https://perma.cc/TNE7-7UAV)

29 M Carney. Building a Private Finance System for Net Zero: Priorities for private finance for COP26, nd. https://ukcop26.org/wp-content/uploads/2020/11/COP26-Private-Finance-Hub-Strategy_Nov-2020v4.1.pdf (archived at https://perma.cc/HAB3-8VCF)

30 ET Energyworld.com. Why 'phasing down' coal is a realistic and optimistic objective, 29 November 2021. https://energy.economictimes.indiatimes.com/news/coal/why-phasing-down-coal-is-a-realistic-and-optimistic-objective/87981741 (archived at https://perma.cc/YMD6-T53E)

31 The Energy Mix. Edelman's covert pro-fossil PR work revealed by coding error, 3 October 2021. www.theenergymix.com/2021/10/03/edelmans-covert-pro-fossil-pr-work-revealed-by-coding-error/ (archived at https://perma.cc/L7YH-8JKC)

32 A Demirbas. The importance of biomass, *Energy Sources*, 2004, 26 (4), pp 361–6. doi: 10.1080/00908310490477406 (archived at https://perma.cc/NUW6-4CHL)

33 The Energy Mix. Smart glass would save 2.19 gigatons of carbon by 2050, The Energy Mix, 26 March 2019, www.theenergymix.com/2019/03/26/smart-glass-would-save-2-19-gigatons-of-carbon-by-2050/ (archived at https://perma.cc/6THK-MVTP)

34 Framework Convention on Climate Change. Mapping of emerging climate technologies: background note, 3 November 2020. https://unfccc.int/ttclear/misc_/StaticFiles/gnwoerk_static/tn_meetings/ef83c3e2cbdc4b16a525a60e3d53014c/b5eb84f99ff845878db9eb7c9e2a2660.pdf (archived at https://perma.cc/XCH4-GWYL)

35 Congress.gov. H.R.776 – Energy Policy Act of 1992. www.congress.gov/bill/102nd-congress/house-bill/776 (archived at https://perma.cc/552D-MQTM)

36 International Energy Agency. The Future of Hydrogen: Seizing today's opportunities, 2019. www.iea.org/reports/the-future-of-hydrogen (archived at https://perma.cc/Q9SV-NHRM)

37 A Chugh and E Taibi. What is green hydrogen and why do we need it? An expert explains, World Economic Forum, 21 December 2021, www.weforum.org/agenda/2021/12/what-is-green-hydrogen-expert-explains-benefits/ (archived at https://perma.cc/YF7E-Y8DP)

38 International Renewable Energy Agency. Green Hydrogen Cost Reduction: Scaling up electrolysers to meet the 1.5°C climate goal, December 2020. www.irena.org/publications/2020/Dec/Green-hydrogen-cost-reduction (archived at https://perma.cc/2SGX-ZLNS)

39 Green Hydrogen Catapult. Home page, nd. https://greenh2catapult.com/ (archived at https://perma.cc/5A7K-ETHM)

40 C Henderson (2021). The hydrogen revolution in the skies, BBC, 8 April 2021, www.bbc.com/future/article/20210401-the-worlds-first-commercial-hydrogen-plane (archived at https://perma.cc/B3WV-Y27C)

41 BBC. California utility PG&E pleads guilty to 84 wildfire deaths, BBC News, 16 June 2020, www.bbc.co.uk/news/world-us-canada-53072946 (archived at https://perma.cc/A7YZ-HVHC)

42 Associated Press. PG&E confesses to killing 84 people in 2018 California fire as part of guilty plea, *Guardian*, 16 June 2020, www.theguardian.com/business/2020/jun/16/pge-california-wildfire-camp-fire-paradise-guilty-plea (archived at https://perma.cc/UQ65-NYTC)

10

Climate stress and scenario testing

This chapter explains how organizations can assess the materiality of the climate risks and opportunities that they have identified through the use of stress and scenario analysis. It is important to remember that the overall purpose of stress and scenario analysis is to explore several plausible and 'best-available' 'what-if' scenarios, rather than to precisely forecast the future.

The main learning outcomes from this chapter are to:

- Align the development of climate scenario analysis within an existing enterprise risk management framework.
- Understand some of the main guidance and expectations of regulators in designing stress and scenario tests across an organization's risk profile.
- Provide details of a climate stress and scenario testing framework that covers six main steps that a risk manager should consider in designing and implementing a framework for assessing the impacts of climate scenarios.
- Appreciate the range of different tools and techniques that can be used, depending on the size and complexity of the climate risks facing an organization, and their associated benefits and limitations.

Introduction

Risk managers can play a vital role in driving the scenario selection and design decisions to assess future scenarios in a rapidly changing world. Risk management isn't about avoiding risks. Instead, it should be focused on understanding the key risks a company faces then taking the right risks at the best time after using the most appropriate mitigation strategies.

'I cannot imagine any condition which would cause a ship to founder. I cannot conceive of any vital disaster happening to this vessel. Modern shipbuilding has gone beyond that.' This famous quotation is attributed to Captain Edward Smith of the *Titanic*. The example highlights that the world does not follow a normal distribution – low-frequency and high-severity events can occur at any time. The discounting of extreme events is very dangerous.

Enterprise risk management should allow for early recognition of risks so as to empower the organization to classify and highlight the risks. The organization can then deal with the threats and opportunities in an effective and timely way. The development of an emerging risk management framework and climate change examples are highlighted in Chapters 8 and 9. It is also important to develop a formal process for designing stress and scenario tests that is aligned to the emerging risk process.

Organizations should start by describing climate-related risk scenarios to which they are exposed, how they are expected to manifest, and (if the scenario occurs) the mechanism/path by which the firm, its external environment and/or its stakeholders would be impacted. Consideration should also be given to the existing internal control environment and the types of remediation that may be required.

Assessing climate change-related risks based on forward-looking information and scenarios is also a central component of the TCFD and regulatory recommendations, and is arguably the most challenging to implement given the complexity of design decisions such as alternative time horizons and climate pathways. However, these scenarios are strengthened when assumptions made are based on learnings from previous events.

10.1 Evolution of stress and scenario analysis – impact of financial crisis

There were many causes of the global financial crisis (GFC) in 2008 that led to corporate failures and bailouts. Many were linked to the failure of risk models to accurately predict future risks in the banking sector. This included the under-pricing of risks in areas such as mortgage portfolios for subprime loans due to increasing defaults. This is accurately represented in the film *The Big Short*.

As with many man-made and natural catastrophic events the GFC led to significant improvements in enterprise risk management.

Rating agencies, which were also at fault, have stated that simply instituting monitored compliance programmes does not address emerging risks. Controls and metrics using historical data are not designed to be predictive of emerging or future risks.

One of the most important areas, particularly for financial institutions, was to develop the more formal emerging risk management frameworks that were covered in Chapters 8 and 9 and stress and scenario testing (SST) frameworks, which will be covered in this chapter.

Designing specific scenarios can help organizations to support strategic planning, improve the setting of risk appetite, tolerance and limits, help develop risk monitoring and management information and support product development.

10.2 Developing a formal stress and scenario framework

Stress and scenario testing (SST) should be a key part of the toolbox of the risk professional. Generally, it is used as a defensive tool to identify actions to protect the business from material losses resulting from adverse events. The process involves taking emerging risks and quantifying the impact on risk assessment, and organizations should seek to develop methodologies and approaches that they can use on an ongoing basis.

It is important to distinguish the two processes:

Stress testing is a process that explores reactions to small (sensitivity) or drastic (stressed) changes in conditions such as financial variables, typically the assumptions in, for example, the business plan.

These are often translated into a number of statistically defined possibilities to determine, for example, a weighted average future forecast based on the probabilities.

This is analogous to, say, stress testing the impact of different future economic scenarios that organizations should undertake if there is an impending recession.

Scenario analysis is the process of evaluating the impact of a specified scenario on the company's financial position. In scenario analysis it is important to provide a narrative (story) behind the scenario, including the risks (events) that generated the scenario sometimes referred to as 'alternative worlds'. Scenario analysis is more granular in nature, in that specific scenarios for events are assessed, such as a future flood event or assessing the impact of a change such as the regulatory change to move to electric vehicles.

It is important to distinguish the two approaches, particularly for climate change, as the methodologies and tools required for each can be significantly different.

There are many sources of good information: The International Actuarial Association have published guidance on stress and scenario testing, 'Stress Testing and Scenario Analysis'. It states that:

> Their use can enhance the risk culture of a firm, as they can alert decision makers to potentially inconvenient truths and provide a framework to enable firms to base their business strategies and risk mitigation activities on a range of forecasts rather than a single best-estimate projected result or an average of stochastic results.[1]

As organizations start to explore a range of future scenarios it will initially improve internal communication and discussions, help to alert decision makers to 'inconvenient truths' and provide a framework to enable firms to inform their future business strategies and risk mitigation activities.

Organizations need to consider a wide range of factors:

- The time frame over which the risk could crystallize (and the window to respond/ adapt)
- The severity of the impact (to the firm, wider environment and stakeholders)

- The anticipated climate change policies from stakeholders, e.g. governments, customers, industry bodies, rating agencies, institutional investors, etc.
- The specificity of impact, e.g. to the organization, whole of market or specific sector

10.3 Design of climate scenario considerations and benefits

It is important to consider designing specific climate change scenarios across the risk taxonomy of physical, transition and liability risks that are material to the risk profile of the organization.

The scope should consider the specific areas of the risk profile that are vulnerable to climate change, and scenarios that are realistic, credible, consistent with regulatory expectations and achievable.

Organizations increasingly need to understand the material impact of climate change to provide support for internal decision-making, including a wider range of metrics that can include changes to profitability, liquidity, capital provisioning and customer confidence, etc.

One of the main benefits of developing a formalized process is that it helps to build consensus among a range of stakeholders about the issues and how to tackle them.

The main benefits are outlined below:

Support business decisions and long-term strategic planning

- Understand the vulnerabilities of business plans to make improved decisions for both business and capital planning.
- Supplement existing ORSA and ICAAP reporting processes (financial services organizations only).
- Provide external stakeholders (such as investors or regulators) with a forward-looking view of climate-related risks.
- Identify gaps in understanding and bring into focus new areas of research required to understand driving forces better.

Improve operational resilience

- Enable management to react better to occurring risks and implement plans, e.g. for triggers and limit breaches, and take action as appropriate. In addition, the exercises will improve monitoring with respect to emerging climate risks.
- Supports improvements in contingency plans.

Comply with growing regulatory expectations

- Embed climate risk considerations within existing strategic and operational processes.

- Climate disclosures, including TCFD.
- Regulatory prescribed scenarios, e.g. the 2021 BES UK climate scenarios (financial services organizations only).

There are a range of other uses and benefits of stress and scenario testing that can support a range of other business applications:

- Manage and plan for multiple adverse events
- Review appropriateness of risk appetite strategy and associated metrics
- Assess interconnected extreme events (discussed in Chapter 6)
- Optimize risk retention and transfer decisions
- Support capital allocation and planning

While is it important to quantify the impacts of climate change, it is also important to recognize how conducting climate scenario analysis is helpful in a broader sense in facilitating greater engagement with internal stakeholders that can in turn lead to significant knowledge transfer across the organization.

10.4 Regulatory guidance and expectations

There is a lot of guidance that has been developed by regulators with respect to designing stress and scenario testing for climate-related risks. Many regulators around the world have been advocating similar approaches and in this section a number of specific examples by different regulators are provided.

There are some common considerations for scenario design across many regulators, including the fact that they need to cover a wide range of risk types across the risk profile and that they need to:

- be realistic, credible, consistent with regulatory expectations, and achievable
- consider short- and long-term time horizons
- assess the impact on key metrics including earnings, solvency and liquidity

Regulators are keen that organizations, particularly in the financial services sector, undertake stress tests to measure financial risks to multiple climate pathways, with different physical and transition effects, over several decades. The main rationale is to stress test the resilience of not only the organizations' own business models but also the financial system itself to the physical and transition risks from climate change.

Regulators acknowledge themselves that this requires new tools and approaches to measure and understand the risks, and in the UK, for example, have been implementing the CBES approaches that we will cover in more detail in this chapter.

A summary of some of the guidance from regulators with respect to scenario analysis is provided below.

Bank of England Prudential Regulatory Authority (PRA) – (PRA Rulebook2 and PRA Supervisory Statements) The PRA expects a firm's board to understand and assess the financial risks from climate change that affect the firm, and to be able to address and oversee these risks within the firm's overall business strategy and risk appetite. The approach should demonstrate an understanding of the distinctive elements of the financial risks from climate change and a sufficiently long-term view of the financial risks that can arise beyond standard business planning horizons.

Where proportionate, the PRA expects firms to conduct scenario analysis to inform their strategic planning and determine the impact of the financial risks from climate change on their overall risk profile and business strategy.

Scenario analysis should also be used to explore the resilience and vulnerabilities of a firm's business model to a range of outcomes.

The PRA expects firms to use these scenarios to understand the impact of the financial risks from climate change on their solvency, liquidity and, for insurers, their ability to pay policyholders.

Generic timeframes have been included (e.g. decades for the long-term time horizon and the business planning horizon for the short-term time horizon).[3]

Climate Biennial Exploratory Scenario (CBES) On 13 November 2020, the PRA announced a programme of planned engagement with firms participating in the Climate Biennial Exploratory Scenario (CBES). The purpose of the exercise is to test the resilience of the current business models of the largest banks, insurers and the financial system to climate change.

Key objectives of the process include enhancing risk management practices of climate-related financial risks to help organizations embedding these risks in business-as-usual risk management, engaging counterparties to understand their vulnerability to climate change, and encouraging boards to take a strategic, long-term approach to managing these risks.

To make these scenarios credible the bank proposes that the CBES examines firms' resilience using fixed balance sheets, focusing on sizing the risks and the scale of business model adjustment required to respond to these risks, rather than testing the adequacy of firms' capital to absorb those risks.

On 24 May 2022 the Bank of England published the results of the 2021 CBES exercise and one of the main findings was that participants need to prioritize investment in climate risk assessment capabilities.

EIOPA – European Insurance and Occupational Pensions Authority EIOPA states that the aim of scenario analysis is to assess and discuss the resilience and robustness of the undertaking's business strategies under different developments of climate change risks over time.

EIOPA also expects organizations to assess the long-term risks of climate change using scenario analysis to inform the strategic planning and business strategy.[4]

Lloyds of London Insurance Market Lloyds uses realistic disaster scenarios (RDS) to stress test both individual insurance companies and the market as a whole to test their resilience to major catastrophe events. These are industry scenarios, termed footprints, that any organization can apply. Lloyds defines the event together with underlying assumptions in terms of industry loss levels and duration of event, which the organization can use to superimpose its own exposures to evaluate the impact. One of its latest RDSs is a 'London flood' event (illustrated in Figure 10.1).

FIGURE 10.1 London flood – event footprint

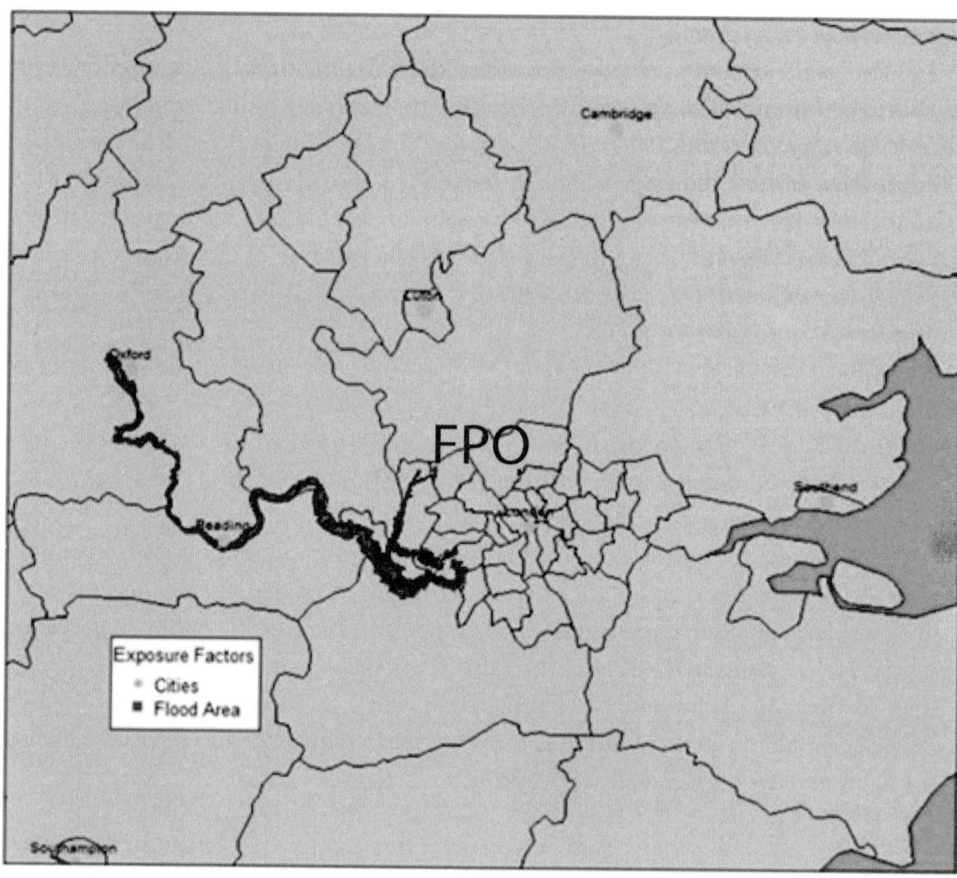

Event definition: The flood scenario is based on a heavy rainfall event. The total flood extent covers 194 km^2 and would cause significant impact on the major populated areas of Oxford, Reading, Slough, Henley and western Greater London.

Lloyds provide underlying assumptions, which managing agents need to then superimpose on their own exposures.

Most regulators expect organizations to develop methodologies to assess the impact of climate change. The time horizon is a key challenge.

10.4.1 Assessing climate scenarios over different time horizons

It is important to distinguish between existing risks that will change over time due to climate change and new emerging climate risks that may impact the organization in the future, i.e., when they are expected to crystallize. As an example, it is important to consider the increases in the frequency and severity of 'acute' weather-related events, such as floods and droughts, as well as longer-term 'chronic' shifts in climate, such as increases in average temperatures and sea-level rise over different time horizons.

In his Lloyds of London address in 2015 Mark Carney stated that 'Climate change is the Tragedy of the Horizon' and that 'once climate change becomes a defining issue for financial stability, it may already be too late.'[5]

Mark Carney points out in his speech that there are not enough actuaries to tell us about the catastrophic impacts of climate change that will be felt beyond the traditional horizons, and that future generations will likely have to bear the cost as there is lack of accountability and related incentives for the current generation to fix the problem. This is mainly due to both the political and business cycles that are relatively short term in nature.

10.4.1.1 HORIZON SCANNING AND THREE HORIZONS MODEL

Climate scenarios should be developed over three distinctive time horizons, namely short, medium and long term, using a range of approaches and tools.

In the context of risk assessment the horizon effectively adds another dimension by capturing when the event will happen. The Institute of Risk Management published a guide on horizon scanning in 2018, which serves as a good reference and details of the tools are provided in Chapter 8, 'Designing an effective emerging risk management process'.

10.4.2 Regulatory guidance on time horizons

Regulators, such as the PRA, provide good guidance and explain that the scenario analysis should include short-term assessments covering the existing planning horizon

FIGURE 10.2 Risk assessment time horizons

Time horizon	Description
Short- near-term 0–3 years	The emerging risk can be expected to occur within a three year time horizon
Medium or mid-term 3–10 years	The emerging risk can be expected to occur within a greater than three and less than 10 years' time horizon
Long-term Over 10 years	Extended modelling horizon for climate risks specifically to capture longer term impacts such as policy changes in excess of the normal business planning horizon

SOURCE OneRisk Consulting

and longer-term assessments of a firm's exposures based on its current business model. They explain that longer-term exercises are not intended to be precise forecasts but are qualitative and used to inform strategic planning and decision-making. Therefore, organizations should seek to develop approximate assessment criteria to describe each time horizon. An example is shown in Figure 10.2.

The Climate Financial Risk Forum Guide issued in June 2020 helps to explain the requirements of scenario assessment by stating that 'This requires leveraging historical data and providing a forward-looking assessment over an extended time horizon, whilst also evaluating the likelihood that extreme climate-related events will become more frequent and severe.'[6]

10.5 Setting the baseline

Another key challenge for climate scenarios is how to set the baseline and there are two main approaches that need to be taken into account:

- 'One-off shock' – Assessing the impact of a one-off shock that has not already been captured or considered on the business.
- Assessing the difference between the central projection and alternative pathways over time.

The context of developing scenarios is to first have a base case and then estimate the impact of these changes over time. Figure 10.3 illustrates the concept of what the outputs need to consider in terms of incremental expected losses and volatility for

FIGURE 10.3 Climate scenario design: setting the baseline – conceptual framework

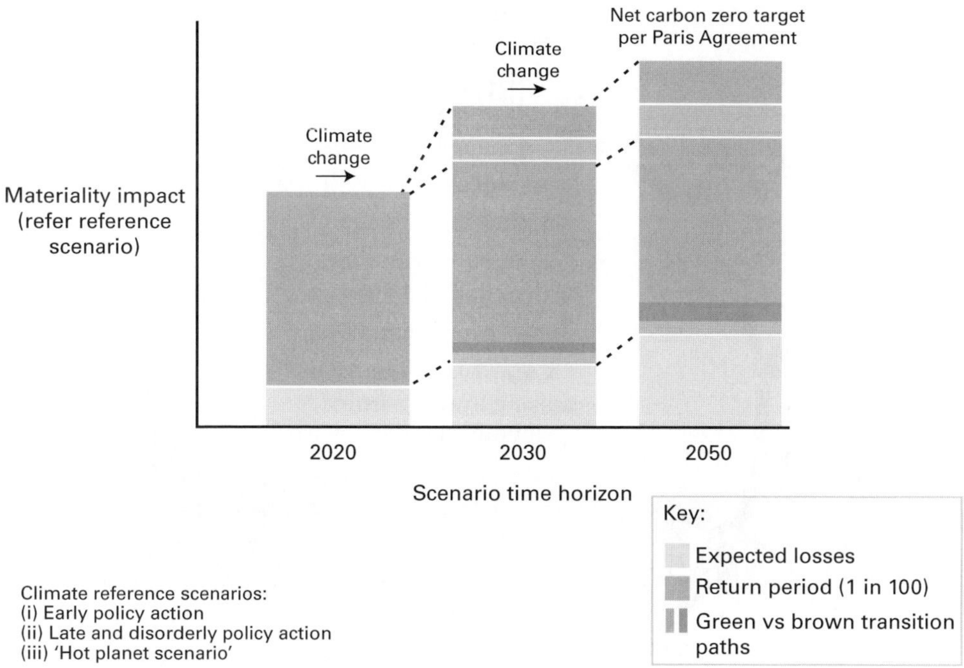

SOURCE © OneRisk Consulting. All rights reserved, 2022

the business. As emissions are expected to continue increasing to 2050 (and beyond) there is an expectation that future volatility of events will continue to worsen. This will in turn lead to the increase in frequency and intensity of certain climate perils, including hurricanes and floods.

This representation is too simplistic in that it tries to explain the impact of physical risks but does not reflect the impact of transition risks that can have both a positive and negative impact on the organization.

The base case from a stress testing perspective should in theory represent the future business plans and then a climate scenario can be superimposed to stress test the impact across the profit and loss and balance sheet. This should include a ground-up approach to stress the impact of climate change in detailed assumptions in the business plan.

10.6 Climate scenario analysis framework

One of the main challenges for risk managers is to develop a framework that includes a robust process for assessing the impacts of specific scenarios on the organization.

FIGURE 10.4 Climate change risk assessment process

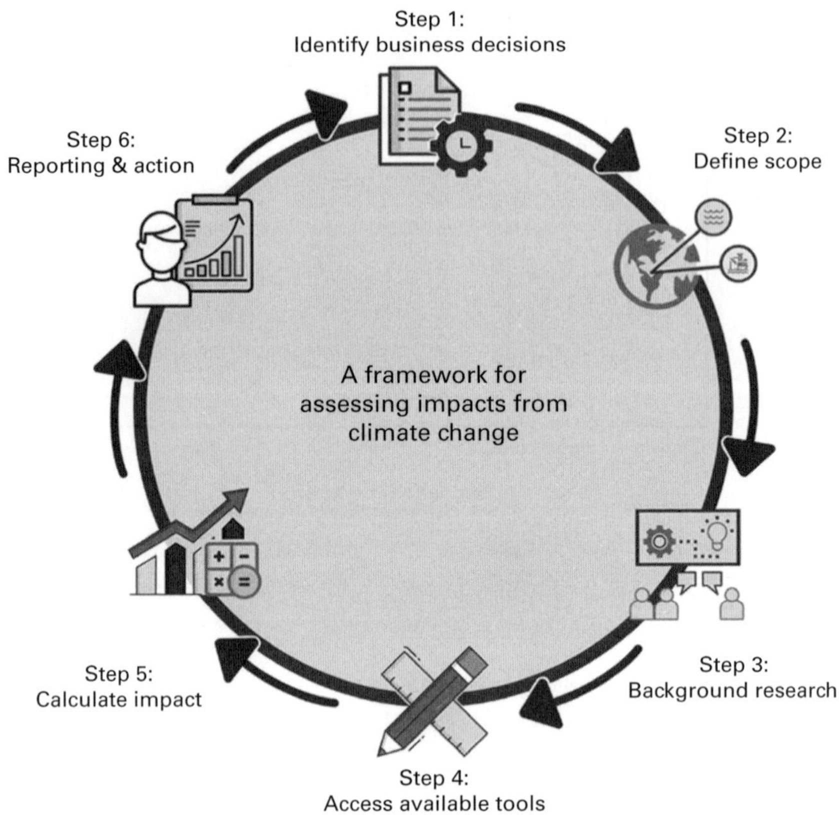

SOURCE © OneRisk Consulting. All rights reserved, 2022

The IRM Climate Change SIG have reviewed a number of frameworks that are being developed to support the design of climate scenarios and we outline a six-step process in Figure 10.4 that organizations can use.

A high-level summary of the main requirements that are important for risk managers to consider within each of the steps is shown in Table 10.1.

10.6.1 Step 1: Identify business decisions

The first phase of the process should seek to link climate issues to specific organizational threats and opportunities that will help to support business decisions and long-term strategic planning.

Organizations should also endeavour to identify and understand the key drivers of their business performance and look to build these into their scenarios. In designing

TABLE 10.1 Framework for scenario analysis – six-step process

Main Steps	Title	Description
Step 1	Identify business decisions	Identify the operational processes and/or business decision that the scenario is intended to inform. This step should also consider the relevant time horizon and metrics
Step 2	Define scope	Define the limits of the scenario including: areas of business, geography, legal entity, time horizon, stakeholders impacted, etc. Acknowledge which area may have a more material impact on your organization
Step 3	Background research	General research and market intelligence is to assess current legislation, regulatory requirements, relevant industry publications to help inform scenario design discussions including climate pathways, data sources and availability, etc
Step 4	Assess available tools	Select the most appropriate scenario analysis methodology and assessment tool(s) for the given scenario
Step 5	Calculate impact	Measure the potential impact (financial and otherwise) of the scenario and monitor against risk thresholds such as risk appetite and tolerance
Step 6	Reporting and action	Communicate the output from the scenario analysis exercise with the aim of informing decisions

the scenarios it is important to understand past climate trends and losses, review the current risk profile in detail and then consider emerging climate risk trends.

Scenario analysis can address multiple purposes while focusing on a range of potential stresses and scenarios, and up front recognition of this diversity encourages the placement of appropriate design elements and controls. Scenario analysis can have important potential applications in a number of areas.

For each area of use, key scenarios must be identified along with a model for analysing the impact of the scenarios. An important point is that the intended use of the analysis should drive the scenario selection and design decisions. By ensuring that objectives are identified and agreed up front, a common reference point is established for communicating and interpreting results.

What makes climate change unique is the wide range of potential business impacts that will need to be considered. They can influence a range of business decision-making and regulatory requirements such as climate disclosures. A list is shown in Figure 10.5 that illustrates the need to support a range of stakeholders both internal and external, such as rating agencies and customers.

From an enterprise risk management perspective one of the main business decisions will be to review and enhance the organization's risk appetite framework and

FIGURE 10.5 Summary of the main business uses and applications

consider changes in both qualitative and quantitative statements and metrics relating to climate change risk.

Another key consideration will include the impact of future changes in concentration and risk aggregation exposures emanating from climate change.

Existing scenario analysis applications, such as inputs within ERM regulatory driven processes (including ORSA or ICAAP for financial services firms), will need to continue with climate change threats being an additional set of inputs required. This process is also applicable to most organizations in assessing the robustness of their solvency or capital position.

10.6.2 Step 2: Define scope

This is a critical phase of the process in which the organization needs to consider the scope of analysis. This will depend on the nature of the business, for example the industry and economic sectors that the organization operates in.

Climate change can affect businesses across legal entities, sectors and geographies and thus the scope of a scenario needs to be carefully thought through.

The TFCD suggests the following considerations:

- The geographic location of the organization's value chain

- The organization's assets and nature of operations
- The structure and dynamics of the organization's supply and demand markets
- The organization's customers
- The organization's other key stakeholders

Significant research is therefore required to support the scoping exercise. Key design considerations are discussed in more detail in Step 3.

10.6.3 Step 3: Conduct background research

This step involves a range of approaches to undertake what is often termed a 'deep-dive' exercise. Detailed research is undertaken into the design of a specific scenario, which can include research into relevant previous climate-related loss events or the extrapolation of known trends. Research into future changes in weather patterns of natural catastrophic events will be an important consideration. For financial services firms, one of the key areas of focus will be to assess the potential concentration of risk exposures relating to these event types within their business.

For many transition risks it is important to conduct market research across the competitive environment, for example to assess how companies in the sector are embracing new technologies to reduce their carbon footprint.

10.6.3.1 CLIMATE SCENARIO TYPES AND ARCHETYPES

There are many types of scenarios to consider and below is some specific scenario terminology that should be helpful to explain the differences. Risk managers should seek to consider and use a range of scenario types.

Types of scenario to consider:

- a 'sentiment shock' in (say) 2025 that prompts sudden and significant change;
- a physical shock, e.g. a major adverse weather event, that could occur at any time; and
- long-term incremental worsening of climate.

The above scenarios can be categorized into the following broad descriptors:

- Slow building – risk factors that are slow to change but which gain momentum (need to be careful not to ignore the scope for non-linear growth).
- De-anchoring – scenarios in which barriers (e.g. regulatory safeguards) are suddenly removed, leading to sharp, sudden changes in the risk factors.
- Point-in-time – scenarios where the probability over the short term is low, but are almost certain to occur at some point.

Even if an organization chooses to use sophisticated statistical models, they aren't always capable of fully capturing such scenarios, so there is always a need for forward-looking expert judgement to develop them.

10.6.3.2 CLIMATE PATHWAYS

In constructing scenarios it is important to factor in alternative scenario pathways that allow for the potential impact of the transition to a low-carbon economy and which utilize published definitions and associated assumptions.

As an introduction to climate pathways, it is important to understand that climate-related scenarios have long been used by scientists and policy analysts to assess future vulnerability to climate change. Producing these scenarios requires estimates of future population levels, economic activity, the structure of governance, social values and patterns of technological change. Economic and energy modelling are also often used to analyse and quantify the effects of such drivers in climate change.

A number of published scenarios are available that outline various plausible pathways to particular target outcomes (e.g. specific temperature increases or CO_2 concentration levels). These scenarios have varying assumptions about the likely timing of policy changes, technology adoption, changes in energy mix and other factors to achieve a climate-friendly economy that may be useful to a company in conducting its own scenario analysis.

The Network for Greening the Financial System (NGFS) has been developing an analytical framework for assessing climate-related risks in order to size the impact of climate-related risks on the economy and the financial stability.[7] The NGFS has concluded that there are two important dimensions to consider when assessing the impact of physical risks and transition risks on the economy and the financial system:

- The total level of mitigation or, in other words, how much action is taken to reduce greenhouse gas emissions (leading to a particular climate outcome)
- Whether the transition occurs in an orderly or disorderly way, i.e. how smoothly and foreseeably the actions are taken

However, they often have limitations for assessing the business implications of climate change at a local or industry sector level.

Regulators have also built on the reference scenarios currently being developed by the NGFS to provide a coherent set of climate pathways and key macroeconomic variables.

The descriptions of the three most common scenario pathways are shown in Figure 10.6.

What is important to recognize is that if governments fail to meet their obligations under the Paris Agreement then the knock-on effects will mean that organizations will need to become more resilient in the face of increasing chronic changes in weather (e.g. rising sea levels), as well as more frequent and extreme weather events (e.g. flash floods).

FIGURE 10.6 Common climate pathway descriptions

Climate pathway	Description
Early policy action	Early and decisive action to reduce global emissions in a gradual way. These actions are sufficient to limit global average temperature increases to below 2 °C. Moderate increase in global temperatures leads to higher physical risks.
Late policy action	The climate target is still met; but due to late action which could include a steep increase in global carbon process, there is a significant degree of disruption to the economy. Physical risks rise more quickly than in the early policy action scenario and transition risks are severe.
No additional policy solution	Governments fail to introduce policies to address climate change other than those already announced. This leads to reduced level of transition risks but with resulting increases in physical risks.

SOURCE

10.6.3.3 USE OF REPRESENTATIVE CONCENTRATION PATHWAYS (RCPS)

There is consistency in methodology that is being applied by aligning the scenarios with, for example, future RCP scenarios. RCP is a greenhouse gas concentration (not emissions) trajectory adopted by the Intergovernmental Panel on Climate Change. Four pathways have been selected for climate modelling, which describe different climate futures. The four RCPs are labelled as a possible range of radiative forcing values in the year 2100 relative to pre-industrial values (+2.6, +4.5, +6.0 and +8.5).

The model results are frequently 'downscaled' to derive potential local-level changes in climate, which are then used to generate scenarios of impacts from climate change (first-order impacts such as flooding or drought, second-order impacts such as loss of crop production and third-order impacts such as famine).

10.6.3.4 DATA SOURCES AND DATA AVAILABILITY

Some of the main climate data types, sources, uses and challenges were discussed in Chapter 7.

One of the immediate challenges in calibrating a climate change scenario arises from the lack of available data and the difficulty in understanding the wide range of data sources that may need consulting and calibrating, for example historical observations, geological records, global climate models, evidence and research from external bodies, etc. For the physical risks, data is often fragmented, there are differences in the level and quality of exposure data across regions and the complexities associated with the physical events may not be captured. For transition risk, it is not possible to tell the extent of climate risks already captured in asset valuations and there is a lack of consistency across the markets.

The data for the financial variables are widely available, but the historical data will not give a reliable indication of the future, hence future estimates will be subject to uncertainty. Expert judgement is required for calibrating on a forward-looking basis. However, government reports, academic research, financial reports and public data can help to inform this judgement.

10.6.3.5 GLOBAL CLIMATE MODELS (GCM)

Global climate models (GCMs) (state-of-the-art numerical weather models) have become an integral tool in meteorological research and help scientists simulate future climates in line with IPCC emission scenarios. While they have not been designed to model scenarios for organizations, their forecasts need to be integrated within predictive tools and techniques.

The importance of the information is that modelling firms are able to take this information and project low, medium and high emission scenarios for flood models, for example, to support the incremental impacts of climate change. These can then be superimposed on an organization's asset portfolio, which is particularly helpful for lenders and insurers. We will discuss this further in the next section, through the use of hazard maps in the UK using flood modelling using flood mapping techniques.

10.6.4 Step 4: Assess available tools

Once the scenario has been defined it is important to use the most appropriate tools to assess the scenario. There are a range of tools and techniques that risk managers can seek to use. These include some quite advanced tools for modelling physical risks, such as natural catastrophe model and hazard mapping techniques.

Organizations need to select appropriate impact assessment tools to analyse the change in the chosen risk metrics for a given scenario. It is important to note that while there are some robust tools for modelling certain risks, there is an expectation that new methodologies and tools need to be developed to help organizations meet the challenges that we have outlined in relation to the uncertainties and complexities involved with modelling transition risks.

10.6.4.1 SELECTION CONSIDERATIONS

The key considerations for selecting a chosen tool or techniques will, of course, vary depending on the size and complexity of the climate risks facing the organization, but some are listed in Figure 10.7.

10.6.5 Step 5: Calculate the impact

With the increasing awareness of climate change risk, organizations should seek to introduce climate scenarios into their existing scenario analysis programmes (in

FIGURE 10.7 Main scenario selection consideration

Key considerations	Description
Qualitative and quantitative methodologies	Consider traditional risk management assessment techniques as well as bespoke proprietary external vendor modelling techniques.
Stress and scenario tests	Use both bespoke scenarios such as future climate events as well as and stress tests across the balance sheet of the organization.
Appropriateness and limitations	Tools should be evaluated to make sure they are appropriate for the specific business decision and scope of the analysis. Methodologies should be used with caution and fully evaluated in the context of the scenario's and model's underlying assumptions.
New innovative methodologies	Be open to consider new methodologies and tools that are currently being developed, tested and evaluated particularly for evaluation of transition and liability risks.

SOURCE

order to incorporate the potential financial impacts into their financial metrics). This is facilitated further if climate risk considerations are included within their risk appetite statements and key risk indicators.

An organization should seek to measure the aggregate impact of climate scenarios into their income statements and balance sheet as well as other key financial metrics, such as risk-weighted-assets ratios or regulatory capital buffers.

Defining meaningful metrics can be challenging. The metrics used in communicating the outcome of an exercise should be driven by the decision they are meant to inform, and their familiarity. Physical scenarios are often aligned to an extreme, or 'tail', event with a return period such as a 1-in-100-year event; that is, the loss event will occur once every 100 years or have a 1 per cent chance of occurrence in a single year.

Metrics will vary by industry and business needs. As an example, insurers may choose to focus on measuring the impact of climate-related financial risks on claims and premiums that drive the profits and losses across their lines of business. Banks may need to assess how climate-related financial risks are to be factored into their measure of risk-weighted asset ratios in order to inform their capital reallocation processes. The quantification of risk may involve reviewing the credit risk profile of customers, changes in counterparty ratings, repricing of collateral and underlying assets, etc.

For example, a mortgage bank would be interested in assessing the potential impact of floods on its mortgage portfolio, quantifying physical damage with metrics that feed into the expected loss models. Likewise, a bank with an oil and gas portfolio would assess how potential carbon price movements may affect the credit risk profile of corporate borrowers and therefore the calculation of loan provisions. For smaller firms, it may be more sensible to start with one aspect of this analysis and build up expertise over time.

10.6.6 Step 6: Reporting and action

Organizations will ultimately need to describe the methodology used for selecting their scenarios – that will include the rationale for choosing the underlying assumptions for each scenario regarding how a particular pathway might develop, for example. It will be important for an organization to disclose and discuss this information, including the sensitivity of various assumptions to changes in key parameters, so that investors and other stakeholders have a clear understanding of the scenario process – not only the outcomes each scenario describes, but the pathway envisioned by an organization that leads to that outcome (i.e., the how and why of those outcomes).

Communicating the quantitative and/or qualitative loss results to decision makers is arguably the most important step and could take the form of a recommendation to 'act' or 'monitor' based on the results presented. The results will need to include a clear indication of the extent to which loss estimates can be relied upon, and appropriate caveats will be necessary to manage the risk of misinterpretation. For instance, 'these results are intended to illustrate loss sensitivity to climate change and do not constitute a prediction or forecast'.

10.7 Types of qualitative and quantitative tools

There are a range of tools and techniques that can be considered and again it is important to align the technique to the type of risk and business decision that the organization is trying to assess. Many organizations are developing assessment capabilities and experimenting with different approaches, and engaging in dialogue to promote cross-learning.

It is important to distinguish between the use of qualitative and quantitative approaches and it can be argued that the best approach for climate change will perhaps be a blend of both. It is also important to recognize the pros and cons of using a particular technique, and its limitations.

There are a growing number of quantitative assessment tools available for organizations and a range of vendor models and tools available for risk practitioners. It is important to point out that models will give different results for modelling the same risks, many are complex and many are termed 'black box' in design. Practitioners therefore need to be careful in both using and interpreting the results.

It is important to have tools for physical, transition and liability risks, and we will consider tools under the following groupings:

- Expert judgement – traditional qualitative scenario analysis
- Hazard maps and footprints
- Probabilistic modelling including catastrophe models
- Integrated stress tests

A summary of each approach follows.

10.7.1 Expert judgement – traditional qualitative scenario analysis

A qualitative assessment typically focuses on understanding what the future world may look like for the organization, based on a set of assumptions that support a potential path for the emergence of climate change risk. With the less rigid nature of qualitative assessments, organizations can more readily consider a variety of transition pathways and implications of changes in the socio-economic environment for business strategy.[8]

In designing scenarios organizations should seek to provide a high-level description together with a synopsis and underlying assumptions that drive the scenario. The scenario should be typically aligned to a specific future risk event.

A good starting point is for organizations to explore exposures to climate change risk for both short- and long-term horizons. Traditional risk management tools, such as risk questionnaires and structured interviews, should be considered and used but probably the most useful tool is to set up working groups and run workshops with key internal stakeholders to brainstorm future climate scenarios.

FIGURE 10.8 Expert judgement – design of climate scenarios

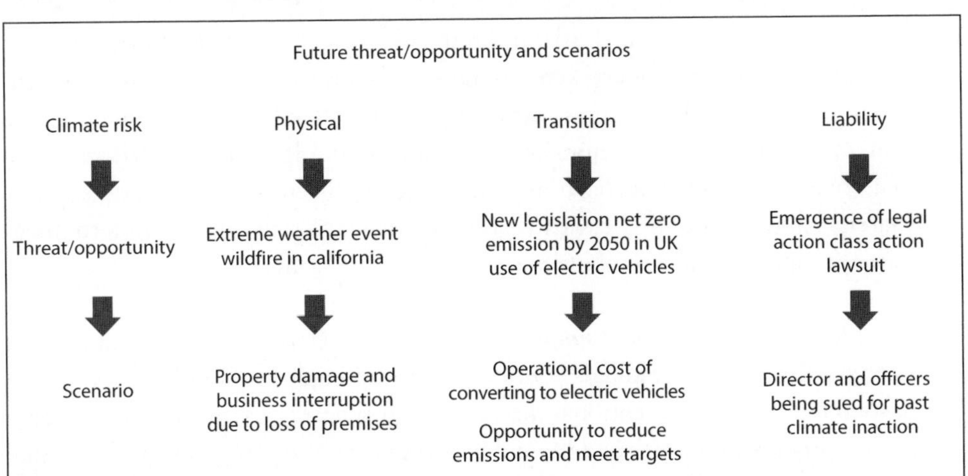

SOURCE OneRisk Consulting

These techniques help in a number of ways. Risk managers can facilitate discussions and gain valuable insights from experienced first-line risk owners who know the business well. Internal brainstorming will typically help to gain buy-in from the senior management, exchange knowledge and help reach a consensus among participants. This approach can be supplemented by external experts who have access to wider industry and global knowledge and insights. In time, as more experience and knowledge is acquired, these assessments can grow in complexity and their ability to generate useful insights is improved.

10.7.1.1 DEVELOPING SCENARIO NARRATIVES – SAMPLE TRANSITION RISKS

A more detailed output that highlights some transition risks and scenario narratives is shown in Table 10.2. It highlights how scenarios should be designed to link transition categories to risk categories.

Developing plausible assumptions Plausible assumptions will need to be made about future developments, so questions should be asked about:

- The development of climate policies: Will there be a direct carbon tax imposed? Will there be regulation on efficiency? Will there be explicit disclosures for carbon emissions? How fast can policy changes be imposed?
- The rate of technology innovation: How much funding will be given to research and development? Can all energy resources be made more efficient? Can technologies reduce the level of carbon in the atmosphere? How quickly will technology changes be adopted?
- Changes in energy mix: How will the proportions of renewable and non-renewable energy change? Will all countries increase renewable energy consumption?
- Changes in society: What will be the secondary effects of changes to the way people live and work? How will people's attitude towards climate change alter?

By developing a set of detailed assumptions, an assessment of the impact on the organization can then be undertaken linking the qualitative assessment to a quantitative output. Overall this process allows for greater flexibility in considering the potential correlations, interrelationships and understanding of the key drivers of the risk. The benefits of this approach are that it generally means that there is better transparency in respect of the scenarios chosen and enables an organization to document an appropriate range of plausible, reasonable scenarios.

Expert judgement – use of heat maps Once a list of scenarios has been developed across physical, transition and liability risk (threats and opportunities) the results can be consolidated into a conventional heat map and then discussed through a workshop. This process helps to validate and prioritize the most relevant and material

TABLE 10.2 Example of transition risks and scenario narratives

Transition category	Root cause/key drivers	Risk title	Scenario of concern/opportunity	Threat or opportunity	Step 1: Identify main business decisions	Risk category
• Policy	Overexposure to sectors that are overpriced (stranded assets)	Decline in creditworthiness of investments	Creditworthiness of investments declines over time due to overexposure to sectors adversely revalued as a consequence of climate change	Threat	Investment ESG strategy	Market
• Reputational	Suppliers are climate inactive and not in line with the organization's onboarding criteria	Noncompliance of climate criteria	The organization uses services from suppliers who are climate change inactive or unaware, for example have poor ESG ratings and are not using recyclable materials	Threat	Supply change management	Reputational and operational risks
• Legal/Liability	Legal actions	Failure to adapt or disclose climate change risks	Legal case brought against the organization though a breach of duty by the boards of directors for not adequately considering or responding to the impacts of climate change	Threat	Compliance	Strategic/legal

FIGURE 10.9 Example heat map

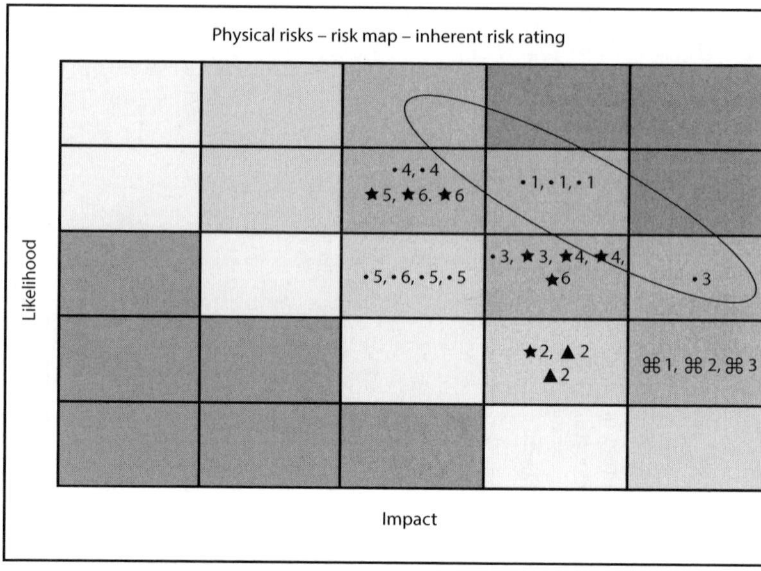

Aggregate qualitative risk description

Extreme risk	Should be brought to the attention of board and immediately progressed
Very high priority	Requires attention of senior management including CEO and an action plan developed as a priority
High risk	Requires action and monitoring by the risk owner
Medium risk	Monitoring the risk by the risk champion along with departmental manager
Low risk	Monitoring the risk by the risk champion along with departmental manager

Climate scenario examples

1 – Major flood event
2 – Major storm event
3 – Droughts leading to increase subsidence
4 – Hot summer – Heatwave
5 – 6 Other

Time horizon

▲ = 0–3 years
● = 3–10 years
★ = +10 years
⌘ – All time horizons

SOURCE OneRisk Consulting

scenario to the current and future risk profile. In Figure 10.9 a hypothetical heat map is shown in which a number of pre-identified physical climate scenarios are mapped against an agreed criteria covering the likelihood, impact and time horizon of the scenario.

In running workshops with key stakeholders it is best to ask participants to provide an initial risk score using the organization's existing risk assessment matrix in respect of an initial 'inherent' impact likelihood score. With climate change this process should be extended to include a third assessment criterion, namely the most applicable time horizon. In the example above the most important scenarios that need to be prioritized against the others are scenario 1, followed by scenarios 3, 4 and 6 that are all classified on a weighted average basis as 'very high'. These should be brought to the attention of senior management and an associated action plan be developed. It is also important to have robust impact criteria that can cover a wide range of potential impacts and that can assess operational, customer, reputational and regulatory impacts as well as financial impacts. The point here is that it is best to take the highest impact across each of the criteria.

It is important to remember that this is a facilitation process to help to provide a basis to prioritize scenarios and gain consensus among key stakeholders.

Once this step has been completed it is then necessary to build out the scenarios, including more detailed risk descriptions and underlying assumptions in order to complete the next step in the process, which may mean using a range of different assessment tools depending on the scenario concerned.

One of the most important areas that risk professionals need to review is the control environment and design of additional mitigation plans (controls and actions) for each scenario. As discussed in Chapter 6, in building out resilience the use of bow tie analysis is a very helpful tool to do this.

10.7.2 Hazard maps and footprints

Hazards such as drought, flood, hurricanes or sea-level rise can be assessed with hazard-specific models. These make use of the outputs of climate models to model changes in risk between present-day and future conditions. For example, models of future flood risk use estimates of the change in likelihood of extreme precipitation events, derived from climate model output.

The example below, provided by JBA Risk Management Limited, for the UK, illustrates a range of specific analytical outputs that help organizations. Data are provided for multiple climate scenarios and time horizons and consist of:

- Climate change index (relative percentage change in flood depths due to climate change)

FIGURE 10.10 Hazard modelling and mapping and future rating

SOURCE JBA Floodability® data. © JBA Risk Management Limited 2022. All rights reserved

- Climate change scores (an easy-to-use scoring system range that summarizes future flood depth and frequency information to show how a property's flood risk may change).
- Climate change rating known as Floodability® (UK Trademark) (an easy-to-use colour rating that shows how a property's flood risk may change, using traffic-light colours such as black, red, amber or green).
- Climate change pricing data (financial metrics showing potential changes in the annual cost of flood to a property due to climate change).

The image in Figure 10.10 shows an example of climate change flood data.

The data points relate to property locations – the shading relates to the level of risk, with areas relating to extreme risk. Some properties which were not currently at risk of flooding are predicted to be at risk in the future. The outputs can help mortgage lenders, for example, assess how flood risk, at the individual property and portfolio level, will likely change over time under different climate scenarios. Increasing flood damage can be correlated to reduced asset valuations and therefore increases in the probability of default on the loan.

The following case studies highlight the use of hazard maps.

CASE STUDY

Fathom: Climate change risk modelling

Fathom

A global authority in flood risk analysis, Fathom is active both in the research and commercial space.

The problem

In June 2021, the Bank of England released its final guidance for the Climate Biennial Exploratory Scenarios (CBES). A large UK insurer and reinsurer approached Fathom to support its submission and fulfil its requirements for UK flood exposure. It needed to know how its portfolio's exposure to flooding might change in the next 10–30 years, under various warming scenarios, to meet the requirements of the CBES.

The solution

Fathom has both flood hazard data and a catastrophe model for the UK, originally launched in January 2021. Underpinned by leading academic research, the models utilize the UK Met Office's UK Climate Projections 2018 (UKCP18) dataset to assess how flood behaviour may change in the future as a result of climate change.

The catastrophe model, Fathom-UK CAT, offers five unique climate scenarios in line with the Bank of England's assessment criteria. This includes the present day, 2030 and 2050 under early action, late action and no additional action warming scenarios.

FIGURE 10.11 Fluvial 'change factors' for river gauges across the UK

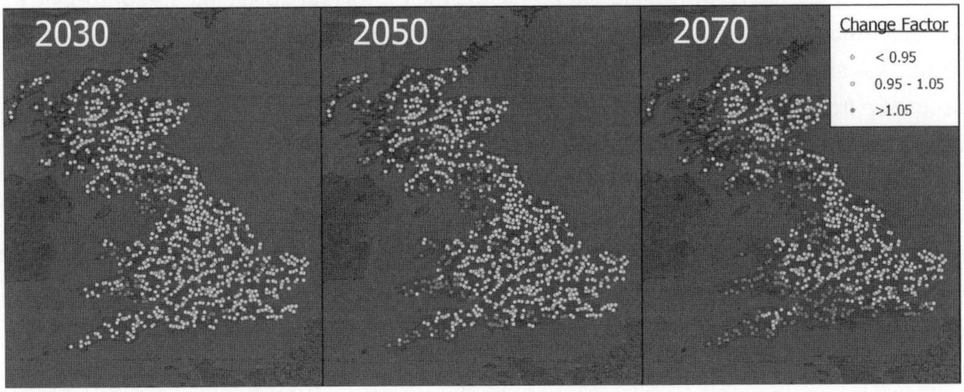

NOTE Values indicate relative change factors at each gauge, through time, e.g. a change factor of 1.1 indicates a 10 per cent increase in peak river flow

To assess its portfolio's present-day and future risk for flood, the insurer ran exposure data through Fathom-UK CAT for around 50,000 properties. Losses were aggregated to the postcode district level, with results for each sub-peril (pluvial, fluvial and coastal flood). Assessments considered insured average annual losses (AAL) and insured 100-year losses for each sub-peril within the five climate scenarios.

The result

The insurer then provided the model outputs as part of its CBES submission for climate-related physical risk. While flooding was just one piece of the puzzle, its submission to the Bank of England was supported by scientifically validated and robust data on the variety of flood-related risks posed to its organization. Users can find out more about the research underpinning Fathom's flood models for the UK by visiting the Knowledge section of the Fathom Global website.

CASE STUDY

A J Gallagher: Future climate scenarios for farmers

This example illustrates the impact of climate change in the UK between 2020 and 2060 using a risk coding applied to four key variables:

- Soil heave
- Storm damage
- Slope failure
- Overheating/humidity

A schedule of locations (with values) at risk across the UK was set up and the risk of specific locations, moving from 'low risk' to 'high risk' categories related to each of the four variables above, was analysed and is summarized in the images that follow (Figure 10.12). The event sets used were from open-source data compiled by the National Trust. The risk impact analysis is reproduced with kind permission from EigenPrism.

The dots in the diagram represent individual farm locations where the values are the sums insured from about 1,050 individual locations and about $450 million of total insured values.

The case study highlights the relative importance of each peril from a climate change perspective. The most impacted peril is risk of 'overheating' (climate zone 3 – hot to very hot dry summer with a cool winter – and higher) that will move from 49 to 956 locations by the year 2060.

This type of analysis can assist the industry in seeking new forms of insurance protection, such as seasonal drought cover, using parametric insurance solutions.

FIGURE 10.12 Overheating and humidity scenario

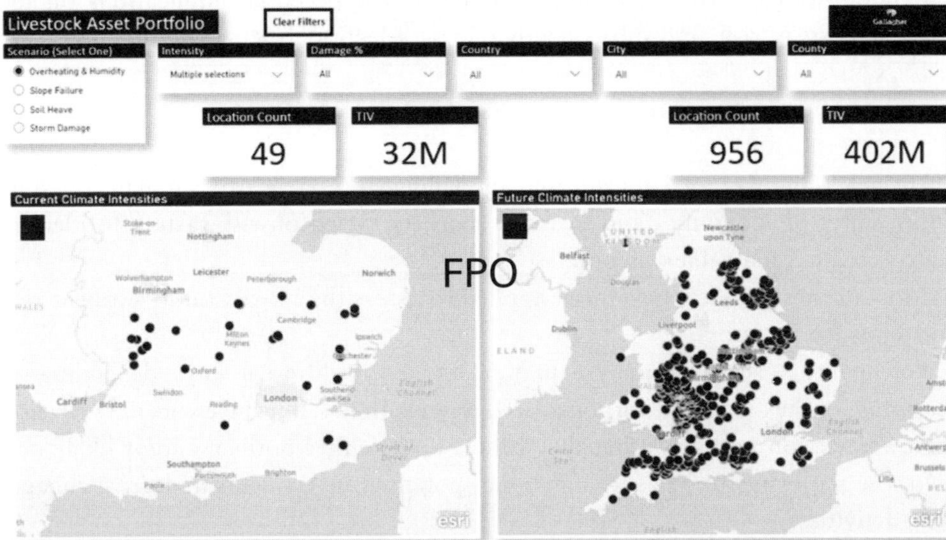

Farmers can start to plan and make better decisions in terms of investments and look to more profitability in new types of crops that can better cope with the changing climate conditions. A good example is wine growers in the south of England.

10.7.3 Probabilistic modelling including catastrophe models

A number of tools are available to help companies anticipate the frequency and severity of potential future catastrophes before they occur so that they can adequately prepare for their financial or social impact.[9]

Catastrophe models are widely used in the insurance industry and have been designed to model many perils that may be impacted by climate change, such as flood and windstorm. Until recently they have focused on present-day modelling.

Climate change modelling is inherently uncertain, especially over the longer term, and this uncertainty is impacted by a number of meteorological, financial and social factors. However, despite this, there is an industry need and increasing regulatory requirements to consider the impacts of climate change on physical hazards over short-, medium- and longer-term scenarios. Catastrophe models are one way of doing so. The models are designed primarily to model 'acute' physical climate risks but are not designed for 'chronic' physical scenarios such as drought and heatwave.

One of the questions that needs to be answered is: how will climate change alter the probability of a severe weather event happening next year? Risk managers also need to consider the impact of climate change in respect of the potential shift in the return period. As an illustration, a 1-in-50-year event in 2020 may become a 1-in-35-year flood event in 10 years' time. This has many potential implications on the financial costs of risk, and subsequently on risk selection, pricing and more.

10.7.3.1 ECONOMIC SCENARIO GENERATORS USING ECONOMETRIC MODELLING TECHNIQUES

There are a number of sophisticated modelling approaches to simulate possible future states of economies and financial markets, based on risk factors to identify unexpected but plausible outcomes.

Most of these models have been applied to assess the impact on investment risk portfolios for investors.

For investors, scenario analysis may be applied in different ways, depending on the nature of the asset(s) being considered. For example, some investors may develop energy transition pathways that they believe to be either optimal and/or likely and use those pathways to measure individual potential investments and drive engagement activities.

Other investors may consider how climate-related scenarios relate to the future performance of particular sectors, regions or asset classes. The results may show that some portions of a portfolio are set to benefit from a particular scenario, while others face a loss in value. Such results, while not conclusive, can be a useful additional factor in determining where to prioritize risk management activities and where to consider making additional allocations.

The UN Environmental Programme (UNEP) issued a comprehensive investor guide about scenario-based methods for climate risk assessment developed in respect of TCFD.

Their report issued in 2019 details the results of the UN Environment Programme Finance Initiative (UNEP FI) Investor Pilot on TCFD Adoption.[10] This was a collaborative effort to explore, enhance and apply a methodology for assessing the impact of physical and transition risks and opportunities on the portfolios of institutional investors.

Investors look into the carbon intensity of investment portfolios, considering the implications of physical and transition risks. There are many tools available for the investment community that can help to assess the impact of an investment strategy of an organization. The focus has been on potential re-pricing of carbon-intensive financial assets, and the speed at which any such re-pricing might occur.

10.7.4 *Integrated stress tests*

Many of these tools are stochastic models that use future econometric models and integrated assessment models to predict the future economic conditions. The UNEP FI report states that climate risks can be incorporated into different financial modelling methodologies. It is important to decide whether to use macroeconomic methodologies (that go from macroeconomic impacts to asset class impacts), bottom-up methodologies (that go from asset-level cash-flow impacts to asset class impacts), or whether to combine the two approaches.

There is a growing need for organizations to stress test the impact of climate change on their current and future business models, which does requires sophisticated methodologies.

There is a recognition that organizations need to identify new tools and approaches to measure and understand climate risks, in order to help them in 'sizing' the risks they are facing and to help ensure a proportionate and coordinated response.

Many organizations are considering and adopting a more integrated and holistic stress testing approach that can assess a range of impacts of physical, transitional and liability climate risk developments by assessing key climate triggers and drivers. This integration would be able to support a wider number of business decisions in areas such as risk appetite, pricing, reserving, risk aggregation/exposure management, new product development, etc.

CASE STUDY

PwC: Transition risk impact assessment for a retailer

PwC UK supported a FTSE250 retailer whose senior management wanted to understand and quantify the future financial impact of climate change risks and opportunities on its business.[11] To assess these impacts, PwC undertook the following steps:

- Risk materiality assessment – understanding the key climate-related physical and transition risks and opportunities to be taken forward to the quantification stage.
- Business lenses – identifying through which lenses of the business the modelling would be targeted. Selected lenses included revenue, energy, carbon, fleet and supply chain.
- Scenario selection – identification of which reference scenarios were to be used for the modelling and any scenario expansions required to supplement the data.
- Impact pathways – development of modelling methodology to calculate the financial impact from scenario variables and data.
- Data gathering – gathering of any internal and external data to help support the modelling, including relevant business plans.
- Assumption setting – agreement of any assumptions to be used to cover data gaps as well as simplify the modelling process.
- Model build – building out the model according to the specification.
- Quantification – using the model built to conduct the scenario analysis and assess the results, linking to potential future management strategies.

FIGURE 10.13 Transition risks

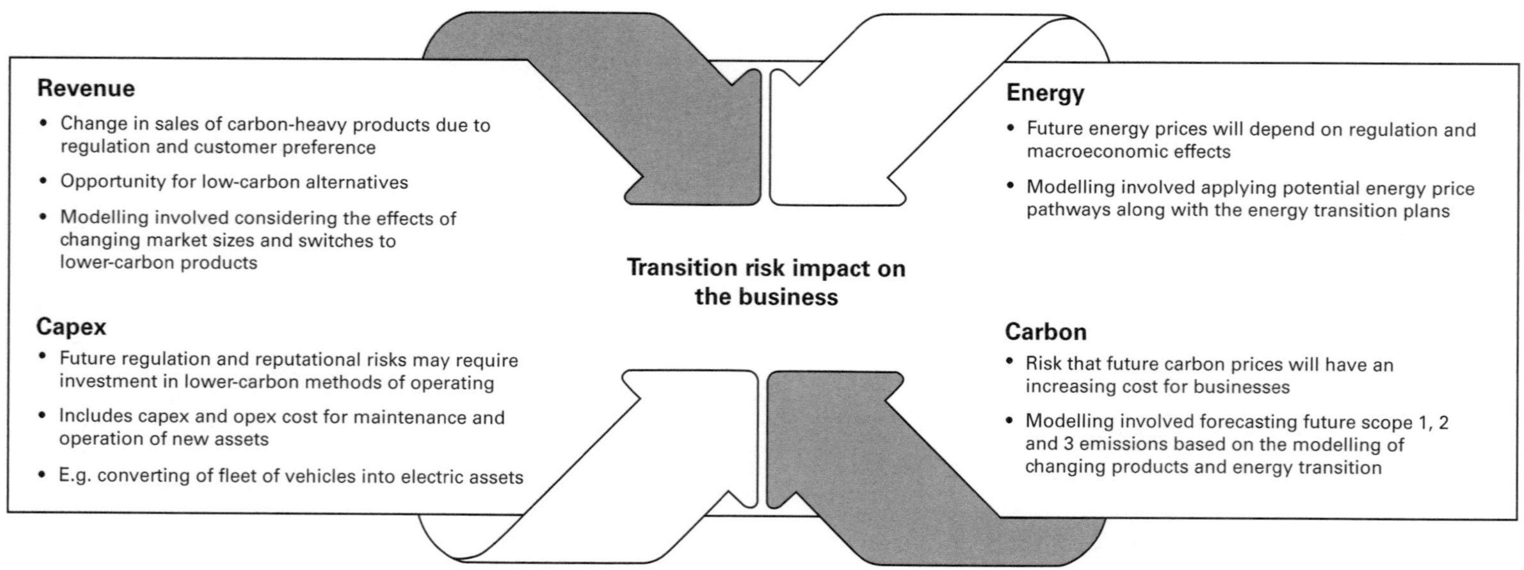

The key transition risks that were identified are shown in Figure 10.13.

A complete scenario analysis impact assessment was provided to the firm and several workshops were held. The results were then used to support the firm's reporting under the Task Force on Climate-related Financial Disclosures (TCFD) requirements. The modelling also enabled the client to understand what the future implications might be for different strategies, and allowed it to make decisions in terms of supply chain, energy transition, and products and markets to invest in.

10.7.5 Scenario templates

For individual scenarios it is helpful to design a bespoke template, typically a one-page output that can capture the information of the scenario and can be used for reporting purposes. Some of the main types of information that should be captured and reported would include:

- Scenario title and description
- Risk types and business area impacted
- Details of underlying assumptions
- Quantitative outputs (gross and net loss after recoveries)
- Probability of occurrence (return period)
- Potential management actions

With respect to the facilitation and discussions with key stakeholders, it's important to provide a template that can capture wider qualitative information that should seek to include key findings and considerations from the stakeholders, such as specific research. Perhaps one of the main areas that risk professionals should focus on is to review the current control effectiveness and then provide findings and future considerations that can then lead to specific recommendations and treatment initiatives.

As an example, given the changes in legislation for electric vehicles in many jurisdictions are likely to impact motor insurers, a scenario description and treatment initiative could be set out as follows, which would form part of a template for reporting ongoing progress:

- **Scenario description** – change in legislation in respect of use of electric cars, i.e. sales of new petrol and diesel cars to end in the UK by 2030, which leads to changing trends in claims and premiums across the motor business.
- **Treatment initiative** – develop a robust and detailed EV strategy in line with the competitive environment.

10.7.6 Climate change dashboards

In terms of internal reporting, it will be important to consider developing bespoke climate risk dashboards that can be used to report risk assessments across the short-, medium- and long-term time horizons to boards. An example was provided in Chapter 3 in Figure 3.5.

It is important to clearly communicate the level of confidence in the modelling outputs for the specific risk. The process will be iterative and it will be important to share and discuss the outputs with stakeholders across the organization. Successful use of the framework should ultimately lead to specific actions being taken by the firm.

Reporting and disclosure complement each other in improving decision making and evidencing that an appropriate process was followed in order to achieve the objective(s).

Over time, organizations should seek to improve reporting and improve disclosure through documenting:

- management's assessment of the resiliency of strategic plans to climate change; and
- the range of scenarios used to inform management's assessment, including key inputs, assumptions, and analytical methods and outputs (including potential business impacts and management responses to them)

Conclusion

Risk managers need to play a pivotal role in driving the scenario selection and design decisions to assess future climate scenarios in a rapidly changing world. As we have discussed, organizations should carefully consider the key parameters, assumptions and other analytical choices.

Scenario analysis is not just about long-term planning but also about supporting improved business decisions in the short term such as risk selection, pricing, reserving, risk transfer, risk appetite, etc that we explored in more depth in Chapter 2.

In conclusion it is important to remember that the overall purpose of scenario analysis is to explore several plausible and 'best-available' 'what-if' scenarios, rather than to precisely forecast the future.

Notes

1 International Actuarial Association. Stress Testing and Scenario Analysis, July 2013. www.actuaries.org/CTTEES_SOLV/Documents/StressTestingPaper.pdf (archived at https://perma.cc/N3XG-U9D8)

2 Bank of England. PRA Rulebook Online, nd. www.prarulebook.co.uk (archived at https://perma.cc/RQ7U-RSXL)

3 Bank of England Prudential Regulation Authority. Enhancing banks' and insurers' approaches to managing the financial risks from climate change, 2019. www.bankofengland.co.uk/-/media/boe/files/prudential-regulation/supervisory-statement/2019/ss319 (archived at https://perma.cc/U2SR-HVNL)

4 European Insurance and Occupational Pensions Authority. Opinion on the supervision of the use of climate change risk scenarios in ORSA, 2021. www.eiopa.europa.eu/sites/default/files/publications/opinions/opinion-on-climate-change-risk-scenarios-in-orsa.pdf (archived at https://perma.cc/KD7H-B6ZK)

5 M Carney. Breaking the Tragedy of the Horizon – climate change and financial stability, Lloyd's of London, 29 September, 2015. www.bankofengland.co.uk/speech/2015/breaking-the-tragedy-of-the-horizon-climate-change-and-financial-stability (archived at https://perma.cc/UWX4-HWQ8)

6 CFRF. Climate Financial Risk Forum Guide 2020: Scenario Analysis Chapter, June 2020. www.fca.org.uk/publication/corporate/climate-financial-risk-forum-guide-2020-scenario-analysis-chapter.pdf (archived at https://perma.cc/563R-LW2V)

7 Network for Greening the Financial System. A call for action: Climate change as a source of financial risk, April 2019. www.ngfs.net/sites/default/files/medias/documents/synthese_ngfs-2019_-_17042019_0.pdf (archived at https://perma.cc/TFD4-SF94)

8 The Geneva Association. Climate Change Risk Assessment for the Insurance Industry, February 2021. www.genevaassociation.org/sites/default/files/research-topics-document-type/pdf_public/climate_risk_web_final_250221.pdf (archived at https://perma.cc/5MAV-2FD8)

9 Lloyds. Catastrophe Modelling and Climate Change, 2014. https://assets.lloyds.com/assets/pdf-modelling-and-climate-change-cc-and-modelling-template-v6/2/pdf-modelling-and-climate-change-CC-and-modelling-template-V6.pdf (archived at https://perma.cc/44YJ-FKS3)

10 UNEP Finance Initiative. Changing Course, October 2019. www.unepfi.org/wordpress/wp-content/uploads/2019/05/TCFD-Changing-Course-Oct-19.pdf (archived at https://perma.cc/46UL-ZCTZ)

11 PWC. Risk Modelling, nd. https://www.pwc.co.uk/services/risk/risk-modelling.html (archived at https://perma.cc/E7PJ-9ZJ2)

11

Climate risk integration into specific business processes

This chapter will cover the integration of climate risk into the mainstream risk management and operational process of organizations.

The main learning outcomes from this chapter are to:

- Recognize approaches to transitioning your organization to a net zero strategy.
- Be able to design a process to map business operations to climate change transition requirements.
- Appreciate the different dimensions required to establish HR protocols with respect to climate change.
- Understanding how climate risk is applied within the financial community across credit, investment and operational risk.
- Provide examples of how climate risk is integrated into 'business as usual' (BAU) processes.
- Recognize the potential for 'greenwashing' to become fraudulent.

Introduction

The previous chapters have outlined the multiple facets of climate change risk management and how it can be incorporated into the wider risk management framework. This chapter focuses on how climate change risk management is being integrated into existing business processes across the corporate value chain as companies transition to net zero.

This will come in many forms and will depend on the organizational structure, the processes undertaken and the various stakeholder groups but it will also be influenced to varying degrees by the climate strategy and ambition of the company, which was discussed in Chapter 2.

The desire to achieve sustainability and effective carbon risk management is driving innovation globally and firms that will benefit most will be those that are prepared to experiment in order to meet their strategic goals (i.e. to increase sustainability or to reduce their carbon footprint). The firms most open to adaptation will develop cleaner business practices and enhanced operational efficiency, which will ultimately flow through to the bottom line in the longer term.

This chapter provides some specific examples of how climate change risk management is integrated into BAU processes focusing on activities that seek to reduce the carbon emission of the organization.

As outlined in Chapter 5, many organizations have been focusing on measuring and monitoring Scope 1 and 2 emissions but the most complex area is Scope 3 emissions that are indirect emissions (not included in Scope 2) that occur in the value chain of the organization.

Scope 3 emissions are from activities that the organization does not own or control and occur across the value chain, and are generally difficult to measure, manage and mitigate. Some of the examples that will be covered in this chapter include customers, suppliers and investment decisions both in relation to capital expenditure and the investment strategies of an organization.

From a risk management perspective, risk managers can support this transition. These are often change programmes in their own right, through climate action plans that should seek to focus specifically on the design of updating risk and operational policies and key risk indicators to manage and monitor the exposures against targets. It is important to develop practices that provide the opportunity to engage with customers or suppliers and to assess the transition risks across the entire value chain of an organization.

11.1 Alignment with business strategy

An organization can make pronouncements with regard to having a climate risk or sustainability strategy, however, this needs to be aligned to what the company does (i.e. its core business) and how it conducts itself. Consequently, it is how this is integrated that will determine the success with regard to the management of climate change risk.

This can be achieved in many different ways and will be contingent on in-depth analysis of the organization's core offerings, the processes undertaken to deliver the product or service, its product range, the behaviours of staff and the establishment of mechanisms to measure its emissions.

Before discussing specific ways that an organization can integrate climate change into specific 'business as usual' (BAU) processes across its risk profile it is important to recognize two important trends that are key drivers for organizations.

First, investing sustainably with an ongoing consideration of climate change is an ongoing process. This applies to companies that are seeking investment and those that will be investing assets. Over time this will become more important to document and demonstrate.

Second, organizations will be affected by climate change in a number of different ways:

- Profitability via the demand for their goods and services.
- Market capitalization (which is driven by profitability, earnings projections, reputation and quality of management).
- Cost of capital will vary, dependent on their maturity in addressing climate change issues. This is due to assessments from the investment community (which consider assessments from the credit rating agencies – who are now considering additional ESG/climate change factors).

11.1.1 Climate change and ESG risk factors

In recent years, sustainable investing as part of environmental, social and governance (ESG) risk factors or with a more explicit focus on climate change and carbon emissions has risen in prominence within risk assessments and investment decision-making processes.

Organizations need to ensure that their approach to ESG considerations takes into account and is consistent with the requirements articulated within the stated overall ambition and risk appetite with regard to climate change.

Companies seeking investment will need to understand that one of the most important components for an investor will be how their portfolio is monitored in terms of ESG ratings and carbon footprint of their investments.

EXAMPLE

A generic process framework that facilitates the change to net zero

As an example of how ESG and in particular climate change can be integrated into corporate strategy and BAU processes, it is necessary to assess the impact of climate change across its activities to help inform strategic decision-making. In 2021 OneRisk Consulting Ltd (OneRisk) with support from Milliman (a global management and actuarial consultancy firm) were commissioned to design a process for transitioning to a net zero strategy. Details of this approach are provided below in general terms in order to show how it can equally be applied in other industries or by other organizations.

Implemented solution

The process framework involved the design of a unique climate risk assessment survey tool, which required different business activities to capture feedback that enabled management to design a conceptual framework to address the changes the business had to make in order to achieve a net zero operating model.

The survey tool has been adapted to ask specific questions that seek to understand the development of ideas, concepts and challenges in addressing how the business could transition to a low-carbon economy and, through understanding from external sources, to develop a process that can then be discussed with senior management as part of the conclusions and recommendations.

The high-level flow chart of the process is shown in Figure 11.1.

FIGURE 11.1 High-level process flow chart of project

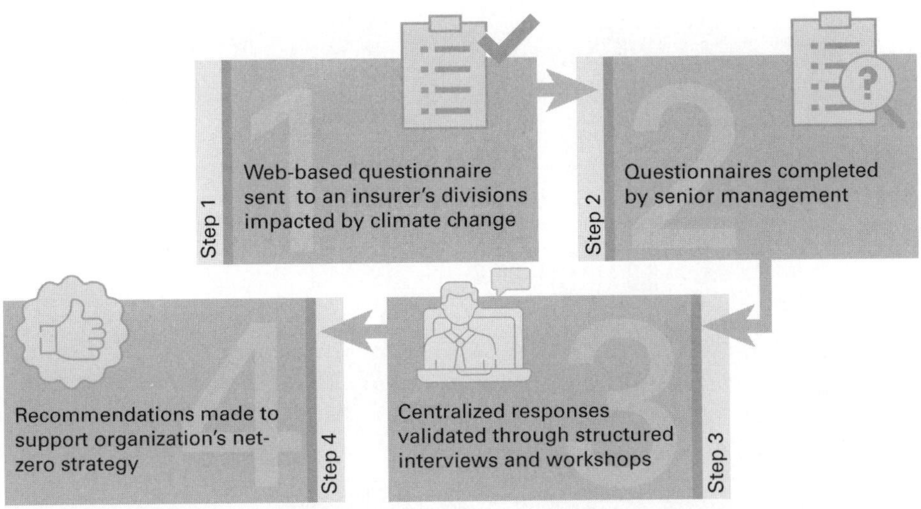

SOURCE OneRisk Consulting

A section of the key questions that were asked included:

- Are you planning to make changes to your business strategy as a direct result of climate change, i.e. changes to business mix and/or risk appetite due to either maintaining or gaining a competitive advantage?
- With respect to the transition to a low-carbon economy, have you made or are you planning to make any changes to your activities to reduce your carbon footprint in line with the Paris Agreement?

The survey captured a wide range of responses from the participants, which enabled the design of an initial process framework, seen in the Figure 11.2. This framework was then used as a basis to articulate and deliver practical strategic approaches to achieve net zero.

FIGURE 11.2 Net zero framework

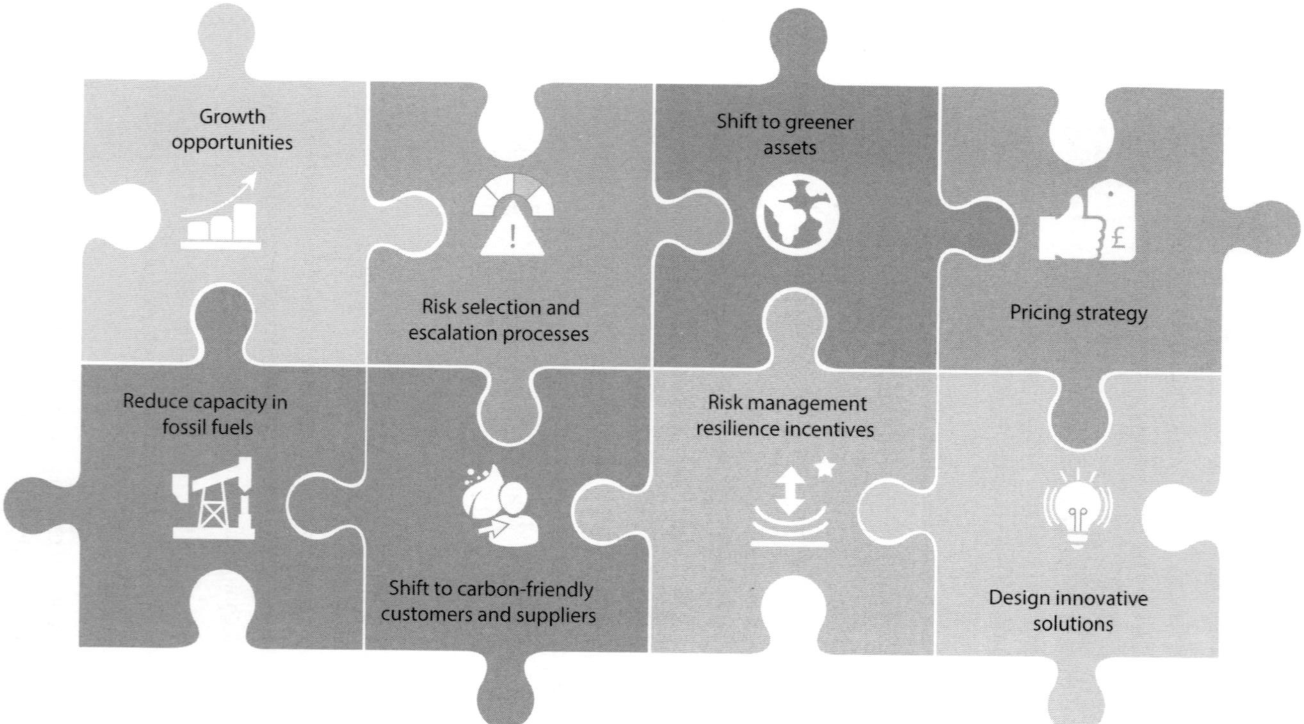

Key:

- Risk appetite strategy
- Tactical implementation levers
- Product innovation

SOURCE

The framework outlined three main areas, which provide insight across all sectors as they address their operations to focus on reducing their carbon footprint:

- **Risk appetite strategy** – The main focus will be to change the organization's risk appetite over time to embrace opportunities arising from sustainable assets and carbon-friendly partnerships as well as reducing exposure to fossil-fuels-related activities.
- **Business resilience** – Other areas of focus include tactical options, which provide incentives for improvements in risk management and enhanced resilience such as 'build back better'.
- **Product innovation** - A third area is product innovation where the organization can develop opportunities in from the transition to a carbon free economy.

In developing opportunities to move to a net zero strategy there will be a need to collaborate across the entire value chain. This will require the development of bespoke tools and techniques and a robust strategy that aligns with wider government targets.

Using tools like these question sets to facilitate discussion can be valuable in raising awareness of climate change across an organization. Multiple responses can be obtained and used to develop a wide range of potential benefits to support internal process changes.

It is likely that discussions held initially will point to the need for collaboration and research to develop industry best practices and common approaches.

11.1.2 Governance arrangements

The most tangible and immediate evidence that climate change risk is fully integrated within an organization will be seen in its governance arrangements, which were discussed in detail in Chapter 3.

It is important to emphasize again here that in terms of facilitating the implementation of climate change plans, robust governance is critical. For example, terms of reference of key working groups, management committees and boards should be embedded within project management practices. It will also be seen in the integration into the agendas and meeting papers from these key meetings and will provide informed influence within the decision-making processes.

When looking for evidence to support this, it will be visible in the role profiles and accountabilities of senior management, terms of reference, meeting agendas (and the accompanying meeting minutes), meeting papers and project documentation. At a more granular level, the more developed and climate-aware organizations will also have incorporated this into corporate and personal objectives (by making it part of staff performance reviews) and thus shaping the attitudes, behaviours and communication flows within an organization.

11.1.3 Sustainable investing – influencing capital expenditure investments

As companies integrate climate risk and sustainability considerations into their investment decision-making, this can be focused on the reduction of energy consumption but it can also be with regard to the sourcing of the energy that they require.

A recent high-profile example of this is Amazon, which in April 2022 reported that it had increased its renewable energy portfolio by nearly 30 per cent, with its announcement of 37 new wind and solar energy projects. Such an approach is required in order to allow it to meet its stated sustainability goals (as part of its stated mission of running 100 per cent of its operations on renewable energy by 2030). It is anticipated that this recent announcement will enable Amazon to achieve this goal by 2025 (five years ahead of the original target).[1]

11.1.4 Integration of carbon pricing mechanism into internal decision-making

As global warming increases, it is likely that government measures will result in the imposition of higher prices for companies' carbon emissions. Increasing costs through the imposition of carbon taxes could directly reduce profitability and returns on capital investments. Consequently, companies are increasingly focusing on introducing their own internal carbon pricing mechanism, in order to better evaluate investments, to manage risk and to shape the strategy.

The carbon footprint impacts of investment options and/or projects can be assessed, based on an internal carbon price, in order to estimate the potential carbon costs going forward. Following such an approach, this allows the expected carbon footprint to be quantified as a financial cost that can be included on the net present valuation of the investment or project. The inclusion of carbon considerations into project evaluation documentation also provides a mechanism for ensuring that this becomes a key consideration and reinforces the message with internal stakeholders of the importance of this.

11.1.5 Acquisitions

Another positive step is for firms to review their due diligence processes when considering acquisitions (for both physical assets and corporate targets), so that consideration is given to the net zero carbon profile of any purchases, and to evaluate sustainability opportunities and risks. The aim should be that they only acquire assets that are lower carbon or can be decarbonized over time. Upon acquisition, the next step is to develop net zero road maps for each asset to ensure alignment with the stated corporate strategy.

11.1.6 Internal carbon pricing (ICP)

ICP is a theoretical price that companies can use to place a monetary value on each tonne of carbon emitted. The setting of the ICP relies on an understanding of carbon economics (i.e. costs of carbon credits, carbon taxes and external carbon costs), operational processes and the company's corporate and climate change strategies.

The benefits of adopting such an approach are threefold. They aim to:

1. Support decision making with regard to capital investments
2. Measure, model and manage the risks (both financial and regulatory) associated with the existing and future government policies
3. Help identify risks and opportunities and provide the chance to adapt strategy

When selecting an ICP, organizations need to choose between the prevailing market rate or another shadow price, based on views of future carbon prices and potential regulatory changes. The price chosen will influence investment decisions and also behaviours within an organization.

As an example of how this could work, if an organization has two different divisions in different countries, their levels of emissions and the cost per tonne of emissions may differ significantly. Consequently, when bidding to be awarded the rights to produce a new product, different ICPs may be applied to each investment proposal and this could significantly influence which division is awarded the contract.

An alternative application of ICPs is when a company imposes a fee on each business per unit of emission. This money is then pooled and can be used to reward those that have the best emission reduction performance over a specified time period. This approach incentivizes the reduction in emissions and promotes the investment in carbon-friendly initiatives (i.e. operational efficiency initiatives, green projects or low-carbon product development) and reinforces a carbon reduction mindset.

11.1.7 Integration into capital allocation decisions

The introduction of carbon pricing will be evidenced in the project and/or investment proposal documentation within more mature organizations and helps generate an element of competition/peer benchmarking between business areas (which further helps integrate climate change considerations into existing processes and approaches). They will also help future-proof operational processes if it has driven the selection of more operationally efficient and lower-emission solutions.

This internal approach is endorsed by one of the world's largest institutional investors (SSGA) in their 'Guidance on climate-related disclosure' article posted on the Harvard Law School Forum on Corporate Governance in January 2022:[2]

> We expect companies in carbon-intensive sectors to incorporate climate considerations into capital allocation decisions, such as for existing or planned projects, portfolio

> decisions, and financial planning. Companies are establishing a price for carbon (also known as "carbon price") to capture and monetize the costs/impacts of their activities as they relate to climate change. It allows for companies to express and incorporate the cost of operations, compliance, and future regulations into strategic decision-making. We evaluate if companies take forecasted carbon pricing into account for project assessment and encourage disclosure of the average and/or range of carbon price assumptions used.

While this market mechanism may not have achieved significant reductions in carbon emissions, it is instilling a means to allow a comparison of investment proposals with a consideration for carbon emissions (both in the marketplace and internally within organizations).

11.1.8 Alignment with the transition to a circular economy

Today's consumers are often making an extra effort to purchase products whose suppliers produce them in an environmentally friendly way, recycle and use natural ingredients. This represents a fundamental societal shift that puts pressure on every organization.

On top of this, there are strict regulations coming from, for example, the European Union (EU) Corporate Sustainability Directive that will make sustainability reporting mandatory in 2023 for thousands of companies. The new rules must be taken seriously, or companies will see severe penalties for violations.

As organizations look to reduce their emissions, the first step is to see how the processes can be optimized/improved, so that they reduce the amount of energy required (thus reducing their consumption).

This requires analysis and optimization of the entire end-to-end production from raw materials to waste product (post-use). This is the concept behind the move to a

FIGURE 11.3 From a linear to a circular economy

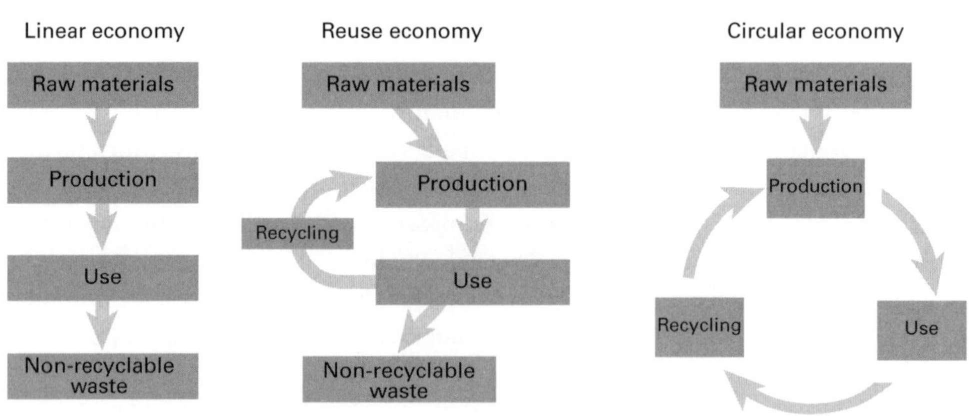

SOURCE Dutch government, Government.nl

'circular economy'. In a circular economy, waste is significantly reduced or does not exist and products and raw materials are (designed to be) reused as long and intensively as possible over and over again. Waste effectively becomes the new raw material.[3]

This approach presents an opportunity for organizations. Looking at how to implement a circular economy is beneficial because it saves raw materials, reduces waste and carbon emissions, promotes product innovation, can create jobs and reduces costs (all of which can improve profitability in the longer term).

The alternative to process change is the use of technology to reduce emissions and promote efficiency. This may involve the substitution or replacement of existing technology/machinery being used across the value chain but it can also include automation of manual or carbon-intensive processes or investment in new technologies or renewable energy sources that can complement each other and result in both reduced emissions and improved efficiency.

This chapter will now focus on the integration of climate change consideration into BAU processes.

11.2 Mapping the risk profile to business activities

In terms of this process, climate change can be considered a cause that leads to many risks and associated impacts. The impacts are the ones that should align with the organization's own risk assessment criteria, which can be developed through workshops in developing climate scenarios that we discuss in Chapter 10.

Organizations should seek to initially map out their risk profile to business processes and then consider how climate change can impact on the business processes both as a threat and an opportunity.

This process can support business resilience (discussed in Chapter 6) but also be used for sustainability purposes and reducing an organization's carbon footprint, which is the focus in this chapter.

One approach is to map out the climate risks against the other principal risks for your organization. This approach helps to identify the key areas of focus and then prioritizes those that are most likely to be impacted by climate risks, including transition risks, but we will also focus discussions on physical risks.

The main output of this review process needs to integrate the internal business and risk information gathered, such as prevailing risk registers, and this is then supplemented by expert judgement, feedback and discussion through risk questionnaires, structured interviews and workshops.

11.3 Operational risk processes

This section provides some general areas that focus on operational risk profiles and operational processes that are applicable to many organizations in terms of climate integration:

- Procurement processes of third-party suppliers
- Human resource processes including recruitment
- Carbon trading

11.3.1 Operational risk – procurement of services from third-party suppliers

One of the main areas of focus for organizations is to integrate climate change and their wider ESG factors within their third-party risk management processes.

Organizations across most sectors should seek to develop processes to be used to assess the ESG/climate change supplier credentials in order to meet certain regulatory standards and be used to track their Scope 3 emissions in line with meeting their strategic net zero goals through a robust supplier procurement process.

The reasons for developing a more robust and integrated process include:

- Meet net zero targets by improving the supports that have a lower carbon footprint
- Meet regulatory requirements and expectations
- Reduce reputational and legal risks
- Gain knowledge of best industry practices through improved communication with suppliers
- Align the procurement process with improved management of risk
- Potential to automate the process to rank suppliers in terms of climate and wider ESG credentials

11.3.1.1 ALIGNMENT WITH CORPORATE VALUES AND RISK-SEEKING PREFERENCES

As outlined in Chapter 2, one of the risk preferences may be to state 'We seek to use suppliers who are climate change active, aligned with our own plans and meeting regulatory standards through a robust supplier procurement process and proactive relationship management.'

Therefore, an association with a supplier that operates counter to your own corporate values may be detrimental to your customers' views of your corporate brand image.

It is important to note that this is equally applicable to existing suppliers and also to prospective suppliers. Companies will want to align themselves with suppliers that share similar corporate values with regard to climate change, and will either decide not to work with (or use) a particular provider or may elect to agree an action plan to remediate any concerns, which can then be monitored over an agreed period.

By incorporating climate change considerations into the process, this flags to your suppliers (or prospective suppliers) the importance that you are placing on climate change considerations and also provides a mechanism for monitoring carbon emissions going forward. This can achieve an organization's due diligence processes during the selection process for a provider but also during their ongoing performance monitoring and when contracts are up for renewal.

Figure 11.4 provides a process flow of the key steps to integrate climate change into a due diligence process.

11.3.1.2 TIERING OF SUPPLIERS

The chosen approach needs to be proportionate to the size of the supplier and the services or products provided, the degree of importance to the overall value chain, the frequency (and value) of the services or products provided and the relative size of the firms involved.

FIGURE 11.4 Supplier due diligence process

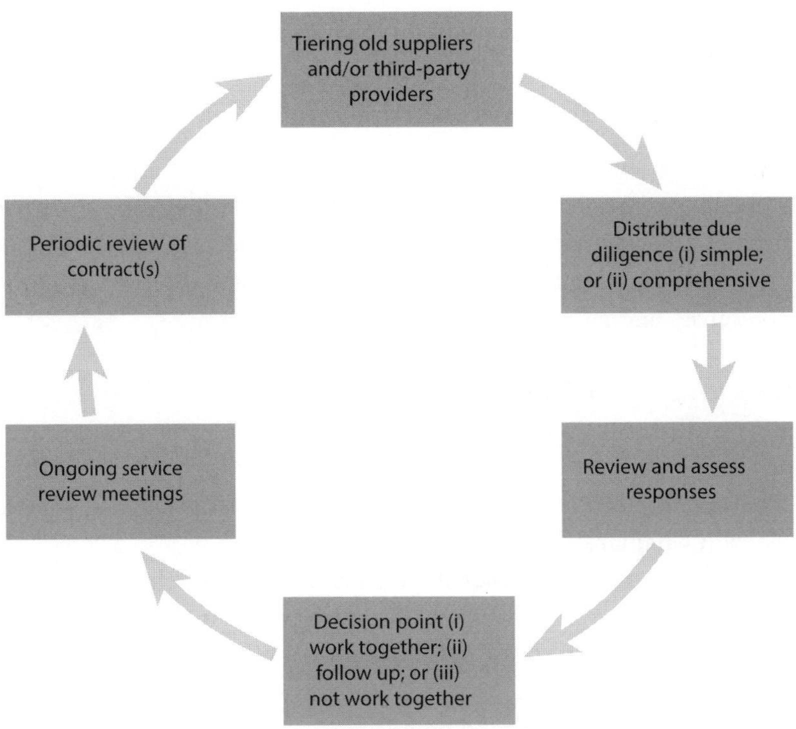

SOURCE

For example, a small company will have limited opportunities to influence a multinational organization that provides its IT equipment. Whereas in the other direction, a multinational organization may be more exacting when requesting certain minimum carbon emission standards from a local printing firm that may be dependent on a significant contract with the multinational.

11.3.1.3 DESIGN OF DUE DILIGENCE QUESTIONNAIRE

The main step in the process is to design a set of questions against specific categories that needs to include a scoring mechanism that can then be escalated. Risk categories can be developed with specific climate change questions; other categories will also be required (e.g. with regard to societal or governance as part of wider ESG considerations). Categories should seek to include the following:

- Climate change strategy and ERM
- Climate change governance and policies
- Supplier management
- Carbon emissions management

Some sample questions could include the following:

- Do you have documented processes and procedures for identifying, managing and mitigating climate-related risks within your organization, (i.e. a climate change policy)?
- Have you engaged with an external third party to calculate your carbon footprint?

Once the due diligence questionnaire is distributed, the recipient firm has to be given time to respond; these responses then need to be reviewed and assessed in an objective way. This will be reliant on having agreed assessment criteria, validation of the responses received and a qualitative overlay.

11.3.1.4 SUPPLIER EVALUATION AND ESCALATION PROCESSES

The supplier evaluation should be based on designing a robust scoring system for each main category and an overall scoring system that is linked to a RAG escalation process and therefore can be used as part of a KRI process in the risk appetite strategy discussed in Chapter 2.

Once a decision is made, it is then important to introduce climate risk considerations into the ongoing review process. This may include incorporation into service review meetings, the review of (or development of) relevant management information that is to be provided going forward, follow-up on agreed actions/remediation, due diligence visits, both regular and ad hoc, and escalation (as required).

11.3.1.5 ALIGNMENT WITH WIDER SUPPLY CHANGE RISK MANAGEMENT

A survey from the IBM Institute for Business Value (published in April 2022) found that top supply chain executives are now recognizing sustainability as a business priority and are reviewing the resilience of their supply chains due to the disruptions in the last few years.[4] In part this is a response to pressures from stakeholder groups but it was also noted that while there may be a short-term profitability impact this is balanced against benefits from complying with environmental regulation, reductions in reputational risk, driving new innovation in the supply chain, reducing waste in the product life cycle, offering opportunities to differentiate their brand and enhancing the opportunities to attract talent (due to having a reputation for sustainability).

11.3.2 Human resource processes (including recruitment)

The role of employees in mitigating climate risk should not be underestimated. As employers examine their role in managing climate change, this involves a rethink of their ways of working. It also increasingly requires an approach that, in the race to attract and retain talent, creates an environment that makes the younger generation want to work for the organization.

The HR function will therefore need to readdress some of the main processes and related policies and procedures, especially covering recruitment and selection, performance management, learning and development, and compensation and benefits in respect of climate change integration.

Some of the areas in which the HR function can influence and shape this is via a range of measures that include:

- Employee accountability and objective setting
- Staff engagement and communication
- Revising HR policies and procedures

11.3.2.1 EMPLOYEE ACCOUNTABILITY AND OBJECTIVE SETTING

In developing and implementing a climate change strategy as discussed in Chapter 2 it is important, and in some instances will be a regulatory requirement, to set clear accountabilities for climate and environmental matters, providing support to the teams tasked with delivering them and developing appropriate mechanisms/metrics so that the progress can be measured. This then forms the basis for performance-related incentives for executives and senior management. It can also be extended to the development and introduction of climate risk and related sustainability objectives into the annual performance review process for all staff (which will also influence behaviours).

By designing specific performance objectives for staff that relate to setting SMART climate-related objectives this should seek to influence behaviours, enhance the employee experience, and improve attraction and retention. This can also be positively encouraged by the targeting of environmentally responsible applicants when recruiting for new employees.

11.3.2.2 STAFF ENGAGEMENT AND COMMUNICATION

There are a number of areas that the HR function can leverage in terms of employee engagement.

It is important to understand the attitudes of employees, which can be assessed through internal surveys and employee focus groups. This can increase their understanding an can also identify opportunities to reduce emissions or address issues where there may be gaps.

Promoting environmental awareness should seek to heighten employee engagement and this should be aligned with a clear corporate climate risk strategy.

Such initiatives are useful tools to increase engagement, to raise the profile of climate change risk and to empower and enable staff to think about how climate risk emissions can be reduced (both in and outside of the workplace), how the risks can be better mitigated or how operational processes can be made more efficient.

This can be achieved with training programmes, lunch and learns, the encouragement of staff to take climate change related qualifications (where applicable), effective and regular communication of what the organization is doing to support climate change initiatives and reduce emissions, and celebrating successes when they occur.

As discussed in the introduction, insurers are in the vanguard of impact on their business from climate change, and we outline here two examples of how different insurers have attempted to address employee communication:[5]

- **Aviva** – Initiated weekly internal climate change updates to inform employees about climate change developments for the insurance sector and globally. This was complemented by 'snapbriefs' for staff, where specific details were provided about what Aviva is doing about climate change and within the domain of influencing public policy.
- **Allianz** – Runs an annual group-wide sustainability forum for all staff to attend and launched an app that allows staff to track their emissions and carbon savings. These then feed into an offset process.

11.3.2.3 HR POLICIES AND PROCEDURES

Organizations, particularly since the Covid-19 crisis, have been reassessing employee policy and procedures to seek to balance issues such as flexible and remote working practices as help to both motivate staff and improve efficiency.

These policy changes also need to be aligned with climate emission targets through initiatives to reduce the overall carbon footprint.

There are numerous additional HR/working practices that are being applied in varying combinations but which are contributing to carbon risk management and the reduction of emissions. Examples of this include:

- Ongoing support for flexible working-from-home initiatives (reducing emissions from commuting)
- Promoting greater use of technology to facilitate meetings (which reduces emissions from business travel)
- Encouraging more environmentally friendly travel to work options
- Choosing sustainable suppliers for office infrastructure and equipment
- Introducing reductions in business travel (which can also have immediate financial benefits)
- Installing EV charging points (or the introduction of electric vehicle schemes – similar to the 'Bike to Work' schemes)
- Replacing regular lighting with LED lights and motion sensors to reduce energy consumption in workplaces

11.3.3 Carbon trading

Another operational consideration for organizations is obtaining the requisite permits for the emissions from their operational processes. This represents a cost of business for organizations and as prices increase, corporate behaviours will change in order to minimize costs incurred.

Carbon trading is the process of buying and selling permits and credits that allow permit holders to emit carbon dioxide (or other GHGs). While not a mechanism to stop the emission of carbon dioxide it is a mechanism to gradually reduce carbon emissions.

Governments or intergovernmental bodies establish an overall limit on emissions for a defined time period (this is known as a 'cap') and a finite number of permits to emit are granted to those firms releasing the emissions. Each permit is considered equivalent to one tonne of CO_2e. Organizations must have sufficient permits to cover the emissions they release. These permits are tradeable on regional trading marketplaces (e.g. the EU Emissions Trading Market) and effectively result in firms putting a price on their emissions. This means that surplus permits can be sold if the firms' own emissions have been reduced (this could be due, for example, to efficiency gains in their own production processes).

The trading of permits allows emitters to exceed their emission caps if an organization elsewhere is reducing their emission (and are prepared to trade any surplus emission permits). Consequently, carbon trading should not be seen as a means to reduce emissions overall, it should be seen as an approach to prevent the situation worsening. It does, therefore, incentivize the adoption of innovative technologies, reward companies that cut their emissions and impose financial costs on companies that do not.

11.4 Credit risk management

The specific credit risk exposure for organizations will vary considerably but some of the principles are very similar.

In terms of moving to a low-carbon economy the banking industry is developing some changes to its lending practices, which we discuss in more detail in the following sections.

11.4.1 Lending practices

Lenders are seeking ways to make a contribution to tackling climate change and the transition to a low-carbon economy in the UK by adapting their credit risk practices and policies.

With regard to governance arrangements, credit risk management policies are being revised to explicitly reference and consider climate risk (or as part of a wider 'responsible lending' policy), climate risk is becoming a standing agenda item at credit risk committees (and included in meeting papers) and the monitoring of credit portfolios is being expanded to cover a variety of additional variables.

11.4.1.1 BARCLAYS BLUETRACK APPROACH

One example of how lenders are making a contribution to tackling climate change and the transition to a low-carbon economy in the UK is where Barclays have introduced 'BlueTrack', which is a dashboard used to measure their financed emissions and track them over time against a decreasing 'carbon limit' on the activity they finance.[6,7] Barclays have a stated ambition to be a net zero bank by 2050 and are already net zero emissions from their own operations, so the focus is now switching to reducing the client emissions that they finance. This approach (based on proprietary methodology) follows a number of steps:

1. The first step constructs Paris-aligned portfolio benchmarks for the sector(s) in which firms operate. These benchmarks define how emissions need to reduce over time. Firms are then benchmarked in absolute terms and/or by emission-intensity.
2. The second step of the model quantifies emissions produced by the client to which finance is provided.
3. The third step attributes emissions to the financing provided (i.e. linking each part of the financing to the client's respective absolute emissions or emissions intensity

metrics), which can lead to Barclays determining their 'fair share' of a company's absolute emissions.

4 The fourth step aggregates company-level emission measurements and financing information into portfolio-level metrics.

The approach will evolve over time as company disclosures improve, as data quality and greater coverage becomes available, by integrating company-level forecasts/commitments and updating benchmarks as they are developed. The success of this integration will nevertheless be contingent on the availability and reliability of the underlying data, and systems to monitor the exposures.

FIGURE 11.5 Barclays BlueTrack approach

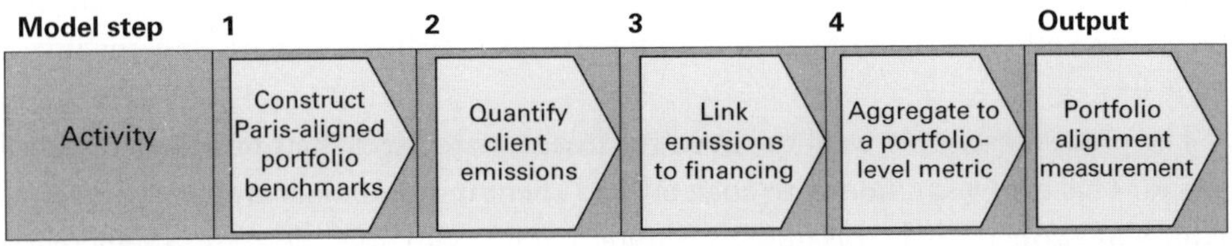

SOURCE Barclays

11.5 Development of a sustainable investment strategy

This section covers the integration of climate change into investment risk strategy. This will be important to companies seeking investment or to those with funds to invest, for example:

1 Investment managers, e.g. pension funds

2 Investment strategy of an organization

11.5.1 Investment risks – stranded assets

One of the most important risks that organizations are facing is stranded assets due to climate change. Stranded assets are assets that have had a premature reduction in value, which can be attributed to changes in legislation, new regulations or unanticipated changes in societal demands and/or production processes.

This can relate to the risk of stranded assets as a direct consequence of climate change, changes in legislation, and indirectly due to changes in consumer demand, which can then influence investors in their decision making.

If we consider the example of regulatory changes relating to GHG emissions and the subsequent impact on the coal industry, this has resulted in sudden and material impacts on operating measures such as revenues, earnings and margins of market participants, all of which contribute to uncertainty relating to the estimation of value of the underlying assets and consequently the shares of the companies involved. An example of this could be the reduction in value of a company's fleet of diesel cars. As certain cities globally restrict the use of diesel vehicles, this reduces the demand for such vehicles and consequently the assets are worth less than expected (which affects both the company balance sheet and income statements).

Such changes can result in credit rating downgrades but also emphasize the importance of valuation committees within the investment management firms in order to determine a 'fair value' for distressed or insolvent assets within their portfolios (albeit under the supervision of a transparent and robust governance framework).

11.5.2 Investment managers

Investment companies need to consider their appetite for risk, their time horizon and the investment objectives of the portfolio of assets they are managing (i.e. the investment strategy).

The process can start with the need for investors to meet their fiduciary responsibilities. This evolves in line with societal and client requirements and can, over time, reduce investment risk (because the underlying companies develop an increased focus on the long term).

11.5.3 Principles for responsible investing

A common approach for investment managers to evidence their responsible investing credentials is to become a signatory to the UN Principles for Responsible Investment (UNPRI). These principles require explicit incorporation of environment, social and governance (ESG) factors into investment decision-making and active ownership.

UNPRI require firms to adhere to the following:

1. We will incorporate ESG issues into investment analysis and decision-making processes.
2. We will be active owners and incorporate ESG issues into our ownership policies and practices.
3. We will seek appropriate disclosure on ESG issues by the entities in which we invest.
4. We will promote acceptance and implementation of the principles within the investment industry.
5. We will work together to enhance our effectiveness in implementing the principles.
6. We will each report on our activities and progress towards implementing the principles.

To be recognized as a signatory, firms are required to report on the implementation of these principles (and this may be subject to external validation). Being a UNPRI signatory is becoming the asset management industry's norm for ESG (including climate change risk management) and it is common practice for this to be a prerequisite prior to an investing party allocating funds to a particular asset management firm. To not be a signatory can place a firm at a competitive disadvantage (because those in control of the funds cannot or will not allocate money to non-signatory firms). Consequently, this form of peer group comparison becomes self-fulfilling and reinforces the investment industry trend towards responsible investment.

11.5.4 Monitoring of investments

Investment managers monitor their portfolios and their investment exposures against their peers, industry benchmarks and stock market indices across a wide variety of data points on an ongoing basis.

Their range of analytics is expanding beyond traditional investment data to also cover climate change/carbon emissions and other ESG analytics. This means that

FIGURE 11.6 Example of a sustainable investment process

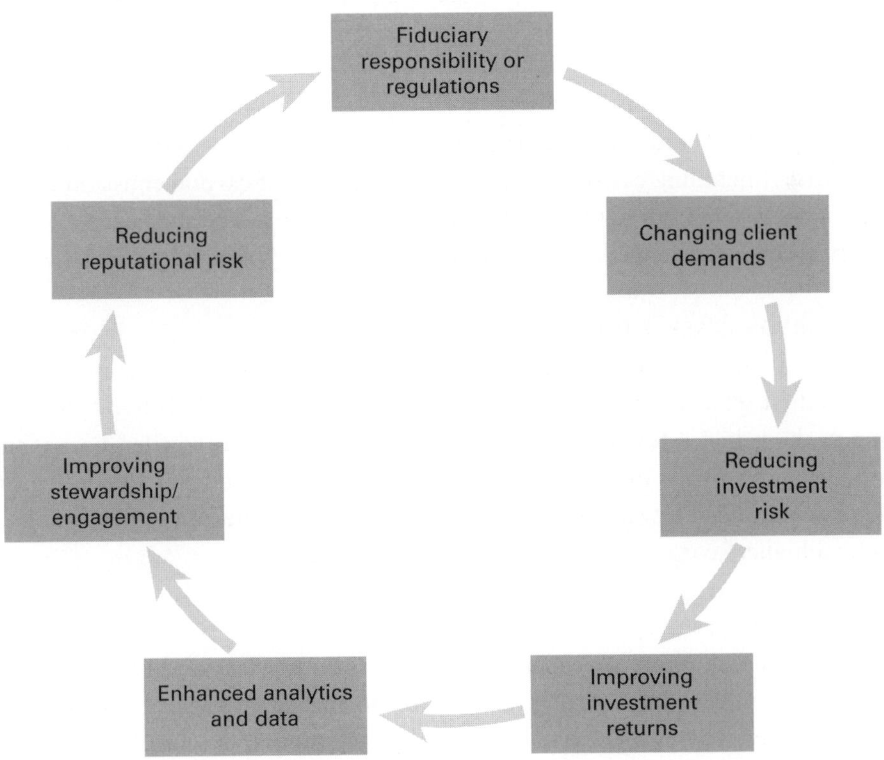

SOURCE © OneRisk Consulting. All rights reserved, 2022

portfolios will now be considering the absolute emissions of the companies they invest in, the highest and lowest emitters, highlighting which industries or geographic areas are better or worse, benchmarking against industry providers (examples include MSCI, Sustainalytics, S&P, Fitch Ratings and Moody's).

In April 2022, credit rating agency Fitch Ratings announced the publication of Climate Vulnerability Scores, which examine sector exposure to low-carbon transition risks for a number of new sectors (i.e. auto manufacturing, aerospace and defence, transportation and technology, media and telecommunications, which builds on their pre-existing coverage of utilities, oil and gas, and chemical sectors).[8] Fitch's Climate Vulnerability Scores provide the agency's view of the creditworthiness impact of sectors, companies and debt securities to a rapid low-carbon transition between 2025 and 2050. According to Fitch, the scores were developed in response to a need by investors for a long-term view of transition risks, recognizing the implications for instruments of different maturities and strategies, to help manage these risks and support security selection, portfolio management, risk management, monitoring and reporting.

11.5.5 *Key monitoring criteria*

Below are some of the indicators for monitoring that may be applied by the various ESG rating agencies.

11.5.5.1 CARBON EMISSIONS INTENSITY

This takes Scope 1 and 2 emissions and divides this by the enterprise value of the organization (including cash) in order to get a measure of carbon emission intensity based on the company's activities (adjusted by company size and sector). A lower intensity relative to the median is favourable and receives a higher score.

11.5.5.2 CARBON RESERVE INTENSITY

This looks at the reserves of fossil fuels that a company owns. This presents two risks. The first relates to the impacts if all of the reserves were burnt and the second relates to the value of fossil fuel assets (which may reduce due to energy transition). Again, the sum value is divided, but the company's enterprise value (including cash) to get a score and a lower intensity score relative to the median is favourable and receives a higher score.

11.5.5.3 GREEN REVENUES

Companies who generate revenues from low-carbon services and technologies are assigned a green revenue score, in proportion to the percentage of the company's 'green' revenues. This is a positive contributor to a company's score.

11.5.5.4 INTERNAL MANAGEMENT VERSUS EXTERNAL OVERSIGHT

Investment companies are in the unusual position of facing climate change risk from two angles. Internally they have to consider how they run their own company and maintain high standards while also overseeing their investee companies, hold them to account and ensure they meet the standards expected of them.

11.5.6 Engagement

Investment firms need to be clear on their engagement strategies with the companies in which they invest. Will they operate on an exclusion basis (i.e. not invest in companies with bad sustainability/climate risk assessments) or choose to actively engage and exert influence over the investee companies?

An example would be ownership of airline shares. One institutional investment manager could decide no longer to invest in airlines due to the amount of emissions that the industry generates. Alternatively, another investor could elect to invest only in the best-in-class airlines (i.e. those with the lowest emissions). Whereas a third investor could choose to invest in the worst-emitting airline with a view to actively engaging management in order to influence them to reduce their emissions.

11.5.6.1 ACTIVE ENGAGEMENT WITH INVESTEE COMPANIES

As climate change risk gains a heightened profile and sense of urgency, investors have a responsibility to exert positive influence over the companies in which they are shareholders. The rise of 'active ownership' is influencing companies to adopt sustainable business practices (which cover all of the facets of ESG), which in turn benefits investors and the wider society.

Active ownership is typically being evidenced by open and transparent reporting of voting records by institutional investors. These results are reported on each company's website and disclosed in their 'active ownership reporting'. This rise in transparency is aiding comparability and consequently it is helping ensure that investment managers are being seen to fulfil their stewardship responsibilities. Part of this is driven by the desire not to be seen unfavourably relative to their peers in the eyes of clients. An example of this is the 'Say on climate' proposals, where shareholders have an opportunity to vote on firms' climate policy and strategy. This can be approved (or disapproved) if a policy or strategy is considered not to be ambitious enough or not sufficient to meet their stated climate strategy.

As investment managers build and manage their portfolios, they need to continually monitor their investments on an ongoing basis in respect of their underlying investment returns and increases in their carbon risk scores. These carbon risk scores need to be considered with regard to their 'fit' with the overall investment strategy of their funds and to ensure that they align with the expectations of their underlying investors or trustees. Institutional investors are now publishing case studies with regard to their approaches in which they provide their assessments (including information relating to their methodology) and details on the individual ratings of companies and sectors, reference to specific historical issues and outlining the voting records on climate change/sustainability initiatives.

A carbon rating could be monitored in isolation but can also be a component of an overall ESG score. Legal & General Investment Management (LGIM), which is one of Europe's largest asset managers, uses 28 key metrics to monitor companies.[9] These are spread across:

- environmental
- social diversity and human capital
- governance (covering board composition, audit oversight and investor rights)
- transparency

Within the environmental component, the primary criteria that are assessed are (i) carbon emissions intensity; (ii) carbon reserve intensity; and (iii) green revenues.

11.5.7 Reducing reputation risk

One of the dangers of seeking investment, due to enhanced sustainability and the business approach to sustainability, is the risk that the approach that is 'advertised' is found not to be as sustainable as intended and should not have been marketed to investors (or to clients of investment companies) as such. This has potential to become fraudulent, as shown below, or certainly to impact the reputation of the organization.

In a market where demand is being driven by consumers for products and services from companies that are actively contributing to carbon reduction and the move to net zero, any perception that this is not the case could have serious reputational (and thus financial) implications.

Two examples are shown here:

1. **Deutsche Bank** – The Frankfurt head offices of Deutsche Bank and DWS (their subsidiary) were raided by the financial regulator 'BaFin' on 31 May 2022 following reports that a whistleblower reported the asset management arm of the firm (DWS) was involved in actively misleading investors by 'greenwashing' their investment strategy. While the subsidiary had been going through 'troubled times', the day after the raid the CEO, Asoka Woerhman, was reported to be 'stepping down' from his role.
2. **HSBC Bank** – At the end of April 2022, it was reported that HSBC had been referred to the Advertising Standards Authority in the UK over its adverts in two

UK cities, which inflated its credentials regarding the provision of financing for clients to transition to net zero and planting trees, without reference to its disclosures relating to the financing of 25.6 million tonnes of CO_2e or reference to the bank's commitments to fund thermal coals until 2040.[10,11]

In generic terms, greenwashing relates to when there is a suggestion that a product or service that is provided by a firm has certain environmental credentials (or meets certain environmental standards), when these standards have not been met. As the appetite for 'green' products grows, this risk increases significantly and consequently the number of legislative and regulatory initiatives increase in order to mitigate the risk of greenwashing. Examples of greenwashing were outlined in Chapter 9.

11.6 Investment strategy of investors

Investment companies recognize that the increased risk from climate change may affect the value of their assets in the future. Over the longer term, as efforts to move away from a carbon-intensive economy gather pace, organizations recognize the possibility that financial market participants may fundamentally reassess the value of carbon-intensive assets and the businesses that rely on them.

Shifts in consumer behaviour may also affect the long-term viability of these businesses and their ability to repay debt. This re-evaluation may lead to impairments to the value of these assets.

Specific transition risks relating an organization's investment portfolio typically include:

- Increased cost associated with production of carbon intensive products
- Impairments in carbon extractive industries due to falling demand, carbon pricing or outright ban
- Higher levels of business investment to support transition
- Failure of businesses to evolve their business models

11.6.1 Investment considerations – selection criteria

One of the common issues in terms of investment decisions is the selection approach of companies within the investment portfolio. Many organizations use a benchmarking approach using an externally based ESG process to seek to exclude investing in certain types of industry sectors or individual companies. This is often termed a 'prohibited list' and by excluding or removing firms that are the highest emitters it may impact upon the risk–return profile and can lead to lower returns or mean that investors do not gain all of the diversification benefits.

An example of this is the Lloyd's Insurance Market. Lloyd's, the world's biggest insurance market, will end new investments in coal-fired power plants, coal mines, oil sands and Arctic energy exploration by 1 January 2022, and phase out existing investments in companies that derive 30 per cent or more of their revenues from this area by the end of 2025. Lloyds has stated that it will align themselves with the UN sustainability development goals and principles.

11.6.1.1 CLIMATE AND ESG 'WATCH LIST'

Many organizations are implementing a process that enables them to develop an 'ESG watch list', which is monitored at each investment committee and is based on ESG monitoring criteria. It is important to note that many issues are related to governance-type issues and not necessarily climate related.

11.6.2 ESG scoring system

There are a number of global industry scoring systems that have developed methodologies to provide an ESG score that is broken down between the E, S and G components. The concept is to provide additional information to investors in addition to conventional financial analysis (discussed in more detail in Chapter 12, which focuses on climate financial reporting and disclosures).

One of the companies that provide ESG ratings is Morgan Stanley Capital International (MSCI) ESG Ratings, which aims to measure a company's management of financially relevant ESG risks and opportunities.

MSCI uses a rules-based methodology to identify industry leaders and laggards according to their exposure to ESG risks and how well they manage those risks relative to peers. However, it should also be noted that there are a multitude of ESG rating companies (all of which use differing methodologies). The MSCI ESG Ratings range from leader (AAA, AA), to average (A, BBB, BB), to laggard (B, CCC).

This represents the following descriptions:

- **Laggard** – A company lagging its industry based on its high exposure and failure to manage significant ESG risks.
- **Average** – A company with a mixed or unexceptional track record of managing the most significant ESG risks and opportunities relative to industry peers.
- **Leader** – A company leading its industry in managing the most significant ESG risks and opportunities.

One of the key points emanating from the rating description is the word 'industry', as the ratings process is based on a score that is relative to industry peers. The benchmarking process aligns with the discussion in respect of climate ambition and strategic positioning (see Chapter 2). The higher the organization's ambition, the more likely the company itself is to have a higher ESG rating.

EXAMPLE

Analysis of a hypothetical investment portfolio

An illustration of how climate risk considerations are now embedded is shown in Figure 11.7. This example of an investment portfolio analysis shows reporting (which breaks down the investment exposures relative to industry benchmarks) and is becoming the norm for portfolio analysis provided to organizations as they monitor their investments, with an additional focus on climate risk considerations.

FIGURE 11.7 Hypothetical portfolio analysis – ESG ratings distribution

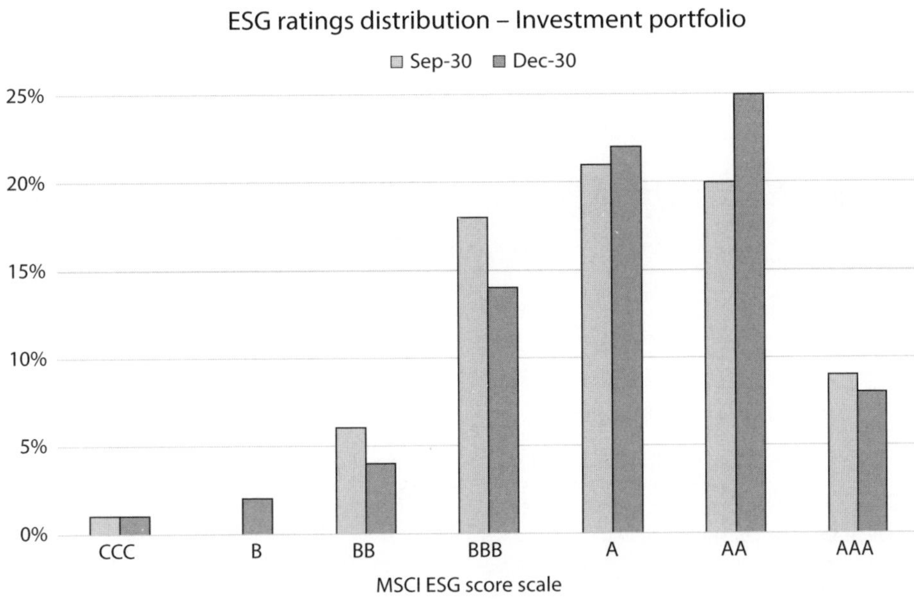

SOURCE OneRisk Consultancy

The analysis helps to develop an overall weighted average score that can then be monitored. For example, if the organization wants to maintain a target of AA, the weighted average score would have to be over 7. The main focus of the analysis is to track the score over time and look at the outliers (i.e. the CCC or Bs) and seek to include them in the watch list, and provide supplementary qualitative data that can then be to presented at the investment committee or board (as required).

An example from May 2022 highlights the differences in approach from the rating agencies with regard to ESG assessments. Tesla, the electric vehicle manufacturer, was removed from the S&P 500 ESG index, while oil companies remain within the index.[12] Notwithstanding the differences in the companies and their relative emissions, it is a notable decision because it highlights the importance of the relative weightings of the different E, S and G components (a company that has a strong environmental record but weaker social and governance standards would most likely be removed from the index, depending on the methodology followed). In this instance, it also highlights the relative importance of industry peer groups and how a firm compares to its direct competitors. For example, if one oil and gas producer compares favourably to others within its industry category this can support its ongoing inclusion within an index.

Figure 11.8 builds on the concept of industry comparators and show how a company can monitor and manage the carbon footprint of its investment portfolio versus relevant sector benchmarks in order to position itself favourably and to increase the likelihood of its ongoing inclusion in various capital-market indices (and thus maintain its access to capital).

FIGURE 11.8 Monitoring of an investment portfolio's carbon footprint

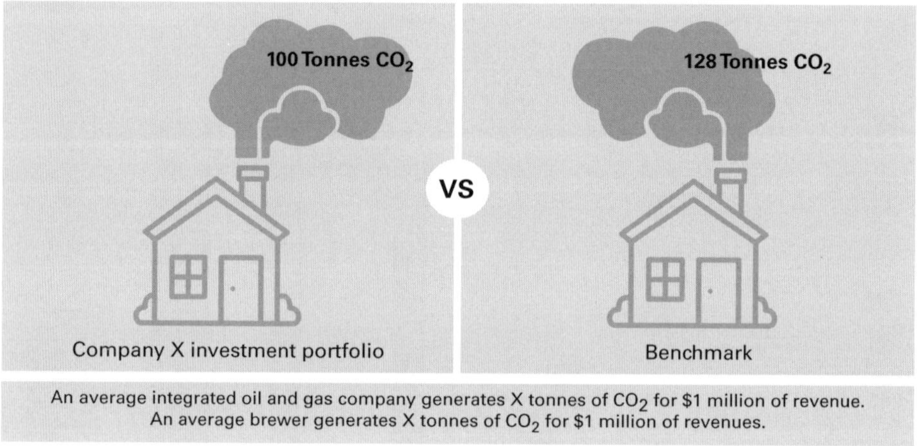

SOURCE OneRisk Consulting

11.6.2.1 PRACTICAL IMPLEMENTATION EXAMPLE

This case study provides a good example of the approach taken by PwC to decarbonize its business activities through integrating climate change and sustainability strategy with existing business processes, such as its supply chain, to reduce its overall carbon footprint across the organization.

CASE STUDY

PwC approach for net zero alignment

PwC UK first started measuring carbon emissions targets back in 2007 and we set our first carbon reduction target in 2012 and have had decarbonization strategies ever since.[13] We have embedded ESG into our day-to-day business (the 'ESG built-in strategy') by supporting our clients' transformation, working collaboratively with our suppliers and, importantly, by pushing ourselves to lead by example.

As a professional services firm, our direct emissions (Scope 1 & 2) are relatively low and are driven predominantly by our energy consumption within our buildings. We recognized early on that to make a real difference we needed to address Scope 3 emissions, in particular business travel and the emissions of our supply chain given this represented a significant proportion of our carbon footprint.

We knew that we didn't have all the data we would need to calculate our emissions, however, we worked out what data we could get hold of quickly to get started (e.g. energy consumption data from utility bills, travel data from centralized bookings). Where we didn't have the data initially we made educated estimations. We then gradually increased the breadth and sophistication of data over time.

To reduce our direct emissions, we adopted four complementary approaches: operating differently; consolidating our office space into fewer properties; refreshing our real estate to adopt sustainable designs and investing in new low-carbon technologies.

In terms of reducing travel, in a service business like ours we recognized the inherent challenges as it is part and parcel of delivering services for our clients. We set about changing behaviours, and started by significantly cutting our non-client-facing internal business travel as this was fully within our control. Our next area of focus is to reduce client related business travel.

With regard to our suppliers we set up a supply chain sustainability programme, which was built around engagement, collaboration and innovation.[14]

- **Upskilling our suppliers** – We have identified our key suppliers and emitters and engaged with them to measure, report and set targets for reducing their emissions (asking them, for example, to subscribe to science-based targets). We use an annual survey to gather insights about our suppliers' performance and hold forums to help them build capabilities to improve.
- **Collaborating with suppliers –** We collaborate with suppliers to find solutions to sustainability challenges: for example, in our BREEAM 'Outstanding' offices, where collaboration led to new technologies for energy, paper and waste. We have also worked with key suppliers to include social enterprises and apprentices in the provision of their service.
- **Building sustainability requirements into our commercial arrangements –** Where appropriate, we seek to embed sustainability considerations with key suppliers through our procurement activities, from developing requests for proposals and evaluation criteria, through to contract schedules, service-level agreements and ongoing relationship management.

We have made excellent progress in reducing the carbon footprint from our direct operations, achieving more than 90 per cent reduction in our Scope 1 and 2 emissions since 2007 – decoupling them from revenue growth. Additionally, we have reduced office energy consumption by 61 per cent, increased renewable energy to over 90 per cent, and have offset any residual emissions to be carbon neutral since 2007.

From a Scope 3 perspective, carbon emissions fell by 40 per cent overall, mainly due to a drop in business travel, with the pandemic driving reduction in associated carbon emissions in 2021. We are exploring ways to limit the bounce back as part of our aim to halve our operational footprint from a new baseline of 2019 – a key element of our commitment to be net zero by 2030. For instance, we intend to maintain our current hybrid model of working and thus expect these positive results to continue.

Our engagement with our suppliers has been remarkably productive. We have an annual supplier forum, and in 2022, over 100 people attended, including 63 supplier representatives across five sectors. Participants rated the event as highly informative, describing it as 'stimulating, inspiring and energising'. 72 per cent of our supplier attendees told us they have already made a net zero public commitment, with a further 17 per cent looking to make a commitment in the next 12 months.

We also want to turn ESG into a driver for all our stakeholders, by helping clients maximize investment opportunities arising from the ESG agenda, launching an ESG platform and committing to upskill our suppliers to build ESG into our client services. We are committed to continuing working with suppliers to measure, report and set targets for reducing their emissions.

Conclusion

Integration of climate change risk management practices is complex and multidimensional. This chapter highlights how it is aligned to operational risk management in the sense that it will be most successful if it is all-encompassing and incorporates people, process and technology considerations simultaneously. Mapping these processes to climate change considerations will be critical to embedding a change programme in future.

Improvements *can* be made by the integration of single initiatives; however comprehensive change will be only be delivered when embedded within governance arrangements. These must be in place to focus on the transition across the business and with reference to the future financing of the organization.

As processes are altered to take account of climate change they will affect the entire value chain of the organization, from the HR processes through the supply chain to end consumer, and increasingly focusing on the importance of marketing 'green' credentials to those end consumers. This will be of increasing importance for the organization as claims of 'greenwashing' become more intense and the need to demonstrate credentials ever more essential.

Investors will play a critical role in ensuring funds are secured for activities in future if those activities can demonstrate their credentials to the transition to a carbon fee economy. We have focused on what investors take into account when deciding to invest their, or their clients', funds. This will be of increasing importance as financial flows are directed only towards sustainable activities, making those that operate only in the short term 'stranded' assets.

Notes

1 E Kerencheva. Amazon unveils big Increase in renewable energy sourcing, on path to 100% by 2025, *ESG Today*, 21 April 2022, www.esgtoday.com/amazon-unveils-big-increase-in-renewable-energy-sourcing-on-path-to-100-by-2025/ (archived at https://perma.cc/CN7S-2A95)

2 B Colton, D Kaul and M Younis. (2022). Guidance on climate-related disclosure, The Harvard Law School Forum on Corporate Governance, 2022. https://corpgov.law.harvard.edu/2022/01/28/guidance-on-climate-related-disclosure/ (archived at https://perma.cc/224S-STUS)

3 Government of the Netherlands. Circular economy. www.government.nl/topics/circular-economy (archived at https://perma.cc/XXV2-WF4N)

4 M Segal. IBM Survey: Supply chain execs willing to trade profitability for sustainability, *ESG Today*, 29 April 2022, www.esgtoday.com/ibm-survey-supply-chain-execs-willing-to-trade-profitability-for-sustainability/ (archived at https://perma.cc/6GZU-HCYV)

5 ClimateWise. The ClimateWise Principles Independent Review 2021: The insurance industry pulling together, 2022. www.cisl.cam.ac.uk/files/cisl_climatewise_principles_2022.pdf (archived at https://perma.cc/M4JS-TRQM)

6 Barclays. Introducing BlueTrack™, nd. https://home.barclays/content/dam/home-barclays/documents/citizenship/ESG/Introducing%20Bluetrack.pdf (archived at https://perma.cc/RWE3-YY7P)

7 Barclays PLC. About BlueTrack™ – an update on our methodology for reducing our financed emissions, 2022. https://home.barclays/content/dam/home-barclays/documents/citizenship/ESG/2022/Barclays_Blue%20Track-White-Paper-2022.pdf (archived at https://perma.cc/5EPF-R8CD)

8 M Segal. Fitch extending climate vulnerability scores for all corporate sectors, *ESG Today*, 25 April 2022. www.esgtoday.com/fitch-extending-climate-vulnerability-scores-for-all-corporate-sectors/ (archived at https://perma.cc/8S58-BRZ5)

9 LGIM. LGIM ESG score, nd. https://esgscores.lgim.com/srp/documents-id/dc2ca5ef-933d-4748-b221-7085515bfa04/Methodologyforratingcompanies.pdf (archived at https://perma.cc/94LZ-RDJD)

10 J Baxter-Derrington. HSBC set to be accused of greenwashing by Advertising Standards Authority – reports, *Investment Week*, 29 April 2022, www.investmentweek.co.uk/news/4048952/hsbc-set-accused-greenwashing-advertising-standards-authority-reports (archived at https://perma.cc/29EV-TFSK)

11 HSBC. HSBC Holdings plc Annual and Accounts 2021, Environmental, social and governance review, 2022, p 48

12 L Kolodny. Why Tesla was kicked out of the S&P 500's ESG index, CNBC, 18 May 2022, www.cnbc.com/2022/05/18/why-tesla-was-kicked-out-of-the-sp-500s-esg-index.html (archived at https://perma.cc/YQL5-TU36)

13 PwC. nd. https://www.pwc.co.uk/ (archived at https://perma.cc/8MLB-MZWH)

14 PwC. Embracing climate technology with our suppliers, nd. https://www.pwc.co.uk/who-we-are/our-purpose/case-studies/climate-tech-supplier-forum.html (archived at https://perma.cc/X9VR-USSF)

12

Financial reporting and climate disclosures

This chapter will cover the growing importance of improving financial reporting and disclosures for climate change risks in line with best practices based on the Task Force on Climate-related Financial Disclosures (TCFD) recommendations, which were established by the Financial Stability Board (FSB) in 2015.

The main learning outcomes from this chapter are to:

- Explain the purpose of climate disclosures in providing information requirements by stakeholders, including investors and regulators.
- Understand the TCFD's four pillars and eleven overarching recommendations across the four pillars.
- Recognize the main financial impact types across different industry sectors.
- Appreciate some of the main benefits, challenges and ongoing industry trends in TCFD reporting.
- Explain the importance of developing disclosures in line with the implementation of an organization's climate strategy including enterprise risk management integration.
- Appreciate the increasing need for climate risks to be integrated into financial reporting standards and included in financial statements.
- Through case studies, explain some of the different disclosure approaches being used to provide decision useful information

Introduction

As outlined in Chapter 1, there has been a significant shift in recent years by governments and organizations to tackle climate change and manage risks as both threats and opportunities. This is due to many external drivers, expectations and pressures. One of the main drivers has been the increase in new international and national legislation and regulations, which includes TCFD reporting.

The Financial Stability Board created the TCFD to improve and increase reporting of climate-related disclosure. According to the TCFD 2021 Status Report, the number of organizations supporting TCFD had grown five-fold in the previous three years at an average annual growth rate of 73 per cent. As of 2021, over 2,600 organizations supported the TCFD framework, with a combined market capitalization of $25 trillion.[1]

In this book, each of the four main pillars of TCFD, namely governance, strategy, risk management, and metrics and targets, has been covered in detail in specific chapters (e.g. governance in Chapter 3).

To some extent disclosure is a way for organizations to report their progress to stakeholders on the implementation of their climate strategy and the road map for providing specific evidence, including how they are performing against their climate targets.

While momentum is increasing, most companies around the world are only just beginning the process of implementation. There are increasingly rising expectations from the spectrum of stakeholders for disclosures to be as insightful as possible while meeting both current and future requirements.

Organizations need to be aware of future legislative changes within their jurisdictions. For example, in the UK the Government intends to roll out mandatory TCFD-aligned climate disclosures across the economy by 2025.

Clearly it is also important to ensure that financial statements reflect the most up-to-date assessment of climate-related risks. The statements are intended to provide information about the financial position and performance of the organization and should provide comprehensive and consistent messaging to a range of stakeholders and regulators.

12.1 Climate change's evolutionary effect on how to account for risk

The following is a statement kindly provided by Rachael Johnson, Global Head of Risk and Corporate Governance at the Association of Chartered Certified Accountants (ACCA), which highlights some of the broader considerations of climate change and the alignment needed within the accounting profession.

> As a profession, accountancy professionals are asking themselves 'to what extent can we use accounting-based methods to more effectively value climate and the other hard to measure transition and physical risks?' This goes for all operational and non-financial risks, which we know are business risks that might not seem material one minute but could be as critical as any other the next.

Given the complexity and speed of risk in today's world, it is necessary to ensure the issues raised by climate change are embedded into all the organization's activities. Environmental and social risks are intertwined with the rest of the risk landscape, and as Mark Carney said at COP26 in November 2021, 'every financial decision needs to take climate change into account'.

As stakeholders increasingly ask how this is done, there is an ever pressing need to place 'a number' on these risks. Making these intangibles visible, in this respect, has become the new frontier of accountancy. The profession is well-positioned to lead this shift in making our primary accounting measure of 'corporate performance' about corporate sustainability rather than short-term profit and verifying how that translates into stronger long-term performance.

Risk accounting

Given the transformations and faster moving risks of today, it is crucial that accountancy professionals provide more foresight and assurance across the connected world, ensuring companies integrate climate change and other existential threats into this assurance. Capital markets, including large institutional investors and prudential regulators, are already requiring this as are other types of policy makers, lenders, insurers, rating agencies, stock exchanges, third parties, customers, and perhaps more than ever before employees and affected communities.

We see more than ever how accountancy plays an essential role in gathering and guarding information that leads to better decision-making and more positive outcomes for stakeholders. It also is clear that those companies focused on the long-term, that measure their externalities and are able to show that they are truly transparent regarding their impacts on stakeholders in value and supply chains, so not only to shareholders, are the ones most capable of attracting investment, loyal custom, and top talent.

The heightened regulation around climate issues, Russia's invasion of Ukraine and record rising inflation have led investors to reflect on how they themselves actually use environmental, social and governance (ESG) as a means of pursuing long-term financial performance. The key challenge for the finance world is how to allocate capital and apply it in a way that fits with a fast-changing world.

This entails choosing to invest in companies that need the capital to make progress in reaching net zero and becoming sustainable. Investors need to ensure they choose the companies which have structured and achievable targets, not only sustainability statements or even seemingly attractive ESG scores. The UNPRI now requires that investors make sure their engagement in helping companies progress is made transparent so all stakeholders can see how investment plays its part in facilitating more positive outcomes.

Lost in translation

Building a common language for financial professionals is also essential to ensuring accountability and effective risk management, and the Task Force on Climate-related Financial Disclosures (TCFD) has been an instrumental impetus. As countries around the world roll out their own TCFD roadmaps, the ACCA continues to advocate consistency, alignment, compatibility, cross-border inter-operability, comparability and interconnectedness of initiatives and standards at national, EU and global levels. In 2022, the ACCA welcomed the collaboration between the IFRS Foundation and GRI on creating a complete and compatible suite of sustainability disclosures.

The same initiatives are being driven in the US where the SEC has made a proposal to move from voluntary to mandatory climate-related risk disclosures. This seems to faithfully reflect the TCFD's widely internationally accepted and adopted recommendations on governance, strategy and risk management, which we believe serves as a general guide for organizations across all industries.

As more disclosure requirements are introduced, the ACCA thinks that further unification is inevitable in order to build trust and transparency into the impact of climate change on the global economy and ensure that decision and policy makers recognize that climate risk is indeed financial risk. Climate change is a global issue and universal standards that allow comparability are crucial to making progress.

The alphabet soup of standards that have existed in the past certainly held many companies back. However, greater cohesiveness in newly proposed standards for climate risk reporting, and enhanced transparency around the world, should as well bring more drive behind getting companies to actually account for the risks better.

Leadership accounting

Boards and C-suite members need to be thinking about purpose, values and vision, in this sense, asking more questions that they may have never asked before if they are to steer their companies in the right direction of creating rather than extracting value. Getting risk into strategy requires more collaboration to understand what information we might already be sitting on and not doing anything about or what additional data is required if we are to understand the various future scenarios and help our decision makers plan effectively for them. An unexpected loss can make a very detrimental dent into the company's finances (and wipe out shareholders' equity), so as these existential risks intensify and accumulate it is imperative that we properly account for them.

What we have been learning through our engagement with ACCA members around the world is that a sustainable organization is one that addresses all potential threats and uncertainties on the horizon by putting risk and risk taking into all decision making. Companies that are focused on being sustainable and creating long-term value are considering all risks into their strategy and by doing that have become much more able to fulfil their purpose and meet stakeholders' changing needs.

12.2 The purpose of climate disclosures

The main purpose of the disclosures requirements is to help meet the information needs of investors' regulators. The regulators expect firms to develop and maintain an appropriate approach to reporting and disclosure that should be constantly monitored and assessed for improvements.

The TCFD guidance implicitly mentions the need for organizations to provide more meaningful information to external stakeholders by better evaluating the potential financial implications associated with transitioning to a lower-carbon economy and climate-related physical risks.

Mark Carney, the former Governor of the Bank of England, and now the United Nations Special Envoy for Climate Action and Finance, stated in 2020: 'Managing climate-related financial risks requires disclosure to go beyond the static (a company's carbon footprint today) to the strategic (their plans to manage down their emissions). Risk management means assessing the forward-looking disclosures to judge the resilience of firms' strategies to the transition.'[2]

Disclosures should include both quantitative and qualitative reporting with transparency around the inputs and assumptions used to generate outputs, and TCFD provides guidance on how the information should be used effectively to help in areas such as risk pricing and capital allocation decisions.

Additionally, as organizations build their climate risk maturity and develop their climate change strategies, they will need to concurrently provide broader and more detailed decision-useful information.

It is, however, important that disclosures are not just 'boiler plate' outputs but provide real and tangible information on the impacts of climate change on both the current and future financial position of the company. This is required to inform various stakeholders on how the company is addressing climate change as well as to understand the threats and opportunities across the organization's risk profile.

TCFD goes a long way towards standardizing approaches to climate-related financial reporting. The more jurisdictions that adopt its recommendations and the more organizations that produce TCFD reports, the more realistic achieving net zero will become. However, until appropriate and relevant data becomes more widely available and easily accessible, the barriers to widespread TCFD adoption will remain.

The concept of disclosures is that it will help companies to better prepare for climate change impacts, and help investors understand risks so that they can make more informed investment decisions. Increased transparency and greater comparability on corporate sustainability performance will help the allocation of financing to sustainable projects. Investors need company data that is comprehensive, comparable and credible.

Ultimately, companies need to assess the impacts of climate change on the value of their assets and liabilities for reporting purposes and we cover this in more detail later in the chapter.

There are several areas that would improve the usefulness of information disclosed on financial impact to support decision making, including:[3]

- Amount of expenditure or capital investment currently deployed towards climate-related risks and opportunities
- Amount of expenditure or capital investment to be deployed to meet targets for addressing climate risks and opportunities, often disclosed in transition plans
- Interconnected reporting linking qualitative disclosures with their actual and potential financial impact

Rating agencies have stated, for example, that climate-related information is an increasingly important input into their financial impact assessments and is a valuable input into informing the rating process.

The UK regulators, the Financial Conduct Authority (FCA) have stated that:[4]

> Better corporate disclosures will help inform market pricing and support business, risk nd capital allocation decisions. And improved disclosures to clients and consumers will help them make more informed financial decisions. This, in turn, will strengthen competition in the interests of consumers, protecting them from buying unsuitable products and driving investment towards greener projects and activities.

This has been reinforced by David Fairs (Executive Director of Regulatory Policy, Analysis and Advice at the Pensions Regulator (TPR) when he stated 'Ultimately, we believe the disclosure requirements should be seen not only as an exercise in compliance but as an exercise in risk (and opportunity) management, which should lead to improved outcomes for scheme members'.[5]

12.3 The evolution and future direction of climate-related financial disclosures

In April 2015, the G20 Finance Ministers and Central Bank Governors asked the Financial Stability Board (FSB) to convene public- and private-sector participants to review how the financial sector can take account of climate-related issues.

Recognizing the risks that climate change may pose to the financial system, the Financial Stability Board (FSB) at request of the G20 launched the industry-led Task Force on Climate-related Financial Disclosures (TCFD) to develop recommendations on climate-related financial disclosures. The TCFD has developed a framework to help public companies and other organizations more effectively disclose climate-related risks and opportunities through their existing reporting processes.[6]

The focus has been on the word 'financial' because the Task Force sought to move the issues related to climate change out of sustainability departments and into the boardrooms of every corporation in the world, no matter how big or small. To achieve this, it was considered necessary for companies to understand what financial risks and opportunities climate change creates for their business

In respect of disclosures requirements, regulators are continuing to request more enhanced disclosures, for example the UK's Financial Conduct Authority proposes in its consultation on 'Enhancing climate-related disclosures by asset managers, life insurers and FCA-regulated pension providers' that 'firms should disclose Scope 3 GHG emissions from no later than 30 June 2024. This is 1 year later than the deadline for the first disclosures in accordance with the rest of our proposals.'[7]

12.3.1 Ongoing global standard-setting proposals on TCFD recommendations

Many organizations consider the TCFD as global standard, although the TCFD is not mandatory and binding. In terms of disclosures in financial reporting or other relevant reports, organizations have commenced complying with the TCFD standards.

As an example of increasing regulatory changes and alignment to TCFD, the US Securities and Exchange Commission (SEC) proposed a draft rule in March 2022 requiring US-listed companies to disclose their climate-related risks and greenhouse gas emissions. This was announced in response to investors seeking more guidance on how they should be reporting on their climate impact.[8]

At the time of writing in 2022, three organizations (the US Securities and Exchange Commission (SEC), European Sustainability Reporting Standards (ESRS) by the European Financial Reporting Advisory Group (EFRAG) and the International Sustainability Standards Board (ISSB) have laid down proposals for climate-related reporting. All these regulators are incorporating both TCFD and GHG protocols recommendations, and TCFD's report on climate disclosure convergence was published on 9 May 2022.[9]

The final standards will be released after the consultation periods close and each body reviews the feedback it has received, which will be a complex and time-consuming process.

Some specific aspects to the proposal in respect to the four pillars are that the greatest degree of alignment between the three proposals and TCFD is with governance but there will be differences in terms of the other pillars. For example, the SEC will require Scope 3 disclosures only if it is financially material or where a company has set Scope 3 reduction targets. Scope 3 is mandatory for both ESRS and ISSB but with some technical differences.

To summarize and compare the proposals in terms of perspective by each organization, ESRS is the most prescriptive, the SEC is the most principles-based and only the SEC is focused on climate.[10]

12.3.2 Task Force on Climate-related Financial Disclosures (TCFD) – recommendations

The main TCFD recommendations were issued in 2017, in which it set out eleven recommended disclosures around four core areas for companies to report material climate-related information to the market via the mainstream financial report,[11] as shown in Figure 12.1 and detailed further in Figure 12.2.

The Task Force encourages organizations to undertake both historical and forward-looking analyses when considering the potential financial impacts of climate change, with a greater focus on forward-looking analyses as the efforts to mitigate and adapt to climate change are without historical precedent.

The recommendations provide clear guidance for risk managers and boards. Under strategy, it includes the need to: 'Disclose the actual and potential impacts of climate-related risks and opportunities on the organization's businesses, strategy, and financial planning where such information is material.' Under risk management, it recommends that organizations need to: 'Disclose how the organisation identifies, assesses, and manages climate-related risks.'

TCFD have provided subsequent updates to date that include:

- Guidance on Risk Management Integration and Disclosure (October 2020)
- TCFD 2021 Status Report (October 2021)
- TCFD Guidance on Metrics, Targets, and Transition Plans (October 2021)

It is important to note that many regulators around the world such as the PRA (Prudential Regulation Authority) in the UK expect organizations to consider engaging with the TCFD framework as well as other initiatives in developing their approaches to climate-related financial disclosures.

12.4 TCFD – main disclosure requirements

The TCFD assessment framework itself is set out in Figure 12.2, which sets out the eleven overarching recommendations for disclosures over the four pillars that can be used to provide information on how the organization is managing material risks and opportunities that arise from climate change.

Some of the main challenges for organizations are to address the following questions:

- How do companies understand what constitutes a material business risk?
- How can organizations categorize the unpredictable, long-term impacts of a changing climate as specific financial risks?

FIGURE 12.1 Core pillars of TCFD recommendations

TCFD disclosures - recommendations

PILLAR	RECOMMENDATION	EXAMPLE
Governance	Disclose organization's governance around climate-related risks and opportunities	Describe board's oversight, management's role, etc
Strategy	Disclose actual/potential impacts of climate-related risks and opportunities	Describe the identified short-, medium- and long-term risks and opportunities, their impact, resilience of organization's strategy considering various scenarios, etc
Risk management	Disclose how the organization identifies, assesses and manages climate-related risks	Describe the identified risks and opportunities and the process to manage, describe the process of how the actions are integrated in risk management, etc
Metrics and targets	Disclose the metrics and targets used to assess and manage the climate-related risks and opportunities where relevant	Describe the metrics used to assess risks and opportunities in line with the strategy and risk management process, Scope 1,2 & 3 of GHG, targets used to assess performance, etc

SOURCE TCFD

12.4.1 Disclosure guidance – TCFD

The TCFD 2017 report provides a helpful guide that maps the recommendations and supporting recommended disclosures (see Figure 12.2).[12] This applies for the financial sector and non-financial groups.

The Task Force developed supplemental guidance for the financial sector, which it organized into four major industries largely based on activities performed. The main rationale for the Task Force was to foster an early assessment of climate-related risks and opportunities, improve pricing of climate-related risks, and lead to more informed capital allocation decisions. However, the Task Force also developed supplemental guidance for non-financial industries, which account for the largest proportion of GHG emissions, energy usage and water usage, and can be used for other industries with similar business activities.

12.4.1.1 GUIDANCE ON FINANCIAL IMPACT BY SECTOR

To assist organizations in understanding which financial impacts are likely to be most relevant to them, Figure 12.3 provides a high-level overview of four areas – revenues, expenditures, assets and liabilities, and capital and financing – where organizations in the financial sector and non-financial groups may be affected.

FIGURE 12.2 TCFD eleven overarching recommendations for disclosures

Recommendations and supporting recommended disclosures			
Governance	Strategy	Risk management	Metrics and targets
Disclose the organization's governance around climate-related risks and opportunities	Disclose the actual and potential impacts of climate related risks and opportunities on the organization's business strategy and financial planning where such information is material	Disclose how the organization identifies, assesses and manages climate–related risks	Disclose the metrics and targets used to assess and manage relevant climate related risks and opportunities where such information is material
Recommended disclosures	Recommended disclosures	Recommended disclosures	Recommended disclosures
a) Describe the board's oversight of climate-related risks and opportunities	a) Describe the climate-related risks and opportunities the organization has identified over the short, medium and long term	a) Describe the organization's processes for identifying and assessing climate-related risks	a) Disclose the metrics used by the organization to assess climate-related risks and opportunities in line with its strategy and risk management process
b) Describe the management's role in assessing and managing climate-related risks and opportunities	b) Describe the impact of climate-related risks and opportunities on the organization's businesses, strategy, and financial planning	b) Describe the organization's processes for managing climate-related risks	b) Disclose scope 1, scope 2 and if appropriate, scope 3 greenhouse gas (GHG) emissions, and the related risks
	c) Describe the resilience of the organization's strategy, taking into consideration different climate-related scenarios, including a 2C or lower scenario	c) Describe how processes for identifying, assessing and managing climate-related risks are integrated into the organization's overall risk management	c) Describe the targets used by the organization to manage climate-related risks and opportunities and performance against targets

SOURCE TCFD

FIGURE 12.3 Potential financial impacts for different sectors

Sector (all industries in this sector)	Potential financial impacts (certain)
Financial	• Revenues • Assets & liabilities
Energy	• Expenditure • Capital & financing
Transportation	• Expenditure • Capital & financing
Materials & building	• Expenditure
Agriculture, food and forest	• Expenditure • Capital & financing

SOURCE TCFD Implementing the recommendations of the Task-Force on Climate-related Financial Disclosure (2017)

The TCFD report states that the impact of climate-related issues will depend on:

- The organization's exposure to, and anticipated effects of, specific climate-related risks and opportunities
- The organization's planned responses to manage (i.e. mitigate, transfer, accept or control) its risks or seize opportunities
- The implications of the organization's planned responses on its income statement, cash flow statement, and balance sheet

It is important for organizations to make sure that they are fully aware of the disclosures they need to make in the context of what information stakeholders such as investors expect.

12.4.2 Disclosure principles

To underpin its recommendations and help guide current and future developments in climate-related financial reporting, the Task Force developed seven principles for effective disclosure. These are described more fully in Appendix 3 of their report:

- Represent relevant information
- Be specific and complete
- Be clear, balanced and understandable
- Be consistent over time
- Be comparable among companies within a sector, industry or portfolio

- Be reliable, verifiable and objective
- Be provided on a timely basis

While considering the TCFD's seven principles, organizations must also carefully consider:

- How their disclosures are viewed, understood and ultimately used by stakeholders such as shareholders.
- How to make disclosures user-friendly for different stakeholders.

The Task Force encourages organizations to consider these principles as they develop climate-related financial disclosures. The Task Force's disclosure principles are largely consistent with internationally accepted frameworks for financial reporting and are generally applicable to most providers of financial disclosures. The principles are designed to assist organizations in making clear the linkages between climate-related issues and their governance, strategy, risk management, and metrics and targets.

12.4.3 Progress and use of TCFD recommendations

There has been significant progress in the development of climate change-related disclosures. The TCFD 2021 Status Report highlights, for example, that 83 of the world's largest 100 companies now support, or report in line with, the TCFD's recommendations.

However, TCFD itself recognizes some shortcomings and the report acknowledged that 'companies continue to struggle to quantify the impacts of climate change, and to source the data they need to fully assess the threats of a changing climate'.

Pursuant to the requirement of larger quantities of data by the organizations, on a positive note, the cost of reporting is expected to fall as data, analysis and knowledge improves.

Mary Schapiro, Head of the TCFD Secretariat and Vice Chair for Global Public Policy at Bloomberg L.P., commented:

> There is clear and growing consensus among investors and regulators on the importance of climate-related disclosure and the need for standardized, transparent data to support capital allocation decisions. As countries and companies around the world set net zero targets, the TCFD framework is increasingly becoming the foundation for standards and requirements needed to chart the transition to the low-carbon economy.

12.4.4 Shift from voluntary to mandatory financial disclosures

The TCFD recommendations have served as a road map for organizations that have already voluntarily adopted them, and we are increasingly seeing countries around the world introduce mandatory versions of their own.

FIGURE 12.4 TCFD disclosure by region, 2020

Regions considered for 2020 reporting – Asia Pacific, Europe, Middle East and Africa, North America, Latin America		
Recommendation	Recommended disclosure	Average disclosure by regions
Governance	Board oversight	23.4%
	Management's role	17.2%
Strategy	Risks and opportunities	49.8%
	Impact on organization	36.2%
	Resilience of strategy	12.4%
Risk management	Risk ID & assessment process	30.2%
	Risk management processes	28%
	Integration into overall risk management	24.6%
Metrics and targets	Climate-related metrics	45%
	Scope 1, 2, 3 GHG emissions	35.6%
	Climate-related targets	31.2%

SOURCE TCFD Status Report, 2021[13]

New Zealand was the first country to announce mandatory TCFD-aligned climate-related financial disclosures in 2020 and many countries, including the United Kingdom, Japan and Switzerland are targeting to have mandates in place before 2025. In 2021, finance ministers and central bank governors from G7 countries agreed to back mandatory disclosures under the TCFD framework for large organizations. Singapore, Brazil and the European Union also announced reporting requirements for certain carbon-intensive sectors.

Since COP26 in Glasgow in November 2021, more countries have announced legislation to enforce mandatory reporting on climate-related risks aligned with the TCFD recommendations, including the United States and Canada.

The United Kingdom will become the first G20 country to make it mandatory and has enacted new legislation whose rules came into force in early 2022. This follows the UK's landmark Net Zero Strategy.

The UK regulator's recent milestone move to mandatory TCFD reporting requirements along with some of the main regulatory timelines are set out in Figure 12.5. These new requirements are provided by the UK Government in its report 'A roadmap towards mandatory climate-related disclosures'.

The implication of governments rolling out regulations for mandatory disclosures is that organizations will need to improve their approaches and methodologies to provide more detailed and transparent reports in the future.

FIGURE 12.5 UK regulatory timelines and implementation of mandatory TCFD requirements

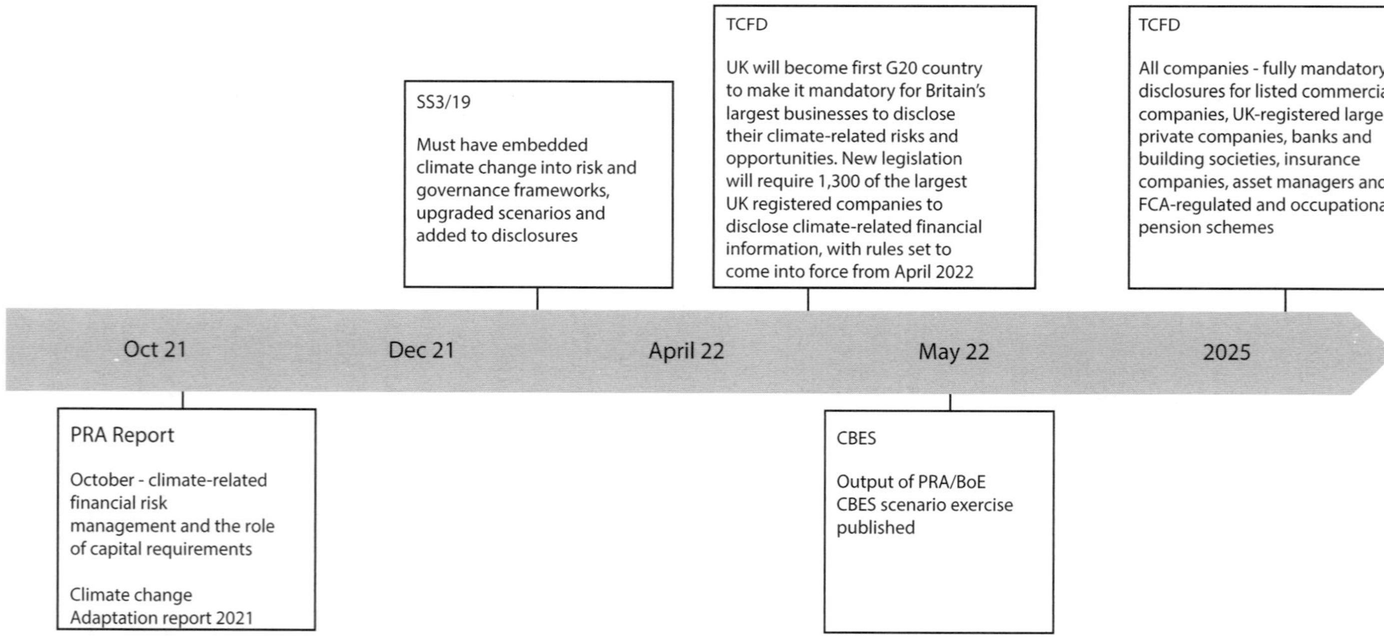

SOURCE © OneRisk Consulting. All rights reserved, 2022

12.4.5 *Time periods and horizons*

TCFD states that metrics need to be developed covering three distinct time periods: historical, current and forward-looking. Figure 12.6 outlines the approach that organizations should adopt.

One of the most important aspects in designing climate change metrics that we have outlined throughout various chapters in this book is that organizations need to consider future time horizons that cover the short, medium and long-term, as the TCFD guidance recommends.

Moreover, TCFD also states that methodologies such as scenario analysis, trend analysis, sensitivity analysis and simulations should be developed. These techniques are discussed throughout the book, in particular in Chapter 10 where we cover the design of stress and scenario testing.

12.5 TCFD summary of recommendations and benefits for organizations

The latest TCFD status report indicates that disclosures of climate-related financial information have increased since 2017 but remain insufficient for investors' needs. Thus, this section provides more insights into each pillar of the main requirements, benefits, and specific challenges and trends observed in implementing disclosures.

TCFD expectations state that 'Through widespread adoption, financial risks and opportunities related to climate change will become a natural part of companies' risk management and strategic planning processes.'[14]

It is important to emphasize that that TCFD is not about reporting in the traditional sense. It involves the ongoing implementation of the climate strategy and plans that have been discussed throughout the book. Organizations can use the opportunity to provide evidence of how their climate change plans are being integrated into business processes and how the material risks are being assessed and managed to make improved business decisions.

FIGURE 12.6 TCFD guidance on reporting time periods and horizons

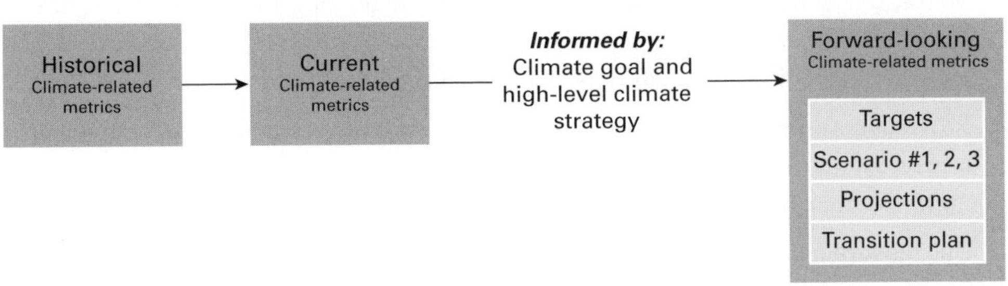

SOURCE TCFD

It is important that organizations consider how climate-related financial risks are integrated into governance and risk management processes, including the process by which a firm has assessed whether these risks are considered material or principal risks.

Regulators expect firms to develop and maintain an appropriate approach to disclosure, reflective of the distinctive elements of the financial risks from climate change. High-quality disclosures should be viewed as a way to gain competitive advantage. It highlights from a risk perspective the ambition and risk maturity of the organization as well as highlighting a good risk culture.

The next section provides more specific recommendations and benefits across each of the four main pillars. Many of the general points are taken from the TCFD report.

12.5.1 TCFD Pillar 1 – Governance

Governance refers to 'the system by which an organization is directed and controlled in the interests of shareholders and other stakeholders.'[15] Best practice climate governance was detailed in Chapter 3.

12.5.1.1 SPECIFIC RECOMMENDATIONS

- Describe the person(s) or committee responsible for climate policies, strategy and information relating to climate.
- Provide information on climate policies and how these are applied in the organization, detailing decisions made through these policies and how the policies are delegated to management.
- Include the processes for informing the board on climate-related issues, and the frequency.
- Describe systems for accountability and incentives.

12.5.1.2 BENEFITS

- Helps investors and other stakeholders to understand i) the role of organization's board, ii) management's role in assessing and managing the issues. This further helps in evaluating whether the board and management are addressed appropriately and have due attention over the relevant issues.
- Provides transparency of an organization's governance structure that can prevent repercussions that weak corporate governance can have on asset values. (e.g. 2007–08 financial crisis).
- The governance principles increase the directors' climate awareness, thereby improving navigation of the risks and opportunities that climate change poses to the business.

- Improved governance supports the ability to meet the increasing expectations and requirements from investors, regulators, customers and employees to provide greater detail and transparency in reporting.

12.5.2 TCFD Pillar 2 – Strategy

12.5.2.1 SPECIFIC RECOMMENDATIONS

- Scenario analysis: an assessment of the resilience of the organization's business model and strategy in a range of different warming scenarios.
- A description of the actual and potential impacts of key climate-related risks and opportunities on a company's strategy and business model.

12.5.2.2 BENEFITS

- Formalizing climate change strategies, commitments or guidelines can help articulate and clarify expectations and outline how they will be achieved.
- It makes very clear to the investors that businesses are considering climate-related impacts on a strategic level.
- Provides a more efficient way of structuring mitigation and adaptation measures, which can provide a competitive advantage over companies moving forward with less focus.
- Opens a pathway and promotes green bonds, innovations and ideas to reduce the carbon footprint and save on operational costs.
- There are different approaches by different companies to implement climate change strategy depending on the organization's strategy and the organization's processes and structure.[16] This helps the company to learn and recognize the suitable strategy for their own organization.
- Disclosure of revenues from products and services designed for a low-carbon economy can help investors to better understand the climate-related changes in the underlying business strategy.

12.5.3 TCFD Pillar 3 – Risk management

12.5.3.1 SPECIFIC RECOMMENDATIONS

- A description of the key climate-related risks and opportunities arising from the organization's operations.
- A description of how the process/measurement of climate-related risks and opportunities are integrated into an organization's overall risk management process.

12.5.3.2 BENEFITS

- Determines the relative significance and prioritization of climate-related risks in relation to other risks.
- Helps to understand the risk mitigation strategies being developed by the organization to improve resilience to physical risks of climate change.
- Markets will be better equipped to evaluate, price and manage climate-related risks.

12.5.4 TCFD Pillar 4 – Metrics and targets

12.5.4.1 MAIN RECOMMENDATIONS

- Details of performance against the targets to date, including a list of the KPIs used to assess progress.
- A list of the organization's targets relating to climate impact reduction, climate risks management and maximizing climate opportunities.
- Metrics and targets should aim to be comparable over time to enable users of disclosures to understand the firm's general direction of travel.

12.5.4.2 MAIN BENEFITS

- Targets can be used to underpin a firm's strategy for shifting the business to help deliver a net zero and climate-resilient global economy.

12.5.5 Disclosure challenges

There are a number of key challenges and we will highlight some of the current broad challenges below, which mainly relate to the quality and reliability of data.

12.5.5.1 GENERAL CHALLENGES

- Obtaining reliable and credible data is a key challenge, particularly for small and medium-size businesses that do not have the access to or the resources to collect and analyse data.
- Organizations need to balance the cost and benefits of obtaining data and set appropriate risk management targets including multiple time horizons.
- There is currently an overreliance on external service providers, which is linked to the challenge of older in-house systems being unable to capture and report disclosures.

- There is often difficulty in determining what constitutes materiality and therefore what needs to be disclosed in terms of risks.
- Disclosing Scope 3 emissions is not mandatory. Therefore, it can get difficult for the investors and other businesses to evaluate an organization's relation with other carbon emitting aspects and the organization's overall carbon footprint.
- Disclosure of targets can lead to the setting of aggressive or unrealistic targets to artificially maintain the organization's reputational standards and therefore makes it difficult to monitor the progress and achieve the desired target. This can lead to the accusation of 'greenwashing' as discussed in Chapter 9.
- There are also ongoing misunderstandings of terminology, metrics and targets, for example in interpreting the difference between the concepts of net zero, science-based targets and carbon neutrality.[17]

Some specific challenges across the four pillars are outlined in Table 12.1.

TABLE 12.1 Specific challenges across the TCFD pillars

Governance	Strategy
• The disclosure requirements are not uniform. TCFD expects the disclosures should be included in annual financial filings, but some organizations provide the disclosure in reports other than financial filings. This is because issuing public financial reports is not mandatory.[18]	• In terms of strategy there is limited knowledge of how much capital expenditure (capex) organizations will need to meet their net zero commitments. • There are currently limited disclosures explaining how business strategies and capital allocation plans have to be adapted and changed to align with the net zero transition.[19]
Risk management	**Metrics and targets**
• Challenges from what constitutes a material risk and therefore what needs to be reported.[20]	• It is much easier to find data on Scope 1 and 2 emissions than it is to find data on Scope 3. This is mainly because Scope 3 data is related to factors outside of an organization's direct control. • A balance has to be struck between providing clear and comprehensive disclosures while climate metrics and methodologies are still being developed. • Metrics should be reliable, verifiable and objective while also supporting effective internal controls for the purposes of data verification and assurance, i.e. for compliance and auditing purposes.

12.6 Current main disclosure observations and trends

On reviewing the current status of disclosures there are a number of common themes in respect of observations and trends, which are discussed below.

12.6.1 General trends and observations

Disclosure reporting is increasingly being used as a basis for benchmarking how an organization compares to its peers.

Many regulators are requesting more concise reporting. For example, the US SEC has advised that if a risk disclosure exceeds 15 pages, companies must include a summary of 'concise, bulleted, or numbered statements' of their risks to enhance readability and usefulness. The summary should not be longer than two pages.[21]

The specific trends across the four pillars are outlined in Table 12.2.

TABLE 12.2 Specific trends and observations across the TCFD pillars

Governance	Strategy
• There is a growing trend in obtaining external validation to the approach in respect of disclosures. • Organizations are increasingly reporting the details of their climate governance in their disclosures. This includes internal committees and structures, roles and responsibilities, frequency of meeting and the activities discussed on climate-related matters. • An increasing number of companies have been putting the company's climate transition plan to a shareholder vote. • Many companies have established a standalone ESG committee.	• Many organizations are developing and reporting more sophisticated approaches to climate scenario analysis. These approaches are, for example, helping to stress test the future resilience across future revenues and costs to provide better insights to support improved strategic decision-making. • Disclosing the impact on financial planning on areas including operating costs, capital allocation and access to capital, including where carbon reduction targets have been set.
Risk management	**Metrics and targets**
• Disclosing the impact of Scope 3 carbon emissions is increasingly helping to support changes in business practices such as procurement, selection of third-party suppliers, responsible investing and engagement with customers. • Data availability is improving through open data sources and an increase in demand, which in turn will lead to more data being produced and collected to support risk identification and assessment processes.	• Targets can more easily emerge once key risk indicators and metrics are in place. Thus, in future the issue of disclosure of targets will have to be revisited as norms evolve.[22] • The current ability of organizations and industries to specify metrics applicable to various categories varies, and they continue to evolve.[23] • Disclosures relating to Scope 3 emissions are improving mainly due to improvements in data capture and enhanced methodologies.

12.6.2 *Industry examples*

This section provides some specific high-level examples, to illustrate how leading organizations such as Tesco and Aviva are reporting their disclosures across the four pillars in their most recent annual reports. Tesco has published its Annual Report and Financial Statements 2022, which includes its climate-related reporting, while Aviva has specifically published a report related to TCFD, Climate-related Financial Disclosure 2021.[24,25]

TESCO – ANNUAL REPORT AND FINANCIAL STATEMENTS 2022

Tesco's Annual Report and Financial Statements 2022 contains a specific section on TCFD. Some significant observations from the report are outlined below.

Governance

Tesco has established a group climate committee, which meets quarterly. Tesco states that the committee is responsible for maintaining oversight of progress made against its interim decarbonization milestones, and for holding the new steering groups to account for delivery of the operational and supply chain decarbonization road maps.

The committee is also responsible for oversight of climate risk management, including assessing and managing climate-related risks and opportunities on the group risk register, where climate is a principal risk, and for its climate-related disclosures.

Strategy

Tesco's operational science-based target was set in 2017. It has realized opportunities through driving greater efficiency in key processes across operations, including improving the efficiency of its refrigeration units and reducing refrigerant emissions across the store and distribution centre network through switching from fluorinated gas to CO_2 systems.

Tesco has also been reducing emissions from logistics through a range of fuel efficiency maximization initiatives, such as improved route planning in which it states that it is also committed to the electrification of transport. As signatories to the Clean Van Commitment and EV100, Tesco has committed to a fully electric home delivery fleet by 2028.

Tesco met its 2030 ambition to switch to 100 per cent renewable electricity across its operations 10 years early, through a combination of direct sourcing and renewable certificates.

Risk management

Tesco established climate change as a stand-alone principal risk in 2020/21. Reviews have been conducted at various levels including the executive committee and the board. This includes the identification and documentation of climate-related risks and the review and consideration of appropriate risk responses.

The report states that the board is conscious of the complexity and scale of its value chain, in conjunction with the expectation for progressive regulatory requirements governing climate reporting, and the executive committee concluded that the risk may accelerate.

Metrics and targets

Tesco has set various targets. Tesco's net zero strategy is underpinned by three key commitments. It has committed to reduce Scope 1 and 2 market-based emissions by 60 per cent by 2025, to be carbon neutral across its own operations by 2035 and to achieve net zero across its value chain by 2050.

AVIVA – CLIMATE-RELATED FINANCIAL DISCLOSURE 2021

Aviva has published its report on Climate-related Financial Disclosure 2021 and some of the significant observations on each pillar are outlined below.

Governance

Aviva has incorporated its climate governance and described its roles and responsibilities in its disclosure report. Some of them include roles in enterprise risk management, external reporting, asset liability management, etc. It has also developed a guide on 'tackling climate change together' that reveals its business practices that could be greener.

Strategy

As explained in Aviva's disclosure report, its strategic focus has been on ensuring a net zero future, decarbonizing its operational and supply chain, embedding climate change across its culture, etc. The report implies that the disclosure helps in recognizing and responding to transition, physical and litigation risk factors and related opportunities.

Time horizon

Aviva has also outlined the time horizon aspect in its report and describes its threshold for each time horizon. They are as follows:

Short time horizon (1–3 years) – general insurance business considers risk in the underwriting and pricing process and in setting the reinsurance strategy.

Medium time horizon (3–5 years) – large catastrophic losses have been explicitly considered in its economic capital modelling to ensure resilience.

Long time horizon (>5 years) – Aviva is considering factors such as life and pension and also in areas such as setting premium rates.

Exclusion policy

By the end of 2022, Aviva claims it will have divested from 202 companies making more than 5 per cent of their revenue from thermal coal, and 7 companies making more than 10 per cent of their revenue from unconventional fossil fuel extraction, unless they sign SBTs (Science Based Targets) or funding is for green project finance.

Risk management

Aviva has revealed its risk appetite to be low for climate-related risks that could have material negative impact on its balance sheet, business models and its customers.

Metrics and targets

Aviva in its TCFD-based disclosure has incorporated several factors such as:

- Weighted average carbon intensity (7 per cent reduction compared to previous year).
- Investment in green assets (refined its definition of green assets and has set a target to invest an additional £6 billion in green assets by 2025 compared to 31 December 2019 timeline).
- Uses portfolio warming methodology (uses MSCI analysis) to capture Scope 1, 2 and 3 emissions and a cooling potential element to capture avoided emission together with the company-reported decarbonization target.[26]
- Weather-related losses – Aviva uses CAT model results supplemented by in-house disaster scenarios and has listed its actual weather-related losses vs expected losses.[27]
- Litigation risks – litigation trends have been classified by Aviva, for example litigation that targets asset owners such as insurance businesses or asset managers in relation to the climate impact of their investments.

12.7 Reporting disclosure information and alignment to TCFD recommendations

Most organizations seek to draft updated disclosures on an annual basis for their annual reports in line with TCFD and other guidance such as CFRF (Climate Financial Risk Forum), as we have outlined.

It is important to emphasize that for many companies it is a mechanism to summarize the progress made in the preceding calendar year and provide a high-level update of progress and developments. The example outlined below is an actual case study from an agricultural insurance mutual in the UK.

Cornish Mutual has kindly provided other contributions to this book in Chapters 2 and 3 covering aspects of its risk strategy and governance structure. The annual TFCD report that is published in its annual report highlights the current and ongoing activities aligned to the progress and implementation of its climate change plans.

It is a reflection of the activities undertaken over the previous year and analogous to a 'school report', highlighting the performance and progress made throughout the year with respect to climate enterprise risk management. One of the most important aspects that is helpful to organizations is the opportunity to provide evidence of ongoing activities and deliverables to improve their climate risk maturity, which was discussed in Chapter 1.

CASE STUDY

Cornish Mutual sample output aligned to TCFD

Climate Change

Internally, and consistent with the regulator's wishes, a significant amount of focus has been on understanding the financial risks of climate change and implementing the recommendations set out by the Task Force on Climate-related Financial Disclosures (TCFD). The TCFD have published their recommendations, which are categorized as Governance, Strategy, Risk Management and Metrics and Targets. For each of these sections we provide an update below.

Governance

The RAC [Risk and Audit Committee] and the wider Board recognizes the tests that Climate Change, as a new but fast-moving risk, will bring to the Company, and we have greatly increased our consideration of the financial risk and opportunities that arise from Climate Change during the year. To enable effective decision making in this area we have undergone a programme of training; engaging with external specialists, attending industrywide talks and reviewing literature specifically aimed at the agricultural industry.

To accompany this, Climate Change has featured as an agenda item at each Board meeting alongside regular updates from our Climate Change Strategy Group on internal developments to promote discussion. The Climate Change Strategy Group has been formed with a wide representation from across the business and is led by our Insurance Director (who also acts as our Chief Risk Officer). He has been allocated responsibility for identifying the financial risks from Climate Change as a Senior Management Function holder, in line with the PRA's expectations. Two further Committees (the Corporate Social Responsibility Committee and Future of Farming Group) feed into the Climate Change Strategy Group, looking at issues from an internal and external point of view at an operational level.

In addition to Board engagement the Climate Change Strategy Group have provided training to all employees. This has embedded knowledge throughout the business and encourages our front-line people to identify risks and opportunity at source and as they emerge, allowing for a quick operational response.

Strategy

Climate Change has the potential to cause inherent risk, not only to Cornish Mutual but to the Membership as a whole, however alongside the challenges which will be posed there will also be opportunities, which if engaged with correctly, can further enforce and support our strategic objectives.

Our core customer base, the agricultural sector, has the chance to respond to Climate Change by embracing changes which will contribute to reducing increasing temperatures. At Cornish Mutual, we want to support farm businesses as they work to deal with both the physical aspects of Climate Change, such as more frequent storms, and transition risks which will help to promote a lower-carbon economy, as well as work to reduce our own impact. To do this, we are engaging with both external providers and the Membership to understand the insurance products and broader risk solution services which are available for the Membership.

Cornish Mutual has engaged with industry consultants and together developed a model which identifies key Climate Change drivers which have the potential to prevent a level of financial risk to the business. These drivers can then be monitored for development over a short and long-term basis and be used to determine prioritization of each risk category. This enables the Company to develop business strategy and financial planning accordingly. To ensure the drivers are relevant both to the Company and the Membership a farm risk survey has taken place to establish levels of priority, areas of concern and current levels of management in place.

On a practical note, we have established an internal loss adjusting provision, which would help us maintain our high service standards in the event of a surge-related event. This improved skillset also contributes to fulfilling one of our core strategic objectives of Empowered people.

As part of our review of the financial risks arising from Climate Change, we have to undertake a review of investment portfolios to ensure that we do not hold carbon heavy assets. We have engaged with our investment manager to understand the risk presented within our current holdings and to understand the way climate change considerations are evaluated in line with regulatory expectations.

Risk Management

In line with emerging best practice, the risk from Climate Change is considered as cross cutting and is integrated into our risk framework in this way. As a specialist niche insurer, we will continue to take a proportionate response that fully recognizes that our core farming Membership will be significantly impacted. Risks within Cornish Mutual are grouped into various categories, which are then reviewed against key considerations to understand which areas present the most risk to the business in terms of the financial impact from climate change. Considerations have been grouped into those which are internally controlled versus those where there is more external influence.

All risk categories within the business have been reviewed by the Management Risk Committee to establish whether they have the propensity to be impacted by Climate Change. 19 specific risk areas were identified within the categories and so an exercise took place with the risk owners to consider the potential short (5-year horizon) and long term (30-year horizon) affects. These will now be monitored within the current framework, engaging with external specialists as and when required enabling us to make decisions on the level of risk which the business is able to absorb and control.

Metrics and Targets

As our response to Climate Change unfolds, we are looking at our own carbon footprint, with plans being developed to both reduce and offset this.

Managing the Financial Risks Arising from Climate Change

In the previous financial year, we raised the increased prominence of Environmental, Social and Governance (ESG) considerations as part of the management of our investments with a particular focus on Climate Change. This year built strongly on this theme with a comprehensive review of our investment holdings and the overall philosophy, tools and processes used by our investment manager to manage these risks. We considered each of the Funds we hold and the extent to which ESG considerations are integrated in the asset selection. As a result, we concluded that our current approach meets, and in some areas exceeds, the minimum regulatory expectations. In particular, we were pleased to find the increased prominence of ESG-screened equity indices being used to achieve equity exposure and a broad range of ESG factors being used to inform the selection of fixed income holdings. We had some reservations about less liquid infrastructure holdings (linked to the aviation sector) within the IBOF fund and undertook to monitor these. Ultimately these holdings were divested so alleviating this concern. We will continue to engage with our investment manager in this arena.

Additionally, we have commenced an exercise to identify what values we may wish to embed over and above the regulatory minimum. This is where our portfolios have historically been constructed solely according to investment criteria (such as risk, return and liquidity) without explicit non-financial objectives. We found broad consensus that as an insurance company our foremost obligation to Members is to deliver attractive investment outcomes. This validates our existing approach for the bulk of our investment assets. There is though appetite to allocate a portion of our Funds to securing positive environmental and social benefits for our members over and above the traditional investment criteria. We will further explore options in this area with a desire to limit activity to the regions we operate in and to achieve clearly quantifiable outcomes that our colleagues and Members can relate to.[28]

12.8 Use of sensitivity analysis for transition scenarios in reporting

Some organizations consider that the impact of climate risk and potential future developments on the entity, including the sustainability of its current business model, is too uncertain to allow for meaningful representation, through measurement and quantified disclosures, in the financial statements. Generally, where there is a high level of uncertainty, entities should consider disclosing their sensitivity analyses. These can be particularly helpful in conveying relevant information in such cases, as illustrated by the example discussed below.

One of the chief risk officers that we interviewed for this book was Robb Eadie of BHP (referred to in Chapter 3). This group provides a good example of the potential impacts of climate change and the transition to a low-carbon economy in its 2021 annual financial statements.

BHP developed two future carbon transition scenarios based on climate pathways, representing management's assumptions regarding the impact of the transition:

- Scenario 1: Central view – most likely view for global economy
- Scenario 2: Lower-carbon view – based on accelerated decarbonization trends.

The most important aspect of the scenarios is that they are used for financial planning and inputs for aspects within the financial statements, for example the valuation of assets and potential impairment charges.

CASE STUDY

BHP Group Limited – 2021 Annual Report (Illustration)

Transition risks

Global transition signposts and commodity impacts

In addition to the Group's targets and goals significant judgments and key estimates are also impacted by the Group's current assessment of the range of economic and climate related conditions that could exist in transitioning to a low carbon economy, considering the current trajectory of society and the global economy as a whole. Despite recent progress, all 1.5°C pathways to 2050 represent a major departure from today's global trajectory and the Group does not believe the technological, regulatory or economic foundations for a rapid transition to net zero emissions are currently in place. Acknowledging these signposts, the Group's current best estimate of the potential impacts of climate change and the transition to a low carbon economy are reflected in the following two scenarios, which consider existing policies, trends and commitments and the Group's view of the most likely range of futures for the global economy and associated sub-systems:

- *Central Energy View*: reflects, and is periodically updated to respond to, existing policy trends in commitments and currently tracks to approximately 3°Celsius temperature increase above pre-industrial levels by 2100.
- *Lower Carbon View*: currently tracks to approximately 2.5°C temperature increase by 2100, and accelerates decarbonization trends and policies, particularly in easier-to-abate sectors such as power generation and light duty vehicles.

These two scenarios are reviewed periodically to reflect new information.

These scenarios are currently being used as inputs to the Group's planning cases, informing updates to the Group's supply, demand and price forecasts, capital allocation and portfolio decisions. As such, these scenarios impact certain significant judgements and key estimates, including the determination of the valuation of assets and potential impairment charges [...], the estimation of the remaining useful economic life of assets for depreciation purposes [...], the timing of closure and rehabilitation activities [...] and the recoverability of certain deferred tax assets [...].

The Group continues to monitor global decarbonization signposts and update its planning cases accordingly. Where such signposts indicate the appropriate measures are in place for achievement of a 1.5°C Paris-aligned scenario, this will be reflected in the Group's planning cases.[29]

12.9 Alignment with financial reporting

As discussed earlier through the commentary from the ACCA, climate change considerations are becoming increasingly important and need to be factored into the preparation and reporting of financial statements. These financial statements need to reflect a multitude of factors and include any assessments that relate to climate change, including any assumptions, and be consistent with any other shareholder and regulatory disclosures. It is important to emphasize that accounting practices need to be forward looking and prepared in accordance with IFRS (International Financial Reporting Standards) standards.

At COP26, the IFRS announced the formation of a new International Sustainability Standards Board (ISSB), which will develop a comprehensive global baseline of sustainability standards. As TCFD will form a part of the ISSB, alignment will help position companies well for compliance with the new standards set out by the ISSB.[30]

The example of BHP provides a good example of how the design of climate transition scenarios that are used in reporting disclosures can lead to better alignment with financial reporting.

The most important issue is materiality and providing external stakeholders, in particular investors, with the most accurate picture. Therefore, information in respect of future uncertainty of outcome and underlying assumption and judgements of those uncertainties will become more and more important.

Recognizing that accounting practices need to be prepared in accordance with IFRS standards, the impacts of climate change may be felt in several ways and could include:

- **Capital requirements** – In the insurance sector for example, the solvency capital requirement (SCR) for climate change is not currently a regulatory requirement. However, many insurance companies are already increasing their SCR to take account of increasing volatility due to increasing uncertainty for future claims payments, for example physical risks from natural catastrophes claims (discussed in Chapter 9) in future climate trends.
- **Asset valuation changes** – The value of property, plant and equipment may change markedly as well as change the useful life of an asset. Examples could be assets used in high-emission industries, i.e. assets related to coal production or the use of coal in their own production processes, which may need to be replaced, depreciated or amortized differently.
- **Provisions** – The nature, timing and amount provisions may change due to climate change through, for example, new legislation or decommissioning costs that introduce unexpected costs or new liabilities that had previously not been provisioned for.
- **Reserving** – The insurance industry is also seeking to strengthen its provisions (that are known as reserves) to pay for potential reserve deterioration. Reserve deterioration could stem from increases in liability losses, which was discussed in Chapter 9, from class action lawsuits against policyholders covering, for example, directors' and officers' insurance.
- **Investment costs** – Heightened investments in technology are likely required to adapt to the changes in the marketplace, consumer demands and regulatory requirements.
- **Residual values** –These may change significantly because of climate change, while depreciation charges may introduce additional volatility from a profit and loss perspective. The balance sheet will also be impacted because there are fewer buyers for assets. An example could be a fleet of diesel cars, which has been

depleted in value due to the switch to electric vehicles, tax increases on diesel vehicles and a shift in consumer demand away from the asset.

- **Repurposing costs** – Assets being repurposed, for example, recent press releases have noted that some old mines are now being repurposed as stores for carbon capture. This represents a notable change in the business model and will necessitate adjustments to the accounting practices deployed. There may be associated costs in undertaking this exercise but there may also be allowable expenses.

These factors, plus others, will be evident to senior management via a range of indicators, over differing periods of time, and need to be monitored as part of business as usual to pre-empt a terminal decline in the commercial viability of the organization. Indicators to monitor include changes to the cost base, i.e. increased costs being passed on from suppliers or increases in own costs that are being absorbed, changes in profitability, deteriorating demand for certain products or services, increases in required investments for new or replacement assets, and costs associated with repurposing or changes to production processes.

Conclusion

There is clearly much progress in the development of climate change disclosures as we have seen through the TCFD 2021 Status Report and the number of new reporting requirements in line with the TCFD recommendations announced by regulators around the world in 2022. These proposals come at a pivotal time as the newly formed ISSB, as a standard-setter, also released its guidance for rule makers across all jurisdictions in its report, released in March 2022, 'General Requirements for Disclosure of Sustainability-related Financial Information and Climate-related Disclosures'. The ISSB is also in line with TCFD recommendations, which helps promote the consistency and comparability necessary for developing quality reporting worldwide.

However, this will be a fast-moving field given the acknowledgement by TCFD that 'companies continue to struggle to quantify the impacts of climate change, and to source the data they need to fully assess the threats of a changing climate.'

Organizations may not have explored the potential impact of climate risk on the entity's financial position and future performance and, therefore, climate risk is not incorporated in the relevant valuations and judgements. In such cases, at the minimum, entities should consider disclosing information clarifying their inability to reflect climate risk in the financial statements, along with an explanation of how they consider the financial statements to present fairly the financial position, financial performance, and cash flows of the entity.

As outlined throughout this chapter, from an enterprise risk management perspective, organizations need to continue to build their climate risk maturity and develop their climate change strategies. This will help to provide broader and more detailed decision-useful information within their disclosures.

Notes

1 FSB. Task Force on Climate-related Financial Disclosures 2021 Status Report, October 2021. https://assets.bbhub.io/company/sites/60/2022/03/GPP_TCFD_Status_Report_2021_Book_v17.pdf (archived at https://perma.cc/H6AX-2MVM)

2 M Carney. The Road to Glasgow, Harvard Law School Forum on Corporate Governance, 12 March 2020. https://corpgov.law.harvard.edu/2020/03/12/the-road-to-glasgow/ (archived at https://perma.cc/7NQE-X97T)

3 FSB. Task Force on Climate-related Financial Disclosures: 2021 Status Report, 2021. www.fsb.org/wp-content/uploads/P141021-1.pdf (archived at https://perma.cc/WE33-5EKZ)

4 FCA. FCA's new rules on climate-related disclosures to help investors, clients and consumers, FCA, 17 December 2021. www.fca.org.uk/news/news-stories/new-rules-climate-related-disclosures-help-investors-clients-consumers (archived at https://perma.cc/2YC7-EH53)

5 S. Smith. TPR highlights first wave TCFD reports as 'opportunity' despite data challenges, *Pensions Age*, 10 June 2022. www.pensionsage.com/pa/TPR-highlights-TCFD-reports-as-opportunity-despite-data-challenges.php (archived at https://perma.cc/HQ98-GLE6)

6 TCFD. Recommendations of the Task Force on Climate-related Financial Disclosures: Final Report, June 2017. https://assets.bbhub.io/company/sites/60/2021/10/FINAL-2017-TCFD-Report.pdf (archived at https://perma.cc/F7TT-MPS4)

7 Financial Conduct Authority. Enhancing climate-related disclosures by asset managers, life insurers and FCA-regulated pension providers: Consultation paper, June 2021, p 32.

8 S Moloney. Data, data, data' remain biggest challenge to TCFD adoption, OMFIF, 4 April 2022. www.omfif.org/2022/04/data-data-data-remain-biggest-challenge-to-tcfd-adoption/ (archived at https://perma.cc/VU36-MXUS)

9 TCFD. Climate Disclosure Convergence: TCFD, SEC, and ISSB, 9 May 2022. https://assets.bbhub.io/company/sites/60/2022/05/TCFD-Webinar-Climate-Disclosure-Convergence-May-2022.pdf (archived at https://perma.cc/D7BM-YW8F)

10 R G Eccles. A comparative analysis of three proposals for climate-related disclosures, *Forbes*, 11 June 2022, www.forbes.com/sites/bobeccles/2022/06/11/a-comparative-analysis-of-three-proposals-for-climate-related-disclosures/?sh=26c40d4e4e89 (archived at https://perma.cc/9GW2-PZ5X)

11 TCFD. Recommendations of the Task Force on Climate-related Financial Disclosures: Final Report, June 2017. https://assets.bbhub.io/company/sites/60/2021/10/FINAL-2017-TCFD-Report.pdf (archived at https://perma.cc/9569-RYM6)

12 FSB. Task Force on Climate-related Financial Disclosures 2021 Status Report, 2021. www.fsb.org/wp-content/uploads/P141021-1.pdf (archived at https://perma.cc/G4GW-EDKQ)

13 FSB. Task Force on Climate-related Financial Disclosures 2021 Status Report, 2021. www.fsb.org/wp-content/uploads/P141021-1.pdf (archived at https://perma.cc/G96G-5RFY)

14 Task Force on Climate-related Financial Disclosures, TCFD, About. https://www.fsb-tcfd.org/about/ (archived at https://perma.cc/7SAB-RMQM)

15 A Cadbury (1992) *Report of the Committee on the Financial Aspects of Corporate Governance*, Gee and Co, London

16 EY. Towards TCFD compliance: Observations on reporting trends, 2021. https://assets.ey.com/content/dam/ey-sites/ey-com/en_uk/topics/assurance/ey-towards-tcfd-compliance-observations-on-reporting-trends-may-2021.pdf (archived at https://perma.cc/45WT-PG7K)

17 EY. Towards TCFD compliance: Observations on reporting trends, 2021. https://assets.ey.com/content/dam/ey-sites/ey-com/en_uk/topics/assurance/ey-towards-tcfd-compliance-observations-on-reporting-trends-may-2021.pdf (archived at https://perma.cc/WLS9-8ZR8)

18 TCFD. Task Force on Climate-related Financial Disclosures: Implementing the recommendations of the Task Force on Climate-related Financial Disclosures, October 2021. www.fsb.org/wp-content/uploads/P141021-4.pdf (archived at https://perma.cc/5Q7M-CD2K)

19 EY. Towards TCFD compliance: Observations on reporting trends, 2021. https://assets.ey.com/content/dam/ey-sites/ey-com/en_uk/topics/assurance/ey-towards-tcfd-compliance-observations-on-reporting-trends-may-2021.pdf (archived at https://perma.cc/BPP5-9GBC)

20 EY. Towards TCFD compliance: Observations on reporting trends, 2021. https://assets.ey.com/content/dam/ey-sites/ey-com/en_uk/topics/assurance/ey-towards-tcfd-compliance-observations-on-reporting-trends-may-2021.pdf (archived at https://perma.cc/3FEX-FMNA)

21 D Kingsley, M Solomon and K Jaconi. Companies have work to do on risk disclosures, *WSJ Risk & Compliance Journal*, 17 March 2021, https://deloitte.wsj.com/articles/companies-have-work-to-do-on-risk-disclosures-01616007730 (archived at https://perma.cc/DD2D-SCXG)

22 CFRF. Climate Financial Risk Forum Guide 2020: Disclosures chapter, 2020. www.fca.org.uk/publication/corporate/climate-financial-risk-forum-guide-2020-disclosures-chapter.pdf (archived at https://perma.cc/D9NB-LUDD)

23 TCFD. Task Force on Climate-related Financial Disclosures: Guidance on metrics, targets, and transition plans, October 2021. https://assets.bbhub.io/company/sites/60/2021/07/2021-Metrics_Targets_Guidance-1.pdf (archived at https://perma.cc/CRR5-6Z85)

24 Tesco PLC. Tesco PLC Annual Report and Financial Statements 2022. www.tescoplc.com/media/759057/tesco-annual-report-2022.pdf (archived at https://perma.cc/GXE5-2CRG)

25 Aviva plc. Climate-related Financial Disclosure 2021. https://static.aviva.io/content/dam/aviva-corporate/documents/socialpurpose/pdfs/climate-related-financial-disclosure-2021-report.pdf (archived at https://perma.cc/S7ZM-8P4P)

26 MSCI. MSCI Real Estate Climate Value-at-Risk (Climate VaR) Methodology: A transparent approach to calculating climate value-at-risk, 2021. https://www.msci.com/documents/1296102/19288350/ClimateVaR_RealEstate_Methodology.pdf (archived at https://perma.cc/U2G6-Q8F5)

27 Insurers typically rely on catastrophe models (CAT models) to help them understand the risk associated with underwriting, setting rates, maintaining a reserve, and other relevant aspects.

28 Cornish Mutual. Annual Report & Financial Statements 2020/2021, December 2021. https://cornishmutual.co.uk/media/3sqn2e2h/financial-statement-2021.pdf (archived at https://perma.cc/W2ZE-RS7M)

29 BHP. Annual Report 2021: The future is clear. www.bhp.com/-/media/documents/investors/annual-reports/2021/210914_bhpannualreport2021.pdf?sc_lang=en&hash=15F0B58BC27ADFA860F0BE29B61E199D (archived at https://perma.cc/2XQL-8Q86)

30 IFRS. IFRS Foundation announces International Sustainability Standards Board, consolidation with CDSB and VRF, and publication of prototype disclosure requirements, 3 November 2021. www.ifrs.org/news-and-events/news/2021/11/ifrs-foundation-announces-issb-consolidation-with-cdsb-vrf-publication-of-prototypes/ (archived at https://perma.cc/HWH5-WX9K)

GLOSSARY

ambition mechanism the Paris Agreement's Ambition Mechanism commits countries to come together every five years to take stock of progress towards the long-term goals and to use this as input to enhance their level of ambition if the stocktake indicates this is necessary.

carbon budget the cumulative amount of carbon dioxide emissions that is tolerable, from a global perspective, over a period of time, to keep within a certain temperature threshold.

carbon capture and storage the process of trapping carbon dioxide before it enters the atmosphere, transporting it, and storing it (carbon sequestration).

carbon credits a permit which allows a country or organization to produce a certain amount of carbon emissions and which can be traded if the full allowance is not used.

carbon extractive industries extractive industries consists of any operations that remove metals, mineral and aggregates from the earth. The most carbon-intensive industries are mining and oil and gas.

carbon footprint the amount of carbon dioxide released into the atmosphere as a result of the activities of a particular individual, organization, or community.

carbon hierarchy a hierarchy by which you find ways to avoid, reduce, replace, sequester and offset in order to reduce carbon emissions.

carbon negative the reduction of an entity's carbon footprint to less than neutral, so that the entity has a net effect of removing carbon dioxide from the atmosphere rather than adding it.

carbon neutral the status achieved when an organization has measured its carbon footprint (CO_2e) and then carries out carbon offsetting activities to remove an equivalent amount of CO_2e from the atmosphere.

carbon pricing mechanisms a mechanism to capture external costs and impacts of greenhouse gas emissions by adding an extra cost to the use of the fossil fuels.

carbon sequestration the process of capturing and storing atmospheric carbon dioxide. There are two main types of processes: geologic and biologic.

carbon sink a natural or artificial reservoir that absorbs and stores the atmosphere's carbon with physical and biological mechanisms.

carbon tax a tax on fossil fuels intended to reduce the emission of carbon dioxide.

carbon trading the process of buying and selling permits and credits that allow permit holders to emit carbon dioxide (or other GHGs), and a mechanism to reduce carbon emissions.

circular economy avoidance of destroying or eliminating the product, but to put the product to use yet again by way of enhancement, refurbishing, reusing, or recycling.

climate action failure relates to the undesired and unanticipated outcome of climate change as against the actions taken to be insufficient for meeting the targets and goals outlined in the Paris Agreement.

climate ambition generally refers to the four levels of ambition that organizations are adopting for their strategic positioning that is dictated by the board. These ambitions are generally termed as Follower, Adapter, Champion and Leader.

climate change – liability risks the potential for litigation if entities do not adequately respond to the impacts of climate change.

climate change – physical risks the risk of direct damage to assets and indirect damage from supply chain disruptions.

climate change – transition risks risk associated with transitioning to 'green economy'.

climate change risk radar a key diagnostic tool used to help identify an organization's key climate-related risks across its risk profile.

climate data value chain a process of data generation, collection and use from identifying climate data needs to its application and potential reuse.

climate disclosure disclosing climate-related financial information by an organization, ensuring that there is consideration of the risks and opportunities an organization faces as a result of climate change while preparing the disclosure.

climate resilience the ability to anticipate, prepare for, and respond to physical risk climate related events, trends, or disturbances related to climate.

climate risk appetite strategy describes an organization's desired risk appetite in the context of articulating the amount and types of risk an organization wishes to seek, minimize, or avoid and defines the boundaries within which risk taking can occur, to in order to meet its strategic objectives and climate-related goals and objectives.

climate risk strategy determines the ambition and sets the strategy of an organization that is typically underpinned by two foundational components namely, 'resilience', and 'sustainability'.

convective storm (also thunderstorm) formed when surface heat causes moisture and other particles to rise into the atmosphere.

covert lobbying setting up and funding 'pseudo-science' research groups who are briefed to blur the edges of any science debate around public policy, or the true extent of social harms resulting from certain products, investments or employment practices.

global climate models (GCM) models that support meteorological research to help scientists simulate future climate conditions in line with IPCC emission scenarios.

global warming an increase in global average temperatures of the Earth's atmosphere through the greenhouse effect, which is caused by increases of pollutants, such as carbon dioxide and methane.

green bonds these enable capital-raising and investment for new and existing projects with environmental benefits.

green energy inflation the contribution that environmental policies make to the cost of delivering goods and services that is passed on via supply chains to consumer prices.

green transition refers to the period of time between now and when human activity will not endanger the health of the planet.

greenwashing a marketing technique aimed at creating an illusion of ecological responsibility.

heating degree day the difference between the actual temperature as determined by the average of the high and low daily temperatures, and 65F. It was created by the energy utility sector to better forecast demand.

hedging the act of reducing risk, often through use of financial derivatives instruments.

horizon scanning a formal process to help to explore what the future might look like, to understand uncertainties better and to analyse whether the organization is adequately prepared for potential opportunities and threats.

hydrogen economy an economy relying on hydrogen as the primary component as a substitute to fossil fuel. For example, hydrogen gas and hydrogen liquid.

internal carbon pricing a mechanism by which companies can put a value on their greenhouse gas emissions in a way that drives positive change in their business.

international sustainability standards board (ISSB) provides a comprehensive global baseline of sustainability-related disclosure standards that are used by investors and other capital market participants with information about companies' sustainability-related risks and opportunities to help them make informed decisions.

low-carbon alternatives the carbon-friendly substitutes to carbon-emitting products/commodities.

low-carbon economy economic activities that deliver goods and services to an economy that generate significantly lower emissions of greenhouse gases; predominantly carbon dioxide.

nationally determined contributions (NDCS) a climate action plan to cut emissions and adapt to climate impacts.

natural capital the world's stocks of natural assets which include geology, soil, air, water and all living things.

natural catastrophe a violent, sudden and destructive change in the environment without cause from human activity, due to phenomena such as floods, earthquakes, fire and hurricanes.

operational resilience the ability of an organization to deliver critical operations through disruption.

parametric (or index-based) insurance solutions a type of insurance that covers the probability of a predefined event/trigger occurring instead of indemnifying actual loss incurred.

risk aggregation a common concept in risk management context, relating to the process of summing and showing the interaction between single or individual risks, to assess the bigger picture. In the context of climate change, this is often used to assess physical risks from natural catastrophe exposures across a portfolio.

scenario analysis a process of examining and evaluating possible events or scenarios that could take place in the future and predicting the various feasible results or possible outcomes.

science based targets targets that align with what the latest climate science says is necessary to meet the goals of the Paris Agreement – currently to limit global warming to well-below 2°C above pre-industrial levels and pursue efforts to limit warming to 1.5°C.

stakeholder mapping the process of identifying, and prioritizing stakeholders by categorization both the organizations influence and importance on a specific area of business activity such as e.g. credit risks.

stranded assets assets that have suffered from unanticipated or premature write-downs, devaluation or conversion to liabilities.

strategic resilience consideration of the implications of the strategic and organizational choices a firm has to make, and the potential implications for long term stability.

sustainability strategy relates to the need to decarbonize, manage and mitigate transition risks as a consequence of transitioning to a lower-carbon or green economy.

sustainable investing investing in progress, and recognizing that companies solving the world's biggest challenges can be the best positioned to grow.

sustainable strategy relates to the organization's strategy to decarbonize and manage and mitigate transition risks, including setting net zero emission targets, as a consequence of transitioning to a lower-carbon or 'green' economy.

task force on climate-related financial disclosures (TCFD) created by the Financial Stability Board in 2015 to provide guidance and improve and increase reporting of climate-related financial information.

the network for greening the financial system (NGFS) NGFS was established by eight central banks and supervisors at the Paris One Planet Summit on 12 December 2017. Its goal is to strengthen the global response required to meet the goals of the Paris Agreement and to enhance the role of the financial system to manage risks and to mobilize capital for green and low-carbon investments.

INDEX